The Mended Mirror
family story and com
deeply human journey from brokenness to wholeness.

Michael Jones,
The Soul of Place: Reimagining Leadership Through Nature, Art and Community

The Mended Mirror is inspirational. Part searing memoir, part spiritual wisdom, and wholly entrancing, this book invites us to glean deep insight from the pains and challenges of our lives.

Tanis Day, PhD,
The Whole You: Healing and Transformation through Energy Awareness

The Mended Mirror goes beyond an interesting read to be inspiring to people dealing with challenges in their lives, to people who have learned to follow their intuitive nudges and to anyone wondering how to bring love and curiosity to those members of our families, or close circles that we might describe as difficult or challenging.

Kathy Jourdain,
A Worldview Intelligence Approach to Building Trust and Relationship at the Speed of Change.

The Mended Mirror weaves together memoir, spirituality and the courage, love and frustration of a unique family life. It brings together Wise Woman teachings, lessons from a mother's fragmented life, and a glimpse of other ways of being in the world. Karen Celeste Hilfman's deft fingers create both tapestry and mosaic that will resonate with readers seeking ways to re-craft their own lives. I highly recommend this book for study groups, writers and seekers of wholeness.

Carolyn Pogue,
Hilwie's Bread

THE MENDED MIRROR

BY

KAREN CELESTE HILFMAN

THE MENDED MIRROR

The impact of
a mother with many personalities and
a shocking DNA test result
on my life and my life's work of
cultivating Authentic Connection Culture:
life-giving community rooted in
creativity, meaningful relationships,
openness to possibilities and
commitment to the well-being of all.

DEDICATION

To All of Us
On the Journey to Wholeness

WHOLENESS:
Coming home to ourselves;
connecting to the Wisdom within us and amongst us
to create Community that reflects our True Essence,
imbuing the world with hope through the power
of the Universal Consciousness of Love
found deep within the centre of who we are.

Through Authentic Connection to Self, Community and the Earth,
through recognizing the Earth, one another and ourselves as Beloved,
through acknowledging and honouring our oneness with all of life,
through deep listening and deepening conversation,
through alignment with the flow of life-giving energy,
—we expand our capacity to create Community and the Commons
where together we imagine and engage possibilities
to journey toward a transformed way of being
rooted in and empowered by love
creating space for the emergence of
a lived vision of the well-being of all.

As a result of connecting in a deeply authentic way
we see life differently;
no longer are we bound by small-ego thinking that is rooted in
limitations, entitlement, blame
and the compulsion to protect our territory;

rather we see creative possibilities, interconnection,
abundance and incredible goodness.

We shift from an ego to an ecological perspective
in order to become resilient and sustainable
in all aspects of life—
economics, ethics, academics, decision-making and politics—
which all reflect the way we
engage in relationships
at personal, local and global levels.

The journey to wholeness awakens us
to the light that emanates from the centre of all of life, which
longs to illuminate a pathway forward
that is empowered by love.
While this light is often covered over by
the demands, destruction, brokenness and noise of life,
it is not extinguished;
it remains constant in its essence and presence.
The experience of wholeness,
arising from developing
an intentional Culture of Authentic Connection,
is a way of being
when we choose to see
our self, one another, the Earth, and all of life
with eyes of love and with hearts open to possibilities.

The Mended Mirror
Copyright ©2019 Karen Celeste Hilfman

Editors: Carolyn Pogue, Julie McGonegal and Peggy Goddard
www.CarolynPogue.ca   www.EditingByJulie.com
Cover Art, Interior Illustrations and Graphics: Anitta Hamming
www.IntoxicatingCanvas.com
Book Design: Pegi Eyers
www.StoneCirclePress.com
Photo of the Author: Bob Millson
Spiral Design Element: Kervin Brisseaux, ©1987 for Adobe 2018
Website Design for Authentic Connection Culture: Nicole Jenney
www.NicoleJenney.com

Library and Archives Canada Cataloguing in Publication

Hilfman, Karen Celeste
The Mended Mirror

Includes Conversations for Book Circles
Also issued in electronic format @ www.AuthenticConnectionCulture.com

ISBN 978-0-2288-0547-2 (Hardcover)
ISBN 978-0-2288-0546-5 (Paperback)
ISBN 978-0-2288-0548-9 (eBook)

Tellwell Talent
www.tellwell.ca

THE MENDED MIRROR

The image of the mended mirror is based on
the art form Kintsugi in which broken ceramic
is mended using gold to emphasize the breaks.

Contemporary Korean Kintsugi artist Yee Sookyung
reflects on the metaphor of her work.
"The cracks between the broken ceramic
symbolize the wound.
The work is a metaphor of the struggle of life
that makes people more mature and beautiful
as they overcome their sufferings."

THE MENDED MIRROR

FRAMING THE MIRROR

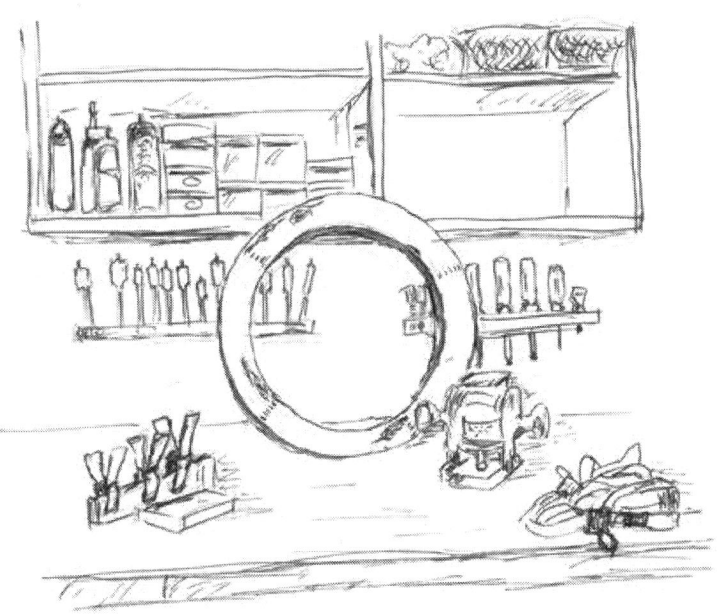

Wısᴅᴏᴍ Cɪʀᴄʟᴇ begins in thirteen minutes. I need at least seven minutes to finish preparing. Waiting impatiently at a red light, I rehearse my strategy to welcome people while completing the set-up.

I pull into the church parking lot. There's an empty spot. My anxiousness begins to subside. I gather my supplies. With arms full, I reach past the bundles to open the door. My phone rings, stopping me from exiting the car. I groan. I consider not answering. But I know I will; I always do. I know who it is because there is only one person who calls me on this phone. As hard as it is to constantly respond, I love my Mom, and I appreciate and respect her incredible capacity to really be there for others. I try to reflect that level of being present and caring back to her.

I fumble in my purse for my phone and answer the call.

"Hi Mom. What's up?"

The sound of screeching pierces my ear. The shock of it takes my breath away. It is a voice I haven't heard in years. She sounds like a raging banshee. At the top of her lungs she is screaming over and over and over again that she hates her Daddy. Mid-scream she hangs up.

The silence throbs with an aching echo.

Stunned, I sit and stare at the phone.

The phone rings again. It is Mom's number. I answer.

The voice is radically different. It is a smooth voice, trying to be charming. She declares that she loves her Daddy.

Then a different voice, monotone and resigned, tells me she needs to talk to me. I remind her that Wisdom Circle is about to begin. She says to come up to see her when I finish leading the Circle.

As I walk into the church, I think of the permission Mom gave me two years ago to record her so that she can see an episode of herself being odd or suicidal. She has no memories of ever being suicidal and is intrigued by my stories of this disruptive reality in our lives. This seems like a good night to provide her with a glimpse of the odd behaviours that have swarmed through our lives. But I don't have any recording devices with me and the equipment at home is packed away with batteries that need recharging.

I arrive at Mom's at 9:15 p.m. I use my key to let myself into the condo complex. I step into the elevator to travel toward a well-known destination, not knowing what I will encounter when I get there. I knock on her door feeling an edge of anxiousness simmering through my body. It is a feeling I always have in the seconds before I engage with Mom. Tonight it is heightened.

She calls out and tells me to come in.

She's in her white chair in the living room. There is a blanket over her lap. She is sitting very still, watching me with an unusual depth of engagement.

Though she doesn't speak, I respond to the firm nod of her head that directs me to sit in the green chair across from her. The large square coffee table is between us.

I look at her and try to find some normalcy in a moment that feels off-kilter. "Mom, why did you need me to come up tonight?"

She doesn't answer.

She stares at me.

It feels like she is assessing me.

We sit in silence, our eyes holding contact.

I wait while she decides whatever it is she needs to decide.

As she continues to hold eye contact, she begins to move, slowly shifting until she is sitting sideways. She curls up in a loose fetal position.

Only then does she break eye contact with me.

She looks down into her lap. She picks up a corner of the blanket. She rubs the edge of the blanket between her fingers.

She speaks in a tiny voice. "Why do people hurt me?"

My heart breaks.

I don't know why I know to ask her, but I do. "How old are you?"

"Three."

"Why are you so sad?"

"Momma is leaving and she won't take me."

I watch her. "Who will take care of you?"

A tiny shrug lifts her shoulder as she sinks further into herself. "Daddy is walking away ... My brothers tell me I can go with them."

"Where are they going?"

"To the back kitchen."

"Is it fun there?"

I ask her this because when I was a child the back kitchen at the house where Mom grew up caused goosebumps of fear to rise on my neck and arms. Going anywhere near it caused my stomach to erupt with a churning sick feeling soured with anxiousness.

She answers so quietly I strain to hear her.

"Sometimes."

A deep fragile silence booms through the room.

Then, in her tiny voice filled with a sigh of acceptance of what life is, she asks, "Why do people want to hurt me?"

A tear rolls down my face.

Her body shifts, moving so fast I am startled. She sits at the edge of the chair with her back straight, her legs spread apart, her hands clutching the arms of the chair, looking like she is ready to lunge at me. There before me is the one I describe as the raging banshee. I've never seen her in her full-blown state before; I've only heard her over the phone. But I recognize the raging voice. I notice that the stiffness in her stance is familiar.

She looks like a young scrapper ready for a fight. Her clothes look different. They have the look of jeans and a t-shirt, rather than the look of a moment before of a smart outfit for a woman in her eighties.

She screams while staring at me, "I hate my Daddy … I hate him I hate him I hate him I hate him."

While the sound of her screeching lingers in the room, she morphs again.

She leans back into the corner of the chair, stretching her legs out in front of her and draping one arm up over the back of the chair so that her body is open and fully seen.

She speaks in an oozing, overly sweet voice of calm, almost like a Southern drawl. "I love my Daddy. I just love my Daddy."

I am stunned. I recognize her. She makes my skin crawl. She looks and sounds like a performer in a nightclub. I am amazed at how the same outfit can look so different simply from the shift in her attitude and her way of engaging life. Her basic green sweater and pants give a totally different impression than a moment ago. They have lost the first impression of being a practical comfortable outfit. They now look like they are intended to highlight her physical assets. Her clothes have a different look to them, she holds herself differently, she sounds different, her focus is different, the energy emanating from her is different.

How have I not recognized this before? They are all so distinct, with clear personalities and perspectives on life.

The feeling is confirmed as she morphs again.

She stops lounging in the chair and turns back toward me.

She slumps. She speaks in a voice filled with whininess. I know the attitude, tone and topic well.

"I just want to die. You would be okay with that, right? There's nothing that I can do for anyone. I don't want to be here anymore."

She slumps more fully into herself.

And then … nothing.

The pose has shifted subtly and the slumped, discouraged-looking body is gone. I feel like I am looking at a blank screen in comparison to the details I have just seen.

She speaks in a bland, non-descript voice. "Thank you for coming over. I need to sleep now."

She curls up and closes her eyes.

I sit and stare at her. I am stunned at what I have seen all my life but never understood.

She falls asleep. I go to her and pick up the blanket that was knocked to the floor. I cover her and tuck her in so she can sleep in her comfy chair. She spends many of her nights here.

I let myself out, closing the door quietly behind me.

I am aware of walking down the hallway in a daze of shock. Thoughts and impressions come like fragmented pieces into my mind. My head is racing with details, yet calm with awareness.

I look at my watch. It is 9:28. Thirteen minutes have passed since my arrival in Mom's parking lot, thirteen minutes that divide my life into two contrasting perspectives: a lifetime of not understanding and an eruption of knowing. A wall that obscured awareness has crumbled, providing a glimpse into a startling reality that radically changes my perception.

A metaphor comes to my mind. It's like hearing a language we don't understand. We are not able to interpret it, no matter how loudly or slowly someone speaks. We have no frame of reference to be able to understand. It appears that has been the case with Mom. I have lacked understanding until now. Now it makes sense.

For a reason that I do not understand, tonight Mom has chosen to intentionally show me how to see and understand a lifetime of reality.

Mom has many personalities. Disconcerting though this reality is, it makes sense of a lifetime of experiences that haven't made sense.

During the moments of Mom morphing from one personality to the next, I had no trouble recognizing the distinct characteristics, focus and physical stance of each one of the personalities. They are deeply familiar as ones who have come and gone through the landscape of my life all my life. Tonight they have shaken me awake. My eyes have been opened to the awareness that life has not been filled with shifting moods and states of Mom like we have always thought; it has been something more. I'm stunned we didn't realize it until now.

As I walk down the hallway, a memory drifts into my mind of my brother Mark saying that when he was a child it felt to him like we had four moms and we'd never know which one would show up.

WHOLENESS IN BROKENNESS; I have become aware through the writing of this book that my relationship with my Mom is a primary source of the learning that is at the core of my life's work, which focuses on the power of connecting to wholeness and authenticity. Mom is also a significant contributor to my life being filled with profound hopefulness. As I look back over my life, I realize these may sound like surprising insights because, from my perspective, my relationship with my mother is impacted by the disruption of a series of disconnected personalities, a reality I do not recognize until a year before her death.

My understanding is that Mom's many personalities form as coping mechanisms when crises and trauma are too much for her to bear. One of the blessings of the alter personalities is that they are the ones who cope with trauma while Mom's core personality remains strong and dynamic. It is through her core personality that Mom impacts the community around her with a passionate vision of inclusivity and her adamant perspective that our world can and must shift toward ways of being that enhance all of life on Earth.

My mother's challenges with mental health impact who I am today, providing me with a perspective on life which includes striving for resilience and seeing possibilities of authentic goodness even when chaos is rampant.

Seeing goodness in the midst of chaos gives hope in a world where good news stories are seldom told by the media. Being able to see goodness and possibilities, even when it appears that the walls that divide us are too high to climb, gives hope in a world where fear, consumerism and blame imprison and immobilize us. Being able to see goodness and possibilities, even when life feels like it is falling apart, is a gift that allows hope to grow and creativity to awaken. I am grateful for the way Mom could see goodness even when others could not. I am grateful to Mom for helping me to develop the ability to see goodness even in the most difficult moments of life.

After Mom's death in 2011, I begin to tell snippets of my story of providing support to my mother for more than 20,000 hours over a period of forty years as she lived with the impact of an unnamed reality. From 2011 until now, the previously untold glimpses of this part of my life were shared only with close confidantes.

To me, sharing stories such as this deepens our awareness of the goodness in us, despite the harsh voices of judgment that erupt in our heads or the brokenness in us with which we struggle. When we risk being open, vulnerable and honest about our struggles and our joys, the fullness of who we are emerges and connects us to one another at a profound, authentic level.

Sharing our stories helps us to risk coming out from behind masks that separate us from each other and from ourselves. Experience has taught me that the pattern of hiding behind masks and disconnecting from authentically engaging in life is at the root of some of our greatest struggles in the times in which we live. We are experiencing an epidemic of loneliness rooted in the destructive powers of judgment, shame, blame and guilt. We are experiencing a culture that is numb to some of the deepest travesties of human history as we soothe ourselves with over-consumption of things, addictive substances and repeated mindless patterns. Too often, we are cut off from the roots of meaning at the core of our being. We strive to survive by fulfilling shallow expectations, rather than allowing ourselves to be nourished by the rich compost of wisdom and the vision of collaboration that is deep within us. Sharing our stories connects us at that deep level of our profound longing for community, creativity, compassion and acceptance.

The story of Mom's many personalities increases in complexity five years after Mom's death, when we discover that as siblings in one family we do not all have the same biological father. When we learn this shocking news, I hear myself make a declaration that startles me but feels true in the place of deep knowing within me: I believe that because of Mom's many personalities she was not aware of the extra biological father in our family. No matter how much others scoff at my interpretation I continue to believe this to be true.

The shock of hearing about the first DNA test result and people's response to it creates a sense of urgency in me for the story of Mom's many personalities to be more fully explored and shared. I immediately find myself scurrying down the "rabbit hole" to seek out the fragmented pieces of our lives, hoping to piece them together to provide clarity and possible explanations for the undercurrents in our lives. Because the results of the DNA information prompt speculation that causes confusion about a story that is more than people know, I feel compelled to ensure that the news of the extra biological father not result in judgment of my mother but rather be received with a deep understanding of the complexity of the story.

Over the years, our family does not talk openly about the difficulties with Mom. When we are children, if we do talk about the disruptive realities of life with Mom, it is rarely more than whispered confusion and pain. The three older kids in the family, Mark, Janis and I, speak with each other about our experiences periodically, but we almost never talk about them with Dad, and we rarely, if ever, discuss them with our younger sister Betsy.

During the worst years, Mark, Janis and I are in our teens. Betsy is young, in the early years of school. Based on my relatively new understanding of Mom, my interpretation of the difficult years in the early 1970s is that the medication Mom is on before and after major surgery sends her into a discordant spiral of revolving personalities, each one filled with more despair and fear. During these difficult times, the older kids in the family take care of our younger sister Betsy to protect her from what we don't understand. Betsy reminds us that her experience of Mom is different than that of her three siblings.

What is clear, based on the conversations and wonderings we have shared, is that we each have our own story, our own perspective and our own experience of how we have each been impacted.

Others would tell this story differently. This is my story, my perspective.

From my perspective, telling the fullness of this story is important. I do not feel that Mom's mental health challenges, which are the result of trauma, need to be hidden in the shadows of our lives. This is a story of struggle that reflects themes of a multitude of stories which weave into the fabric of our life in community. It is also a story filled with resilience and Mom's amazing capacity for goodness even in the midst of struggle. While there is despair, there is also hope.

———————————————————

In the year of my sixtieth birthday, when the news of the shocking DNA data barrels into our lives, the writing of this book propels me into a deepening awareness of who I am and the depth of the influence of Mom on my life's work about how to create life-giving, creative and meaningful community.

Writing this story has been a time of identifying learnings and insights which inform my perspective about life as a direct result of my relationship with Mom. Engaging with Mom awakened a longing in me to discover how to be in relationship with myself and others where we are authentic, where we can risk showing up as the person we are deep within us. This longing develops, in part, by watching Mom show up in a multitude of ways I do not understand.

My central learning that impacts my life is that: when we connect to our true essence, to our authentic self, we connect to a reservoir of power deep within us that is filled with love and creativity; when we risk connecting to one another in a deeply authentic way, we see life differently—no longer are we bound by small-ego thinking that is rooted in limitations, entitlement, blame, judgment and the compulsion to protect our territory, rather we see creative possibilities, abundance and incredible goodness; and when we connect at an authentic level as a community by creating a commons where everyone is respected and belongs that is rooted in a communal agreement, the wisdom within us and amongst us has the opportunity to emerge to enable us to recognize future possibilities that enhance life when we work together.

The brokenness and the richness in my relationship with my Mom has helped me to identify principles and practices about how to create healthy, life-giving authentic community so that we can address the brokenness in our world by choosing to live together in ways that reflect our deep longing for the well-being of all.

I learn again and again that though life can be demanding and appear to be fractured or even crushed, somewhere in the midst of the rubble there is goodness and a longing to be whole that yearns to emerge amongst us. This is a story that explores how to connect to that power of wholeness, the power of love, in the midst of the brokenness in our world today.

While this is the story of my ongoing journey home to who I am, rerouted by unexpected detours, it is also a glimpse into our shared story as humans as we seek to be in healthy relationship with ourselves, each other and the Earth; as we seek to create space for love to emerge, acceptance to expand, possibilities of an alternative vision to be considered, and creativity to be our response when pathways to wholeness and the common good become obscured.

———

Before you follow me down the "rabbit hole" described in *Alice in Wonderland* as a place filled with unexpected turns and bizarre realities, I think it would be good for you to hear two stories to help you know aspects of who I am that impact how this story unfolds.

The first story reflects a central theme and perspective which dances and weaves through my life. It arises from a mystical moment that happens the summer I am three.

I am in a glorious meadow where warm sunshine fills the air. Butterflies are flitting everywhere. I hear the song of a multitude of birds and the splashing dance of the creek. I hear the voices of others in the meadow. I can see them out of the corner of my eye as I run and twirl with delight amongst the flowers that blow in the gentle breeze. The breeze carries the warmth of the sun and kisses my face. When I come to the centre of the meadow, I stop. Everywhere I look I see light: light pouring out of the people; light flowing like a wave around the butterflies and blossoms; light emanating from me. I see light all around me, coming from within me and from within every living thing.

I don't exactly see the light with my eyes, but I see the light with an inner vision that feels more real than what my eyes see. This guiding vision makes the world a magical, mystical place filled with possibilities, potential beyond our imaginings, and peace that is deep and profound. For me, the light is the energy of the Divine. I know deep within me that the light all around us and within us is the power of Love.

In the early years of my life this is how I think everyone sees the world.

Throughout my life, this memory informs how I see people and how I engage life. It is a reflection of my profound sense of knowing that the Divine is intimately present and can be found deep within all of us. It is an energy that connects us to life rooted in love. I return to the feeling of this experience in moments when I am challenged to see the light and goodness that are within all of us. This memory roots me in an awareness that even in the midst of the struggles of life we have the amazing capacity to let love shine and creativity flow through our lives. The result is that I am often puzzled by behaviours, masks and walls that cover over the depth of goodness that is everywhere. I am often outraged by injustice, and filled with a longing for what is possible. In the midst of my frustrations, I am sustained by the awareness that the energy of love is all around us, and that no matter how broken life can seem there is still wholeness present.

The second story provides insights into my detailed memory that goes back to when I am very young, a reality that you need to know in order to make sense of the stories I tell. I know my earliest memories go back a long way because of a picture in the family box of photos.

When I am eight or nine years old, my family spends an evening around the dining room table digging into the box of family photos to find treasures. I ask if anyone has seen the pictures from the time we went to Algonquin Park. Mom and Dad both respond. Without looking up, they both say that we've never been there. I am surprised. I have such clear memories of going to Algonquin Park. I remember stopping on the side of the highway to feed a fawn sugar cookies. I distinctly remember trying to scramble out of the car with my tiny body seeking to keep up with my sister and brother. I remember being on the beach and seeing a teenager asleep on an air mattress that is drifting far out into the lake. I alert my brother, tugging at him until he looks to where I am pointing, so he will see the danger she might be in. I remember that we are there for Janis's and Mark's birthdays and that Janis receives a painted cardboard in the shape of a doll designed to thread wool through to complete the picture. I remember Janis won't let me play with her cardboard doll. She turns her back to me as we sit on the top of a picnic table, hiding her gift in front of her, ignoring my demand to be included.

We continue to sort through the photos, showing each other pictures filled with memories. And then someone finds a booklet of pictures where the first picture is of Janis and Mark feeding a fawn while Mom stands in the background holding the cookie tin. Apparently, my little legs did not scramble fast enough to get to the fawn in time to be in the picture. The next picture in the booklet shows the gate into Algonquin Park. My parents are shocked because they have forgotten we stayed there and shocked because I remembered.

The date on the pictures is August 1957. I am eighteen months old.

This book has been described as both intimate and intricate. While it feels risky to share it, it also feels like a call, a nudge, or more accurately a push I cannot ignore. I could keep silent, leaving people with the interpretation that Mom and the extra biological father in our family simply had an affair, but the story is filled with so many more layers of complexity and insights into life. The push to write this story is strong. It will not leave me alone, awakening me each day with new edits, guiding me to write with only the skeleton outline that divides the book into five sections. The story flows out of me, continuously surprising me with the memories and reflections that emerge. Pieces of the story click into place, often startling me with how the puzzle fits together to create a picture filled with textures, contours, depth and colours permeated with nuances that illuminate the beauty at the core of life.

I have pondered how Mom might feel about this story being told. I am aware that telling it provides details that we often don't share in our society. For me, telling this story provides potential for greater appreciation of the incredible resilience in my Mom. She truly was an amazing woman.

After prayerful consideration, my deep intuitive sense is that Mom would be more than okay with me telling this story. Mom always wanted to write a book about her life, to be a source of learning, support and insight for other people. Comments have been made that this story has the potential to help other families dealing with mental health challenges, as well as people who work in the mental health field. Mom would appreciate knowing that her story has the potential to help others. Already, my sister Janis has shared that reading this book has given her greater understanding of Mom and the challenges she lived with. As a result, her heart has softened toward Mom. This story is also filled with Mom's significant impact on the development of my life's work of the importance of creating Authentic Connection Culture, learned through both her struggles and her strengths. She would love for it to be known that she has been one of my greatest teachers.

A rich tapestry of life emerges as the strands of the story are woven together. Some strands are light and flowing, others are colourful and zany, some are golden and filled with sparkles, others are thick and heavy and hard to handle. The beauty and strength of the tapestry emerge from the deepening insights and learnings, creating a reflection of life that shows the potential we have within us for life to be filled with both love and wholeness.

One of my hopes for our one Earth community is that we awaken more fully to the transformational power of love, a power that longs to engage our passions, teaches us to celebrate diversity, and compels us to risk imagining a way of being together that leads to wholeness. Awakening to this power within equips us to co-create a world committed to the well-being of all. For me this story of connecting to wholeness even in the midst of brokenness, of experiencing resilience even when life shows up with difficulties, deepens our hope as we work together to mend the world.

The moment that creates the impetus for me to tell this story erupts on the morning of April 18, 2016.

THE MIRROR SHATTERS

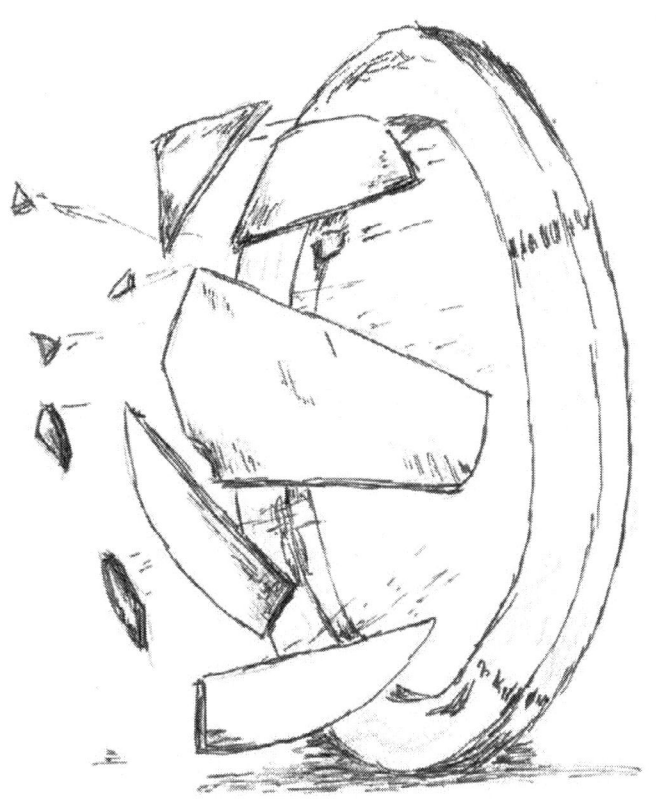

Early Morning Monday, April 18, 2016, the sound of a whistle cracks the silence. A text message has arrived. I groan. My body, mind and spirit are exhausted, drained from the demands of a busy life and the months of directing *Joseph and the Amazing Technicolor Dreamcoat*. This is my first day to sleep in after the show closes.

I lie in bed, sinking more deeply into the mattress and pillows. My slightly awakened mind conjures images of the impact of the musical on the small town of six thousand people north of where I live. Over one thousand people were in the audience over a four-night run. The cast and crew of one hundred people all invested a magnitude of hours to lift the production to a professional standard. A tiny smile wants to crack my face. I'm too tired to smile.

Instead, I let visuals flash through my mind of how we deepened the meaning of the story. Throughout the show, most of the cast wore scarves made of camouflage material. In the final song, Joseph and the narrator help the rest of the cast to discover that on the inside of their camouflage scarves there is a lining made of the same material as Joseph's coat. The side of the scarves that has been hidden throughout the show is a replica of the scarf Joseph and the narrator have been wearing. Each member of the cast turns their scarf over to the bright colours. They realize the beauty has been on the inside from the beginning.

On a metaphorical level, the beauty within, represented by the colourful side of the scarf, has been camouflaged by the small-self attitudes of jealousy and a sense of entitlement that most of the characters express for much of the story. The material of the beautiful lining that they have unknowingly been wearing identifies the whole cast as beloved in the same way that the coat, made of the same bright material, identifies Joseph as Jacob's beloved son. It is intended to remind the people on stage and the people in the audience that we are all beloved; that we can choose to share love in the world rather than cover over the love within us with hatred and greed. My mind wanders to the bookmarks we gave everyone in the audience as a keepsake. Each bookmark has some of the material of the coat attached to it along with the words "Colour the World with Love." A tiny smile finally curves my mouth.

I drift back toward sleep in a glow of satisfaction.

I stop myself from drifting too far because I know I need to do something about the text message. I consider ignoring it, but it will awaken me every fifteen minutes with a persistent intrusion.

I groan, thinking, "I really need to figure out how to change the settings on text message notifications so they stop after one alert."

I reach out blindly and grab the phone. I anticipate that once I open the message to stop the notification whistle, I will fall back to sleep. The text is from my sister Janis. I am instantly awake. Our busy lives don't allow us to talk often. I don't want to miss a chance to connect.

I read the message.

"Good morning, Karen. I have a question. Do you remember the last name of 'uncle' Scott, a family friend when we were little?"

I respond without needing to give it any thought. "Pretty sure it is McDonald." I look at what I have written and think, "That's spelled wrong. It should be Macdonald with an 'a.' But what difference could the spelling possibly make?"

I press the send button, then write, "What prompted you to think of him?"

Immediate response: "I need to talk to you."

The phone rings. Without telling me why, Janis asks me about my memories of our family friend we called 'uncle' Scott.

Though puzzled by the question I rhyme off a list of my memories:

I remember going to his cottage as kids. We loved it there, and it seems to me that we went often. I remember 'uncle' Scott and his wife coming to all the adult parties at Mom and Dad's. I also remember Mom flirting with him sometimes, and other times she treated him like her buddy.

When we were still quite young, there was a huge fight at the cottage on the weekend that Grandma came up with us. I don't remember going back to the cottage after that or seeing 'uncle' Scott at the parties at our home. I do remember hearing updates about his kids when Dad came home after golfing with him.

There were two other times when we saw 'uncle' Scott again. The first time was when I was eight. He gave each of us a necklace watch. The second time was when we were teenagers. He took each of us out for a full-day visit that included dining at a very exclusive restaurant.

Scott's name came up during the really bad years when I sat up with Mom night after night while she was distraught to the point of being suicidal. Mom begged me one night to call him at midnight. She pleaded with me, declaring, "He is the only one who understands me."

I pause.

Janis fills the pause with a sentence that stuns me. "I'm pretty sure 'uncle' Scott is my biological father."

I press pause on life for a flickering second to absorb what Janis has said.

Then a multitude of questions rush into my head.

Janis tells me that she received an email late last night from a person identified on her Family Tree DNA report as her "first cousin once removed." Janis has chatted back and forth with this Greg

Macdonald on email since being connected by Family Tree earlier in the year.

In last night's email, he notes that he doesn't want to upset her, but he has been investigating their DNA connection since it is such a close relationship. He has determined that markers in her DNA indicate that she has to have a Macdonald as a parent.

She shares that after receiving the email and experiencing the shock of this new information based on her DNA data, she kneels down in prayer. In answer to her question for guidance about this startling information she immediately receives the name 'uncle' Scott. She remembers a family friend we called 'uncle' Scott in our childhood. But she does not know his last name. The answer to her prayer comes at 2 a.m. my time. She spends a wakeful night waiting to send me a text at a reasonable hour.

The stories I share about 'uncle' Scott Macdonald confirm for Janis that Mom and he were close, so close Mom reaches out to him when her life is tumbling into chaos.

Later that day Janis finds out that the "first cousin once removed" on her DNA family list also has a favourite 'uncle' Scott. Greg's 'uncle' Scott is actually his cousin, but he has always called him uncle because of their age difference. It turns out that his 'uncle' Scott is the 'uncle' Scott family friend of our childhood.

The name of 'uncle' Scott coming to Janis in prayer, combined with my memories of Mom and 'uncle' Scott being close, and the DNA marker information that identifies Janis's strong relationship with his cousin, all support this startling awareness that the family friend we called 'uncle' Scott is Janis's biological father.

In our childhood it was normal to give Mom and Dad's closest friends the honourary title of uncle or aunt. 'Uncle' Scott was one of the people included in that circle of close family friends. For clarity I will simply call him Scott throughout the telling of the rest of this story of the shocking DNA test result.

Janis's purpose for doing the DNA test was to try to find information about our Dad's side of the family in order to develop our family tree. We were surprised in the 1990s to discover through a contact on Facebook that our Dad's family name is Russian Jewish. Previous to gaining this insight Janis had not been able to find information about our family name. Once she started using information from Jewish synagogues, she made some headway. Although she finds our family name, she cannot find our grandfather.

With this lack of clarity about the place of origin of our family, Janis decides to deepen her investigation through DNA testing.

We have always known there are missing pieces in our family story. Our paternal grandfather came to Canada from the United States in 1918. He never talked about his life before arriving in Canada. He never talked about the family he left behind in the States. He came to Canada with a secret that he does not reveal. As kids we wonder if maybe he was running from the law, but since he is such an upstanding citizen that doesn't make sense.

It turns out that his secret is that he is Jewish. In the early 1900s, persecution against Jewish people was accelerating. He comes to Canada and his heritage is hidden when he marries a devout Christian woman and becomes active in a Christian church. Maybe he falls in love with Grandma and knows she won't marry him if he is Jewish, or maybe he wants to hide his heritage from the community. Whatever the reason, his secret remains a secret until four decades after his death.

In the nineties, Mark shares with Janis that people often think he has Jewish heritage based on his appearance. Not long after Mark tells her that, Janis attends a Bar Mitzvah. When she looks around the room, the people have a familiar look that is like our family. When I go to the Holocaust Museum in Washington, DC, the faces staring out of the bleak pictures startle me with glimpses of resemblance to people who gather around the table at our family dinners.

Delving for details about one secret has now uncovered a totally unexpected outcome.

It feels like the lined-up pieces of our lives are being scattered in a multitude of unknown directions.

An image like a video clip erupts in my mind in the middle of that first early morning call with Janis.

The video begins with the image of the wedding present of silverware that Alan and I were given from my parents and grandmother. It is stored in a beautiful wooden chest lined with velvet. The chest is designed to securely hold each piece of cutlery in an orderly fashion.

In the video clip that is playing in my head, that very organized, structured box is held up high, then turned over and given a strong shake to dump all the silverware on the floor. The pieces crash with painful echoes as they clatter everywhere.

The clattering of the silverware echoes the feeling deep within me which is erupting in the midst of the phone call—a feeling of the foundational stories that organize our lives crashing apart and scattering, shattering our preconceived notions about who we are as family.

In the weeks and months to come it is shocking, yet satisfying, to pick up the pieces and try to find the place they fit. The life-long curiosity that Janis and I share about genetic lineage and dynamics of relationships compels us to see how the pieces of this puzzle fit together.

In the midst of the fascination of piecing the story together, I experience a heavy anxiousness rolling inside me. I describe the feeling to Janis because it is pushing its way into the conversation, refusing to be silent. In that first call, I blurt out that I think that if Scott is her father, then he must be mine too. Over the next few days, I periodically toss that thought into the conversation and then withdraw it, not wanting to take away from this moment of discovery for Janis. I quickly shift the conversation back to the information we know about her DNA and try to keep my wonderings to myself.

I agree to do my own DNA test. Janis plans to ask our younger sister Betsy to do one too.

I tell Janis that I still have my watch from Scott. I tell her I will give it to her so she has something from her "bio Dad," as she calls him. She suggests that I keep it until my DNA test results come in, just in case he is my father too. I'm relieved that she accepts the possibility that Scott might be my father because it feels like a real probability to me.

From the moment of hearing the news in the early morning of April 18, I feel out of sorts, like someone has pushed my core pillar off its foundation, leaving me off-kilter and uncomfortable. I can't imagine that Janis and I are not full sisters. I can't imagine how I could be more related to Mark and Betsy than I am to Janis. My energy and perspectives in life align with Janis's in a way that is very different from how I connect with Mark and Betsy.

Energetically I have always been aware of feeling different than Betsy and Mark. I love them both dearly, but to me, it has always felt like there are two uniquely defined pairs of siblings in our family; Mark and Betsy is one pair, with Janis and me being the other pair. As a kid, I think that the two distinct pairs of siblings in our family might have something to do with Janis and me sharing a bedroom and Mark and Betsy cuddling early in the morning when Mark gets Betsy from her crib as soon as she makes a sound. I feel the difference between the two pairs of siblings even when I am six years old.

Now I am struggling with the possibility that Janis and I are not full sisters. If I am not Janis's full sister, the way I interpret and understand my life feels like it will shift drastically and shatter because space will need to be created for something new to emerge.

I actually find it easy to believe that Scott is Janis's father. It explains a lot about who she is. I do not find it easy to imagine that Janis and I are not full sisters.

DURING THE FIRST EARLY MORNING CALL when Janis realizes that Scott is her biological father, a way of interpreting and explaining this new reality rises up in me. It is based on years of experience of caring for Mom as she moved in and out of her various personalities. But the sense of certainty of this explanation comes from more than logical analysis. It feels like a deep knowing that bypasses thinking mode and erupts into words that gush from my mouth.

Deep within me, I am quite certain that Mom did not know that Janis is Scott's daughter. People argue with me, saying that isn't possible, but there is a certainty in me that shocks even me.

Since my sense of certainty is so strong, even in face of the protests of others, I am compelled to delve into this mystery like a detective seeking clues and insights that might shed light on this hidden story from long ago that is disrupting our lives today.

My immediate response to this new DNA information is that the many personalities play a significant part in this story. As I ponder, hints of memories rise up that send me deeper into the story, seeking forgotten information thought to be unimportant to provide insights into this new reality.

The personality who I think is at the centre of this mystery is the one I now refer to as the Partying One. In my experience she only shows up if Mom has more than one drink of hard liquor, resulting in Mom quickly becoming inebriated and shifting into another state of being. An intriguing and confusing aspect about the personality of the Partying One is that she does not seem to have any memories. After she has spent an evening partying, the next day Mom acts like she doesn't have any memories of the night before. Of course, that is not unusual when people are drunk, but in Mom there seems to be a total lack of awareness.

From the day I find out about the extra biological father in our family, my mind keeps wandering through the well-remembered but little-explored details of Mom's different personalities, trying to see more deeply into the story than I have ever seen before.

I share details with family members of my experiences with Mom. I rarely shared them before because previously people did not want to hear about them. I tell them what I have been aware of since October 2010 when Mom morphed into distinct and recognizable personalities. I share how that experience allowed me to see the distinctive natures of the different personalities who have shown up all our lives, with behaviours and characteristics that we have been describing as moods or states.

I tell them about how my experience points to Mom having a core personality and how Mark, Janis and I have been referring to her as our "real Mom" for years, including using the air quotes to indicate that Mom is not in one of her states but is present as "real Mom." This is the personality most people meet outside our home. This is the one who is an amazing community leader. She helps to banish the use of the strap in schools in Toronto. She is presented with the Queen's Silver Jubilee Award for her work with the mentally and physically handicapped association—work that includes being on the national committee that proposes federal legislation for mandatory wheelchair accessible washrooms and medical parking spots. She is an amazing dynamo, passionate about including everyone, with a delightful presence that makes her a good leader.

I share with them, as I will share with you, the pieces of the puzzle of the many personalities that keep swirling through my mind after finding out that Scott is Janis's biological father. Later I will provide a summary of all the personalities and the crises that I think triggered their presence, but here I want to share the development of my thoughts as I try to piece together the story.

My sense is that the Partying One, who is at the centre of this mystery, forms when Mom is nineteen years old as a result of a pregnancy and a broken engagement. Mom is engaged to a man from a prominent family who has big dreams for him in politics. Mom becomes pregnant by her fiancé. His family decrees that because she is pregnant, she is not good enough for him. She is rejected as sexually easy. In the midst of the trauma of being rejected and left alone in her pregnancy, I suspect the new personality forms to protect the wounded place within her to help her cope with this crisis. The personality that emerges is sexually uninhibited, an expression of the way others describe her and treat her.

Mom never tells her parents that she is pregnant at nineteen. She leaves home on her sixteenth birthday. I am not aware of any stories that suggest that she keeps in contact with her parents over those late teen years. She lives with an older sister during her pregnancy.

On the day Mom gives birth to a baby girl, her former fiancé sends her a bouquet of flowers. Otherwise, she is alone.

After ten days of nursing her baby, Mom is told to leave the hospital and to do it quickly because the baby's mother is coming to pick her up.

This part of the story breaks my heart. I can't imagine what it would feel like for Mom to walk away from the hospital on that day in early May 1948, leaving behind a baby she loves. No matter how clear she is that it is better for her child to be cared for by a couple who have resources and a relationship, it breaks her heart. The one time that I hear Mom talk about the experience, I sense a hollow place within her that is filled with unshed tears.

It is our "real Mom" who deals with the trauma of choosing to allow her child to be adopted. It is from the strength within her core personality that she makes this decision. Unlike the crises that create the alternative personalities, this experience is rooted in an internal choice. She is the one who chooses. The traumas that result in the formation of the alter personalities are all external crises caused by people or circumstances over which Mom had no choice or control. The personalities that emerge in order to cope with an external crisis are rooted in very different circumstances than this internal moment of struggle to make a choice for the sake of the well-being of her child.

And so it is our "real Mom" who carries the sorrow of the moment of leaving the hospital. The trauma and sadness of the choice she makes to give her child up for adoption create an angst in her heart that never leaves her until she meets that baby again decades later. That pain, which she tries to keep hidden, is something I feel as a young child. I sense that she is hiding something horrible. In my child's mind, the most horrible thing I can imagine is that she is trying to hide the fact that she does not love me. Before I am very old, her secret creates a feeling of deep fear within me.

After Mom leaves the hospital without her baby, one of my much-loved aunts, another one of Mom's sisters, gives Mom a job for the summer at her lodge. Dad is playing drums at a local dance hall in the same summer tourist town. He stays at the lodge where Mom is working. That summer Mom meets my Dad, and Scott.

Dad falls in love with Mom, our "real Mom," her core self. But there are also hints of memories and impressions that point to Scott having a strong connection with Mom. What I always notice is that the two of them are great buddies when Mom is our "real Mom." Our "real Mom" chooses Dad to marry. But there is another side to the relationship between Mom and Scott; I clearly remember Mom flirting with him.

I think that Mom is in her partying personality when she is intimate with Scott. Mark and I both observe that the morning after an episode of actions associated with the partying personality, we don't remember Mom identifying regret for her odd and disturbing behaviour of the night before. It's like there is a huge hole in her memory. To us, as children, we are surprised that she seems to have no memory of her "weird" behaviour, which is how Mark describes these types of episodes.

But there is another personality who also connects with Scott, the personality who I refer to as the Suicidal One. I believe the Suicidal One emerges in response to another tragedy that breaks Mom's heart.

On a fateful night in September 1960, Mom decides not to go as planned with her youngest sister for an evening out. When her sister is driving home, she pulls into an intersection on a green light. Mom is certain that if she had been there, she would have checked oncoming traffic. Her sister's car is hit and crushed by a young driver trying to outrun the police in a high-speed chase. Mom's sister is killed. The suicidal personality that emerges from this experience is sad, whiny, demanding and feels profoundly sorry for herself, constantly saying that she has nothing to give and that she has no value to offer to anyone.

In the early seventies, Mom is medicated before and after major surgery, and the medication triggers the presence of a cyclone of personalities. I remember that one night Mom asks me to call Scott. It is a particularly difficult night. It is filled with different erupting personalities, including the overwhelming sadness of the Suicidal One.

Although, as a fifteen-year-old there is a part of me that would love to talk to Scott and have someone else help Mom on this night of devastating disruption, I tell Mom I can't call him. It is midnight. I'm not even going upstairs to wake up Dad or Janis. I don't want to wake up anyone and I certainly don't want to make a call this late. Social etiquette, which Mom vehemently taught us, is that all calls must be complete before 9 p.m. I can't call this late. Everyone in the house will be in bed. In most homes, there is only one phone in a central place where it permanently hangs on the wall. Even during the day it is not used often. If I call at midnight that means someone will have to get out of bed and stumble through a dark house. They will be anxious because calls at midnight are always foreboding. No one calls at this hour unless something extreme has happened. Mom demands that I call anyway, declaring, with a passionate plea, "Scott is the only one who understands me."

I find the number, lingering over the task, hoping Mom will change her mind. I dial the number, checking carefully to ensure that I am doing a long distance call correctly. The phone rings. I hold my breath, not knowing what I will say if someone answers. We never talk about these episodes, even amongst those of us who live together. What do I say? I have no practiced words to describe the reality I will be asking Scott to enter. I let the phone ring the required five rings, no more, no less. No one answers. I hang up. I exhale. There is great relief that I do not have to talk to someone whose night I have disrupted.

The memory of that incomplete phone call is a key piece that confirms for Janis that Scott is her biological father. When Mom's life is crashing down around her, the person she reaches out to is Scott.

There's another memory as I ponder this mystery which is connected to the personality I call the Suicidal One. I shared with Janis during the early morning call on April 18 about a fight that happened at Scott's cottage when we were quite young. I comment that I don't think we ever went to the cottage again after the fight.

My friend Tanis reminds me of a process in her system for healing which I can use to tap into the fullness of my memory of the night that I described to Janis as the "fight" at the cottage.

The fight happens on a weekend when our paternal grandmother comes with us to the cottage, which is extremely odd. We rarely see our Grandma. She treats Mom with a sense of disdain because Mom comes from a lower class in society than our Dad. I heard it said in my childhood that Dad came from an upper-class home and Mom came from a lower middle-class home. There were whispers of servants in the house where Dad grew up, while it was said that Mom's Momma looked old before her time from taking care of ten kids in a tiny home. At Mom and Dad's wedding Grandma refused to speak to anyone from Mom's family because they were beneath her.

Janis and I try to imagine the reason for the fight. With his mother at his side, did Dad confront his good friend and charge him and Mom with infidelity? That does not feel right.

So on an afternoon during the summer of discovery in 2016, I enter into the process that Tanis taught me, going back into that moment in my timeline. We each carry an energetic memory line within our bodies, which Tanis has learned to access through her process. She has already helped me with the key step of identifying where I carry the memory in my body. Alone in my living room on a quiet summer's afternoon, I feel into that spot below my lower left rib where I carry this memory, confirming where it is. There is a feeling of tenderness there. As Tanis taught, I pull my point of consciousness back from my mental body where our imaginations are informed by probable answers and past experiences, moving back from the place where we form opinions and arguments about what likely happened. I feel myself entering into the still point of calm at the centre of my brain. I then journey down into my body to the place of my memory.

I feel myself in my child's body sitting outside the cottage in the early dusk. I listen to the conversation amongst the adults.

At the end of the conversation, which has provided me with a whole new way of understanding what happened, I return to awareness of my adult body sitting in my living room. I am astounded at the strong feelings surging through me.

What I have heard makes sense to me of my Mom and Dad and Scott. In that moment of the "fight," Scott tells Dad that Mom is in really rough shape to the point of being suicidal. He confronts Dad, saying Dad needs to do something to help Mom.

———————————

As I sit and feel into this new awareness, sobs rise up within me because I realize I am not alone in my concern for Mom back in the early years of my life.

During my teens I feel very alone in my desire to acknowledge and respond to the depth of despair in Mom.

Mark leaves home at sixteen because he can't take what he calls Mom's weird behaviour. He writes about that experience in a letter we give to her doctor in 2008 when we realize she really needs help.

Janis leaves home two weeks after turning eighteen. However, two years before she moves away from home, she writes Mom a letter telling her she can't cope with providing support anymore and asks Mom to leave her alone.

During the most tumultuous years Betsy is very young. On the rare occasion we talk as adults about Mom's struggles she reminds me that her experience of Mom is not like mine, Janis's or Mark's. She is aware of Mom's struggles, but her awareness comes from a different time in Mom's life. During the years Betsy and her husband live with Mom and Mom's second husband, Betsy sees the impact on Mom of living with a man with a drinking problem. She is a major support to Mom in those difficult times. Unlike my other siblings, who struggle to stay in relationship with Mom, Betsy's connection to and support for Mom is constant and strong. However, she is young during the particularly difficult years when I am in my teens, and so I can't turn to her when I feel alone in my support of Mom through those years.

During the sixties and early seventies, Dad strongly considers divorcing Mom. He speaks about it openly in the fall of 1971 through 1972. I plead with him to give her more time to move through whatever this is that she is going through.

Sitting alone in my living room in the summer of 2016, I am now aware that I was not alone in wanting to respond to the despair in those hard years of the sixties and early seventies. Scott was also watching out for Mom as early as 1961. Tears pour down my face. Sobs rise up and consume me with a power that shocks me.

Like me, Scott is not only aware of Mom's turmoil in those difficult years, he feels she is worth supporting rather than leaving her to cope on her own. I am aware of why some of my family members need to not deal with Mom but I feel their absence profoundly.

When I call Tanis to debrief the experience, she asks me how I feel as the adult. Tears flow because of the solace I am experiencing that is rooted in a sense of kinship with Scott.

I text my sister Janis and tell her I have a different perspective on what I now call the "confrontation" rather than the "fight." I tell her

I am not prepared to share this deep sense of knowing with everyone because I don't want to have it ripped apart with disbelief. I am willing to share it with her if she wants to hear it.

Janis texts me to say she can call me in a few minutes but she has an appointment in half an hour. Is it still okay if she calls?

I immediately respond with, "Yup."

Moments later my phone rings. With little time to spare, Janis asks me what I remember. I tell her in as much detail as I can. I pause to sort out what else she might want to know.

Janis immediately jumps in to say my memory makes so much sense in light of who we know Mom and Dad and Scott to be.

Tingles rush through my body, which for me is a confirmation from Spirit that we have named a truth.

My voice becomes muffled. Tears impact my capacity to speak. Janis needs to go but says she will call me back.

———————

When I haven't heard from Janis by the middle of the next day, I send her a text. I tell her that it is forty-five years ago to the day when Scott picks her up to spend the day with him. I share my memories of her special dress that she wore. Then I share details of my experience the next day with him. I name all the special foods I order at the elegant place where he takes each of us for dinner.

I am able to determine the date of our excursions based on when the band The Guess Who performed at the CNE in 1971. After our extravagant restaurant dinner Scott drops me off at the house of some friends I met while camping with Mom, Dad and Betsy. They take me to that Guess Who concert the next day.

When Janis first tells me that Scott is her biological father, I tell her that I think I had time away with him because I needed a ride to the city to my friend's house the day after Janis went out with him. Dad is away, and Mom is not well. In the early evolution of understanding this story I interpret my day with Scott as him helping Mom.

After sending my chatty text to Janis, it is another five hours before I hear from her. She makes no comment about my babbling details about the forty-fifth anniversary. The text responds to our conversation from the day before when I shared with her that the "fight" at the cottage turns out to be a "confrontation" between Scott and Dad about Scott's concern that Mom is suicidal.

In her text, Janis says, "I appreciate your memory, Karen. I truly believe that my way of coping with a mentally and emotionally compromised mother was to remain aloof. When I became a mother, I was saved from the tendency of being aloof, which meant that for most of my life it has not been too damaging. But it was you who saved me from Mom. I think you have remembered the motivation of what actually transpired that day."

A sigh rushes out of me, releasing long-held feelings. My heart surges. It's me who saved her from Mom.

Up until that moment, Janis and Mark have each made one comment over the years to express their awareness of what I do with Mom.

In the last few years of Mom's life, Janis tells me that the only way Mom can come and stay with her in Florida is if I come too. She can no longer cope with Mom on her own. The previous time Mom was there she consumed conversations with details of her health and was obsessed with wanting to help to the point where she was washing clothes that she had already washed.

Mark told me once that he talks to Mom every six weeks for about thirty minutes. It takes him the full six weeks to get over the call. He comments that he doesn't know how I cope with her every day for over two hours.

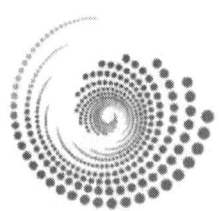

OVER THE SUMMER OF DISCOVERY IN 2016, I begin to give voice to this story that I have held inside me for most of a lifetime. I discover I have a surprising amount of awareness about some of the alternative personalities within Mom, as well as some significant wonderings and questions.

The use of the phrase "many personalities" to describe my experience of Mom only emerges in 2010, the year before her death. As much as I now talk about these personalities having an impact on my entire life, I go through most of my life thinking that when Mom exhibits "weird" behaviours, as Mark calls them, we interpret them as shifts or changes in mood and describe them as her being in one of her states.

We all engage the world differently at different times, depending on the circumstances and other realities in our lives in that moment. For most of my life, that is my interpretation of Mom's life: she is moving along a spectrum of different responses to life depending on circumstances and other realities in her life.

In 2008, information is gathered about mental health challenges in our family because of the possibility that someone in the family might be dealing with bipolar disorder. This is the first time I consider that Mom might have an actual mental illness.

Based on the information we gather about Mom, we begin to wonder if perhaps rapid cycling bipolar disorder explains the shifts in Mom's state, which can change rapidly from manic behaviour to depressed response.

It shocks me that it takes so long to consider that Mom might be dealing with some sort of mental illness even though she has expressed suicidal thoughts most of my life.

When I now read the information in a letter to Mom's doctor in 2008 about our concern that Mom may have a mental illness, it amazes me that it is not considered then that Mom might have dissociative identity disorder (DID), which is the proper name for an official diagnosis of someone with alter personalities. It is in that letter that Mark talks about feeling like he has four moms.

I am intrigued that I don't consider this possibility sooner based on my experience of engaging extensively with a woman who is diagnosed with DID; although it is not something I figure out on my own in her case either. It is years into our relationship when I learn about her diagnosis with DID, which significantly impacts her life.

In the early years of my relationship with this woman, I interpret her shifts and changes as moods. When she tells me that she has the diagnosis of DID it makes sense to me.

After my experience with Mom in 2010, when I finally see details of Mom's life that point to her having many personalities, I phone this woman and talk to her about my experiences with Mom.

I share with her that I wonder if one personality holds the memories and provides details and information when another personality needs it. I describe how there are times when I ask Mom about something, and she looks confused as though she has no idea what I am referring to. And then all of a sudden she shifts and responds appropriately to the topic. I interpret her behaviour as being a normal gap in memory. I share with this woman that I now wonder if, in that moment between confusion and full knowledge, the required information is being downloaded to her from the one who holds the memories. The woman tells me that my description fits her experience. She also tells me that the one who holds the memories is referred to as the host personality.

Before the experience in October 2010, I do not see similarities between the woman with DID and Mom's struggles. However, when I provide support to someone else, I see similarities in them with the woman diagnosed with DID. In this new person, I recognize two distinct personalities who are different ages by their own definition.

The two personalities have very distinct ways of walking and talking. I can see it in them, but at that time I don't see it in Mom.

I don't see, or I can't see, the concept of Mom having many personalities until that October evening in 2010 when I am confronted with a reality that helps me to see that the presence of many personalities describes my experiences of Mom.

I have spent a lot of time reflecting on the different personalities since 2010, with significantly increased interest during the summer of 2016.

My interpretation is that each personality forms as a result of dealing with a crisis in Mom's life. In my mind, I associate a particular crisis with each personality based on what appears to be the age of each personality, the behaviour of each one, and the crisis in Mom's life around that age.

I acknowledge that these are all simply my interpretations. Even when Mom is still alive, I can't test my theory by asking her questions, since she doesn't have memories of the different personalities. All I can do is watch and gather details by looking through this new lens.

My reflections and wonderings have deepened as a result of my hope to make some sense of the fragmented pieces of the story of an extra biological father in our family.

It has been intriguing to witness how, in the midst of my curiosity, long-forgotten memories have emerged that have previously seemed like random snippets. They now help me to see the various pieces in a new light and provide insights into how things might fit together.

I feel like a detective sorting through the landscape of my mind as I seek to find a story or to remember a conversation which sheds some light on how this story might have unfolded.

As more information rises to the surface, long-held perceptions give way to seeing different possibilities of unexpected dynamics.

Details that once seemed trivial now point to cracks in the façades of interpretations.

Based on my experience I identify eight alter personalities plus Mom's core personality. It is interesting to me that we have referred to Mom's core personality as our "real Mom" for years.

The nine personalities are labelled according to their behaviour. I now refer to them as our "real Mom," the Three-Year-Old, the Flirty One, the Aggressive One, the Wild One, the Partying One, the Suicidal One, the Angelic Presence, and the Mundane Organizer. When I simply use the term "Mom" I am referring to the combo of all nine personalities with the recognition that the one I am engaging could be any one of the nine personalities.

Before we get to the descriptions of each personality and the crisis that might have created them, I want to sort through the layers of one particular personality who I think is the host. She is the most elusive of all the personalities. I need to sort out the details of this more complex character before I can be clear about descriptions of each personality.

The host personality carries the memories of all the personalities. I think it is the one I call the Aggressive One.

I use two descriptors to describe the end points of the spectrum of behaviours of the Aggressive One, which all carry the same energy. The sense that there is a spectrum of behaviours reflects the complexity of this personality. The other personalities are single topic-focused with a consistent pattern of behaviours.

The description at the far end of the spectrum of the Aggressive One is that she can be like a raging banshee, wildly screeching and out of control.

On the other end of the spectrum is a protector with the strength of a warrior. She functions as one who protects the "many personalities" by ensuring they have the required information and details which are rooted in the memories of other personalities. She makes sure they have the information they need to be able to function. The memories are not shared, only the information.

In 2008, Mark talks about having four moms. He describes one of the four moms as "mean Mom." It takes me a while to put this together, but I think that the character Mark describes as the "mean Mom" is part of the spectrum of the Aggressive One.

After sifting through my memories of each personality's presence and energy in our lives, I am now aware that the Aggressive One showed up far more often than I thought at first. There are many moments in our family's life when a stern, unsympathetic character, who has clearly run out of patience at how things are unfolding, shows up to move a situation along.

She feels very different from our "real Mom." Our "real Mom" might actually be the one we are engaging when suddenly her energy shifts. She sounds different than our "real Mom" and behaves in a particular, consistent way that is characteristic of the Aggressive One.

As I think about the presence of the host personality of the Aggressive One I get a sense of this personality popping in and out of our lives by suddenly erupting into a moment with a gruff and abrupt tone and then leaving just as abruptly. It is the same energy that I experience when she is in the mode of the raging banshee. When she comes as the protector the raging tone is absent, which is why there are different words that describe her: the raging banshee, the protector, mean Mom, the aggressor. There is also the interesting, demanding, fun side that shows up on a rare occasion. All these describe this more complex personality of the Aggressive One.

Memories of the presence of the Aggressive One go back a lifetime. They often include a repeated physical action; when the Aggressive One is present I am often taken by the arm and moved to where she thinks I am supposed to be. I have memories of being physically moved as a child and memories as an adult of being firmly led by a strong hold on the upper part of my arm. I have particularly clear memories of this action during the final years of Mom's life.

The move is very decisive as she takes control. At one time I surmised that this action is part of our "real Mom," but as I go back in my memories I realize that in these moments she feels very different than the part of our "real Mom" that can be assertive as well. The behaviour of the Aggressive One feels more like aggressiveness than the assertiveness that is more typical of our "real Mom." The attitude exhibited is different than "real Mom" in its level of impatience and lack of tolerance for the input of others.

I am quite sure it is the host personality who tells me to come over on the night I am allowed to see the personalities morphing from one to another. The host personality is the only one who could choose to show me the different personalities because she is the only one who is aware of all the personalities. It is intriguing to me that on that night I don't see the Partying One, which feels like a confirmation that the host doesn't have clear memories of her. I also don't see the Wild One, but it is rare when she shows up in life.

The eight splinter personalities that I identify and the crises that I think may have caused them to form are listed below after my description of our "real Mom." These are my conclusions, after working extensively to try to put pieces together based on my experiences. Some of these descriptions are already familiar to you; parts of the stories have already been told. This is a summary of the details because I know from talking to people that it is good to repeat these stories so that the personalities are clear. It has also been noted that it would be helpful to have them listed in one place. So, eight personalities plus the original core personality are described below. For some of the personalities, this is the only place their possible origin is described. For other personalities, the stories of their origins and their characteristics are a repeat of stories told elsewhere in the book.

SUMMARY OF THE NINE PERSONALITIES & POSSIBLE ORIGINS

OUR "REAL MOM"

I think of our "real Mom" as Mom's core personality. She has a very distinct, recognizable way of engaging the world. She is well put together, dynamic, a leader, organized, dependable. She sees tasks that need to be done, and she does them. She cares for her children well, ensuring we have clean nice clothes, bedtime stories, polite manners, and are well fed. She is a leader in the community. She is involved and interesting. She has a delightful sense of humour. She is fun to be around.

I notice that one of the things that prompts our "real Mom" to show up when she hasn't been around for a while is the presence of Betsy. Betsy's birth brought Mom back to us out of the abyss of the Suicidal One, and now in my experience, Betsy's presence prompts our "real Mom" to show up.

I am intrigued by the awareness that, long before the experience on the night in October 2010 when I am smacked in the head by my new understanding of Mom living with many personalities, Janis, Mark and I have been using air quotes around the phrase "real Mom" since we were teenagers. The air quotes acknowledge that Mom is not in one of her "weird" states; our "real Mom" is present, the one we know and love and understand.

THE THREE-YEAR-OLD

Research suggests that people who have DID usually form their first alternative personality as a result of a significant childhood trauma, with the most common trauma being sexual abuse.

Mom does not have a diagnosis of DID, but since her youngest personality is three by her own description, I do wonder about the trauma in Mom's life at that young age. Whatever it was, I think it was the beginning of a journey of personalities forming to protect Mom in tragic circumstances.

On the night the personalities morph from one to another in front of me, it is only the Three-Year-Old who allows me to ask her questions. When I ask, she tells me she is three years old.

She has a question of her own that she repeats two times: "Why do people want to hurt me?"

When I go to my grandfather's house as a child, I find it painfully difficult to go anywhere near the door that leads to the back kitchen. Terror and fear course through me, causing the hair on my arms to stand up any time I head in that direction. In my childhood mind, the back kitchen feels like a place where something horrible happened to my Mom when she lived in that house.

When I have the opportunity to speak to the Three-Year-Old, she tells me her brothers are taking her to the back kitchen on the day when my grandmother leaves with the twins and won't let Mom go with them. The back kitchen is where Mom's brothers sleep during the warm months of the year.

Whenever the Three-Year-Old shows up, which is rare, tenderness rises in me toward Mom. To me, she appears fragile and confused by whatever is happening. She tends to show up in the midst of times when the sad Suicidal One is present. Her tiny, wondering voice flits in and out of the long, meandering conversations typical of the Suicidal One. Their energies seem to align with the depths of their sadness.

THE FLIRTY ONE

In speaking with an energy healer who has worked with people with many personalities, I learn that it is common for a child to adopt a second alter personality who is quite sexual and flirtatious as a result of two things: early engagement in sexual activities before there is emotional maturity, and their perpetrator's encouragement to enjoy the attention they are receiving for being sexual. For many months I do not want to consider the possibility that the Flirty One is a child. But the longer I think about this possibility, the more it becomes clear to me that this personality is quite young even though her focus is very sexual. I now wonder if the Flirty One emerged when Mom was in childhood, somewhere around six to eight years old.

The Flirty One is constantly sexual in her engagement with the world. She is bold and brassy and demands attention. The topic of sex is a common focus of her conversations. She has a slurring Southern-belle type of voice that oozes with a smooth, fake sweetness that makes my teeth ache. Her body is boldly open and seductive. I notice her physical characteristics most distinctly when she is sitting. She spreads her arms wide and leans back into the corner of the chair or couch. Her legs are stretched out in front of her so that her entire body is lounging on display. The difference between her and our "real Mom" is extremely evident in this posture. Our "real Mom" sits up straight with eyes engaged with interest on the people and activities around her. The focus of the Flirty One feels like she is trying to entice people in order to get their attention.

The Flirty One sounds like she has been drinking, at least that is how her speech patterns have been interpreted by family over the years. I wonder if her sensual dialect is what makes her sound like she's been drinking. She does not sound like our "real Mom" at all. She also does not engage life with the level of intelligence that our "real Mom" exhibits and so it sounds like her thinking is incapacitated, which is presumed to be the result of drinking. I think it is because she is younger and does not have the intellectual capacity of our "real Mom."

When the Flirty One shows up, she gives me the creeps. Much about her flirtatious personality is a mask or a façade. She feels the opposite of authentic. While other personalities are hard to take, they are consistent in their presence. They are not phony like this personality. I suspect my reaction to her has to do with the phoniness that is a consequence of a young girl trying to fit in with the reality of her life, especially if there were ongoing sexual encounters. With this new perspective that the Flirty One is a child trying to cope with a reality that she should not be dealing with, I feel badly for my very strong negative reaction to this personality.

I cannot isolate one trigger that causes her to show up. But she shows up often. I do notice she shows up more often with other people than with me. It is like she is trying to please someone so that they will engage with her, a behaviour that is immature and rooted in a childhood pattern which keeps playing out through this personality. I recognize her presence even back when I think of the differing behaviours as moods and states. When the behaviours of the Flirty One are present I stay as disengaged from Mom as possible. I watch from a distance, embarrassed by her actions and embarrassed for the person she is engaging.

THE AGGRESSIVE ONE (The Host Personality)

I suspect the personality of the Aggressive One emerges when Mom is eleven or twelve years of age. She has the feel of a young, angry girl just heading into her teen years. Research suggests that a personality often forms when the youngest personality feels at risk. I can see how the Aggressive One might form to protect the delicate Three-Year-Old. I wonder if it has to do with reaching puberty that makes her feel threatened.

This personality is the only personality that has a spectrum of behaviour. The Aggressive One is the personality who screams how much she hates her father on the night I see the personalities one after another, but I think she was also the bland resigned voice that I heard at the end of the episode that night. There is also a part of this personality that shows up like a protective warrior who is gruff and demanding to make sure situations move along. So this personality ranges on a spectrum from gruff and impatient to raging banshee where screaming is a distinct characteristic.

The trauma that causes this personality to form is unclear.

I know that Grandpa uses his belt on his kids when he is displeased with their behaviour, but that happens all through their lives. So I don't suspect that is the cause for this splinter or the anger expressed by the raging banshee part of this character.

When Mom is eleven, her beloved older sister dies of tuberculosis. Her sister has been living in the sanatorium on and off for four years. My memory is that permission is given by the staff at the sanatorium for Mom's sister to come home to live as her life draws to a close.

Grandpa declares he won't let her come home. Mom is livid. Her sister dies in the sanatorium.

If it is accurate that this personality is eleven or twelve that is also right around the time that Grandpa comes home inebriated on a Friday night and in a fit of rage throws Mom's much-loved violin into the coal bin.

However, after living with awareness of this personality for a number of months I now wonder if her anger at her father might be for not protecting her from the sexual abuse which I suspect happened in the back kitchen where her brothers slept in the summer. As a child I notice that she does not have a good relationship with her eldest brother. It feels to me like she barely tolerates him. When Mom is eleven or twelve her brothers go to war. Is it then that she realizes that whatever has gone on in the back kitchen should have been stopped immediately? Is that why at this age she is raging at her father, because he didn't protect her?

Whatever the crisis that creates this personality, the level of anger, and the need to shift situations that are unjust, fit the behaviour and focus of the Aggressive One. It makes sense to me that she could have emerged simply to protect the Three-Year-Old. Her aggressive energy to protect is at the core of Mom's work as an amazing advocate for vulnerable people in our society, which includes anyone who is excluded or mistreated in life.

I now recognize that this personality pops in and out of our lives on a fairly regular basis. As the one who holds the memories of all but one of the personalities, she protects each personality by ensuring they have details they need to function in the world.

In some ways, I like it when the Aggressive One shows up because she pops in during the moments of life when things are unravelling. There are times it is a relief that she shows up and sets life back on a reasonable track.

Mark talks about a mean Mom. I think his experiences of the mean Mom, which go back to when he is four years old, are of the Aggressive One who regularly steps into our lives with an abrupt attitude. Her tone can be hard to take when we are hoping for the much sunnier personality of our "real Mom."

The one time this host personality who I call the Aggressive One does not carry memories is when Mom has two or more drinks of hard liquor, which causes the partying personality to emerge. The Partying One is always inebriated; when she is present all aspects of Mom are inebriated. The Aggressive One who is the host personality does not hold the memories of the Partying One similar to the way people don't remember details if they drink to the point of blacking out. The lack of memory seems even more profound in Mom. There doesn't appear to be even a foggy recollection of anything that happens when the Partying One is present.

THE WILD ONE

The Wild One is the personality I have the greatest difficulty sharing because she is so different than the Mom we all know and love. There is a part of me that longs for the behaviour I describe below to be the result of a reaction to medications rather than an actual personality. If it is a personality, I shudder to think what the crisis is that creates her because this personality is filled with terror.

If this is a personality, I wonder if she emerges when Mom is fifteen. Mom very abruptly leaves home on the day she turns sixteen. Could something so horrible have happened the spring when she turns sixteen to cause this personality?

The Wild One focuses on death, though she is quite different from the Suicidal One. She is the most disconnected of all the personalities. Her long hair, which our "real Mom" always ties back, hangs long and straggly to her waist. She walks with her shoulders hunched over, creating a moving curtain of hair in front of her face. She is filled with terror. She clutches at anyone close by and asks charged anxious-filled questions again and again. Death is a frequent topic of her charged agitation.

When I have described her to a few people I have been asked if she terrifies me. The question shocks me because such a possibility never enters my head; she is my Mom. She does not terrify me. No matter how changed her looks and behaviour, I can still see the light of love inside my Mom. What I am clear about is that she is obviously terrified, and so I long for her to find a way to return to the place of stillness that we all carry within us where we connect to the power of love.

I wonder what might have happened to Mom at fifteen that would be horrible enough to create this personality. What I know is that when Mom leaves home on the day of her sixteenth birthday, she only has five weeks before she graduates from grade ten. I remember hearing a comment once that something happened that was so significant she could not stay long enough to graduate.

There are two stories that I am aware of from this time of her life.

VE Day is May 8, 1945, when victory is declared, signifying the end of the war in Europe. Two of Mom's brothers are in Italy during the war, where they are on the frontlines of brutal trench battles which confront them with the depth of the horrors of war. Six days after the declaration of victory in Europe, Mom leaves home. It is her sixteenth birthday.

Does she have a fight with her father about her eldest brother, who I suspect is the one who abused her, coming from war and being allowed to live in the family home? Does she leave in anger because her father is not willing to protect her? Is she furious because he will let his son come home, but he wouldn't let his daughter come home from the sanitarium five years earlier when she was dying?

I don't know for sure what happened that made Mom feel like "she had no choice," which is what she often said about leaving home the day she could legally leave, but I do know that Mom's eldest brother lives in the house with Grandpa when I am a kid.

I also know that Mom has a very strained relationship with her eldest brother. Anytime we go to pick up Grandpa, Mom barely speaks to her brother, who is always sitting in the living room right beside the door where we enter the house. He is never invited to come to our home for dinner with Grandpa—though I recently watched our family movies, which show that at least once he did come for Christmas dinner, in a year when almost all the aunts and uncles and cousins were there, making it a particularly large crowd.

The other story I am aware of during this time period in Mom's life is a story I only hear her tell once. Although I know five of the people who are present on the day this story unfolds, I do not hear any of the rest of them talk about the experience. When Mom tells me the story, it feels like she is telling a story that has only ever been shared in whispers.

In grade ten Mom plays hooky with a whole group of kids. Two of the other people there are her twin sisters, her younger and youngest sisters, along with the boys who will become their husbands and my uncles. Some of the cousins who live on their block are also there.

During that day one of the boys in the group, who is not related to Mom's family, lands on a cemented hill below a viaduct. He dies as a result of the fall.

Did the horror of that day splinter Mom into this personality? I wonder if the way the Wild One frantically asks questions, grabbing at others as though seeking assurance in a terrifying moment, demanding to know where someone is, might be an echo of the experience of the tragic and senseless death of a friend on that horrible day in grade ten. What happened on that day? Did he choose to jump down to the cemented hill below the viaduct, thinking it was safe? Did he choose to jump to his death? Did he get pushed onto the hill? Did Mom, along with others, feel responsible for what happened that day?

In the early 1970s, her repeated question on nights that were filled with the Wild One is "Where's Mark?" The question is filled with terror as she clutches onto my arm, grabbing at me in panic.

I don't know the details of what happened that day long ago. I do feel that if this personality forms as a result of this tragedy, it makes sense as to the level of horror that the Wild One expresses. The story seems to make sense of her persistent, frantic quest to find someone when she is in this state.

What I do know is that when I think about the Wild One, I experience a sense of discordant anguish reverberating through my mind and my heart.

I know that the most common trigger for the appearance of this personality is medication, but it is not always a factor when she appears. Whatever crisis it is that caused her reality to splinter fills Mom with a terror that consumes her.

The first time I see this personality is in the seventies. She does not present as having a specific age. So she could be younger than I think or she could be older.

I don't know a lot of details about Mom's life after she leaves home at sixteen.

I do know that she works at a hardware store where she falls through a trap door and sustains an injury to her back, which she suffers from for a lifetime.

I know that she lives with her older sister. Once I learn about Lynda, Mom's first daughter, I learn that Mom was engaged during those later teen years and had a baby whom she gave up for adoption.

While I do think that Mom forms a new alternative personality as a result of being deserted when she becomes pregnant, that personality is the one I call the Partying One, not the Wild One.

THE PARTYING ONE

The crisis that I think causes the Partying One to emerge is Mom grappling with the reality of being pregnant when she is nineteen and rejected by her baby's father. Mom's fiancé's parents decide that since she is pregnant before marriage, she is not worthy of marrying their son.

The Partying One shows up in my experience when Mom drinks hard liquor. In my memories Mom is not affected by wine or beer like she is by hard liquor. The behaviour of this personality includes an extravagant interest in sexual flirtation and fun. However, she is different from the demanding and sensual Flirty One. She has a sense of delight about life. She is fun and engaging. I like her better than the Flirty One. She feels more genuine. While the Flirty One always sounds like she is drinking, this one actually is inebriated when she shows up. The consumption of hard liquor seems to be the trigger that prompts the Partying One to emerge. For her to continue to be present hard liquor needs to continue to be consumed. The more hard liquor she consumes, the more the fun-loving side of this personality is obliterated. She becomes irritating in her demands to be reassured that she is loved and loveable. She does not show up very often. In my memory the drinking of hard liquor resulting in the partying personality showing up happens only at parties in her younger adult years.

The Partying One is different from other personalities regarding her memory. The other personalities have memories from the different times in Mom's life when they are present, except for the host personality who carries fuller memories. The Partying One personality, however, does not seem to have memories of any of the times she has shown up. The host personality also does not have memories of the actions of the Partying One because all the personalities are inebriated.

It is important in my interpretation of this story to be aware of my sense of this lack of memories in the Partying One and the lack of memories about the Partying One in the host personality. Understanding this is critical to understanding the reason why, I believe, Mom does not know that Scott is an extra biological father in our family. In my assessment neither the host personality nor the Partying One carries memories of the actions of the Partying One. I believe it is the Partying One who is intimate with Scott.

A question stirs in the midst of this description. How do I know that the one who shows up when she is inebriated is different than our "real Mom"? Could the Partying One not just be our "real Mom" impacted by liquor since the uninhibited attitude of the Partying One sounds like descriptions that could be used for many people when they are drunk?

Each of the alternative personalities has a different way of engaging the world than our "real Mom." The differences between the personalities are so subtle I don't see for years that the changes in Mom are something more than shifts in mood.

Subtle though the differences are, they become extremely clear in my mind on the night I am shown some of the predominant personalities. Now, I can't *not* see the differences.

The only comparison that I can think of is that it is like figuring out the difference between twins: once you see a difference in twins, like a subtle variance in their attitude toward life or a minor difference in their physical stance, or a different feel to their energy you can't not see it.

The same is true for me in the difference between our "real Mom" and the Partying One; their energy, perspectives, focus in life and physical stance feel like the two of them are distinctly different.

THE SUICIDAL ONE

I think that this personality is created when Mom is thirty-one in response to the death of her sister, who is killed as a result of a high-speed police chase. Mom is supposed to go with her youngest sister that night, but doesn't, and so she is not there to see the oncoming vehicle that crashes into her sister and kills her.

It is evident in many ways that Mom feels profound grief over her youngest sister's death. She offers incredible support to her sister's children, which she does for anyone who needs help, but in this case it feels like her response is intensified.

My sense that this alter personality comes into existence after the death of her sister is associated both with the tone and focus of this personality but also with the timing of her arrival. It is eight to nine months after her sister's death that Scott confronts Dad and Grandma with the need to support Mom because she has become suicidal. Scott believes her suicidal tendency is a result of the death of her youngest sister intensified by her sense of guilt for cancelling going with her sister that night. If she had gone she felt she could have saved her sister because as a passenger she still would have checked traffic as they entered the intersection.

In the early seventies, Mom often speaks to her sister who died ten years earlier. On nights when Mom is totally falling apart, I regularly sit and listen to a one-sided conversation between Mom and my deceased aunt. In those conversations Mom talks about wanting to die as well.

The most repeated question and statement of this personality is, "What value do I have? I am of no value to anyone."

This personality does not obviously have one specific trigger. She sometimes shows up in moments when life is not unfolding the way our "real Mom" expects it to. It seems to me that if our "real Mom" feels that she has not adequately accomplished something the Suicidal One will show up. The Suicidal One always shows up when Mom is on prescription drugs beyond her standard daily medication. Whatever the triggers are, she shows up often.

This personality consumes much of my life as I continuously respond to her despair. When I discover in 2008 that Mom has no awareness of ever being suicidal, I stop responding to this personality (which I do not understand to be a personality in 2008 since it is still a time when I think of all these different manifestations as moods). Instead, when the behaviour shows up, I suggest that she contact an emergency phone line to deal with her feelings.

The shocking reality to me is that once I stop engaging with this personality she stops showing up as often or demanding attention. I am stunned by the awareness that I may have been feeding this personality with attention, which for so many years kept her thriving.

This is the personality who is whiny and demands constant reassurance that she has value. She moans and groans that she has little reason to live at all. She consumes massive amounts of energy, absorbing it from anyone who is willing to stay with her when she is in this state.

THE MUNDANE ORGANIZER

Based on my experiences with Mom's many personalities, I think there is one that forms after the death of her third husband in 2005, on the day when Mom is leaving their home. She is moving to a condo in the community where I live in order to be close to me. This has been the plan since before her third husband's death. At the time she is seventy-six years old.

I am on the phone with her when the splintering into this personality begins. She is overwhelmingly distressed. She speaks of hearing her dead husband. She's filled with anguish over finding a lost piece of jewellery that she is certain wasn't there a day ago when she thoroughly vacuumed everything. How did it get there? Who put it there?

Over the next seven weeks, I watch the disintegration as this new personality emerges. The changes in Mom could be attributed to the implications of getting older, but in my experience this personality is quite distinct from the core personality we call our "real Mom." And the changes happen abruptly rather than over a period of time, which would be a more common flow to the aging process.

The Mundane Organizer is extremely self-absorbed and, in my experience, boring. Her time and conversations are filled—to the point of obsession—with making sure she is organized. A key component of her conversation focuses on passing on detailed medical information to family members so that we are all appropriately informed.

This personality expands during the years that Mom lives in the community where I live. During that time a number of physical manifestations emerge. She begins to walk in an odd, choppy way, a gait that mirrors other choppy actions, including her speaking patterns. It is like she has lost a sense of flow in life. Her movements are almost robotic, like those of a mechanical being.

This personality also has a different way of writing. Mom has beautiful handwriting. If she is in the suicidal personality, her handwriting can be a bit sloppy, but it is still recognizable as Mom's handwriting. In this new personality, she periodically has a radically different way of writing. It is very square in its design in comparison to the flow of Mom's usual handwriting style. It shows up at odd angles on a page, with no consistency of size in the letters, even in one word.

During these latter years of Mom's life, the Mundane Organizer is significantly present, although the other personalities continue to show up regularly.

THE ANGELIC PRESENCE

The personality of the Angelic Presence is intriguing when she shows up. I love her presence. It is warm, welcoming, serene and undemanding. Her energy feels like pure light. The energy fields around her and within her are clear; they are not filled with past wounds, small-ego self or issues that lurk in the background. She is simply clear—clear like an angel might be. When I feel back into my memories as a kid, I sense her presence showing up once in a while. The feelings of those moments stand out in my mind because she is such a delight.

She doesn't get caught in any of the mundane realities of life. She focuses on whoever is right in front of her. When she shows up, it is usually for a significant period of time, like a respite from life as usual. As I begin exploring the personalities at first I think that the last time I see her is in the fall of 2008, when I am pretty sure she stays around for over five weeks.

Since there is no distress in her energy field, it seems to me there is no external crisis to associate with this personality. I wonder if she shows up when the host personality is overwhelmed by the other personalities, with their various obsessions about day-to-day life. Did she emerge to create respite space for the host personality? It is interesting that when the Angelic Presence is around she is the only alter personality who acknowledges being conscious of information that she does not know. When she is here, if it is a time of respite for the host personality, maybe the host personality isn't as engaged with the Angelic Presence personality as she is with the other personalities to whom she seems to regularly pass required information. Or maybe it's that the other personalities are so small-ego self-centred they don't realize they have gaps in information. The Angelic Presence is definitely the most "together" of the alternate personalities.

Engaging with her is like connecting with Mom at the core of her being, where none of the struggles and issues of this life intrude. She feels like the eternal part of Mom, and since the only thing that is eternal is love, she totally emanates love. What I do know is that I like it when she is present. Relationships matter to her. It's as if she glides on waters that are calm and still. Nothing troubles her.

She does, however, lack the complexity of our "real Mom." Her attention is not captured by future plans like we experience with our "real Mom." She is also quite different in that she does not engage in the life of the community around her like our "real Mom."

It is only after I see the many personalities in Mom and really begin to explore memories of the different personalities that I realize that it is this personality who tells me in August 2008 that she has never been suicidal. She tells me that if I ever see such behaviour in her again I have her permission to record it so that she can see this part of herself of which she is totally unaware.

It is when she is in this personality in 2008 that I share with her that we wonder if there is a possibility that she might be experiencing the impact of rapid cycling bipolar disorder. I tell her we have been gathering experiences of different people in our family who have had episodes of odd behaviour because there is a member of our extended family being checked for a mental illness. She tells me it would be nice if he were to have someone in the family with whom he could relate and who could help him discover strategies that would help. She says she would be pleased to provide support by trying the medicine if she does have this rapid cycling bipolar, an offer that is huge considering the negative impact of medication on her life.

I talk to her about this possibility while we are in the emergency ward for what turns out to be an obstructed bowel. I tell her we want to share the information we have gathered with her doctor. She listens as I talk to the doctor and nods her head to indicate she is okay with what I am saying. She does tell the doctor that she has no memory of the odd behaviours.

It is this personality who I think endures the test run of the medication for bipolar in the fall of 2008, until the raging banshee part of the Aggressive One or the host personality steps in and declares, "Enough of this being sick and having constant diarrhea."

It is during this time in the fall of 2008 when Mom and I talk about how I once spoke with her third husband about her odd behaviour. She is stunned, saying she always thought the two of them had no secrets and so she can't imagine him not telling her. I tell her she was not only part of the conversation, she was the one who initiated it. She sinks into silence, puzzled over this new awareness.

As I ponder her strong sense of connection to her third husband, I wonder if it is the Angelic Presence who is present during the years of that marriage. Mom is good during those years. She is serene and content. She spends all her time caring for her home, her husband, welcoming family for gatherings and reading to two little girls from down the street. These are all tendencies and characteristics of the Angelic Presence. I remember noticing her lack of engagement with her community, which is also a typical characteristic of the Angelic Presence personality.

If the Angelic Presence provides a time of respite for the host personality, and since the five years of Mom's third marriage follow the seventeen years of hell of her second marriage, it makes sense that the host personality needs time for recovery and respite. I am intrigued with the idea that this alter personality could stay around constantly for five years, with the exception of one five-day period when the Suicidal One shows up, prompting the call to me from Mom and her third husband. I realize now how much I enjoyed her delightful presence during those five years but also that I missed the more dynamic presence of our "real Mom."

As I complete the descriptions of the eight splinter personalities, I am aware that I am, in an odd way, grateful to them.

One way I am grateful to them is that I learn a great deal about engaging with various perspectives on life simply by engaging with Mom. Mom's differing insights on topics have honed my skills and commitment to tap into the many perspectives that swirl amongst us so that we can find the best way forward. Engaging with Mom has taught me to anticipate that there will be gems of wisdom if we are willing to listen to all the voices, which results in hearing the wisdom within us and amongst us.

The key aspect of my gratitude, however, has to do with my awareness that I believe the personalities protect the core strength of our "real Mom." They each take on the burden of a crisis in her life. As a result the crises in her life do not diminish Mom's core strength.

I wonder what Mom's life would have been like if the personalities had not emerged to deal with traumas, if they had not emerged as a coping mechanism. If the personalities had not dealt with the really tough stuff of life, how would Mom have coped? If alternative personalities had not formed, what might have happened to that strong core presence of our "real Mom" in the face of the many crises? I wonder how she would have responded. Any of the options that I can imagine may well have resulted in us not being graced by the gifts of her core personality.

During the summer of 2016, while I am pondering the different distinct personalities, I do a small amount of reading about the experience of people with dissociative identity disorder (DID). I am aware that this diagnosis is considered to be a response to trauma, so it is not genetically passed on. It is like the impact of post-traumatic stress disorder (PTSD), which also emerges as a result of trauma.

As I read about DID I look for distinctive characteristics consistent with people dealing with this disruptive reality to see if presenting issues are in any way consistent with my experience of Mom. If they are, it could explain a lot. Such insights could help us to more fully celebrate and understand Mom's life. However, we will never categorically know for sure if DID was part of her reality because a medical professional is required to provide a diagnosis of a specific mental illness. That never happened in Mom's lifetime.

In my reading, I have learned that the concept of multiple personalities, which was an earlier description of DID, was never fully accepted by the medical community because of a suspicion that patients had different personalities emerge while under hypnosis due to suggestions from their doctor. Mom was never under a doctor's care for this potential disorder in her life, and so there was never any possibility of a doctor impacting the development of personalities.

I have also read that it is thought that the formation of a variety of different personalities happens as a result of a childhood trauma. In my experience with Mom, the personalities seem to emerge at different times as a result of different crises in life, though the first one formed as a result of a childhood trauma. Based on what I have observed, it seems to me that once the pattern is established of a new personality forming in response to an early trauma, the formation of alternative personalities becomes the response to cope with extreme crises in life.

Although I have done some reading on this topic I have chosen to not do in-depth reading or research into other people's experiences. I think it is important to not distort the unusual position I am in to share my experiences of Mom without being influenced by wider perspectives or interpretations.

After developing my own awareness of the different personalities in Mom, I did check one prominent website called "Healthy Place,"[1] which provides mental health support, resources and information. The website includes a description of the new designation

---

[1] For more information, visit www.HealthyPlace.com.

of dissociative identity disorder (DID) based on the *Diagnostic and Statistical Manual of Mental Disorders, 5th Edition.*[2]

Some of the characteristics described for DID seem to align with my experience of Mom. In my experience Mom did have: "more than two distinct personalities with their own memories and ways of engaging with the world"; "gaps in her memory about realities in her life"; "difficulties in functioning"; "personalities who present in ways that are opposite to each other"; "transitions that can happen rapidly from one personality to another often brought on by stress"; "increased sexual behaviour"; "different handwriting"; "auditory hallucinations"; "a sense of fear and betrayal."[3]

I don't know for sure if Mom would have been diagnosed with DID. However, I have shared my thoughts and interpretations of my experiences with Mom with a highly respected now-retired senior staff person of a mental health unit. After reading this section of my manuscript, his first comment to me is that he thinks I missed my calling in diagnosing people. He comments that my in-depth insights, intuition and observations are more complete than those of many practitioners.

When I talk about a mother with many personalities, it is not a diagnosis, it is a way of describing my experience of my Mom. The phrase "many personalities" is a description that captures what I experienced in my life with Mom.

[2] *Diagnostic and Statistical Manual of Mental Disorders, 5th edition* (Washington, DC: American Psychiatric Association, 2013).
[3] Ibid.

REFLECTING ON IMPACT

EACH MEMBER OF OUR FAMILY experiences and responds differently to the varying mental states that Mom presents. In October 2016, when Janis and her husband come to Canada from their home in the States for Janis's mother-in-law's funeral, we talk about how different people respond to the reality of life with Mom. Janis's husband sums up Janis's and my differing responses by saying, "Janis left, and you, Karen, dealt with Mom from a different realm."

To me the different responses amongst family members always seemed more circumstantial than deliberate.   But Janis's husband's comment intrigues me. It causes me to stop and ponder what it means that I dealt with Mom "from a different realm."

My wonderings prompt me to return to the mystical moment in the meadow at age three when I experience light emanating from everything and everyone. At first I think everyone sees life this way. However, over time the experience feels like I am connecting to something different than the landscape of ordinary, everyday interactions. When I am connected to this realm, I can see and sense the light in people. No matter how shattered or broken a person is, I still see the light within them. No matter how shattered or broken I am, I still sense the light in me.

Throughout my life, I am very aware of when I am connected to this realm or to this place of the power of love within me which allows me to see goodness and light in life. I am also aware of when I am not connected to this place of power within me. Past wounds and their triggers, combined with the voices of judgment and fear that I carry inside my head, disconnect me from this place of connection to the power that is love. When disconnection happens, I am a captive in a landscape of expectations and of judgment rooted in fear, which slowly drain my energy and suck the life and the love out of me.

We can get mired in a way of engaging the world that is informed by the voices of judgment and fear that swarm through our world and our minds, which prompts us to see only what is wrong. At the other end of the spectrum we can engage the world from this place within us that is rooted in love, a love filled with a passion for justice nourished by deep caring, and with a commitment to choose to see goodness so that possibilities of a way forward can emerge. This is not to say that when we look at the world with eyes of love we do not see the destruction and dysfunction. Love demands that we allow ourselves to be broken-hearted when we observe how far we have strayed from the path of wholeness. Our awareness of our disconnection from the vision of wholeness carried deep within us inspires us to choose alternative possibilities which allow us to become a reflection of love together.

My description of the experience of engaging the world rooted in love is that it happens when we are connected to our true essence, our higher consciousness, to the universal consciousness of love, to the Divine within us. When I am rooted in fear rather than love, I am connected to my small-ego self where I allow external expectations and judgments to define me, which diminishes and dismantles my core strength. In such moments I am off-kilter and not centred.

I know that in my life I move along a spectrum of these ways of engaging in life. I also know that I can observe which way of being I am engaging from.

In the one state when I am connected to the Divine I feel like all the layers of the expectations that are external to my true essence give way and I remember who I am. I can see more clearly, my gifts flow through me with greater ease, and I feel a sense of connection to the awe and beauty all around me. In the state when I am drawn in by my small-ego self, it is like I am wearing layers of cumbersome clothing that obscure my true essence. I get caught up in how I think other people will think of me. I give away my power of choice to a whole list of expectations that feel alien to who I know myself to be. In my experience, connecting to the transforming power of love takes time and intention, but once this state or place is known, when connection is lost, it is a small step away.

Janis's husband's description of me dealing with Mom "from a different realm" makes me wonder: if my life had not been filled with meditation, an abundance of spiritual practices, large blocks of time spent in retreat deep in the heart of nature, mystical experiences and the support of a mature community committed to upholding each other on the journey of life, would my experience of my relationship with Mom have been different? What would my life have been like if I hadn't found nourishment for my spiritual well-being? Would I have completely burned out rather than just being on the brink, like I was a few times? Would I have been so caught in the circle of the needs of day-to-day demands and expectations that I would have missed the joy of life? Or would the mystical experience from when I was three be enough to sustain me?

Connecting to the transforming power of love that is at the source of life has been central to my journey. It nourishes me in my day-to-day life and empowers me to live connected to who I really am. Living the way of love is so much more than soft, cuddly, nice thoughts. It is demanding, challenging, freeing and life-giving—and it has the power to change the world. It is a core message of the teachings of Jesus: to love with all our heart and all our strength, to create a world filled with the Kindom of God where the power that reigns is love. Using the Principles of Circle Practices to awaken us to Authentic Connection Culture,[4] where love is at the centre of all we do, holds the power to transform life on a personal and a communal level.

Finding love and joy changes our perspective. Even in the most difficult moments, Mom and I find a spark of laughter or discover an insight about life and relationships that has a positive effect somewhere else in my life. I often have the very unusual and unique opportunity to

---

[4] See Appendix.

hear wisdom and thoughts from more than one perspective while simply sitting with Mom as the conversation is engaged by different personalities. In the disruptive and confusing moments, I intentionally choose to turn toward gratitude. I choose to focus on the goodness that is emerging, using a variety of methods to be centred to ensure that fear, judgment or cynicism will not overwhelm me.

In the midst of the stresses of life, there has been a constant certainty in me that the power of love carries the vision and the potential for the power of transformation and wholeness. This sense of certainty has allowed me to see potential even when life is shattering.

When I look back over the years, I see streams of light weaving in and out of my relationship with Mom. Those streams of light illuminate a path filled with love even when our reality is overwhelming, disturbing or confusing.

In the midst of the reality of life with Mom, I strive to connect to the core place within me where I am grounded and feel a sense of wholeness. In my life's work and during the writing of this book I identify lessons I have learned from Mom about finding wholeness in the midst of brokenness.

13 LIFE LESSONS THAT HAVE EMERGED IN MY RELATIONSHIP WITH MY MOM

- o Deal with issues when they arise.
- o Follow the flow of energy. If you meet resistance, be like a river and keep searching for a place that allows you to move with ease so that you are flowing with the energy of life rather than fighting the underlying currents.
- o Choose to see differently by shifting your focus.
- o Listen for, and to, inner wisdom and intuition.
- o Pause so that as many people as possible know where we are trying to go.
- o Trust that there is goodness trying to emerge.

- o Reconnect to your core essence and the Divine.
- o See the light within yourself and others even if you have to look beneath the rubble.
- o Allow curiosity to lead you rather than judgment or expectations.
- o Listen for the wisdom and voices of all perspectives.
- o Stop "shoulding" on yourself or on others.
- o Let gratitude and beauty fill you.
- o Focus on what you want to grow.

These life lessons weave in and out of the stories of the fractured reality of life with Mom; they are insights for which I am deeply grateful. They are strands of a story that weave together a tapestry of wholeness even in the midst of brokenness.

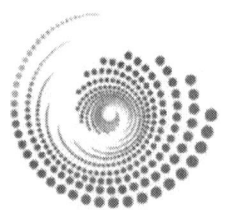

AS I WANDER THROUGH THE REALITY OF LIFE WITH MOM, the first experience I go back to, which impacts me and my relationship with my Mom, is when I am six months old. I have no conscious memories of the experience, but I carry the impact of that time inside my energy fields. I discover this in my early forties when I do energy healing work. I keep being guided to do healing to the time in my life when I am six months old. For years I don't know why.

In 1999 when Mom and I are on the final leg of our journey through Israel and Palestine, I ask her if she remembers something happening in my life when I was six months old that would cause me distress. We are in Tel Aviv standing on the balcony of our hotel room. It is the night of April 27, the sixteenth anniversary of Dad's death.

Mom tells me that it is when I am six months old that she almost died because of complications from the pregnancy that followed my birth. I know the story—I just didn't know it happened when I was six months old. No wonder Mom repeatedly tells us that nursing a baby is not dependable birth control. She knows from personal experience.

Mom tells me the full story as we stand on the balcony.

She is rushed to the hospital. Any time she shares this story she tells us that the baby was moving up into her organs, a description that seems odd but that's how she describes it. During the night she remembers an out-of-body experience of looking down at herself from the corner of the hospital room. Then she turns because she feels drawn beyond the room. Part way to someplace else, my face flashes before her. She remembers the ache of her milk-swollen breasts and turns back.

She looks at me that night out on the balcony and says, "You brought me back that night. I was in the hospital for seven days. I don't even know who took care of you and your sister and brother while I was gone."

I ask her if she was able to breastfeed me when she got home. She responds quietly, "No."

So my inner child carries the wound of this experience.

When Mom comes home from the hospital, she has two lively kids, a two-year-old and a four-year-old along with me at six months old. She is also healing from the impact of a pregnancy gone wrong, as well as any medicine they had her on during the seven days in the hospital.

If I imagine myself in that situation, with no grandparents to help, I am sure I would be in survival mode, making sure the kids are fed and safe, then withdrawing into myself to contain some energy for my own healing.

For me as the six-month-old, I am dealing with being put on formula and introduced quickly to solid food. I am also dealing with the reality of a totally absent Mom for the seven days and, I suspect, to quite a degree after the seven days.

I speculate out loud to Mom that my guess is that she uses much of her energy to engage the two- and four-year-olds when she comes home, hoping that the six-month-old will stay put. When I describe the scene in my imagination to Mom, she agrees it is pretty accurate.

Mom and I stand on the balcony side by side pondering our shared experience. We are gazing out at the Mediterranean Sea. Something catches my eye. A white dove is flying down toward us. It hovers over us for a moment, and then flies away.

The imagery in the story of Jesus's baptism—the description of a dove like the Spirit descending upon him—is not lost on me. It is in that moment of the appearance of the dove that the scripture story says Jesus hears God claiming him as a beloved child of God.

The assurance that we are all beloved is a key understanding that sustains me in the tough moments of life.

A deep peace comes over me. The moment feels like a gift after all the angst of struggles Mom and I have shared together. I wonder if perhaps the depth of our connection begins on that night long ago when Mom almost dies. It seems to make some sense as to why our lives continuously intertwine.

———————————

My mind meanders down the pathway of my life-memories to a few years after Mom's near-death experience.

The strongest conscious memory of our early relationship of just the two of us comes from the time when Janis and Mark are both in school. I am three. It is 1959. I feel myself back in my three-year-old body as memories flood through me: watching Captain Kangaroo on TV while Mom works in the kitchen; playing with my china dish set at the kitchen table while Mom creates something wonderful for lunch; going out for tea with Mom to my best friend's house across the fence in our backyard; kneeling on a red leather chair in the front window of Mom's hairdresser watching people go by every Thursday morning from 10 to 10:45 a.m., or longer on the weeks Mom gets a perm.

There is a moment from this time in my life that stands out in my memory. It is the first time I am allowed to go outside by myself without being in the fenced-in backyard.

I sit primly on the top step of the veranda where I have been told, firmly, to stay. I am delighted to be alone and not have a fence blocking my view of the world. I love being able to stare deeply into the area across the road that we call the Pit, due to it having been a gravel pit at one time. To my sister and brother and me, it is a huge area of incredible marshlands filled with intriguing foliage. It has the most amazing toboggan hill. It is in the Pit that I first experience the magic of fireflies. It is from the Pit that my night-time lullaby emerges, filled with the sounds of crickets and frogs.

I look down the street to the right. I can see the entrance to the cemetery across the road. The Pit is on one side of it, and the river is on the other. I know that if you turn the corner at the end of our road, you come to a park that overlooks the river. There's a cliff that extends down from the park's edge to the water's edge. I have wonderful memories in that park: making grass hula skirts at a camp Mom helps to run; Dad bringing a vending truck to the fireworks so the neighbourhood can buy ice cream and hotdogs; my best friend and I going to the park alone to play on the teeter-totter as long as we promise to stay away from the edge of the cliff that looks down over a rushing river.

After a few moments of savouring this time alone and enjoying the neighbourhood where we live, I begin to play a game in my mind. I imagine people coming up the front walk toward me. They ask for help to find their way home. After listening attentively, I point them in the right direction and tell them what to watch for so they can find their way home.

I am intrigued when I think about this memory because so much of my work focuses on finding our way home to who we are, finding our way back into authentic relationship with our self and with each other. At three years of age I am already imagining helping people find their way home to the place where they are meant to be.

I remember sometimes going to church when we are young. Dad is something called a steward. I don't like church very much. My earliest memory of church is when I am three. I am first in line in the children's choir, dutifully following the adult choir down the centre aisle. When we get to the front of the church the adult in front of me slams a gate shut, blocking the way of the children's choir. We are directed to seats behind the gate. I don't much like that some people get to go into the special area at the front while others are shut out.

The impact of that moment echoes across the memory line of my life, making me sensitive to actions that might cause people to feel they are not respected or included, particularly in church, which becomes the place of my sphere of influence.

Life changes in September 1960. My favourite aunt, Mom's youngest sister, is killed when a car, being chased by the police speeds into an intersection, crashing into the car she is driving.

I am four. I remember the day with clarity. It is filled with the anguish and the pain of Mom and my aunt's two children. I stand at the bottom of the driveway with Janis, Mark and my two cousins and watch them try to find something normal to say. The grief enfolds us in a sacred moment of connection, a connection so profound the bond lingers through the years. Later I stand at the edge of the living room and experience my mother completely falling apart on the inside, yet rising up to take care of everyone else.

On that day and in the months to come, Mom begins to disappear, to withdraw from life and us. She's there physically but the Mom we long for is absent. Our aunt is gone, and now Mom is leaving too. I feel an ache in the centre of my chest that won't go away.

Mom still engages in everyday life; she helps us find rhubarb hidden under the trees at the edge of our yard, she goes bowling with Dad every Thursday night and is part of the Parent Teacher Association. But even in the midst of normal everyday activities, I am aware that Mom is fragile. Her energy is dissipating. It feels like she could fade away or shatter into a million pieces.

My sense as a five-year-old that Mom could shatter at any time is confirmed one day. I am standing beside Mom when the breadman comes to the front door carrying his wide wicker basket full of fresh baking. He has red hair. My hair was black when I was born, then it turned red, then orange on its way to white blond before turning chestnut brown with the highlights from the earlier colours. I remember being teased that the breadman must be my father. How else could I have such red hair? I wonder if people are right that he is my Dad. That day he looks at my Mom with sad eyes and says he sees in the paper that the man who crashed into her sister has been sent to prison for two years. Mom crumbles and weeps. His presence is kind as he stays with her for the moment it takes for her to compose herself.

In the summer of 1961 life shifts again.

In the conversation the morning of April 18 in 2016 when Janis asks me about Scott to try to figure out if he is her biological father, I tell her that I remember a big fight at his cottage. The 1961 shift in life happens as a result of that big fight.

Our Grandma is there that weekend, which is very odd because we rarely see Grandma even at home, never mind at a cottage hours north of Toronto. The trip up to the cottage that weekend is painful. The car is filled with undefined strife, in stark contrast to the usual excitement that travels with us to the cottage on a normal weekend.

This is the story that I delve into during the summer of 2016 when I tap into the timeline of my memories, so I can access the full memory of what happened during the big fight.

The people present are Scott and his wife, their two kids, my parents, Mark and Janis, me, and then the very odd character of our Grandma, Dad's Mom.

As soon as I go to the place in my body where I carry the memory, the details come rushing in. I can feel myself drawn into the moment. The details are sharp in their intensity.

Dinner is over. The five kids are shooed outside. It is dusk. The light is dimming.

It is a relief to leave the tension-filled cottage even though I find my attention drawn to the window that peers into the depth of what is happening in the cottage. Janis and Scott's daughter are beside me, chatting and playing. Mark and Scott's son are lying on the dock, hanging their heads over the edge to explore life below the surface of the water.

I am sitting looking up the hill at the cottage. I am painfully aware of the irritation of the sand beneath me, but I don't want to move. I sit, waiting. The screen door of the cottage slams, making the sharp sound that echoes across lakes in cottage country everywhere. I hear the voices of Mom and Scott's wife drift off down the road.

As their footsteps fade, my grandmother speaks sharply. "What's this all about, Scott? Why did you demand that I come here?" She is clearly beyond annoyed.

Scott turns his attention to my Dad. "I'm worried about Ellie. She's fading away. She's like a dark shadow filled with grief. And now she's talking about not wanting to be here, not wanting to live."

His statement is met with silence.

"You have to do something, Max! You can't just keep hoping it will get better! She's going deeper and deeper into despair. It feels like she's just going to slip away, and you can't let that happen!"

"What am I supposed to do?" Dad's question is quiet, but filled with the anguish of his not knowing.

"You need to talk to her, let her tell you what she's feeling. Do you know how guilty she feels that she didn't go with her sister that night? She's convinced that if she went like she was supposed to, as a passenger she would have looked both ways before they pulled into the intersection and she would have seen the two cars racing toward them. She's convinced she could have saved her sister if she kept her word and gone that night."

Dad groans. "Oh, no wonder she's so despondent. It's bad enough to lose a sister without feeling like you could have stopped it from happening."

Silence.

Dad stands up. I can see him in the window. "What are we going do?"

Scott rises, and the two of them stand face to face. "I think you need to start getting her to talk to you, so you can show her you care by listening to her. She needs you to understand what she is going through."

"How do you know how she feels?"

"She talks to me. I listen. She feels that I understand her … and nobody else does."

Dad steps toward Scott. "Well, maybe it would help if you stopped being available for her to talk to."

Reflecting On Impact   Page 77

Scott steps back. "Fair enough. How about if we put your visits to the cottage on hold for a time, and we stop coming to the parties for a while? You and I will still see each other for golf, but we won't all get together."

"Okay," Dad nods, "that seems good."

Scott moves toward Dad, directing passionate energy at him. "I will encourage her to talk to you before you leave tomorrow. But, he points a finger at Dad, "if you aren't there for her ... if you don't provide her with the support she needs ... if she lets me know she is falling apart ... I will respond."

Grandma stands. "You just stay away from her. My son is her husband. Now that he knows, he can take care of her."

Scott turns to Grandma. "He'll need your support. Another part of her being upset revolves around you. Why are you so mean to her? What she wants, what she needs, is a caring, supportive family and you are not helping."

They glare at each other.

Then Scott steps back. "The women are coming back."

I hear the voices of Mom and Scott's wife coming closer.

Scott looks at Dad and Grandma. "Do we have a deal?" They both nod.

The squeak of the cottage door echoes into the charged atmosphere. The slamming of the door cracks through the silence, shattering the scene. It is replaced by pleasant questions from Scott about their walk.

During the night I hear murmurings from Mom and Dad's room.

The next morning the atmosphere is subdued. By the time we kids get up, the car is packed. We are fed breakfast and told we are leaving. As we stand by the car Mom pushes us forward to say goodbye. We do. It feels strange. It feels more permanent than other times of saying goodbye to this family we have been so close to.

We get in the car. It is a silent trip home.

We never see Scott's family again. I ask for updates about Scott's daughter every time Dad goes golfing with Scott.

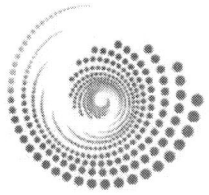

DAD AND GRANDMA BOTH KEEP THEIR WORD from the night of the confrontation, which is how I now refer to the big fight. Things in our life change as they both intentionally find ways to be more supportive of Mom.

I don't remember Grandma in our life much before that summer. I do remember asking Mom why. She tells me Grandma goes to Florida for a lot of the year. As young as I am I know it is an excuse.

But after the confrontation Grandma comes to visit. She teaches us how to knit. She even knits clothes for our Barbies. I still have a pink-fitted dress that has sparkles on the quite risqué low ruffle at the neckline. My granddaughter plays with it with her Barbies. Grandma also makes us fuzzy delightful slippers and awful poodle cover-ups for toilet paper.

I am not sure if I like having her around with her authoritarian, snobbish perspective, but in some ways, it feels better than the empty void that had been there before.

Dad responds by making significant shifts in our life. In September of 1961, Mom becomes pregnant, even though the doctors told her not to have any more children after the last pregnancy when she almost died. She tells us Dad really wants another baby.

I remember thinking as a child that Dad wanting another baby was incredibly selfish since it put Mom at risk, but now I see it differently. Now I wonder if choosing to have another baby is Dad's attempt to give Mom new purpose in her life. It works. Mom begins to re-emerge, though veils of fragility still surround her.

I remember my first day of school in September of 1961.

Mom walks with me to the bus stop. I hold her hand. I stare at her feet ensconced in high heels. I am amazed at her capacity to walk in high heels with such ease. I'm not often with her when she wears high heels, but she needs to be well-dressed to go to the school because she is the president of the Parent Teacher Association, the PTA. I feel a warm glow inside of me because she is the president of the PTA. I have noticed that she likes to be in charge and she likes it when people notice her gifts.

But it is because of a meeting of the PTA that I learn crucial and painful lessons about life.

I am part way through kindergarten when an episode at a PTA meeting causes me to identify ways of being in relationship that are not healthy and not life-giving. The experiences associated with that time start me on a life-long journey of searching for key concepts about how to be in community in a way that is healthy and life-giving.

One of the significant lessons I learn is the importance of dealing with issues before they fester. Issues need to be dealt with no matter how fragile I assess another person to be—in this case, my mother. The experience weaves together many lessons that become strands in my life's work around being intentional about developing good communication skills to aid us in creating space for wholeness to emerge.

The experience begins innocently in the kitchen in our home. I am telling Mom all about my day at school, including how I went into the storage closet to change into my toy high heels and mink stole for show-and-tell.

The phone rings in the middle of my story. Mom excuses herself to answer the phone. I stand and listen, waiting impatiently to finish my story. By the time she gets off the phone, she is in a hurry to get ready for the PTA meeting that night.

She calls us all to the table for dinner. We say grace together, then the conversation goes in all sorts of different directions, and there is no obvious time for me to finish telling my story.

The next morning in circle time I am delighted to hear my teacher say that she talked to my Mom last night at the PTA meeting and how I told her about going to the storage closet the day before. I smile, thinking it is great that Mom remembered my story that was interrupted.

But then the teacher gets mad at me. "Why did you tell your mother you were sent to the storage closet? Why did you lie to her? She asked me last night to explain what happened and I couldn't answer her."

I am so shocked, I sit there silenced.

"Why did you lie to your mother?"

The whole situation is bizarre. The storage room is where you are sent if you are bad. Why would I lie to my mother and tell her I had been sent there if it wasn't for something like getting dressed up for show-and-tell? I am shocked at what is happening. I am so stunned I don't speak. The teacher tells me I have to tell my Mom that I lied. I nod my head.

Every day for the next three weeks at circle time, in front of the whole class, the teacher asks me if I have told my mother that I lied. I haven't because I rarely think about it when I am at home, since in my mind it is just so strange. If I do think about it when I am at home, it seems to me that Mom is too fragile to deal with it. I decide to protect Mom from having to deal with a problem she has caused by going to someone else to ask questions about my unfinished story instead of having a conversation with me.

The teacher keeps persisting with an anger that seems unreasonable. She tells me one day that she doesn't like being made to feel like a fool, especially in front of the president of the PTA, and I need to fix the situation.

I finally tell my teacher that I have told my mother. That is my first lie. I don't want my teacher to feel like a fool, so I lie to her. I don't want my fragile mother to have to deal with something that I think is unimportant, so I don't tell her.

There are so many lessons wrapped up in this story about how not to have a healthy relationship—starting with me accepting that there is no time to finish sharing my story, continuing with Mom seeking information about what I said from someone other than me, expanding through a teacher who is triggered and so doesn't handle a situation well, and compounded by my sense of responsibility for everyone else's well-being. These are all ingredients and practices that guarantee the development of unhealthy relationships.

The story doesn't end here. The impact of it continues to unravel over the next few years in two different schools. The experience plants within me a seed that germinates and blossoms through my life's work. I am passionate about the development of principles and practices to create a culture where we can trust that we can speak openly and honestly, where we can have significant conversations rather than allow grumblings, secrets and projections to structure our relationships. What starts as a tiny misunderstanding becomes a significant impact in my life.

I am amazed at how strong my commitment is to not allow issues to fester. I am still quite young the first time I really see this commitment within myself. I am in grade six. I am twelve years old.

My class has decided to prepare the play *Cinderella* for the younger grades. No one wants to be the director, so I offer. I share my ideas of a way we might do the play. Everyone agrees and is enthusiastic. I think the rehearsals are going well. People have volunteered to be actors and to take care of technical aspects. The play is coming together.

Then one morning when I get off the school bus, a friend meets me to tell me, "None of the kids in the class will talk to you."

I ask her, "Why?"

She says, "I'm not allowed to tell you."

A strong feeling surges through me. I tell her, "You have to tell me. How else can we solve the issue?"

This is my worst nightmare. I am being totally rejected.

She reluctantly says, "Everyone is mad because you get to do everything."

I'm shocked, but at least I know what I am dealing with.

I go to where everyone has gathered for the early morning rehearsal. I stand at the side of the group and look at them. They stare back at me and then turn away and chat amongst themselves.

I speak over the hubbub and tell them I understand they aren't speaking to me because I get to do stuff they don't get to do. I ask them to give me some examples. They are silent for the longest time. I stare at them, waiting.

Then one girl emerges from the group spitting mad and rhymes off a list.

As I listen to the list I acknowledge it is true: I do get to do some things they don't. I admit some of what they are saying is true.

But I also tell them that some of the tasks I do are things I have no control over. I am aware that I get to do certain things because our teacher, who is also our principal, thinks that my dream of becoming a teacher and principal suits who I am, so he keeps giving me a chance to discover what that role entails. It includes being one of three people who fill in for teachers when they have an appointment and helping to lock up the exterior doors at the end of the day. I am chosen for those jobs.

However, I point out that the rest of the list are jobs that they all did at the beginning of the year but then decided they didn't want to do anymore. Anytime the teacher asked if someone else was willing to take a task on, I waited to see if anyone else was willing. When no one offered, I put up my hand. I ask if anyone wants to do any of the tasks. They are welcome to any of them. No one wants to.

The final item on the list is that I get to direct the play. I ask if they remember how that happened. They acknowledge that it happened basically the same way all the other jobs ended up being mine. No one else wanted to direct.

Though my next words feel like they are breaking my twelve-year-old heart, I tell them that I am willing to step aside for someone else to direct. They look amongst themselves. No one steps forward. They slouch in acceptance.

I ask them what I can do to make the experience better. They tell me to listen to them more, give them a chance to share their ideas.

I nod, and then ask, "Should I stop sharing my ideas?"

I am told forcefully, "No, your ideas are good; we just want to add in ours."

On that day, I make two critical discoveries about how to work with groups and create a sense of community.

One of the discoveries is that a leader is actually more effective if they gather the thoughts and insights of the whole group, rather than feeling like everyone expects them to know all the answers and lead the way.

This is a huge learning that has impacted my work through the years. It's the basis of my commitment to being a Facilitator of Significant Conversations: to intentionally ensure that the wisdom and creativity amongst the group has the opportunity to emerge.[5] When we create safe space for all voices to be heard, the result is that we tap into the wisdom and creativity that are within us and amongst us, which moves us toward future possibilities that are more than any one person can develop alone.

To this day when I direct a play I intentionally invite the insights of the cast. We are usually very close to the opening night before I request that input stop.

The second discovery from this tumultuous day in my twelve-year-old world is the difference it makes when we connect to the power of honesty and kindness that is at our very core and allow those powers to flow through us to reach out to the world. I experience one of my greatest fears that day in grade six: I am being completely rejected by everyone around me. However, something happens that day that surprises me—I do not let the fear consume me but rather, based on what I learned from my Mom through the incident in kindergarten, I choose to deal with the issue rather than let it fester.

---

[5] See Appendix.

Somehow a power deep within me breaks through the fear and speaks through me in a way that is authentic and real. The importance of speaking from my authentic self has been an awareness that I have intentionally tried to use since that day.

So I learn the importance of speaking openingly and honestly from an experience when Mom skewed good communication practices and I ended up wrongly being called a liar. I also learn that issues not dealt with can spiral out in unexpected and destructive directions. Life teaches me at a young age that not dealing with an important issue for fear of upsetting someone can cause far greater problems than risking hurting someone's feelings by being honest.

In the fall of 1961, when I am still in my early months of kindergarten, Mom and Dad search for a larger home to accommodate our soon-to-be larger family. They find a house that is just being built. As Mom's pregnancy progresses, the feeling that she is returning to us grows stronger. By the time we move into our new home in March 1962, it feels like she has come back home to us.

When we move, we go to a new school. Mark, Janis and I go to the office with Mom when she registers us. She hands the school secretary a file folder for each of us that contains academic information from our last school. I am in my final months of kindergarten and quite happy to be out of the setting where I had been labelled as a liar.

Three weeks later I am shocked to discover that the label of liar has followed me to this new school. I discover this disconcerting reality one day when we are told to move into our reading groups.

As I am heading to my group the teacher stops me. She tells me I am not going to the right group. I tell her I am going to the group where she put me on my first day. She bends down, looks me in the eye and in a very angry voice tells me I am a liar.

As I stare into her accusing eyes it seems to me that the unbalanced way that my first kindergarten teacher dealt with the incident when she thought I was lying must be documented in my file that follows me wherever I go. My new teacher believes my former teacher.

She directs me to a different reading group. I sit down because she tells me to. I look around at all the new faces. I had just gotten to know the kids in the other group.

I am so upset at being called a liar again and being put amongst a bunch of strangers I pee on the carpet. The teacher's assistant notices and takes me away to get cleaned up. She tells the teacher that I was right that I was placed in the other group. I am returned to my original group.

But I don't feel comfortable anymore. I have been called a liar, again.

I continue to pee on the carpet on a fairly regular basis, at least it seems that way to me. I remember a day when I feel like I can't cope for another moment because of the discord inside of me created by being mislabelled. I see that the teacher's assistant is watching me with kind eyes. She asks me if I would like to leave the room for a moment. I go with her into the area where we hang up our coats.

I begin to cry. It quickly becomes a wail. She asks me if I want her to call my Mom. I tell her I do.

Mom arrives.

Instead of taking me home, Mom takes me to the big mall. We go to the baby section in the large department store. I get to pick out a real baby dress and booties for my beloved, life-size baby doll.

When we get home, I go to the bedroom I share with my sister. I am all alone, and I get to play with my doll without having to fit someone else into my make-believe scenario.

That afternoon I discover how much I love to be alone. It feels like a lovely counterbalance to the demands of being in community where people have all sorts of expectations of one another that to me feel aggressive and controlling and lack awareness of the goodness that is longing to emerge. Big words to imagine in the mind of a six-year-old, but the feelings that those words describe are definitely swirling within my little body, filling me with a sense of confusion and sadness at what we humans do to each other.

To this day kindergarten is the year in my school life I hate the most.

Home feels much safer than school.

The feeling of a loving and stable home deepens when Betsy is born in May of 1962. She is a month early. According to Mom, her early arrival is a result of Mom shovelling a truckload of gravel out of the way so that she can get her car out of the garage to drive the three of us to school.

With Betsy's birth, the memories of Mom withdrawing from us fade even more.

When Mom holds Betsy and nurses her she looks down at her with eyes filled with love. I can imagine her doing that with me in a time of my life that I cannot remember. It fills me with a warm feeling of being loved.

When I am in grade one we go to the newly built school in our newly built neighbourhood. My teacher becomes one of my most dearly beloved teachers. I adore her so much, she and her daughter come to my birthday party. I am over the moon with happiness when I get her again in grade two. I love being in her class for many reasons, including the fact that we are experimenting with the new idea of students working in groups.

But then, part way through grade two, one of my friends tells her mother that I keep talking to her in our table group, and she can't get any work done. Her mother writes a note to the teacher.

The teacher calls me up to her desk and tells me about the note. She then tells me she is very disappointed in me and now she will have to put me in the single row for kids who can't work in a group.

I tell her I don't know what my friend is talking about.

She looks at me with sadness and says, "Don't lie, Karen."

There it is again. I am stunned and silenced.

I sit in abject misery in the single row for a few days. I have been incorrectly labelled once again. By being put in the single row, I am visibly mislabelled as a liar for all to see.

Before this happens I am already feeling awkward amongst the kids in the class because I keep being sent out for special tests for my reading. Apparently, I am not reading like the other kids. I don't read phonetically. When I see "pretty," I say "beautiful," which is not considered the proper way to read. The adults think it is intriguing. I think it makes me dumb.

And now I have to sit in the row that tells my grade two world that I can't get along in a group. It feels like a double whammy. I am devastated.

Then my teacher receives another note from my friend's Mom saying her daughter made the story up. I am moved back into the group.

No one apologizes to me but I am so delighted to be back in a group I don't notice at first. But the group doesn't feel the same. No one knows quite what to do with someone who has been accused of lying or with a friend who admits to lying. There is a feeling of discord in the group. The group doesn't feel like a fun or safe or kind place anymore.

I look over at the kids who sit alone in the centre row. I realize I feel lonelier in the group than I did when I was in the single row. At least in the single row, no one is expected to get along and there is even a sense of solidarity at being cast out together. Here in the group I just feel alone.

Years later I find out that the reason my friend's mother writes the second note to the teacher is that my Mom asks my friend's mother about the situation, saying she is surprised that I am disturbing another student. When I finally hear that story, I wonder why Mom didn't tell me at the time that she had been an advocate for me. It would have meant a lot to me to know that she stood up for me.

During those early years of school, in kindergarten and then in grade two, I am returned to two different groups innocent of the charge of being a liar. Both times I am returned to a group where it feels to me like the sense of community that had been in the group is now gone. I'm glad the truth came out that I didn't lie. I am glad I am returned to my group. I wish someone realized that kids don't have naturally developed skills to sort out healthy relationships. I wish that someone had done something to reconnect us in a healthy way.

These experiences plant a seed within me about the importance of actually talking about how we will be in community, so that when things break down we can figure out how to get back to being in healthy relationship.

Deliberately deciding together how we will build community and how we will deal with issues is a key principle in my life's work of identifying how to create Intentional Circles that provide the experience and skills of Authentic Connection Culture.

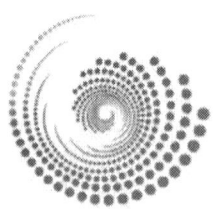

AT HOME THINGS SEEM TO BE BASICALLY GOOD for the next few years.

We live in a neighbourhood where the families hang out together. One time, prompted by Janis, the whole neighbourhood creates a circus to raise money for a charity. We discover we have amazing talent amongst us. After the circus the neighbourhood gathers regularly to watch the unending shows that the kids create.

Our lives are filled with sleepovers and sleeping out on the deck above our garage where we watch for falling stars. My days are filled with playing school in the basement where my very own classroom has been set up. Once in a while I let others play with me, but I prefer playing on my own.

Our weeks are filled with guitar lessons for Janis and Mark, dance lessons for me and trips to the chiropractor to help Mom cope with the back injury she sustained when she was seventeen.

Special occasions fill the house with extended family, great food and music. Camping trips become explorations of exciting new places.

However, it is during this time period that I begin to have a disconcerting feeling. The feeling lurks at the edge of my life and stays with me right up until the early nineties. For all the outward appearance of a loving household, I begin to live with the fear that Mom will pull off her mask of kindness and laugh at me for believing my parents love me. This feeling arises out of my sense that Mom has a secret. The worst secret that I can imagine is that she does not love me. Actually the secret is that she chose to allow her baby to be adopted and she doesn't want us to think she could do the same with us.

In 1964, Mom is injured. The accident happens on the night Mark goes to the first-ever Beatles concert at Maple Leaf Gardens to celebrate a friend's birthday. When the boys are being picked up after the party, Mom is chatting with one of the other moms at her car window. Mom steps back as the other mom prepares to pull away, but she doesn't step back far enough. The car runs over her foot.

The next morning Dad wakes up Janis and me. It is odd because he never wakes us up. Normally he barely even enters our room. He tells us Mom has her foot in a cast. We are to go see her in their bedroom.

I can see in her face that the pain is bad. She has medication to cope.

For the next several weeks Mom sits with her casted leg on the couch in the big bay window in the living room. She is knitting a sweater with a Maple Leaf hockey player on the back for Mark. It is grey with royal blue trim. I don't have any other memories of Mom ever knitting before or after those weeks of recovery.

Mom is different during these weeks. Most of the time, it is like she just wants a big party to be happening. She laughs a lot. She is loud and seems to be having fun. She calls out to us and demands that we join her in the living room to sing or dance for her. Usually Mom is totally consumed with her list of tasks and responsibilities. Now she is engaging and her face lights up with delight.

But there are other times during these weeks of healing when she is so sad it breaks my heart. I enter the living room hoping to find the happy, fun Mom. If she hasn't noticed me coming into the room I approach her quietly. I know that the fact that she hasn't noticed me is an indication that I will find the sad face when I get closer.

The difference between the happy one and the sad one is extreme. When the sad one is present it is almost like she is gone, leaving behind a thin veneer of the mother sitting in the living room window. There is a half-finished grey sweater with blue trim on her lap, pierced with knitting needles that lie still.

I watch one day when Janis goes into the room when Mom is sad. Mom looks up and talks to her. After a few moments Janis walks away. I go in and sit by Mom and hold her hand. She doesn't look at me.

From years of experience, I now suspect that the medication for the pain in her foot probably flipped Mom into two of her alternate personalities: the Aggressive One who can be like a demanding protective warrior who sometimes shows up with a wonderfully fun but demanding side, and the sad Suicidal One. They are distinctly different. Both the happy one and the sad one show up alternately while Mom is recovering.

Somewhere in the midst of these weeks Scott shows up. It is the middle of the afternoon. From the vantage point of years later, I think Scott is keeping the promise he made the night of the confrontation three years before—that if Mom lets him know that she needs him, he will respond.

Mom calls Janis and me downstairs. I come part way down the stairs that are covered in the gold broadloom that Mom and Dad so proudly chose for our new house. I peer through the white and gold metal stair spindles at Scott. He comes over to me. We are eye to eye. I haven't seen him in such a long time. We hear about him because he and Dad still golf. I miss him. He has always been one of the most adored adults in the circle of people in my life. But as I sit looking at him I feel shy because it has been so long since I have seen him. When I look into his eyes I can see that he is sad too.

I wonder what he thinks of our new home. It is the first time he has been here. Memories flash through my mind of the parties Mom and Dad have hosted here when I sit in their bedroom and wait for Scott to come upstairs to leave his coat on the bed. But he never comes. I see all the other adults who are Mom and Dad's friends. They are happy to see me and think it's sweet that I am there to greet them. I am disappointed when Mom comes upstairs in one of her party dresses to tell me it's time to go to bed because everyone has arrived. The dress I remember the best is the turquoise fitted dress that she always wore with the shiny broach, which as an adult I learn came from the father of her first child. Since her arrival in the bedroom means everyone has arrived I trudge off to bed sad that Scott yet again has not come to the party.

In the middle of that afternoon when Scott comes and looks at me through the white and gold metal stair spindles he asks me how I am doing. He listens to my hesitant answer. His attention does not waiver from my face. Then he tells me he has a gift for me.

He hands me a box. I open it. Nestled in the soft cotton is a watch on a chain to be worn as a necklace. The gold glitters in the soft afternoon light. My mouth forms a silent "O." I look up at him in delight. I tell him I just received my first watch on my last birthday, which I love because having a watch makes me feel so grown up.

I look down at the beautiful watch necklace. It feels almost too grown up. I put it on. I look up at him with a shy smile and a sense of deep joy.

He returns my smile and says, "I picked the gold one for you. It's shaped like the sun. Light sparkles from it just like you sparkle with light."

I smile even more. It feels like a wonderful reflection of the golden light that I saw in the meadow on that day long ago, a golden light that carries a song of love within its energy.

Then he says something odd. "I know things aren't easy for you with Janis being the favoured daughter between the two of you these days."

I cock my head sideways while my smile fades, thinking that is an odd thing to say. But I know it is true. Mom must have told him, or maybe Dad. Hearing him say it hurts, but it also helps me feel like I am seen and known and still loved.

I have been noticing that over the weeks before Mom's injury, she keeps me in the kitchen when Dad comes home at night. The other three kids still greet him with shouts of enthusiasm. Dad lifts them up and twirls them around. I feel left out.

I used to be part of that chorus of welcome but now Mom asks me to stay with her to help. I like being with her so I agree, but it feels like my relationship with my Dad is slowly disintegrating.

When Dad comes into the kitchen to give Mom a kiss, I get a brief hello. Mom tells him what a great help I am.

From the time I am eight until I am fourteen, this discord between Dad and me continuously impacts our relationship.

In looking back, I realize that Dad's desire to not engage with me begins at a time in his life when things are not going well at work. It is right around this time that he leaves one company, tries to start a business of his own which doesn't get off the ground, and then ends up at a second company.

It is a difficult time of transition in his career, weighed down with the reality of a new house and four children. Someone suggests that maybe I become like a family scapegoat for his frustration. My interpretation of the tradition of the scapegoat is that you pour all your frustration and anger onto the goat, and then send it out into the wilderness where you can't see it, which allows you to cope with the rest of your life. It's an interesting thought and perhaps explains these very odd six years. Eventually our discordant relationship completely turns around, but it consumes significant years of my childhood.

It is when I am fourteen that things shift with Dad. I get to a point where I am tired of him keeping me at a distance so he doesn't have to spend too much time with me and tired of him being constantly annoyed at whatever I am doing.

Having reached the limit of my tolerance for his lack of connection to me, I look at him one day and in the echo chamber of my fourteen-year-old mind I scream at him, "F--- YOU!" I decide to stop trying to earn his approval. I stop trying to please him.

I am shocked but delighted that from that point on Dad and I start having a relationship that grows and deepens over the years. When I am in my later teens Dad and I become extremely close, forming a relationship rooted in deep respect and love for each other. His desire to stay disconnected from me in earlier years takes a radical shift as he finds as many ways as possible to connect with me, like surprising me one night by showing up when I am at university doing my drama degree. He wants to watch me direct a rehearsal. Later as a young adult, I spend all day Sunday and usually one night a week with Dad and Mom and my soon-to-be husband.

Dad comments more than once that he thinks that the years when he didn't like me made me a stronger person. It certainly helps me to stop trying to please people to the point where I lose myself. Years later, Dad shares how he is surprised that we became extremely close once I hit my mid-teens, considering how much he didn't like me as a child.

So, Scott is right. When I am eight years old Janis is the favoured daughter between the two of us. Dad clearly doesn't like me and doesn't want me around him. Dad delights in Janis's quick wit. Mom confides in Janis about things that probably no ten-year-old should be told. I feel left out.

The gold watch from Scott feels like someone can see me. Much of the time I feel invisible to the people around me.

Someone feeling invisible is a reality that puzzles me as a child. I know from that moment in the meadow long ago that we are all connected by the golden light. If we are all connected, how can some of us be invisible? The golden light is constantly streaming through us and amongst us, calling us to see ourselves and each other with eyes of love. It connects us to one another at the very core of our being. My child-like heart breaks when I see the world around me disregarding what is possible; if only we would really see each other and understand that we are connected, I am sure we would treat each other differently. As I watch the way we fail to notice that we are connected, I am continuously saddened by lost opportunities for love to flow.

Janis comes crashing into my moment with Scott. She comes barrelling down the stairs and flops down beside me, clearly annoyed at being interrupted from whatever she has been doing.

Scott gives Janis a box similar to the one he has given me. She walks down the stairs and opens it. The voice of judgment inside of me rumbles awake. Why did I stay on the stairs to open my gift? Now I feel awkward and dumb for just sitting here. But it did mean I got to be eye to eye with Scott without him having to crouch down. That felt good. I like having full eye contact with him.

Janis's gift is a beautiful, modern-looking, silver watch necklace. I watch Janis and Scott with their heads together and think about what Scott said about Janis being the favoured daughter between the two of us. I know it is true.

But the fact that I have been given the gold watch is a sign to my eight-year-old heart that to Scott I am special; gold is the colour of affirmation according to how we use gold stars and gold ribbons.

After Scott leaves that day we don't see him again for seven years.

I think that by showing up that day, Scott is keeping his promise to not see Mom unless she calls. I think she reaches out to him when the sad personality peeks out under the influence of the pain medication because of her foot. Good to his word, Scott shows up when she calls.

Life returns to normal a few weeks after Mom gets the cast off her foot. We go back to the very scheduled life of housewives from Mom's generation—of laundry on Monday, groceries on Tuesday, and meatloaf on Thursday, with dinners served already on our plates. Every Sunday we have roast beef as we watch *Lassie*, *Walt Disney* and *The Ed Sullivan Show*, including the first live North American TV performance of the Beatles.

In the midst of the regular pattern of our lives, I experience Mom as being detached. I notice it and presume that it is how adults act, but I don't like it. She can be in the room next to some awful childhood behaviour amongst siblings but she never seems to notice. She has a way of detaching from the things going on around her. I experience this behaviour as a kid and when I am an adult.

A simple example from my adult years is when she is in my home and I am on the phone dealing with an issue from the church.

While I talk on the phone she is in the room puttering away at some task, usually hanging up my overwhelming number of clothes. In my mind it is clear that this is not a confidential call or I would have left the room. After I get off the phone, I talk to her about the conversation I just had. She reminds me that she doesn't listen to other people's calls so she doesn't know what I am talking about. I am a person who has to work really hard to not hear everything that is being said around me. For Mom it seems like second nature to stay detached from what is going on around her. I wonder if she learns to stay detached from her own Mom, who lived in a tiny house with many people.

There are times when we are kids that I long for her to engage more in the everyday flow of conversation and activities, but particularly in arguments amongst the kids.

Mom is in the next room one day when Janis screams at me that I can't come into the closet with her and two of our cousins because I'm too young to be part of the conversation. I protest loudly through the closed door, reminding them I am the same age as one of the cousins. They ignore me. Mom wanders into the room where I am protesting at the closet door and she simply goes about her task of putting away laundry, totally detached from what is happening.

That is, until someone uses the forbidden words.

I am in the basement one day with a girl from our neighbourhood. We are standing in the middle of my schoolroom area. Mom is in the kitchen upstairs at the other end of the house. I know the words are forbidden but I am so mad that I risk whispering them to my friend since Mom is so far away.

"Shut up!" I scream in a restrained whisper.

She stares at me. Her face changes as her eyes grow wide. I think I am making my point.

But then I feel a fierce hand on my upper arm. Mom moves me to one side, creating space for my friend to pass by us. Mom tells her it's time to go home. She scurries up the stairs as fast as her nine-year-old legs will carry her.

When the back door closes Mom turns me around to face her.

She screams at me, with each word spoken with space around it for emphasis. "Never [pause] tell [pause] anyone [pause] to SHUT UP!"

She grabs hold of my shoulders and shakes me. She shakes me so hard I can't hear anything she is saying. She shakes me so long I have trouble catching my breath. She is livid beyond anything I have ever seen.

She lets go of me and tells me to get upstairs. I race ahead of her. When I get to the second set of stairs that go to the bedroom level I slow down because Mom's gone into the kitchen. But then she charges at me with a wooden spoon, telling me to get moving.

I dash into my bedroom and climb onto my bed as far away from the door as I can get. She stands near the doorway, waving the wooden spoon at me and telling me to stay there until I am ready to say I am sorry. She leaves and slams the door. I am relieved she is gone.

I stay in my room for as long as I think I can without making her angry again. I finally make my way downstairs. Mom is in the kitchen. I enter with trepidation, going no farther than the doorframe. I tell Mom I am sorry. Without turning around Mom tells me to go and play. Her voice is calm.

I wander back downstairs. I never tell my friend that I am sorry. It seems Mom is the person I need to say sorry to. I've said it, but not to the Mom who was raging mad. She seems to be gone. Mom has shifted back into the mood where she focuses on running the house, which includes being detached from the kids so she can accomplish her list of tasks.

From the perspective of today, I recognize the behaviour as part of the Aggressive One I describe as the raging banshee, who is mean and furious and clearly triggers to the phrase "shut up." Mom's behaviour that day is totally inconsistent from that of our "real Mom." Our "real Mom" is a strong advocate for the abolishment of the strap in school. But every once in a while, Mom, who does not seem like our "real Mom," threatens us with the wooden spoon and shakes us uncontrollably.

IN 1965, WHEN I AM ABOUT TO TURN NINE, I have to have some medical tests. Mom is extremely thorough in giving us information about what we can expect when we will be interacting with doctors. It seems to be one of her fascinations in life. I wonder if she might have been a nurse if she hadn't left high school so abruptly when she turned sixteen.

By the time I arrive at the clinic I am filled with terror of the big black belt that they will put over me to hold me down, and equally terrified of the equipment they will use for the test. It is simply a chest X-ray, but with all of Mom's detailed descriptions I have created a laboratory of horror in my head.

I am diagnosed with pneumonia. The doctor orders that I stay at home for two weeks. For the first three days I totally love being at home while Mark and Janis are at school. Mom, Betsy and I spend the whole day in the house, Mom doing her thing with the house and Betsy and me upstairs alone in the bedroom I share with Janis.

Then Janis starts exhibiting the same symptoms. She doesn't have to go through the tests I went through. She is simply told to stay at home as well. She ruins the very delightful experience I have been having. Her presence feels like torment to my solitude.

After two weeks I return to school. A week later Mom calls to me to tell me to come downstairs. I have been upstairs playing Barbies with my best friend. I run down to the kitchen. Mom tells me she has forgotten that she is supposed to take my temperature regularly. She sticks a thermometer in my mouth, turns back to cutting potatoes, turns back to me, takes the thermometer out, stares at it, shakes it, puts it back in my mouth, stands still beside me, takes the thermometer out, looks at it and reaches for the phone.

It is only the second time I have heard Mom call Dad at work. The first time is when she is in labour with Betsy and even then she doesn't call him until 4:45 p.m., when his work day will be done in fifteen minutes. Betsy is born shortly after 6:00 p.m. This time she tells him he has to leave work right away so he can buy some rubbing alcohol and bring it home.

She grabs me by the hand and rushes me upstairs, explaining to me that my temperature is over 104 degrees Fahrenheit, which is very high.

In an agitated state she yells at me to get undressed, while she runs a bath.

"Get in," she demands.

There's hardly any water yet so I think it is odd. I step in. The water is freezing. She tells me I have to stay in it to try to get my temperature down. She scoops up water in a small pail and pours it over my shivering body.

Moments later, Dad comes running in with the rubbing alcohol and asks Mom how I am doing. Mom tells him to stay with me and pour water over me while she makes up my bed with sheets that have been out on the line in the blustery winter wind. It is weird to be alone with Dad with me in the tub because he's never been part of bath time. It is weird to have him focused on me like this.

When Mom returns to the bathroom I am hauled out of the tub and not allowed to be warmed by a towel. The two of them frantically rub rubbing alcohol all over me. I am taken to a freshly made bed that is freezing cold.

They stand over me for a moment while I lie there shaking. My temperature is taken two more times, silencing any of my questions.

They decide they have done all they can do. They walk away.

The memories of that late afternoon are strong. It is a rare moment to have both my parents focusing on me. I actually feel fine physically. A part of me is sad that it takes me being really sick for them to focus on me. Another part of me simply soaks up this moment of attention. But another part of me observes that their attention is very detached as they ponder the problem objectively. I so wish that we could connect at a deeper level. I am tired of engaging at a surface level. I am frustrated by the perspective that problem solving is about finding the right mechanical or technical solution. Don't other people long like I do for relationship and connection? Why do we create these walls of detachment? Why won't we risk really being present to one another and to ourselves?

For Valentine's Day that year I use my allowance to buy everyone in the family a heart-shaped sucker. I also buy a piece of white bristol board to make a big card for my family. I cry as I make the card because of the depth of my love which I am trying to express. I love every one of them profoundly to the point where it almost hurts because the feeling is so strong. After pouring my heart into creating the card, I give it to them at dinner that night. I am thanked politely, told it is nice, and asked to sit down.

And I wonder, even as a child soon to be nine, how do we get past the masks we all wear to really get through to each other? I feel a sense of resignation. As I look at the world around me, it seems like all my friends live in families like mine where we follow the rules of our roles. It seems so shallow to me.

———————————

Life continues to be filled with listening to CHUM radio, developing a collection of 45 rpm records, wearing go-go boots, learning to do the twist, watching Ed Sullivan on TV Sunday night, following the rise of the Beatles, stopping conversations every ten minutes for the drone of the planes coming in for landing at the nearby Pearson Airport in Toronto whose pathway is directly above our backyard, and learning to carefully budget my $5 a week allowance to ensure I can pay for my dance lessons, make an offering at church if I go, save some money for things I want and buy a new 45 every week.

Every once in a while Dad takes one or more of us to church on a Sunday morning. Mom stopped going to church after her youngest sister died in the car crash. After my experience as a three-year-old of having the gate to the front of the church closed in my face, church is somewhat redeemed by the Sunday school superintendent at a new church. On the day the Bibles are to be handed out to the grade four students, our Sunday school teacher carefully explains that only those who regularly come to church will receive a Bible. I look around the group. I realize that according to this rule, the people who will receive a Bible will be everybody but me. But on that day the superintendent calls my name and gives me my very own Bible. It has my name on the first page along with her signature. I still have that Bible.

In 1966, my brother puts together a band. He also starts working at a horse ranch. He is living with the reality of being in his second go-round of grade eight. Mom is keen to find things that interest him so that staying a year behind doesn't have a negative impact. She repeats the story often of how having mononucleosis plays a significant part in Mark not completing grade eight the first time.

In the band Mark plays guitar. Friends bring other instrumental and singing skills. Because one friend plays drums and we have Dad's drums at our house, the band practices at our house.

I notice that, although Mom encourages the band, as she encourages each of us in whatever interests us, when the band gathers to practice at our home, her anxiety level is high.

One day in that fall of 1966, the band is practicing when a terrible storm begins to rage. Mom tells the boys to call their parents for rides. None of their parents are at home.

Mom tells us all to get in the car. I am sitting in the middle in the backseat. We drop off one of the boys, and then head to another house. Mom's anxiety level is going through the roof. I can feel her anxiety deep within me. It is not something I see or hear. It is a feeling. We pull into a driveway. Another member of the band gets out of the car and runs to his house through the downpour. We pull away. Mom's anxiety lowers immediately, although she is still very agitated.

It is decades later before we understand the stressful impact of that member of Mark's band on our lives. As kids we did not know that he connects us to a part of Mom's life that she keeps hidden, to a time when his father played the major role in Mom's life as the father of the baby she put up for adoption.

As a child I intuitively feel that Mom is not sharing all of herself with us, which is why I have the fear that she is wearing a mask that hides something horrible, like the fact that she really doesn't love me. Years later, after we find out about the daughter Mom gave up for adoption, Mom tells me that she didn't tell us about her first daughter for fear that we might think she could give us up as well. It is sad that the very fear that prompts Mom to not tell us about her first baby actually fills me with the fear that she could reject me because she doesn't love me.

As a kid, I never understand how people think that the stuff that swirls around inside of them is hidden. Don't they know that other people can feel it and sense it? Don't they realize that knowing the fullness of a story is far more manageable than surmising horrible possibilities?

In late fall of 1966, Mom and Dad search for a new home. Dad's work has just opened offices in two larger towns west of Toronto; we are told it will be easier for him if we move further out of the city. I have very few memories of Dad going to the two outlying offices after we move. He still travels back to Toronto most days. They look at farms, saying that we need somewhere we can have a horse because Mark loves his work at the ranch.

In 2014, Janis, Mark and I make plans to spend a day together. I pick up Janis at an airport after driving seven hours. We spend much of our day remembering our childhood. In the conversation we ponder the reason for the move to the farm. We realize we each had different ideas when we were kids about why we move. Janis says that she has thought for years that we moved because of the father of Mom's first baby not only living in our neighbourhood but now connected to us through Mark's band. But we don't know there is anything significant about that member of the band being in our lives until the spring of 1993. It is in 1993 that we find out about our half sister and we learn that the member of Mark's band and our half sister have the same father. I now think that, from the vantage point of decades later, Janis's perspective is right: the presence of the father of Mom's first baby encroaching on our lives did significantly impact us and was probably part of what prompted the move to the farm, but we didn't know that as kids.

In a recent conversation with my husband Alan about this topic of the impact of my half sister's father on our lives, we encounter an example of the kind of conflicting details that periodically emerge around stories in the life of my family.

I share my perspective with Alan on the story about the move to the farm, including my understanding that Dad knew about the baby Mom gave up for adoption. I comment that I think Dad was being supportive of Mom in his willingness to move to the farm so that she didn't have to be in the same neighbourhood as the father of her first baby.

In the early days of finding out about Lynda we did not know that Dad knew about her. We periodically commented that it was maybe a good thing that Dad was not around when Lynda entered back into Mom's life. But at some point over the years Mom told me that when she first met Dad she told him about her first baby. Alan, however, remembers conversations with Mom in the latter years of her life when she told him that Dad did not know about her first baby. I now wonder if only one or two personalities knew that Dad knew about Mom's first baby.

These kinds of conflicting details reflect some of the discombobulating realities that have woven in and out of our lives. Our lives were often filled with this type of disconnected detail where the information did not line up in neat, linear rows of insight. This is a small example, but there are other instances when conflicting information impacts our lives in significant ways. Perspectives, expectations and information can change depending on which personality is present. For most of our lives we do not understand that we are dealing with many personalities, and so life often feels disruptive when details lack integrity.

WE MOVE TO THE FARM on December 2, 1966 in the midst of a huge snowstorm. The moving van gets stuck at the bottom of the lane. When we enter the empty house we stand together in silence in the kitchen at the centre of the house. Each of us wanders toward a doorway to peek into the different rooms. Clearly a lot of work will be required to bring the house up to a reasonable living standard. But this is now home. For me it will quickly feel more like home than either of the houses we lived in previously.

We each go to find the space that will be ours. I have already claimed the bedroom with the built-in furniture and two windows. The promise of this room was the way my parents consoled me when we first looked at this house. Earlier that day I fell in love with the land of another farm and so I had no interest in this place. Mom found me sobbing upstairs when they toured the house.

She pointed out that this house is a good choice because all the kids will have their own room.

I look at her and ask, "Can I have this room?"

My tone is defiant. I am sitting on the counter of the room with the built-in furniture. It has two windows and is the largest bedroom.

Mom looks around and then turns back to me and says, "Yes."

I stay in the room and begin to dream of all I will do here.

In the early months of moving to the farm, I am labelled and rejected by my classmates as the stuck-up city kid. I remember one night wandering into the living room and sitting by myself. I look at the bookshelf beside me. The Bible I was given in grade four is sitting there. I received it when the wonderful Sunday school superintendent defied all the rules and gave it to me even though I didn't go to church regularly.

I open the book. I turn to the last part of the Bible where the New Testament stories about Jesus begin. I read the first four chapters. I am intrigued by the story where Jesus goes out into the wilderness to figure out how to not be affected by external expectations and possibilities. At eleven years of age I am struggling with what it means to be me in the midst of the demands and expectations of others who imbue me with descriptions and expectations that don't fit me at all.

I memorize the story of the temptation of Jesus from the gospel of Matthew. It is the only scripture passage I know by heart until I become a minister. The way Jesus wrestles in the story with options of how to live his life appeals to me. Though he might have been tempted to follow the path Satan laid out for him in the story, he instead chooses what is right for him and for who he is and who he wants to be. He chooses a pathway that leads him to a sense of wholeness. I am struggling to listen for that kind of certainty within myself. It feels like I am being tossed about by a multitude of external expectations that crash into me and constantly demand attention, continuously feeling like they don't fit who I am. The teacher expects maps to be coloured a very specific way rather than allowing creative expression. Kids label me as a snob and so won't explore becoming friends, which is my deepest longing. People expect polite conversation that bores me to tears when there are so many ways to engage imaginative wonderings. I am definitely struggling, like Jesus did in that story, longing to find my path that will lead to a sense of wholeness.

Mom is struggling too. By the spring of 1967 our new doctors tell Mom that the difficulties that are impacting her life are all "in her head." The recent move from the city to a farming community is huge and so they say it makes sense that she is experiencing distress. They suggest that she simply has not found her place yet. Plus her husband is gone for many hours of each day with his work in the city. She is told that it will take time. She will feel better once she gets settled.

The doctors' pronouncements seem inconsistent with what I know of Mom. Being in the country actually suits her. She fits in much better than Dad. And Dad being gone for long hours every day is not new to her.

One area in my mind in which their insight contains some truth is that she has not found her place in the community yet; instead of being the president of the PTA, she now volunteers in a less public way by working in the library at our school to mend the books that are falling apart. She repairs them with something that looks like duct tape, but she does it with pride and a real sense of delight. I remember her showing me just how particular you have to be if the book is going to continue to be usable. The doctors might be right that she has not yet found the fullness of her call of how she will be in public life in this new community, but she chooses to find joy in what she is doing.

During that first year of living on the farm a television film crew comes to the school to film the students skating on our rink. One of the moms connected to the school is to be in a television documentary. I wish our Mom could be on the show. It would make her happy to be the centre of attention.

When the show airs Mom makes sure that we get to watch it so we can see ourselves on television.

I am taken aback by the show. I'm not sure what the focus of the show is but it includes footage of this woman's life on a farm. A quick glimpse of her kids at our school on the skating rink is included. The rest of the segment tells the story of this woman's day-to-day life. Her day begins with getting her kids ready for the school bus in the morning while she stays in her pyjamas. It shows the kids grabbing a Pop-Tart for breakfast as they head out the door after their mom yelled at them from the bottom of the stairs to get moving. Once they are on the bus, which the mom watches them do from the living room window, she goes back to bed and reads a Harlequin novel. By mid-morning she gets up and starts preparing dinner. Then she sits down for a break with a coffee and a magazine. After she puts in a load of laundry and does a bit of cleaning up in the kitchen, she watches a soap opera amidst the clutter that is everywhere while she waits for her kids to come home.

I am astonished that she is chosen to be on this TV show. What is it about her life that prompts them to choose her? And why does she do so little in the day? It is so inconsistent with my experience of my Mom.

I'm shocked at how deeply I move into a stance of judgment toward this television show. Negative judgment toward another person is a perspective that rarely enters my field of awareness. Usually I move to a stance of curiosity. But on this day I feel judgment surging through me, providing me with an experience of how ferocious it can be.

The other part of feeling stunned and off-kilter in this moment is that I am shocked to realize that not all homes are run like the one I live in where there is never any clutter.

When Mom gets us ready for school she is fully dressed with makeup on. She gently awakens each one of us by chatting with us about the day as she opens our blinds. When we go downstairs the table is set, ready for us to sit down for breakfast together. In the winter we have hot oatmeal and toast along with Tang for juice. Mom walks out to the driveway to watch us get on the bus.

I don't know all that Mom does in a day. What I do know is that the house is immaculate, though I never see Mom clean. The laundry often waits for late evening because the rest of Mom's day is filled with other things.

When we get home at the end of the school day, Mom has placed piles of our things on the stairs that we are expected to put away. While we are at school I know Mom feeds the pigs, the chickens, the dog and the cats, but she also checks on the calves, the horse, the pony and the rabbits that others are supposed to feed.

Mom is the one who paints all the rooms in the farmhouse and puts up wallpaper. The painting is never bland. Janis's room is purple with red and peachy-pink accents that go with a bedspread that Janis found in the Sears catalogue. The older furniture that Janis and I once shared is all painted to match the colour scheme. It's quite a transformation considering the room had once been a chicken coop.

Mom wallpapers the kitchen by herself. It has nine-foot ceilings and is large enough to have five doorways and two windows. I don't have many memories of her doing this work while we are home so I'm guessing that's what fills her days.

I know that in the summer when we are home she is constantly cooking, baking, taking care of animals and kids, hanging clothes on the line so they hold the scent of the wind, chasing down the calves, horse and pony when the pony yet again finds an escape route, tending her incredible rock gardens that are a profusion of colour from her abundance of petunias, and planting a huge vegetable garden each year which exhausts me just thinking about all the weeding that Janis and I will do, though Mom does most of the weeding along with preserving and freezing the vegetables.

As an adult with an overflowing clothes closet, I realize Mom must have regularly discarded clothes I no longer wore. I have no memory of missing clothes, so I have no idea that is a task she does. It is a shock for me to discover that such a task needs to be tended to regularly. To this day I am not good at it. The limited things Mom teaches me about tending a house are learned on Saturday morning when I am expected to do the dusting in one room while Janis vacuums another room, or each evening when we either have to set the table or help with the dishes. From my childhood experiences I have no idea what taking care of a house actually entails.

A few weeks after moving to the farm, everyone except Mark goes to a United Church that Dad wants to check out. We become involved. It is a fairly progressive church. It's one of the churches that support the New Curriculum of the United Church in the mid-1960s, which teaches a metaphorical interpretation of scripture rather than the more common literal interpretation.

As progressive as the church is supposed to be, I struggle in Sunday school. I want to fit in, but the lessons are filled with understandings about life that are different from my profound experience of the presence of God. My experience of God fills my life with the golden light of divine love which I encounter in everyone I meet. In Sunday school I hear statements that declare that we cannot know God, we can only know "about" God.

Lessons are filled with information to teach us about God so that we will have understanding that leads to correct belief. These lessons, filled with doctrine and explanations of a faraway God, feel like a "second-hand set of beliefs" they are trying to cram down my throat. In the process of cramming them down my throat they are choking me and silencing me.

In my experience, the divine presence of love comes as a "first-hand way of knowing," not as a "second-hand set of beliefs."

My struggle at eleven years of age foreshadows my struggle at seminary years later where my hackles rise up at the systematic theology that is presented as being rooted in the value of academic interpretations of God without regard for personal experiences of God. Absolute attitudes and standards of belief feel like they are in diametric conflict with my living faith, which is experienced and expressed through the day-to-day moments of life. In those moments I have a strong sense of knowing God rather than just knowing about God.

Dad delights in the intellectual debates that are shared in the pulpit in this new church. To me they are like gymnastics for the mind rooted in centuries of theological ponderings. Mom is clear. Her faith is simple. God is love. That's it. From her perspective all the rest of the discussions are rooted in academic proficiency for which she has little time. If I were asked to pick a perspective, I would agree with my mother. If faith does not speak to the essence of everyday life what value does it have? But I enjoy discussions that reflect Dad's love of debate so long as personal experience is allowed to enter the conversation rather than the conversation being filled only with the perspectives of scholars.

We are active in the church as a family for a few years until a conflict around the new minister erupts. Dad and Mom leave the church because they feel the minister has been treated poorly. I choose to stay.

IN 1967, MOM'S DAD COMES TO LIVE WITH US for two-month intervals twice a year. He moves between his daughters. He takes over Mark's bedroom. Mom gives up her office space for Mark to sleep there when Grandpa stays with us.

I notice that Mom's relationship with her Dad is odd. There are times when she adores him, times when she tolerates him and takes care of him, and there are times when he isn't around that she clearly detests him. The year before she dies, I finally understand that the differing perspectives that Mom had toward her Dad are rooted in the different personalities she carries inside her. On the night she morphs from one personality to another and another, a key focus of conversation is about her Dad. One personality hates him, one personality loves him, and one childhood personality is overwhelmed with sadness because people hurt her. Back in my childhood I am puzzled over the contrasting ways Mom interacts with Grandpa. I know we can feel differently about people at different times, but her feelings seem extreme.

Mom's excessively conflictual feelings toward Grandpa crash through our lives, imbued with emotions we don't understand.

I remember going to Grandpa's house as a kid. It is hard for me to sit in the living room and politely visit because I sense lingering feelings that are disturbing. When Mom is a kid this is the room where she and her two sisters sleep on a pull-out couch. There are stories of how Grandpa uses his belt on his three daughters when they don't go to sleep fast enough. I know that the youngest twin always sleeps in the middle which means the strap doesn't touch her. But the older twin and my Mom feel that belt deep in the marrow of their bones; they talk about it every time they share stories about their childhood. As I sit in this room, the stories continually grab at my awareness and make me uncomfortable.

There are also stories of Grandpa coming home drunk on Friday nights. One time when he is in a rage he throws Mom's much beloved violin into the coal bin. I can see the entrance to the bin from where I am sitting in his living room. I feel painfully awkward sitting here with the energy of that night echoing through my mind.

But in many ways Grandpa seems kind. He brings a block of ice cream for dessert anytime he comes for dinner. He serves it by opening the whole box and cutting it up so everyone gets an equal share.

It is hard to look at Grandpa with his one eye stitched shut. When Grandpa is a baby his brother twirls a string with a piece of sharp metal on it beside Grandpa's carriage. His brother releases one end, and the metal flies off the string into the carriage. It takes out Grandpa's eye. The cavernous look of the closed eye socket fills me with a sense of loss that creates a lingering melancholy for how quickly life can change.

Grandpa had a hard life in many ways, though probably not very different from others in his generation. By the crash of 1929 he has eight kids, with two more to be born less than a year later. After his death we discover that he and Grandma are expecting their second child when they get married. He is just sixteen and she is nineteen. His three sons go to war. Two are on the front lines in Italy, one of the most brutal places in the war. His second-eldest daughter dies of tuberculosis in her twenties. A grandson kills himself while cleaning his gun. Another daughter dies in a car crash.

But there are stories of his life that are filled with wonderful memories as well. There are stories of huge gardens that overflow to the point where produce is shared with all the relatives who live on the block. There are memories of a multitude of cousins playing through the backyards. There are also memories of gratitude that his kids never have to stand in the breadlines during the Depression years in the thirties. Grandpa had steady work painting all the buildings at the

Canadian National Exhibition. It is a matter of pride to Mom that none of Grandpa's kids had to wear the red sweater-coats that brashly declare that a family has received aid from the community.

This red sweater story illuminates two conflicting attitudes in Mom that don't align in my thinking. On one hand, Mom demonstrates incredible compassion toward other people in her commitment to not judge anyone as less valuable than others. On the other hand, she has a sense of personal pride that she and her family do not have to wear the red sweater coats, an attitude that seems to suggest a sense of judgment toward those who have to wear the red sweaters.

This attitude of pride often shows up in her life, particularly in regard to ensuring that her children have the best of everything. It causes confusion in my teenage and adult brain over the years—how she wants everyone to be treated equally but then wants her family to be better off than others. It is extremely important to her to be the best she can be and have the best of whatever is available. I wonder now if what I am encountering in this feeling of disconnect is actually conflicting sets of values that are held by the different personalities, values that I desperately try to mesh into one set of values.

At Grandpa's house there is one room that gives me the creeps when we make our rare journeys there. It is the back kitchen, a closed-in area where my uncles sleep during Mom's childhood summers. The only bathroom in the house is at the end of the main kitchen, right by the door to the back kitchen. I try not to use the bathroom very often because the hair stands up on the back of my neck any time I approach that area.

I only go through the back kitchen once. Mom insists we go into the backyard to see Grandpa's raspberries. Feelings of extreme anxiety sweep through me as I get close to the door. The energy that emanates from that room suggests to me that something horrible happened there.

I get to know Grandpa well when he lives with us. I discover that I quite like him.

He has a distinct smell. I later learn it is the smell of whisky.

When we get home from school, I run to Grandpa's room to tell him about my day. He wants to know all that I have learned. Some nights he's sitting in the living room when we get home. I sneak in and peek to see if he is awake and then tiptoe away, forgetting that his permanently closed eye is on the side where I glance. He calls me back.

I remember one night sitting with my big, cuddly teddy bear coat on for over an hour while Grandpa and I search through the encyclopedia to learn more about whatever topic I have been studying that day. I don't want to take the chance that he will stop engaging with me, so I don't interrupt the conversation to take off my coat. Being hot is better than someone else taking over his attention.

The conversations with Grandpa add an element of stability during the year he stays with us before his death on March 1, 1968.

Strange things are happening through the later years of the sixties. Mom starts to talk a lot about there being a ghost in the house.

My first memory of the idea that there is a ghost in the house happens one day when I ask to wear one of Mom's necklaces. She searches through her jewellery box but can't find it. She finally tells me to go without it or I will miss the school bus. The two of us dash downstairs. I run down the driveway just as the bus is coming over the hill. I turn and wave to Mom on the patio. I run up the next hill where the bus waits impatiently for my arrival. When I get home that night Mom tells me a strange story. After saying goodbye to me she returns to her bedroom to put away her jewellery properly. She had dumped everything back into the box before we left for me to catch the bus. But when she reaches for the contents in the box upon her return to the room she is shocked to see all the jewellery pushed to one side. The necklace I asked for that morning is sitting in a corner all by itself. She blames the ghost.

A few months later, Mom loses her watch. Two weeks later while sitting in the chair where she watches the evening news, reads the newspaper, and has her before-dinner beer, she feels something stick into her spine. She reaches down and pulls out her watch. She credits the ghost with its return.

The watch scenario can be explained with a number of theories. The story of the necklace, however, is just odd. In later years such occurrences happen often. Mom will set things out to run errands and when she prepares to walk out the door, the items are no longer on the bench at the front door. In retrospect I suspect that the host personality of the Aggressive One, who includes the part of her that I describe as the raging banshee, likes to play tricks on Mom. If that is true, it is Mom's body that does the action, but only the host personality has awareness of the action. In moments when she decides not to tell the other personalities where she has moved something, it is almost as though it provides her with a bit of fun. Otherwise her tasks are probably demanding to keep all the details straight and provide information as needed. I did meet the fun side of this personality back when I was eight and Mom was recovering from the injury when her foot was run over. She definitely has an edge to her that likes to joke and play tricks on people.

During the early years at the farm, I rediscover the wonder of solitude as a way of grounding myself so I can cope with the upheavals of day-to-day life. I often go out alone to the apple orchard to swing as high as I can, feeling myself soaring with ease as though I am flying. Or I climb the old apple tree where the meadow and the lawn meet and let the gentle breeze and the sounds of nature wash over me to help me release the feelings of confusion and uncertainty that stir within me about life.

In 1967, Mark wants to take courses that are unavailable at the local high school. Mom drives him and four other students to the next town for a year so they can take their courses. Mom begins a petition for a school bus to take kids to the next town for the courses they want. She is like a dog with a bone when she sees a situation where the system does not respond to the needs of the people.

By the time I am ready for high school in 1970, there is a bus transporting students from the local high school to the high school in the other town. It is recommended when I am in grade eight that I go to the high school in the next town where there are advanced English courses. When I travel from the local school to the school in the other town the bus is full of kids who are seeking a variety of courses. It is mostly boys who want to take the tech courses. I am the odd kid wanting an enriched course in English.

In 1969, before the end of grade ten, Mark decides to head out west to take a job on a huge farm. He will turn seventeen that summer. I don't think he finishes his school year before heading west since planting begins in the spring. He never lives in our family home again on a permanent basis. In later years he tells me that moving away from home is an intentional choice to create distance between him and Mom.

In the summer of 1969, our family travels by car to visit Mark out west. We plan our trip to coincide with time he can take off to go with us to the Calgary Stampede and the mountains for a week of camping.

The whole trip is demanding. Other than the one week in the mountains with Mark, we move campsites every day. Every move requires setting up the large cumbersome tent, blowing up the air mattresses and repacking the car with great care the next morning because of the limited space. The challenge of space is impacted by Mark's request for us to bring out some large mechanical pieces for his car. Mom thrives on the constant demand of this organizing even though she has not been well over the past two years. She doesn't even complain when Mark decides he doesn't want to keep the large mechanical pieces for his car. They travel back home with us.

———————————————

Mom is never a person to sit still. She stays up long hours, often ironing until the wee hours of the morning. From the time I am very young Mom does laundry late at night. She even puts it away in our rooms while we sleep. For much of my childhood I awaken to see her silhouette over by the dressers in my bedroom.

Mom's constant high energy and commitment to tasks become a story in a family cookbook which I finish writing in 2004. It contains recipes from Alan's and my extended families. For each recipe there is a story. I decide I want to include Mom's recipe for macaroni and cheese. I write a story to go with it, but I am concerned that Mom might be offended by the story. However, I decide that I will include the memory because it is the only story I can think of around this recipe. After I give everyone a copy of the cookbook Mom comments more than once how she loves the story I wrote about her macaroni and cheese recipe best of all. Her comments provide me with a huge insight into how much she sees her constant activity as a major value in her life.

This is the story I wrote that it turns out she loves:

When we are kids Mom
has a regular menu for the week
including, like many families,
roast beef on Sundays
—to which Mark always responds
"it's the best roast beef you've ever made."
But one of my favourite nights
is macaroni and cheese night
particularly because of the moments
when Mom is grating the cheese.
It is a time when Mom stands in one place
and I get a chance to chat with her.

In the fall of 1969, when Betsy is in grade two and I am in grade eight, Mom has a terrible experience as a result of her persistent activity. The experience impacts her for years both physically and emotionally. Any time she is in physical pain her emotional stability suffers significantly.

On the day of the terrible episode she decides she wants to fix a problem that has been going on in the house for quite some time. There is a squeak coming from the furnace. She goes downstairs to the basement to vacuum the floor. We have one of the cleanest basements I have ever seen. While she is down there she opens the furnace door to see if she can figure out where the squeak is coming from. She leans deep inside to get a closer look. As she tips her head back, the wheel of the fan belt grabs her waist-long ponytail and pulls her in. She is bent backwards from her waist. When she feels her hair starting to rip from her head she imagines her seven-year-old daughter coming home and finding her mother scalped and dead on the basement floor. With a rush of fear, she reaches behind her head and yanks the massive fan out of the floor with a surge of adrenaline created by maternal instincts. Later she is told that she pulled a 250-pound part out of the cement.

By the time I get home Mom is hyperventilating wildly. She tells me something horrible has happened. She can't tell me what it is because sobs are consuming her. I imagine all kinds of scenarios, including rotating imaginings of the death of each family member. After my imagination runs wild it is a relief to finally hear what actually happened. No one is dead. The person in the horrible accident is standing in front of me looking fairly normal. Later Mom estimates that she lost a third of her hair that day. We find out much later that she also tore the muscle off her sternum, which results in her being rushed to the hospital with a suspected heart attack more than once over the years.

The combination of this injury, plus one from earlier years, has a huge impact on her life. The first injury is the one she sustains to her back when she is seventeen years old. She is working in a hardware store. She falls through an open trap door, landing on the cement floor below. She lives with pain ranging from constant discomfort to extreme agony for the rest of her life. The description of this injury that I hear is that her spine jumped out of position and created a new hole to sit in. From that time on it could slip in and out of the two holes at the base of her spine. As I think about it I actually can't imagine her functioning at all with such an injury, but that is the description that I remember.

The combination of that severe injury when she is seventeen, and the experience of pulling the fan of the furnace out of the cement that horrifying day, plays havoc in Mom's life.

These injuries do not, however, explain the third pain that she is also dealing with during these years. The third pain, which begins around the time we move to the farm—the one that doctors say is all in her head—is in her abdomen.

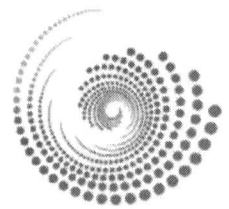

A MEMORY KEEPS NUDGING ME from these years when Mom is dealing with so much pain. It is February 1970. I am in grade eight. The memory makes me wonder if I am feeling the strain in our home more than I am conscious of at the time.

The memory begins with Mom coming into my room to wake me up one morning. I tell her I am not feeling great. She asks me if I want to stay home. I say I do. The next day the scenario is repeated. After a couple of days I am actually feeling better, but for some reason Mom doesn't wake me up that morning. She asks me later in the day if I feel like going back to school yet.

Since I seem to have an option I respond by saying, "No. I think it would be good for me to stay home a bit longer."

My memory is that I stay home for many weeks without being regularly asked if I am ready to go back. It is almost like Mom ignores my presence, or maybe she is just not well enough to notice how bizarre it is that I am staying home for such a long time.

I am totally enjoying my life. I stay in bed and read. I mostly spend the day in my bedroom, though I do begin to get hooked on Mom's soap opera that she irons through each afternoon. I don't go anywhere. It is a time of total respite from life, and I love it.

It is during this time of being alone that I begin to check all the books I am reading to see if I can find one that starts and ends with the same word. Although I acknowledge it is an odd thing to do, I check books for years. When I recently shared my quirky search with a friend her observation was that a circle starts and ends in the same place. It makes sense to her, knowing my passion for the power of circle, that I would seek out a book that starts in one place and circles around through wisdom and experience to end in the same place, changed by the fullness and the wholeness of the insights that have been engaged. I appreciate her interpretation of why I feel called to search. It is wholeness and connection that I am seeking.

To find such a book, I had to write it.

After five weeks at home the doctor decides to put me in the hospital to see if they can figure out what's going on. At the end of a week I am sent home.

Mom is livid when she comes to pick me up. She has only visited me once during the week. She tells me I am returning to school on Monday. I don't know what the doctor told her, but her response feels to me like her pride of being a good parent may have been wounded in the assessment.

On the day I go back to school my homeroom teacher makes a big deal about the return of another student who has been away for a much shorter time than I have been away. The teacher says nothing about my return. A couple of classmates comment on this, and tell me they, at least, are glad to see me.

I remember suspecting that the adults in my life have been told not to fuss over my return. I suspect that it is because they find nothing wrong with me while I am in the hospital, and they don't want to encourage a repeat performance of me choosing to stay away from school.

When I enter back into my memory line of that time I am intrigued to notice how much their assessment and concern about my behaviour do not bother me. I refuse to feel that I have done anything wrong. The weeks away have been good for me. Disconnecting from the world helps ensure that I stay mentally strong and healthy. It has been a time to reconnect with myself. Back in kindergarten I learned that I need retreat time in order to deal with life. Too often we get caught in details and lose sight of the things that really matter, like caring for each other and connecting at a deep level where life is far more interesting than only engaging surface issues.

But there may have been another reason for me choosing to stay at home after I feel better.

I remember that it is close to the end of grade eight that the principal and the guidance counsellor tell me that my test results indicate that my reading comprehension is equivalent to the beginning of second-year university. They apologize to me for their lack of awareness and declare that I must have been bored out of my mind. I am shocked by their response. I share with them that I am never bored. I do the work as required, but my real interest is in the dynamics of relationships. I spend my time doing what I love most, watching and observing people, continually exploring the levels of connection or the profound sense of disconnection going on all around me.

I now wonder if, once they receive the information that my reading comprehension is higher than expected, they think that might be why I needed a break and so stopped coming to school. There might be some merit in that possibility.

Was I getting bored with the frivolity of school life? Is that part of the reason why a long break felt so good? It seems to me that may have played a part in my enjoyment of not having to engage with the world for a while. As much as I like to observe the connections or lack of connections between the people around me, it is not hard for me to imagine eventually being bored, or at least not missing my times of observing when I am given the opportunity to remove myself from everyday life for a time.

I remember that when I return to school after six weeks away, the only thing that I feel a little stressed about catching up on is the independent studies in history. History is a concern because the course load is designed to do one fairly in-depth project every week. However, I end up quite enjoying having a shorter deadline to complete the work. There really isn't enough meaty information in our textbook about any one of the topics to keep my attention for a whole week. The shortened time helps to keep me focused rather than letting my mind wander to what might be more interesting in the present moment.

Since that experience I have quite enjoyed tight deadlines that spur me on to do my work. This pattern has been annoying or surprising to other people over the years. Only once in all the years of following this rhythm do I run into trouble.

It is 9 a.m. Sunday morning. I have been up since my usual 4 a.m. to write my sermon. Although I have been mulling over the sermon all week and have been gathering ideas and stories, I do not have any cohesive thoughts about my sermon for the service that begins at 10:30. With panic swirling through me I get off my dining room chair and go down on my knees to pray. I rarely kneel to pray. I can only remember one other time in my life, outside of being in a Catholic monastery. I ask for guidance to see what I am supposed to say today. I stand up and sit at the table. I pick up my pen trusting that something will emerge. It does. I needed to get out of the way for it to arise.

For some reason my small-ego self has gotten in the way of Spirit's insights that want to flow through me. Forty minutes later I have a full script for my sermon. I feel good about it. It captures insights and learnings that are timely, things that I was trying not to say as I sat and pondered the sermon while deeply connected to small-ego self. I suspect it will speak to at least one person's life, perhaps more, but when I am guided by Spirit so strongly I know that if it only speaks to one person, I need to accept that as my task in this moment.

Over the years people try to break me of this practice of waiting for the last minute to write things. Sometimes they try to break me of this habit by providing an artificial deadline, which to me feels like I am being lied to. I have little tolerance for false deadlines, though I have learned to make sure I honour the true deadline so that I don't mess up other people.

Throughout my life I have no tolerance when it feels like someone is lying to me. My kids know that they can tell me anything but a lie.

This theme of the importance of being truthful is huge in my life. My strongest spiritual gift is discernment. This spiritual gift, identified through a spiritual gift inventory tool, means I am very aware when people, including me, are being phony. As a result it can feel to me like people are telling lies with their words and their lives, hiding what is true behind complex masks that disconnect us from our own truth.

I constantly seek the gems of authentic truth. These gems are often covered over by the agitated energies of discord in our world. But searching amongst the chaos can provide a harvest of insight. In the metaphor of one of the biblical stories of Creation, new life emerges out of chaos. The Chinese characters for chaos and opportunity are the same. Seeking truth in the midst of the chaotic energy of life is to search for the beauty, wholeness and future possibilities at the centre of who we are, at the core of our true essence.

Speaking and living our truth is rooted in connecting to our authentic self, to our true essence, to enable us to live without masks and façades that cover over the truth of who we are, that cover over the wisdom within us.

A way that helps me to live more fully connected to my true essence is to seek to live in the present moment. One of the masks that my Mom often hid behind was the mask of being busy, an unending striving to meet some unnamed or false deadline, which meant she often missed savouring the present moment.

I don't want to miss the critical moments of my life because my mind is off taking care of future details, like Mom did and I used to do. I don't want to miss the wisdom that is trying to emerge from within me or the people around me because I am focused on somewhere and sometime other than here and now.

Early in my adult years I realize that Mom, Janis and I are all similar in that we have a lot of energy. We tend to have a lot of projects on the go all the time. Our lives are full of activity, so I understand the inclination to allow our attention to be constantly pulled ahead. But even as a young child I puzzle over Mom's lack of attention on the moment in front of her. I often wonder why she is focusing on the things in the future and not enjoying the moment.

I remember saying to Janis at a time in our lives when we are both moms to young kids that I have discovered how important it is to really be present to our kids. She asks me what I mean. I tell her that I strive to be really focused on the present moment, right down to and including when we are helping our kids get into their coats and boots to go do errands. I find there is a tendency in me to be thinking ahead to the next two minutes when I will need to make sure everything gets in the car. I realize that even if I am only thinking about two minutes into the future it still means I am not there in the hallway with my kids. As women of this culture we are good at multi-tasking, but when it comes to the precious moments with our kids or grandkids we need to savour them and be present. I learn this from watching Mom. It is something she almost never does.

Mom's lack of attention to the present moment impacts the way I engage life. Her pattern shows me what I don't want to do. While I suspect that Mom's reality of many personalities may play a part in this, I also know it is a tendency in our culture to not be present to the moment we are in.

Over the past two and a half decades it has been good to see people developing the practice of mindfulness, which develops our skills to be present. Being present allows us to connect to our authentic self, empowering us to fully engage with life.

The time of retreat that Mom helps me to create for myself in grade eight provides me with a rich time to reconnect to me. It helps me to not get lost in the expectations and cultural norms that otherwise might have hooked me at a significant time in life when I am figuring out how to be true to me in the midst of a demanding world. I am grateful that she didn't notice how odd it was that I was not going to school.

FROM THE FALL OF 1970 TO JUNE 13, 1971, Mom co-leads a class for confirmation with the minister of our church. Although Mom left the church after her youngest sister's death, she returns to active involvement when we move to the farm. Janis and I are members of the confirmation group, along with twenty other high school students.

Through most of these classes Mom is able to stay reasonably focused. But by the summer of 1971 Mom is really struggling.

The significant pain Mom has been in since our move to the farm continues to escalate. The doctors continue to diagnose it as "just being in her head."

Following Grandpa's example of delving deeply into information in the encyclopedia, she persistently does research until she identifies her physical problem. In the spring of 1971 doctors agree that she is probably correct in her diagnosis of her symptoms. Plans are made to have her gall bladder removed.

The date for the surgery is set for October, in seven months' time. Until then she is given medication to cope with the pain. Mom and medication are rarely a good combination.

It is in the summer of 1971 that Scott shows up in our life again. My interpretation at the time is that he has come to provide us with a special summer event since Mom is not well enough to do anything and Dad is away.

Plans are made for Scott to take first Janis, then me, for a full-day visit. Mom is in really bad shape. As I look back it is clear she is enmeshed in the difficult personalities, and basically not functioning. Being taken out by Scott does not seem odd to us. Even though we have not seen him for years we still hear about him often from Dad, and we have memories of Scott and Mom being buddies. Whenever

Dad comes home after golfing with Scott, I look forward to hearing about what his daughter is doing.

On each of our special days out with Scott, we are taken to the same elegant and exclusive restaurant for dinner, Janis on the first night, me on the second night. We each wear our confirmation dresses from June so that we are appropriately dressed up.

On Janis's day away Scott lets her drive his creamy yellow Cadillac convertible, though she only has her beginner's licence. She tells the story of how he directs her to a large parking lot so he can help her develop her driving skills. She loves it, thoroughly enjoying herself.

A few months later when Mom is in hospital, I have a memory of Janis driving us home with Dad as her licensed driver. He is urging her to do things correctly because she will need her licence when Mom comes home from the hospital. Janis is annoyed, slams on the brakes, gets out of the driver's seat right in the middle of the road, goes around to the passenger side and tells Dad to get out and do the driving himself. She starts taking lessons from a driving school the next week.

On my day with Scott, I remember entering the elegant penthouse restaurant and being introduced to Scott's uncle, who is the doorman. He greets us as the elevator opens. It turns out that he is the father of Greg, who identifies Janis as a Macdonald.

I remember how Scott encourages me to try whatever interests me. I order Vichyssoise, filet mignon, asparagus with Hollandaise sauce, and roasted root vegetables—my first-ever taste of parsnips. Scott prompts me to be adventurous and try the baked Alaska. It all feels decadent. It is a perfect setting to spend the evening with my much missed and very charismatic 'uncle' Scott, who always makes me feel like I matter.

I now suspect that the reason Scott shows up at this time is because Mom reaches out to him in the midst of her turmoil that summer. And good to his word on the night of the confrontation ten years before, he comes when she calls.

As much as Mom is going through a very difficult time, she is amazing in her support when a close friend of mine is killed in a car crash in September 1971. The day after his funeral I am in the kitchen with Janis and Mom setting the table for dinner. Mom speaks to me with a sharp tone. I start to cry. I run to the bathroom and slam the door, leaving Janis and Mom in the kitchen.

Janis declares to Mom that she isn't being very kind considering what I am going through.

Mom's comment back is, "She needs to cry. It won't do her any good to hold it all in. I know just how important it is to really cry when something like this happens when you are young."

That overheard conversation shocks me.

First it shocks me because Janis stands up for me, which is a rare occurrence in our lives. She is normally trying to stay as detached from me as possible, unless she has a story she wants to tell or an outfit she wants to borrow.

Mom's comment also surprises me. She has been so out of it for so many months, it shocks me to hear her be so astute about the need for me to cry. Then I remember that she also had a friend die when she was my age. It happened on the only day she ever skipped school. I tilt my head a little because I am pondering that there is something odd about what she just said. Then I realize it's not so much what she said as it is the tone of her voice. When she makes the comment that I need to cry, her voice sounds very different than the sad, depleted voice we have heard all summer. In this moment she sounds like our "real Mom" who hasn't been around for a while.

———————

In the fall of 1971, before Mom's gall-bladder surgery, Janis writes Mom a letter to say she can no longer provide her with support. The last straw for Janis is when Mom begs Janis to tell Dad that she wants a divorce, that her life isn't worth living and it's his fault. Janis waits up for Dad to come home after work that night. She relays Mom's message. Dad acts like this is normal behaviour that should be ignored.

Mom is in bad shape before the surgery. There are nights that are very disturbing.

One night the Wild One, who wears her hair loose and straggly, shows up. She repeatedly grabs me in panic. Her fingers feel like the talons of a powerful bird of prey. "Where's Mark?" she demands. I remind her that Mark is away on one of his long-distance truck runs. She calms momentarily, then grabs me again, and again, and again, demanding "Where's Mark?"

The raging outbursts that show extreme disconnection from life multiply and intensify after the surgery. While Mom is in the hospital she pulls out the intravenous tubes and screams about caterpillars crawling all over her and under her skin. The pain medication before the surgery, exacerbated by the medication they give her during the surgery, triggers a year of hell. Throughout the year her alternate personalities become stronger and much more present. The one we describe as our "real Mom" rarely shows up.

When Mom comes home from the hospital after her surgery I begin a nightly vigil, sitting beside the couch where she curls up. I am fifteen years old. After Betsy goes to bed, Mom spirals into despair. Janis retreats to her bedroom. Dad doesn't come home until it is late.

Many nights Mom talks to her youngest sister who died a decade earlier. It's like I am sitting listening to a one-sided phone conversation. Other nights she is very serene. On these nights she asks me to understand if she can't be here anymore. These conversations seem scariest of all, as though she has already decided that she won't stay. I am anxious that she has plans in place to attempt suicide.

Most nights Mom drifts off to sleep between 1:00 and 2:00 a.m.

As I sit by the couch into the wee hours of the morning, I often see Mom thrash and struggle as if filled with torment as she tries to sleep. I long for her to experience some sense of peace.

At first I just sit and watch. Over time I begin to develop a process that I think might be helpful to Mom. I know it is helpful to me; at least I am trying to do something. I imagine holding Mom in soothing energy that is filled with light and love. I hold her in this energy that flows out of me to surround her and infuse her.

When I connect with her energy through this process it feels like a part of her is missing. I know that the way she is engaging with life is not all of her. I am sure that the part that seems to be missing is still there. She just can't find it at the moment. It's disconnected but not gone.

Though the darkness of despair overwhelms her, I still see light within Mom. Her light seems to be reflected off a fractured mirror that shatters her energy in a multitude of directions, but it is there. At times, much of the light within her is covered over. But even in the midst of her wailing and desire to end it all, I can sense a glimmer of the light.

I connect to that glimmer of light as I sit beside her. I urge the part of her that is connected to that light to rise to the surface rather than be lost in the maze of tunnels within her that lead only to deeper darkness. There are moments when she returns, but they are fleeting. She is quickly sucked back down. As I sit beside her, I intentionally try to connect to her energy, hoping to keep her from falling too deeply into the abyss.

Years later, this experience with Mom comes back to me when I stand in an intensive care unit beside a woman in a coma. I find myself searching to connect to the light within her, to connect to her life energy. It feels like it is lost in a maze of tunnels. After much searching through gloomy tunnels I finally find her. I stay with her in the darkness for a while, recognizing that, in an odd way, this place feels comfortable to her, like she is safe in the midst of so many disruptions and losses in her life. I ask her if she would like to travel with me back up toward her life. I suggest we travel on the wings of an eagle. I know one of her favourite songs is based on the poetic image from Psalm 91 of the wings of the eagle that raise us up and hold us in light. She agrees to travel with me.

The tunnels are dark and long and filled with a sense of despair. Just as we are rising to the surface, a nurse comes in to say she needs to do vitals. I anchor the woman's energy close to the surface, hoping she will hold on rather than slip back under. When I return to the room I connect to her energy again. She opens her eyes. She is only there in a very faint way. I go out to the hall to tell her family. They rush into the room and look deep in her eyes. I remind them that the nurse said that this can happen sometimes but it isn't necessarily a sign of her coming out of the coma. I work intentionally to help her energy stay for as long as possible. It is hard. It feels like she wants to return to the place of comfort deep within her but she is staying out of a sense of love. She stays with her son and husband for a very few moments.

She slips away. I feel her energy slowly sink into the depths of the darkness within her to weave its way into the protection and comfort of the maze of tunnels beneath the surface of the life she once knew.

The experience with this woman is so similar to the nights I sit by Mom and try to hold her energy from slipping into the abyss. A part of me thinks these experiences are totally bizarre, but there's another part of me that knows they are real in a way that is not explainable by logic or reason.

It is in this time period, on an evening when Mom is beyond frantic, that she asks me to call Scott at midnight. I resist. She pushes. I try. No one answers.

Most nights Dad comes home around 10:00 p.m. after working late or playing a game of golf or going to a jazz club or seeing a movie. While Mom stays on the couch in the family room, I sit with him as he eats the dinner that has been kept warm for him. Some nights we go into the living room and he tells me about the issues that are going on at work. Sometimes he talks about divorcing Mom. I encourage him to give her time.

I am somewhat aware that I am living a bizarre reality. I speak about it once in English class in grade ten. Later that year I dance my feelings about it in a creative project. I dance to the tragic music of *Romeo and Juliet*.

Otherwise I just carry on. I listen to Dad when he comes home late in the evening as if I am an appropriate companion. I sit with Mom, hoping she will not choose to end her life.

In the summer of 2016 I learn that in the spring of 1972 Scott shows up one final time. It is only Janis who sees him. After Janis is accepted into the drama program at college Scott takes her out and buys her a whole new wardrobe for college.

In the early days of finding out Scott is her biological father I question Janis's description that he bought her a whole new wardrobe, thinking she is exaggerating terribly. I do remember her getting a sheepskin coat to go to college, though I had no awareness that it came from Scott.

Later I feel badly that I questioned her description of her experience. As different stories are shared in the summer of 2016, a first reaction to a new story or perspective is often met with a sense of disbelief and resistance. My first reaction to Janis's story is to correct the details. I notice that my reaction to this story is similar to what others have done throughout the summer when they hear the stories and perspectives that I share: they want to correct me or deny what I have said. I now know that it is more common to resist stories than to change our own version of events. I notice that when we are willing to sit with each new insight, the pieces begin to make sense, our resistance fades, and we weave the new piece into our understanding.

When Alan and I are camping during the spring of 2016, I can't get to sleep one night because a memory keeps nudging at me. I start to remember the most bizarre shopping trip that Mom takes me on in the fall of 1972.

Mom isn't in good shape. She is still regularly talking about dying, but she insists we have to go clothes shopping. It is odd in many ways, including the fact that I have been buying my own clothes since I started to work three years ago at a boutique and an agricultural dealership. I have been choosing my own clothes even longer.

That day Mom buys me a sheepskin coat with orange embroidery on it. I already have three winter coats. Then she chooses a pair of orange and brown wool pants with a houndstooth design and a short-sleeve brown sweater. I don't like short-sleeve sweaters and I don't like how the pants fit or feel. I am so shocked by what Mom is doing I keep silent. She adds a wool plaid pant suit in burgundy to the pile and a rose-colour sweater with a white Peter Pan collar to wear with it. The pile of clothes is growing. One might describe it as a "mini wardrobe." I wonder now if it is just like the wardrobe Janis talks about that Scott bought her. Then Mom chooses a dusty rose and black skirt with a matching jacket that has great, big, fluffy cuffs and collar. I tell her I like it, which I do. It is soft and comfortable. But I also tell her I can't imagine where I will wear it. She tells me it is good quality so it will keep until I go to university, just like the rest of the clothes. She is right. I have pictures of me in that suit after the birth of our first child more than a decade later.

On that spring night in 2016, lying awake until 4 a.m. in our trailer, I begin to wonder about the financial resources for that bizarre shopping trip. Did Scott give money to Mom and ask her to buy me a new wardrobe when I go to college or university just like he did for Janis? Scott is already having difficulties with his heart. Perhaps he is looking ahead thinking he might not be around when I go to university.

I don't know for sure which personality is with me that day on the shopping spree. It feels like it is the bossy Aggressive One. She is definitely demanding that day, with no tolerance for questions about what we are doing and no patience to look at options.

As I lie awake in the trailer in the early hours of the morning, I abruptly realize that it is on that bizarre shopping spree that Mom also buys herself a sheepskin coat; it is just like the coat she chooses for me and just like the one Janis chooses when she is shopping with Scott. It is weird that we all have the same coat. However, it is the eleven- or twelve-year-old personality there that day. I wonder if it makes sense to her for us all to have the same coat; I remember as a twelve-year-old buying matching clothes with my friends. But it doesn't actually make sense in our lives. Janis is eighteen and in college, I am sixteen, and Mom is forty-three.

THE PATTERN OF NIGHTLY VIGILS with Mom continues all the way through my year in grade ten and lingers over into grade eleven.

At some point during the early spring of my year in grade eleven, Mom begins to emerge from her cocoon of despair. She starts volunteering at a nursery for mentally and physically handicapped children. It gives her a renewed sense of purpose. Things are still tense at home, but at least she is once again engaging with the community.

As Mom's commitment to her volunteer position grows, her stability grows. She takes college courses to become a certified support worker for children who require special education. She eventually becomes the president of the association that supports the programs with which she works. By this time she is once again thriving.

During her tenure as president of the Association for the Mentally and Physically Handicapped, the residential institutions in Ontario begin the process of reintegrating some of their residents into the community. Under Mom's leadership, a home is built in our area. Residents from a regional centre up north who have families in our area are moved to this new home with twenty-four-hour support.

I remember the first Christmas after the residents move into the home. The plan is that all the residents will go home to spend Christmas Day with their families.

But the family of one of the residents doesn't want him at their Christmas celebrations. He is in his late forties. He has Down Syndrome and has lived in the centre all his life. Though he is now close to home and able to go out for the day, his family doesn't want him. Mom is livid. First, because his family is rejecting him, and second, because one of her staff will have to stay at the home with him and miss Christmas Day with her family.

Mom decides that isn't going to happen. The resident will spend the day with our family.

When Dad hears the plan that a resident from the home will spend Christmas Day with us, he is livid. He is adamant that he doesn't want one of those people coming to our home on such a special day. He declares that it is fine for Mom to choose to do things like bring them to our pool to swim when he is away at work, but not when he is home. Mom is furious right back at him. She tells Dad that if he doesn't want to be there when the resident is there he can go somewhere else. The resident doesn't have that choice.

Christmas dinner that year stands out stark and clear in my memory. Our extended family gathers as usual at the dining room table. Our new guest sits two seats down from Dad. Dad is clearly grouchy. Alan observes years later that Mom rarely sits for very long at the table for family dinners, which is something I don't notice until he points it out. Going back into this memory I notice that for this dinner Mom stays at the table. She periodically glares all the way down the table at Dad. I can feel the energy of their combined angst zooming back and forth down the length of the table.

And then, in the middle of the tension, our new guest stands up. He toasts our family and says, "This is the best Christmas I have ever had." Then he says, "Thank you."

Everyone laughs with surprise and delight. I watch Dad. He looks around at the scene and melts. He joins in the laughter, raises his glass, and says with a sigh of resignation, "You're welcome."

As our new guest looks at all the happy faces, he responds, "So I'm going to celebrate with you all the time, every Easter and Thanksgiving and birthday and Christmas and Thanksgiving and Easter and …."

We all laugh with him, enjoying his boyish joy, including Dad. Mom smiles at Dad at the other end of the table, and lets down her guard that bristled at the thought that someone would not be welcome at our Christmas feast.

And our new guest is right: he shares all our holidays with us every year for the next decade, right up until Dad dies. After Dad dies, he thinks that means he will be the man at the head of the family now, and so he and Mom need to get married. Mom has to set a boundary. It's a firm one. We never see him again.

When I look back into my later teen years to the time when Mom is past the really difficult years, I realize that she becomes the cool Mom she always wanted to be.

When I am in grade eleven she supports my boyfriend in his plan to arrange a surprise party for me out in the bush at the back of our farm on the day that I get out of two weeks of quarantine because of scarlet fever. I am totally surprised. I remember heading out to the meadow on wobbling legs that have spent most of the last two weeks in bed. It's not long after I get there that my boyfriend is carrying me back to the house. I have learned the hard way that drinking white rum in a white Styrofoam cup when the night is dark does not provide clarity as to how much rum is going in the cup. I also learn that drinking after being sick is not a good idea. When Mom holds my hair while I am being sick, she's not terribly sympathetic; in fact I'm pretty sure that she actually laughs at me.

When I am in grade twelve a whole gang of us want to go up to a hunt camp to stay for the weekend. Mom agrees to go with us so that some of the girls' parents will let them go. Nobody else wants their parent there but my boyfriend and I are fine with Mom coming.

When I am in grade thirteen my graduating class plans a major event every month for us to party together. The final event for this class of a hundred and eighty kids is held at our farm. People hang around in the house or out in the yard by the fire and the pool. It is a great party. At 1:00 a.m. I look around and realize I don't know any of the people who are still there. Up till then I haven't realized the party has been crashed. I watch as Mom takes one room and Janis's boyfriend takes another room to herd people out. Though Mom is only five foot four she stands up to the tall hulky young men and won't let them bully her. I'm impressed.

In the fall of 1975, when I am nineteen years old, I begin university. I am engaged to be married. My fiancé is not pleased that I am going to university since he's seen many relationships break up when people go away to school. So I live at home and carpool with other students for the thirty minutes to the university. One day a week I am the driver, using Mom's turquoise-blue Mustang.

On Thanksgiving weekend I break off my engagement with my long-time boyfriend. Mom is wonderfully supportive. She encourages me to head out and create a new social life without him. She tells me it will be good for me.

At that time I don't yet know the part of her story of when she is nineteen and has to create a new social life without the man she has been engaged to. Within an hour of my broken engagement she nudges me out the door to go find my high school friends at the local pub. Everyone is home from university for Thanksgiving. I am nervous about going out because my former fiancé kicked down part of a fence when I told him I was ending our engagement. What if he is still out there on the dark country road where we live? Mom scoffs at me and tells me I can't let fear like that consume my life. She is right. I go out for the evening and have a great time.

———————————————

At the end of my first semester at university I switch my major from English to drama. My hours at the university will become more erratic for the rest of my years at school because I will have to stay late at night to prepare for plays. I find an apartment to share with a new friend who I meet through a high school friend. We will move into the apartment in early January.

For Christmas Eve that year I am invited to prepare and lead the late Christmas Eve service at my home church. On December 23, I finally have the opportunity to look for material for the service. My search is frantic. I want to create something that will be significant for the congregation. I long for the service to crack them open to the power of this incredible story of Divine love coming in human form to live amongst us, calling us to embody the Divine love within each of us. I am searching for materials that are not from the anticipated perspectives. I want readings and prayers that go much deeper than a traditional way of engaging the story of the birth of Jesus.

As I stand in the pulpit late Christmas Eve with candlelight all around me, I pause and look out over this community who has encouraged me and delighted in my gifts. In that moment, an awareness rushes over me that profoundly impacts me for the rest of my life.

I am very conscious of the façade I became aware of just a few months ago that I present to the world. I refer to it as the 'golden girl façade.' It feels like a larger than life cut-out of me. The 'golden girl façade' reflects the sense that my life is filled with goodness. It is rooted in what people know me for: being one of three from our confirmation class of twenty-two kids back in 1971 who is still active in the church; the kid in the family who is the rule follower; the first runner-up in the posture contest at high school; a member of the senior dance troupe in my dance school and a dance teacher; the most recent fall fair queen, who is the only contestant that year at the Miss CNE contest who has her own reporter with her because the town was so sure I would win. My sense is that people experience me as a golden girl. I think they expect me to uphold this role of a young woman who successfully does what is expected of her.

I know, however, that there is more to me; behind the façade there is another part of me. Up till now it has been hidden, even to me to a certain extent. But now it is getting stronger and bigger. As it is emerging it feels uncomfortable and unacceptable because it is such a contrast to how I think others perceive me and how I think others expect me to be. I describe this emerging part of me as my 'dirty, grungy self.' It is a description filled with negative judgment because I do not think that the world would want to get to know this part of me.

And now it feels like the 'golden girl façade' has begun to separate from me. It feels like it is moving farther and farther out in front of me to the point where I can no longer reach it, a smiling façade that is disconnected from who I really am.

As I stand there in the candlelight that Christmas Eve, I become aware that the façade is so far out in front of me it may no longer hide this other part of me. With the façade so far out, people may be able to glimpse behind it and see that side of me that is not particularly kind and at times thinks awful thoughts that do not reflect the sweet me that people have come to expect. What will happen when they discover that I am not as sweet as they think, and that I have a mind that is discerning, that has the capacity to be critical beyond their imaginings? What will happen when they discover that I rebel against their theology and the times when they resist broader perspectives?

On one hand, I am filled with angst that people are not seeing the real me; they are engaging with a well-rehearsed thin veneer. I am concerned that their expectations of me are causing their perceptions to be a phony interpretation of who I am. I have never felt comfortable when someone is being phony and now I think I am being perceived in a way that is not true to who I am. On the other hand, in this moment when it feels like the 'dirty, grungy' me is at risk of being exposed, I am aware that I want to choose how I will share this part of myself with the world rather than have people stumble upon it. As I stand there in the depths of the night when we remember that God's love comes in human form not once but again and again, I decide that I will not live with this fear of rejection. I will not hide a part of me even though I risk being rejected by sharing it. I decide in that moment that with the dawning of the New Year I will live out of my 'dirty, grungy self' to discover the fullness of who I am. I will no longer hide behind the 'golden girl façade.' I will not live behind a pre-formed mask. I know what it is like to live with the fear that my mother will take off a mask and laugh at me for thinking she loves me. I will be fully and honestly who I am and if the world doesn't like it, at least I will not be harbouring a secret that disturbs relationships and creates distrust.

In the midst of this momentous decision, the worship service continues to unfurl. People speak for years about that service, observing that something powerful was happening. They are right. On that night I am like a midwife standing by waiting for the emergence of my 'dirty, grungy self.'

The next four months, my first months of living away from home, are filled with lots of lessons as I live out my 'dirty, grungy self' and discover greater clarity about how to be my authentic self.

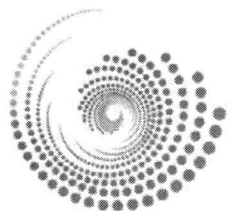

Betsy is fourteen when I move half an hour away from home in order to be closer to the drama department at the university where we often work into the wee hours of the morning. Mom sometimes kids that it is hard for three people all born under the sign of Taurus the bull, which Mom, Dad and Betsy are, to get along without the Pisces fish personality, which I am, swimming amongst them calming the waters. But all is going fine at home.

So fine in fact that when I start to have a tough time in those four months I realize I haven't talked to Mom, Dad or Betsy in weeks. I call to see how things are going at home and to share that things are rough for me. As much as I want to discover the part of me that has been hidden, it is not an easy time. I ask if someone can pick me up for Sunday night dinner. Mom tells me, "No, we have other plans."

Nobody calls later to check on me. Clearly Mom doesn't need my support anymore, which is a good thing, but a part of me wishes I could have someone to comfort me. Janis and Mark have been observing for a long time that one of the ways that Mom copes with life is by only focusing on the project that is currently capturing her enthusiasm. It takes me years to realize they are right.

At different times after I leave home Janis and Mark try to help me see how off-kilter Mom is. While I can see their point I don't know what difference this awareness will make. I am planning to stay in regular contact with Mom even if they feel they can't. I think they are concerned that I will get hurt.

While it is true that lots of things happen in my relationship with Mom that are filled with potential hurt, the greatest impact of Mom in my life is the multitude of lessons that I learn about how to be and how to not be in healthy relationships with myself and others.

Mom's mental health challenges provide me with a deep and abiding passion to engage the world from my authentic self. Later in life this passion becomes a core component of my call to invite and teach others to connect to their authentic self, to their true essence, that part of us that is rooted in love which enables us to create healthy, life-giving relationships and communities.

There are so many lessons that I learn from Mom.

I learn from observing the eight alter personalities that it is okay to show up as who we are and that even with all our frailties we will still be accepted. I realize that we don't need to struggle to try to fit predefined roles or fulfill expectations that are external or opposed to who we know ourselves to be. I recognize that playing a role based on what we think is expected of us is unhelpful; a lack of depth and creativity is the result when we try to create a picture-perfect facsimile of who we think we "should" be. Mom's alternate personalities provide examples of people who don't get hooked by roles based on external expectations. However, in their less-than-mature perspective on life, they miss the nuances that are necessary for healthy relationships, such as holding space for others to also fully show up. Some of Mom's alternate personalities tend to arrive expecting everyone to focus on them, making it very difficult for rich mutual relationships to develop. Our "real Mom" models how to genuinely care for others by engaging with them and delighting in who they are. The various realities of Mom provide me with practices and attitudes that help me discern ways I want to engage with the world and ways I do not want to engage with the world.

The search for how to live in authentic relationship with myself and with others during that first year of university provides a crisis that is an opportunity to learn about myself and life. Longing to be the "me" I know deep within, and not wanting to live behind any kind of mask, I choose to live out of the part of me that I call my 'dirty, grungy self' during the first four months of living away from home. I discover that buried within this side of me, which I had tried to hide, is an abundance of creativity and amazing insights about life.

It is startling for me to discover that, though I feel like I am engaging the world in a radically different way during these four months, no one seems to notice the difference. I wonder if maybe they have always seen the fullness of me, including that part that I label the 'dirty, grungy self.' Or maybe they are simply accepting that I am growing up.

There are only two examples of a person observing a difference in me during the four months of living solely out of my 'dirty, grungy self.'

The first one is at the end of the four months. My high school friend who introduced me to my roommate has now become my roommate's boyfriend. The two of them are going to take over our apartment to live there together. My high school friend phones me in mid-April to find out how fast I can move out of the apartment so they can move his stuff in. I've paid to the end of the month, so I tell him I am not moving until then. I am firm and insistent and annoyed by his request. I stand up to him and won't let him push me around. I hang up the phone with a loud slam.

The phone rings almost immediately. I answer it. It is my friend again. He is phoning to check to see if he actually just had a conversation with me or someone else. He tells me it didn't sound like me. I tell him it was me. I pull back from the strong, assertive attitude once he acknowledges that I have the right to stay in the apartment. I tell him I am okay with him moving in with us in the apartment. For ten days the three of us share the apartment, sleeping in the one bedroom together. It is a final defiant move toward being only my 'dirty, grungy self' who has little willingness to be accommodating to anyone.

The second time it happens is when I am sitting at the kitchen table at my parents' home months later. There is a black out. We are sitting by candlelight. I am reading an Ibsen play while my current sort-of-boyfriend is sketching a picture of me.

When he's almost done he looks up at me and says with a voice filled with surprise, "I have sketched you before. I just realized it as I am finishing the details of your cheekbone. How can it be that I haven't recognized you?"

He delves for his portfolio of art and leafs through it. He pulls out a sketch.

He looks at it closely and says, "I think this is you. We were at the same party in March. You were sitting alone on the other side of the room from me. Wow! Did you ever look different! I wouldn't even recognize you now from this picture. What was going on in your life back in March that makes you look so awful?"

Awww ... a portrait of my 'dirty, grungy self.'

After fully living as my 'dirty, grungy self' for four months I discover it feels as inappropriate as engaging the world with the thin veneer of the 'golden girl façade.' I intentionally begin to reintegrate what I once saw as two separate parts of me.

I realize that the 'golden girl façade' and the 'dirty, grungy self' are not two unconnected parts of me or even false projections of who I am; they are simply different parts of me. I discover that when they are reconnected to each other my life and my contribution in the world are much richer, fuller and filled with greater potential. I recognize that I am a person who is kind and caring and smiles often like the 'golden girl,' and I am capable of critical thinking and filled with creativity like the part of me I once called the 'dirty, grungy self.' I am actually more than a combination of them.

I begin to recognize that some of my greatest assets reside in that part of me that I was hiding behind the 'golden girl façade.' It would have been a loss if I had left those gifts stranded in the depths of who I am to wither away through lack of use. I shift from thinking of that part of me as my 'dirty, grungy self' to describing it as the 'creative, critical' part of who I am. The 'creative, critical' part of me, combined with the 'golden girl' part of me, is a much better reflection of who I am. Integrating both parts is an important step on my journey to living from a place of wholeness.

I know I have successfully reintegrated the different parts of me to create a cohesive whole from a comment one of my professors makes during my fourth year at university.

Others say that this particular professor can't stand students. He sees us as inadequate bothers. I find it unbelievable that a professor can't stand students, until I experience it one day when I go to his office to pick up an essay.

He doesn't look up from his desk when I enter. When I reach for my paper he asks if my paper is the one on top, still not looking up from his desk. I tell him it is.

His comment back to me is, "If you had some letters behind your name that paper would be worth publishing."

I'm shocked. He continues to work and ignores me. I leave.

As I go down the stairs a question goes through my mind: "Why do I have to be an academic with a degree in order for the paper to be published?"

I snort in disgust at his academic snobbishness.

It is in our next encounter that he shows me I have reintegrated the different parts of me. We are at the cast party following the closing of three one-act plays. I directed a George Bernard Shaw play.

This professor who has such disdain toward students comes up to me and tells me with a voice that has a slight slur from drinking, "You know I always thought you were just an empty-headed party girl with your perky little ponytail and constantly smiling face. I had no idea you had such depth of thought. I directed that Shaw play myself a few years ago, and your version is far superior … far deeper. Where did you find all the layers of meaning that I missed?"

He shakes his head and wanders away.

As he goes I think to myself, "Yes … I did it … the 'golden girl' and the 'creative, critical' one are now integrated!"

During the years of university, evidence emerges a few times when I encounter a perspective about who I am and what I am capable of that is contrary to my perception of myself. My perception of myself is that I lack valuable insights. I am intrigued now when I look back to realize how little I allowed evidence of a contrary perspective to penetrate my awareness.

During my second-semester psychology course I hear a whisper of insight which I ignore. I continue to walk around thinking I am not capable of providing new or in-depth insights into the world around me.

The incident happens one morning when I go to my psych tutorial seminar. I have not been in weeks. When I arrive, the group is not in our designated room. I find the new room. I try to slip in without being noticed because I am late. It does not work. I apologize. The tutorial leader sends me a sharp look. She tells me they are trying to find a volunteer to do an analysis on levels of intelligence. I tell her that I am willing to be the guinea pig as a way of apologizing for disturbing the class. The student seminar leaders are trying to show us a theory that has consistent, proven results based on people's ability to repeat series of numbers. They are expecting a volunteer who will not be able to repeat back the full series of numbers but will get a higher tally each time one particular number is repeated in the series.

It turns out I am not a helpful participant. I can repeat back all twenty numbers each time a series is given to me. After class the tutorial leader walks with me down the hall. She tells me she is amazed at my capacity to be able to remember numbers. She tells me my ability shows a high level of a certain type of intelligence. I explain to her that the reason I can remember so many numbers is simply because I have worked in a parts department for five years where remembering numbers is a necessity.

Later when I am back in the parts department I realize that all the series I am working with are only seven to nine numbers long. I still brush off the high-test results as being based in a skill that I have developed rather than being based on my intelligence. As I write this book I am realizing that I have walked through my life with a skewed sense of who I am in the world. I have lacked recognition of some of my strengths, including my intellectual capacities.

Recognizing and celebrating our gifts becomes a key concept that reverberates through my philosophy of Authentic Connection Culture. Deeply rooted in the invitation to connect to our authentic self as the starting point to create this culture is the strong encouragement for people to claim and honour their gifts, as well as celebrate and acknowledge the gifts of others.

I now wonder if my passion to infuse this awareness of claiming and celebrating our strengths is one of many examples of being called to teach a particular perspective because the lesson is one that I need to learn. I needed to learn to claim my level of intelligence that again and again I discount because my type of intelligence does not fit the expectations for intelligence identified by our society.

As I ponder this ongoing self-perception of having a deficit in my thinking ability, I recognize that I have grown up in a world that values logic and rational thought. The primary and preferred way that I see the world is through the lens of creative metaphor, intuitive insights and relational perspectives. As a result, the contrast between my preferred style of engaging the world and what the world values causes me to judge myself as not a particularly capable thinker. There is a voice of judgment inside my head saying that I have little to add to subjects of substance.

My passion for ensuring that we hear all the different voices, thoughts and perspectives in a discussion comes from my knowledge that I am not alone in carrying this negative judgment inside my head; like me others downplay the value of the perspective that they could bring to a conversation. This voice of judgment echoes through the minds of many people raised in a world where we value certain skills and abilities, rather than recognizing that we need the wisdom, insight and skills of everyone for the circle of community to be whole. It is through the combination of all our gifts, insights and talents that life is enriched. This voice of judgment created by our cultural expectations silences far too many people, cutting us off from creative possibilities that could assist us in these times when our world is crumbling as our demands consume the foundations of our way of life. We need the perspectives of the many different voices. This realization eventually helps me to acknowledge the value of my own intelligence, but it still takes a number of years.

In the spring of 1976, at the end of my second semester at university, I move back home. Mom and I delve with excitement into planning a huge party for Dad's fiftieth birthday. It is good to see Mom functioning well. Dad is thrilled with the party, which is filled with a huge jam session of live music. We actually manage to pull it off as a surprise.

Mom and Dad are back on track. Mom is significantly better than she was two years ago when Dad and I planned a twenty-fifth wedding anniversary celebration for them. Signs of the ongoing improvement in Mom's state are evident when comparing pictures of the two events.

In the fall of 1976, I move away from home again. Janis and I become roommates. We are students at the same university. We have a great time. We haven't lived together in four years. We share the top floor of an old house. Janis is just starting to regain her childhood memories, which she lost as a result of a car crash when she was eighteen, four years before. When we lie in bed at night she shouts out a memory from the other room to see if it is a true memory or one of the ones she made up so that she had stories to share when she was at college. I laugh at some of the stories she made up and delight with her when a memory is actually rooted in our childhood.

We move to a larger place in January of 1977, which Janis and her husband take over when they get married that fall.

Two months before Janis is married Alan and I begin to develop our relationship. He is at their wedding reception. He helps me to move out of the place Janis and I have shared and get my new apartment set up.

My RELATIONSHIP WITH ALAN SHIFTS on August 22, 1977 when we explore the attraction that has been bubbling between us all summer while we worked and while he helped me move into my new place. On the night our relationship shifts we spend ten hours talking.

Six hours into our conversation, around 4 a.m., Alan tells me about the death of his mother. It happened fourteen years earlier. After sharing his memories, intermingled with a deluge of tears, he tells me he's never told the story before. He notices that he feels good for sharing it.

When I start to get to know Alan's family, I am struck by how little they have talked about the tragic death of their Mom. Since I suspect that I am going to hang around them a lot, I feel a nudge to do something about the story no one speaks about. To me the untold story feels like chaotic energy swirling amongst us whenever we gather. To them it is normal, but to me it feels like a pressing weight that fills the air.

Experience has already taught me to be sensitive to the impact of ignored grief. From the time I am thirteen until I am twenty-one, twenty young people I know die in tragic circumstances—mostly car crashes but also two suicides, one drowning and two by cancer. Ten of them are friends and ten are acquaintances. Two other young people end up in wheelchairs as a result of two of the deadly crashes. I know the feeling of grief lingering in the air. It hangs like a pall over conversations where no one talks about it even though it is present in the room.

I also carry the burden of many unspoken stories about my Mom. I long to help others avoid doing the same. I know the pain of untold stories that stir below the surface of life.

As a result of my own experiences, I wonder if, in my relationship with Alan's family, it is worth the risk to try to broach the conversation about their Mom's death, especially since Alan observed that he feels better for having shared the story.

I think it might be best to speak to each of Alan's siblings alone. When they indicate they are willing to share their memories, I ask what they remember about the day of the accident. They are very open about telling me. The story is usually told without a lot of emotion.

More than once I hear that when they think back to the day they remember it is Mother's Day. "We were in the barn playing tag, though I'm not sure who all was there."

No one is sure who all was there.

It turns out all six kids are there that day. They ranged in age from four to fourteen years old. The details that I hear are that their Mom joins in a game of tag. She runs by the board that covers the hole from the hayloft to the cow stalls below. Her foot hits the board and it flips over. She slips and goes through the open hole. She dies a week later from her injuries. The details beyond that, including who is present at her funeral, differ from person to person. I am able to confirm that they are all at the funeral.

Over a couple of months, I listen to the stories from the perspectives of each of the kids, Alan's Dad, as well as some aunts. I piece together the fragments of what they tell me, much like I am attempting to do with the story of this book. I then go back to each person to share what I have heard. The story I share is a communal version of the story, which is a fuller perspective than any one of them have on their own. My hope is that the communal story will mean they won't feel alone in their memories.

Afterwards I am amazed that, for me, there is a shift in the energy at family gatherings. It's quite possible no one else notices. But I think there is impact from the simple opportunity for people to tell the story. At the time of the tragedy, they all agreed through silent consent not to spend a lot of time focusing on what happened. Their

Dad and their two aunts who came to live with them felt that, as a family, they needed to get on with their life, which they did in amazing ways.

A year and a bit after the tragedy Alan's Dad married the schoolteacher of the one-room school where all but the youngest child attended.

On the day of the wedding, seven-year-old Alan looks up at his one-time teacher, smiles at her, and says, "Hi Mommy." She smiles back at him.

Two sisters are added to the family through this marriage. Alan is adamant that they are simply his sisters. There is no differentiation in his mind between the kids in the original family and these younger sisters.

I adore Alan's family, and once I complete the process of listening to the stories of the tragedy of their Mom's death and then weaving together the many perspectives to retell the fullness of the story, it feels more comfortable to hang out with them.

The opportunity to hear the stories of Alan's family helps me to deepen my understanding of the importance of gathering different perspectives. My learning is that for people who are grieving, hearing the perspectives of the people who share their grief brings them together. It lifts the burden of feeling alone and isolated.

Sharing stories is a powerful way to move toward acceptance, healing, forgiveness and connection. Experience has confirmed that a significant way to initiate the healing journey is through sharing our memories and stories. I work with many families in tragic situations over the years as a minister, and I learn that people are willing to share their memories when an open-ended question is asked so they can choose what they want to talk about. A key intention behind asking them to share stories is that they share their memories with each other. They willingly do it so I can get to know the person who has died; but I know that sharing stories is even more beneficial for them than it is for me as I prepare the funeral service.

This awareness of the importance of gathering the multitude of perspectives through open-ended questions also helps me when I am dealing with a person or a small group of people who think they carry the knowledge of the whole group. I learn that it is rarely true that a small group carries the wisdom of the whole group. My facilitating style in my more recent role as a consultant is designed to ensure that we hear the many perspectives to add depth and a richness of insights, which often cracks a group open to creative ideas and solutions.

This learning also informs how I interact with Mom. I now understand that the different personalities within Mom carry differing perspectives and opinions about things. But for many years I did not understand that that was what was going on. My inclination to remind her of things she has said about a topic in the past doesn't always turn out well, even though I think it is important to have all perspectives on the table. I can now see that she did not find it helpful to hear the differing perspectives because she had no awareness that they all came from her.

In the process of encouraging people to share their stories I become aware of the power of the stories we tell ourselves and each other. Over the years of encouraging people to tell their stories, I begin to realize that we can choose the perspective from which we tell our stories. We can choose to tell stories from a perspective that lifts us up and helps us see future possibilities together. But we can also choose to tell stories from a narrow or judgmental perspective that can hook us into thinking of ourselves as a victim, or that identifies us as broken to the point where there is no hope, or fills us with fear to the point where we are immobilized. The perspective from which we choose to tell the stories of our lives impacts our lives.

Too many times I have spent energy on unfounded fear or misinformed judgment that come crashing into my mind, stirring a sense of anxiousness rooted in fear. The way we think about things matters. It impacts how we engage the world. We need to be intentional about what we give power to, including our own thoughts.

The beliefs we carry inform how we engage life. We need to notice them so that we can decide if we want to give them power or not.

A simple example of unfounded fear that once consumed me happened when Alan and I were first married. We shift his life insurance from his agent to the agent my family has used my entire life. But his agent had been the leader of the youth group at the church of which he had been a member for a number of years. For weeks I carry a huge fear in the pit of my stomach that his former youth group leader will confront him for his lack of loyalty by switching to a different insurance agent. It is a story that I keep telling myself. It gets so bad that I hesitate to answer the phone in case it is him. When an unexpected car pulls into the driveway I become anxious. I carry the concern inside of me until I can't bear it any longer. I finally tell Alan that I think he needs to return his life insurance policy to the person he bought it from. Alan is confused. I tell him what I have been feeling. He explains to me why he does not feel obligated to his original insurance agent, why he feels good about the decision we made, and his sense of certainty that we are not going to hear from the leader of his youth group because this is simply a reality of business.

I am shocked by the weight that lifts from my shoulders through a simple conversation that helps me realize that I can see things differently and that I can tell myself a different story.

I once again answer the phone with a sense of anticipation rather than dread.

When we carry fearful interpretations about life experiences without exploring them to determine if our interpretation has validity, our narrow interpretations and judgments can become a burden lurking deep within us, creating wounds rooted in anxiousness that consume us. I remind myself that in the Bible the phrases "fear not" or "do not be afraid" are apparently repeated 365 times, once for every day of the year. Fear can warn us about unsafe situations. Fear can also drain us of energy that might have been otherwise used to focus on gratitude, curiosity, or creativity, or to figure out how to deal with an unjust or inappropriate situation. These days, when I am caught by fear, I move to connect to the place of light and love within me to listen for guidance as I allow the fear to unwind and dissipate; that way the energy is free to be used for a helpful response.

When we choose to be intentional about seeing a story from different perspectives, including the perspective of seeing with eyes of love that have the capacity to detect hope and light and possibility, incredible shifts can happen inside of us.

I have been amazed at the insights that keep emerging as I spend time pondering the details of the story in this book, details that have enhanced my perspective in helpful and positive ways. When I am able to look at my life and the people around me with eyes of love rather than judgment, blame or resistance, compassion and curiosity crack me open to engage life differently.

I am aware from experience that the weight of secrets is a burden that has the potential to become lighter when we can find a safe place to share. It's intriguing to me to notice how many people tell me one of their parents also lives with mental health challenges when I share my story. Sharing our stories connects us at the level of authenticity, which has the potential to dispel the feeling of being isolated and alone.

I continue to be amazed at the power of untold stories. They create energetic havoc when we walk through this world carrying the burden of our silence.

The power of sharing our stories is a power that can change the world. Untold and unexamined stories can quietly suck the life out of us by allowing us to nurse unacknowledged wounds of the past. But sharing stories releases creative energy which allows future possibilities to emerge.

Both Janis and I remember Mom phoning us when Scott dies. He is only fifty-two years old. He dies of a massive heart attack. My memory of that conversation is that Mom speaks of him as though he has been her buddy. In her core personality, that is Mom's relationship with Scott.

Almost a year after Scott's death, Mom turns fifty. A week prior to her birthday she is rushed to the hospital with a suspected heart attack. It is determined that it is not a heart attack. They transfer her to a hospital in Toronto. She remains there for close to two weeks.

I never hear a reason why they keep her in hospital. I later wonder if they were seeing the weird way Mom behaves, even though she is in the midst of some particularly good years. It strikes me as odd that the staff tell us that we are not allowed to visit her. We can periodically chat on the phone with her. Dad is allowed to go see her once, on the day of her birthday.

From my experience as a minister, the scenario set up by the hospital staff sounds like a strategy that I have seen with patients in psych wards when the family is asked not to visit so that the patient has time to move through the issues with which they are dealing.

Mom has little awareness of her time in the hospital other than the fact that her window looked out onto a busy street that she enjoys watching. She is not aware of the medical staff coming to any conclusions as to why she is in the hospital other than recognizing that the pain she experiences suggests a heart attack. I think it is during this hospital stay that she finds out that the muscle had detached from her sternum when she ripped part of the furnace out of the floor years before. When Mom comes home she does not have any meds and she does not have any follow-up appointments.

Generally life with Mom stays relatively good over the next few years.

ALAN AND I ARE STILL TOGETHER, though with the wisdom of a twenty-one-year-old and a twenty-two-year-old we have decided that there are too many significant differences for us to consider marriage—differences of economic background, education, and level of connection to church. A year and a half into our relationship we decide that we will not get married. But we continue to hang out together, certain that it will be clear when we are to go our separate ways. From 1978 on, we don't talk about marriage.

Then on a wintery Sunday morning in January 1980, I am awakened in the early morning hours. I feel a sense of certainty within me that I am supposed to marry Alan. The message that is rising up is that he is the right partner for me in the life I will live. This is the first time I feel a strong sense of call in my life. I decide I will sit with it for a month on my own before I say anything to Alan, since this is far outside of our agreed-upon plan.

Later that day, we go to a zoo where you drive through the landscape where animals roam. As we drive through the buffalo herd, Alan turns to me and says, "So are you going to marry me?"

I turn and look at him, shocked. "Yes."

Alan and I buy a ring three weeks later. After leaving the jewellers we go to my parents' home. He stops the car at the top of the hill overlooking the farm.

He asks, "Will you marry me and be the mother of my children?" I say "yes" with a sense of certainty that this is what I am being called to do.

Soon after our engagement Mom's younger sister, the one surviving twin, is diagnosed with cancer. Mom steps up in an incredible way to provide care and support to her sister. Mom basically spends all her time in my aunt and uncle's home to care for her.

Alan and I are to be married in August 1980. Mom is so busy with her younger sister she has little time to be part of organizing our wedding, so when she says she wants to be there to pick out my dress and the material for the bridesmaids' dresses, I am thrilled.

I get to try on three wedding dresses. She picks the second one. She is so delighted with it, I say yes, even though I had dreams of a princess-style dress. But as she notes, the style is elegant and classic.

Next we head to Toronto to find material for the wedding party. Though I would have chosen a brighter colour for our wedding party, Mom is very practical, saying the deep country blue will mean that the women can all use the two-piece outfits other times. None of them ever wear the outfit again, but it is so good to actually have Mom there and present, I just want to soak up these attentive moments with her. I am careful not to do anything to rock the boat and trigger a different reality. I feel I need to be gentle and supportive because it seems to me that Mom is close to snapping, which I think is understandable considering the reality of her sister dying and the support she is providing.

In retrospect, I am pretty sure that the energy I pick up that day is the impatient Aggressive One who does not tolerate hesitation or have any desire to explore a variety of options. Without fully understanding what is happening in the moments when the Aggressive One shows up, I learn over a lifetime of experiences to tippy-toe around her so that I will not exacerbate the anger I feel rumbling just below the surface.

On the evening before our wedding, Mom is fairly relaxed. The whole family is home and staying together at the farm. It is the first time we are all together in ten years. It turns out to be the last time we will all be together. Mark almost didn't come because of the cost of the flight. I buy him his ticket because we can't have our five brothers and five sisters as our wedding party if Mark doesn't come.

After getting home from Alan's family's farm where the rehearsal dinner was held, we all sit at the kitchen table. Mom goes to bed first, which is so odd since she normally outlasts all of us. I suspect she's not getting much sleep at her sister's house. The rest of us stay up until after 2 a.m. Janis curls my hair with the old pink rollers that we used every night as kids so that I don't have to get up as early as planned to go to the hairdresser.

Our wedding day dawns warm and muggy. Mom has prepared an orange juice and champagne brunch for my side of the wedding party. Then we all spread out to get ready in the upstairs bedrooms.

I remember being alone in the midst of the sound of activity coming from the other rooms. Mom doesn't come to help me put on my veil like she said she wants to. Janis has to nurse her daughter and so is in another room.

When I am ready, I wander downstairs to the kitchen. Mom is there. She's piping mad. The person who picked up Grandma has brought her to the farm rather than going to the church as planned. Mom barely notices my arrival in the room. I got more reaction as a teenager for the creative outfits I put together each day for school.

As I observe Mom's frustration, I decide I am not going to fuss about details that turn out differently than I planned for this day. It turns out to be a good decision. Very few of our well-laid plans unfold as expected. No one reads the detailed information sheet I gave everyone at the rehearsal. Instead they make up things as they go.

My memories of the day are kind of odd. It is almost like I am in a bubble. The noise of the day seems to be off in the distance which is sometimes what happens to me as a result of the impact of my allergies. I notice the unexpected turns in our plans with a sense of detachment. I focus on the things that are most important to me, with Alan being my primary focus.

I have been aware for the three years that Alan and I have been together that people find us an odd couple. My friends don't understand why we are together. My sister's husband questions me about our suitability for each other. In the early years, Dad makes comments about my former fiancé, noting things like the great new car he is driving. Our minister isn't sure we are right for each other.

But somewhere deep down inside of us we know that we are to be together. It might not look right on the outside, but at a place deep in our souls we are connected.

When I walk down the aisle, my best friends are singing the processional from the balcony, the ones who would have been in my wedding party if our five sisters and five brothers had not been our wedding party. The song is John Denver's "Annie's Song." It still brings me to tears. That summer I remember driving with my Dad and making him listen to the song over and over again as I share my exuberance about why it touches my heart.

The words capture the feeling of the connection I experience with Alan. It uses images of nature that fill us up like love fills us up. In a way that we don't fully understand, Alan and I fill each other up, encouraging each other to be all we can be.

On the occasion of our first anniversary, Alan makes me a card out of wood with a sketch of a glorious tree. His declaration and encouragement to me is to "Branch Out and Be Loved."

This connection we have with each other is reflected in our vows.

Alan and I plan to write our vows to each other and memorize them. Alan is able to put his thoughts on paper first. We decide we will both use the opening paragraph and the closing statement that he wrote.

During the ceremony Alan says his vows first:

From this day on, I shall be your husband and you my wife.
Together, we will grow in many ways,
both as strong individuals and as a team working as one.
Our Christian faith and our growth in it
will be something that, together, we shall expand and strengthen.
We shall develop our relationship on the basis
of both love and truth.

Karen, in this life together, I shall love you always.
I will support you in your decisions and life ambitions.
When you need me, I will be there to comfort you and care for you.
I will help strengthen our friendship,
so that our days together will be happy and fulfilling.
Through God's guidance and God's help,
may our lives be ever enthusiastic and truthful.

Alan says his vows word perfect, looking deep into my eyes with his love flowing like a gentle ray of sunshine toward me.
Next it is my turn.

From this day on, I shall be your wife and you my husband.

I stop. No other words will come to me. Alan stares into my eyes. Then he realizes what is happening. His face fills with concern. I smile at him and turn to the minister for a prompt. Alan has worried so much about not being able to remember his vows, it never dawns on him that I might be the one to go blank. All the worry he had about not being able to remember himself reaches out to me to let me know it is okay. A quick prompt captures the rest.

Together, we will grow in many ways,
both as strong individuals and as a team working as one.
Our Christian faith and our growth in it
will be something that, together, we shall expand and strengthen.
We shall develop our relationship on the basis
of both love and truth.

Alan, I shall love you, care for you and be by you always.
I will give you strength and support
in whatever you endeavour to do.
When you need me, I will be there
to share with you the joys and sorrows in this life.
With God's support may our days be filled

with our love and friendship.
Through God's guidance and God's help,
may our lives be ever enthusiastic and truthful.

Three moments from the wedding celebration stand out in my mind.

The first moment is when we are dancing our first dance; the lyrics of "Can't Help Falling in Love" feel right, declaring to all who are gathered that we can't help falling in love with each other, and no matter how odd our match, it feels like we are meant to be together.

Another moment is when all the grandkids on Alan's side of the family gather to surprise his maternal Grandma with a cake and to sing "Happy Birthday." It is her eightieth birthday. I'm so glad to be part of another family for whom family matters.

The other moment is dancing with my Dad. It is just past midnight. Alan and I are about to leave. Dad asks me to jive with him to "In the Mood." At the end of the dance everyone forms a circle for Alan and me to say our goodbyes. When we get all the way around back to Dad he is crying. I have only seen him cry once before. It was when our dog Mike died. I saw a single tear roll down his cheek. But this time his tears are pouring down his face. He hugs me tight. I wonder when he will let me go. When he does, he tells me he loves me.

We have to go back to the farm. No one read the instruction sheet I prepared for the day, so my suitcase is not with us. I decide to make a quick call to the hotel where we are going for our wedding night. They were just about to give away our room since we hadn't arrived yet. It's the last room in the building on a night when all the inns in the city are full. They agree to continue holding it for us. I ask if our bottle of champagne is in our room. It is not. Good thing I called when I did because the bar is still open for two more minutes.

For all the well-planned details that keep being fumbled, it has been a magical day. We open our champagne and share memories of the special moments.

I am excited when it is time to put on my white peignoir set that my mother insisted I have for my wedding night. It's beautiful and flows and feels very special.

When we make love it feels like the most incredible sacramental moment, a sealing of our covenant of love that is so profound it brings me to tears.

Our wedding is the last event that my Mom's younger sister goes to. She dies on December 2, 1980.

Mom comes home after spending months caring for her sister.

Mom, Dad, Alan and I hang out together more and more. Most Sundays are spent at the farm in the backroom that Dad remodelled within the structure of the old woodshed at the back of the house. It is during the remodelling project that Dad finally comes to recognize and respect Alan's gifts, even though they are not those of a business executive like Dad's favourite son-in-law, Janis's husband. Alan's gifts catch Dad's attention in Alan's commitment to excellence in building and woodworking. The room that the two of them work on together becomes a special place for the four of us to gather.

In the early years of our marriage before I feel called to ministry, Alan and I agree to work with the minister of our church to lead a confirmation class for youth. On the day the group is confirmed, Alan and I are each invited to speak to the confirmands. We both do. Alan is asked by several people for a copy of his part of the sermon. I am not asked by anyone for a copy of what I said. I have kept his sermon all these years because it captures Alan's philosophy of life, which has made him such an incredible partner for me. Although Alan and I often talk about these fundamental concepts as a way of understanding life, this is the only time they are articulated in one place and shared in such a public way. I checked with him recently to see if he used any resources to write the sermon. He did not. He is twenty-four when he shares these thoughts that come from deep within his heart. The year is 1981.

This is what he said:

Life is a pure flame and we live by an invisible sun within us.
The past, the present and the future are really one—they are all today.
Greet each new day with love in your heart.

Consider nothing as impossible.
Reach for goals until you succeed.
Remove words from your vocabulary
such as can't, unable, impossible.
Know that each failure
will increase your chance of success at the next attempt.
Keep trying.

Human life is a miracle.
No one before you or after you has been or will be the same as you.
Take advantage of this and grow to your full capacity.

Live this day as if it is your last.
Don't think about yesterday's defeats and pains.
Don't try to see what tomorrow will bring.
Live today to your fullest. You will be a better person for it.

Laugh and be happy.
Share your happiness with others.
Show people that you really care
about your life and the people in it.

Enrich your values.
Don't settle for something less than what you are.

Don't leave your goals and ambitions sitting still.
Take action.
It is better to try and fail
than never to have tried at all.

Choose to grow rather than rot.
Choose to live rather than die.
Choose to give rather than steal.
Choose to persevere rather than quit.
Choose to laugh rather than cry.
Choose to love rather than hate.

Cultivate
a pure heart so you may see Love,
a humble heart so you may hear Love,
a heart of love so you may serve Life,
a heart of faith so you may love Life.

Remember to go through each day with purpose,
but also go through each day with happiness and love.

Dad, Mom, Alan and I all love the opportunity to have in-depth conversations about life as we sit in the backroom that Dad allowed Alan to help him build.

In the beginning we also have lots of conversations about Alan's and my woodworking business, which Mom and Dad are both actively helping to grow.

As time goes on the conversation focuses on new directions for our business because Alan is getting frustrated doing custom work. Too often people want him to replicate other poorly designed items. He can do it but it doesn't fulfill his desire to be creative and make things that are beautiful.

A SIGNIFICANT CHANGE IN MY LIFE'S PATHWAY shifts the focus of our conversations.

On Sunday June 25, 1982, on Mom and Dad's thirty-third wedding anniversary, I go to church alone, which is unusual because Mom, Dad and Alan often go with me. The minister, who has been a big part of my life, is leading his final service before he moves. While I am sitting alone in the pew I have an experience that changes the direction of our lives.

At fifteen I had an experience of a voice rising up within me that tells me that in my work I will be with people in times of joy and times of sorrow, that I will teach although I will not be a teacher, and that I will recognize the work I am supposed to do when I see it.

That morning, sitting alone in the pew listening to the sermon, a telegram type of message prints across the inside of my forehead. It tells me the work I am supposed to do is to be a minister. As a minister I will be with people in times of joy and sorrow and I will teach. I am shocked.

I decide I will sit with this sense of call for a while on my own. However, before dinner at Mom and Dad's, I take Alan aside into the living room. I tell him what I have sensed. He encourages me to follow the nudge. Throughout the evening as we celebrate Mom and Dad's anniversary dinner, they talk about their dream of going to Hawaii for their thirty-fifth wedding anniversary. Alan and I catch each other's eye, knowing we are carrying a dream as well, one that could change everything.

Tuesday I meet with the minister. He explains the process to me to become a minister and tells me that if I want to explore this possibility it would be good for me to be interviewed by the church elders before he leaves at the end of the week. That night Alan and I have dinner with Mom and Dad. I tell them about my sense of call, including the advice of the minister to "not give into the call for as long as possible" to ensure it is right.

By July 10, 1982, Alan closes our woodworking business, we sell a van that we have had for sale for six months, Alan finds work in the middle of a recession, I find a professor from my years at university for my bachelor's degree to write a letter of recommendation for me, I am accepted at Emmanuel College to start in the fall, and I become an intended candidate for ministry.

When I fill out the forms for my candidacy I don't even know what a Presbytery is, never mind which one I am in. There would be many in the United Church who would shake their head at someone feeling called to ministry in a church about which the most basic structural information is not known. But I have learned not to argue with nudges and calls from Spirit.

The conversations in the backroom at the farm shift focus. The four of us have deep theological discussions and arguments. Dad asks lots of questions once I start seminary in the fall of 1982.

I have lots of questions too.

Most of my classmates have already taken introductory courses in things like biblical studies. I haven't taken any such courses. When I did my bachelor's degree I was totally focused on the demanding and creative aspects of drama as my area of specialization. And so when I am faced with writing a paper every week for a course called English Bible, which is an alternative course to learning Hebrew or Latin, thank goodness, I do not have background that helps me to see the Bible differently from what I learned in Sunday school.

I don't want to appear clueless, so one day I casually ask a classmate, "Which duplicated stories in Genesis did you choose to reflect on in your paper this week?"

When she answers that she chose the two creation stories my comment back is, "That's a good choice."

But in my head a screaming rampage is going on. I knew there had to be duplicate stories in Genesis because the question for our paper is to pick two stories in Genesis and explain why the story is told two different ways.

Questions rush through my brain, causing pain similar to the rush of too much frozen yogurt. "Two creation stories? What is she talking about?"

As soon as I am on my own, I pull out a Bible and look at the opening chapters of Genesis. I had never thought of the story of the seven days of creation and the Adam and Eve story as two different stories. To me the Adam and Eve story is just fleshing out details of the seven days of creation. But as I look at them more closely I can see different styles of writing and different intentions behind the stories. It amazes me. I can hardly wait to explore more.

I listen closely to all the conversations going on around me while hiding my lack of knowledge. I offer questions only to keep a conversation going in the hope that I will be able to figure out what they are talking about. That is until we get close to the end of the first semester, and I finally burst in total frustration at words used and concepts discussed that do not connect to everyday life.

My explosion is around the casual and repeated use of the phrase "eschatological hope." These are the days before Google. I have tried to figure out what everyone is talking about when they refer to eschatological hope because it is difficult to research a topic when I don't know how to spell the word. A few times I ask questions, trying to get at what people mean, but their answers are as confusing as the rest of the conversation. I am in class when I blow up.

Everyone pauses as my outburst rolls off my tongue. I bemoan how our conversations do not, in my mind, provide nourishment for or connect to everyday lives. The professor finally provides me with a simple explanation of what is meant by "eschatological hope."

I sigh and ask, "Why don't you just say that instead of using long, fancy words that are heard only in the halls of this building?" Exclusionary academic language irritates me still.

In another class, my partner for a project has an outburst similar to mine. We are discussing the development of our paper for an ethics course.

For each new insight offered into our conversation he is able to name one or two theologians and their perspective on the topic. What I offer are stories from real life, applying the concepts and identifying how they will be helpful to the way we engage the world.

After a couple of hours of working together, he abruptly pushes back his chair, jumps up yelling and cursing, asking why it is that I am always able to come up with a story and all he offers are the theories of theologians. It takes me a moment to understand his point. At first I think he is complaining that I am not adding any academic insights into our work because I am very conscious that I am not.

Once I digest what he has said about his frustration that he is not able to come up with stories from real life like I am, I tell him that I think his gift of being able to identify different theories is not only helpful but amazing. I tell him that I am not able to identify the perspectives of different theologians because once I hear a concept or interpretation that makes sense to me I integrate it into my thinking and no longer retain the particular person it comes from. I point out how unhelpful that is in an academic world.

He sits down. We continue. But now we are conscious of helping the other develop their capacity to either find stories or name theologians by asking questions that encourage each of us to see things through different lenses.

The most shattering experience of those early months at seminary happens outside of course work.

There is a group of women who are migrating toward each other as we find similarities in our thoughts and perspectives rooted in feminist theology. We plan to go to a film together that is being offered at one of the other colleges on campus. *Not a Love Story* focuses on the industry of eroticism and pornography. It includes the perspectives of women who are part of the industry as it explores the impact of the industry on attitudes toward women.

The film shakes my foundations. It cracks me open to see what I have not seen before, to know what I have not previously noticed. It shatters all my preconceived ideas that we live in a culture where equality is integrated and every person is treated with respect for the gift of who they are.

I cry for what I have not seen. I weep for what I did not want to know. I mourn for the acceptance of norms that I have adopted so that I will fit into the culture around me. I sob for how blind I have been, molded into accepting a worldview that is causing systemic issues of injustice, oppression and a distortion of our humanity.

When I arrive at home that night I stumble upstairs to our attic bedroom. I go to the far side of the room and lean into the corner, slowly collapsing to the ground to curl into a fetal position of despair while I am reborn with eyes capable of critiquing our reality. The scales fall from my eyes. It is painful to have my eyes opened more fully.

Even while acknowledging the traumas of our culture of domination, control and consumerism, I do not lose sight of the goodness or what is possible.

However, three months into my program I feel like my faith is crumbling, jarred by a curriculum of sledgehammer-like critical interpretations and historical realities that are inconsistent to my core experience of God being love. It used to feel like my faith was built on a strong foundation, but now it feels like the pillars it stood upon are disintegrating.

The things that I learn in my first semester cause me to question whether I actually want to be part of the church at all, never mind a minister.

———————————

There is one particularly difficult night when I am overwhelmed with a feeling that the foundations of my life are crumbling. It is at the end of the first semester, which has been filled with deep chasms and high mountains of unexpected awakening.

My home church has invited the wider community to gather for the ancient Christmas celebration of the Boar's Head Dinner Feast. It is an annual celebration that I find slightly distasteful. Even so, we always go as a family. This year it feels very uncomfortable. I am one of the servers for the evening and so have to engage people amidst the frivolous antics of jesters while a papier mâché boar's head is paraded around on a platter. There are moments when the theology and life perspective that are being expressed bring me to tears. I find myself in tears as I rush around trying to look busy so no one will bother me.

These strong feelings probably have to do with the cracking open of my worldview that has happened in this first semester at school. It also probably has something to do with discovering that morning that I am not pregnant like we hoped.

Later that night, I am shocked out of my rare melancholy.

When we are leaving the legion where the dinner is held, Dad asks Alan and me if we are coming to the ongoing celebration at their neighbour's house. I groan inside.

Alan says we would love to, since that was our plan.

As Alan is driving around a fairly significant bend in the country road we realize that the roads are slipperier than we thought. Alan can't make the turn. He heads into the swamp. But we don't come to the expected abrupt stop. He somehow manages to dodge around trees that are coming at us from every direction. We bump over stumps and rocks and pass through long, icy grass that whips at our headlights.

And then we are back on the road. And we are fine.

We turn and look at each other in the now still car. We don't know how we got through the swamp.

We both acknowledge that it felt like there was a power beyond us that maneuvered us as we twisted and turned through a landscape that we should not have been able to travel through. As we sit at the edge of the road with a sense of being safe, my feeling of life being in a state of upheaval lifts. I feel a profound sense of reassurance that when the swampy and difficult places in life are encountered I need to seek ways to move forward and never give up hope that somewhere in the muckiness there is a way through.

In early 1983, the Sunday conversations with Mom and Dad shift again when Alan and I announce we are pregnant. Mom is pleased. Dad is thrilled.

These first three years of our marriage are good years between Alan and me. They are also good in regard to Mom's state of being.

Though Mom can't always focus and can be agitated, she is mainly present. There are times when she can go a bit squirrely, but in my mind I chalk that up to simply being human since at this stage I do not understand that there is more going on inside her than just the ups and downs with which we all deal.

The memories of these two and half years since Mom's younger sister's death are filled with the four of us enjoying good food, good conversation, and the odd card game if Mom can focus long enough. There are also fun adventures like going to see the new James Bond movie followed by Mom and Dad coming for a sleepover at our house to join us in the tent in our backyard where we sleep for six months of the year.

We practically live in our backyard, so it is fun to have Mom and Dad join us there. The tent is set up next to our huge vegetable garden that produces an abundance of produce. There are also red and black current bushes, a gooseberry bush for jam, a cherry tree that provides amazing fruit for pie, and abundant rhubarb. The yard is bordered by fields filled with soy beans. Each year we scoop a bucket of beans. It is great, since our budget is tight. Plus we love to learn new recipes.

Life in our home feels rich and magical.

LIFE SHIFTS AGAIN, ABRUPTLY. It is April 27, 1983.

I am exhausted. It is the last day of exams at the end of my first year of my Master of Divinity degree in preparation to become a minister. On top of all the upheaval of being a student again and the pulling apart of my faith to the point of wondering where it has gone, I am four months pregnant.

I am curled up in a deep sleep when Dad phones me just after 7 p.m. He has been away on a trip with the committee he sits on with the national church.

He tells me that he is so disappointed to hear that the ultrasound I had on Monday shows that I am not pregnant with twins like everyone thought. He says that he wanted one baby for him and one for Mom.

He has been planning to retire as president of the company in Toronto so that he can become a minister too, though it won't be in a congregation. He plans to be a pastor in pubs so that he still has lots of time for his family.

He tells me that he has talked to Mark about Mark and his family coming home from out west to live in a trailer on the farm.

Dad seems to want his family around him to share the day-to-day stuff of life that he missed while we were growing up.

Mark is staying with them at the moment, and Betsy is going to come over for the evening so they can watch the family movies. He asks me if we can come. I tell him I'm too tired. I never say no to Dad, but in that moment I can't imagine getting off the bed.

Dad tells me that his new car has come in, so I will be able to buy his current car from the leasing company the next day.

Then Dad tells me a joke about candidates for ministry and their total lack of knowledge about the story of the resurrection, infusing it with images from Halloween, Christmas and finally Groundhog Day. The best part about Dad's jokes is his laughter. His eyes squint to the point of disappearing because he laughs so hard.

After we hang up, his laughter echoes in my head as I sink back into the mattress and drift into a deep sleep, thinking it will be nice for Betsy and Mark to be with Mom and Dad. They definitely don't get to hang out with them as much as we do.

A little over an hour after our phone call, Dad has a massive heart attack. The doctor is called. When he arrives he calls for an ambulance. Mark and Betsy talk to Dad as they carry him out of the house on the stretcher.

The phone ringing doesn't wake me from my deep sleep. Alan comes upstairs to tell me the news.

As we drive through the dark night toward the hospital, I remember the last time I saw Dad. It was just before Dad went away. Mom had come up earlier in the day to help me at the house. Dad arrived after work to join us for dinner. After dinner we discussed life beyond death and Dad's sense of the importance of not being cremated. Mom left for home before Dad. Dad lingered, chatting with Alan about his miniature trains.

I have a strong memory of the moment he leaves. He is wearing a red sweater. He gives me a big hug and tells me he loves me, something he doesn't often say. When Dad goes out to his car we walk to the driveway with him.

As his taillights head down the lane I have a profound experience: I am filled with a sense that this will be the last time I will ever see my Dad. I turn away, not allowing myself to watch him go, trying to ignore the morbid thought.

And now, less than two weeks later, Alan and I are rushing through the darkness toward the hospital. I know whatever has happened is serious because Dad has been sent to the closest hospital rather than the bigger hospital that we usually go to that is farther away. I begin to plan Dad's funeral.

Alan and I arrive at the hospital and rush to where Mom, Mark and Betsy are standing outside. Mark says a prayer. He asks that we be given the strength to accept whatever is to come. The surge of a silent scream rushes through me, furious that the prayer is about acceptance rather than expectation that Dad will make it.

Moments later the doctor comes out and says, "I'm sorry."

I turn into Alan's arms with my great big pregnant belly, and pound my fist against his shoulder.

But then … I have an incredible experience. I sense Dad going down a long, velvet, black tunnel. I feel like I am standing still watching him, but I'm staying with him as he travels. I see a large light at the end of the tunnel. Then his presence moves beyond me, heading toward the light. A figure steps into the edge of the light to welcome him.

I look up at Alan and then turn to my brother and sister and say, "He's okay. He knows now."

One of Dad's favourite conversations was to speculate on life beyond death. And now he knows.

The experience Dad and I share that night, of going down the black, velvet tunnel together toward the light, is beautiful and comforting.

I ride with Mom, Mark and Betsy to the farm while Alan follows. During the drive Mom declares that it will be important for everyone to pitch in to help so I don't have to do too much since I am pregnant.

It is a nice sentiment, but it doesn't happen. Mom quickly falls into the pattern of depending on me, not just with the funeral arrangements but on a day-to-day basis for much of the rest of her life. Immediately after the funeral we engage in long conversations as Mom deals with her grief. At times the suicidal tendency shows up, but it is mainly just genuine grief. We talk for at least two hours each day.

Mom's increasing dependency on me begins as soon as we wake up the morning after Dad's death. I make the calls to the extended family and to Mom and Dad's friends. I go with Mom to pick out the casket and to choose the cemetery plot. I help her pick the clothes Dad will be buried in. We all help rewrite the obituary after a standard one is published by the funeral home the first day. I deal with Grandma, who is extremely upset because she thinks we have pushed her out of the centre of activity around the casket, as we have directed her to a comfy chair in another room. I explain to her that no one is standing by the casket. The family members are spread out throughout the funeral home. As people arrive I greet them at the door and tell them which room each family member is in. People are free to go to the casket if they wish and free to just see the family members they know. Over eight hundred people come through the funeral home. It would have been brutal if we stood by the casket in a line. Grandma huffs her disgust at our choice to ignore proper etiquette.

On the day of the funeral I watch as they take off Dad's wedding band and close the casket. It is the first time I have had time to myself to really face what has happened. Tears pour down my face.

The minister puts his arm around me and says he thinks I shouldn't try to do the reading in the service because I am clearly too upset. I nod, unable to speak. Later I am furious that he took that option out of my hands in a moment when it is expected that people will be emotional.

I learn that day how important it is to always tell family members at a Celebration of Life service that before I announce their part in the service I will look at them so they can nod to me to indicate if they are okay to come up or not. I also provide them with strategies ahead of time if they find themselves overwhelmed with tears when they are speaking.

I would have been okay to get up to read during Dad's service. When it is time for the reading I am composed and engaged in the service.

Just as the service is ending, there is a huge crash of thunder. The power goes out. The organ music fades away. The jazz band keeps playing.

The crowd is told to remain at the church because of the storm. Only the family will go to the cemetery.

My sisters and I are told to stay in the car when we get to the grave. I lean back in the seat for a brief moment until I realize that I do not want to stay in the car and that I do not have to stay in the car.

Alan puts his arm around me as we brave the wind which turns out to be a mini tornado. It strikes me that Dad would have loved the drama of the moment.

BY THE MIDDLE OF JULY I am aware that there is a sense of exhaustion deep within me. The combination of the demanding impact of first year at seminary, my grief, Mom's grief and my pregnancy have created a constant simmering of tiredness that feels like it penetrates down into the very marrow of my bones. It is an unknown experience to me to engage the world with this lingering tiredness that draws on my energy. I decide to stop working and take the rest of the summer off. Alan supports my decision.

The company I work for agrees to hire my brother to replace me. For a month I train Mark to take over the parts manager job I have done for thirteen years. The deal is that while I train him during the bosses' holiday, I can sit and work on my sermons for the summer pulpit supply that I am doing. Mark loves to hear what I am writing. He encourages me with his questions and his joy at the way I weave stories into my sermons.

Once I complete my work at the dealership, the conversations with Mom expand because I am more available.

In mid-September 1983, I begin to experience the hints of labour early on a Monday morning. I tell Alan before he goes to work that things are beginning to happen.

An hour and a half later I am lying on our bed after a walk down the lane on the farm where we live. Alan comes bounding up the steps to our bedroom. I tell him he doesn't need to be at home yet; things are just starting.

He tells me he has just lost his job. He challenged the service manager for not ordering required parts for customer machines as promptly as possible. The owner appropriately stood behind the service manager, though a few months later the owner calls Alan to offer him his job back because the service manager has been let go.

I look back to that moment and marvel at how calm we stay. Between us we have no job, no income and I am in labour for our first baby.

I am actually glad to not be alone even in these early stages of labour. In the early hours of Tuesday morning we drive to the hospital. By 10 a.m. we are sent home. Sometime during the afternoon the contractions become stronger. Alan begins to massage me.

By 10 p.m. we feel that it is time to go back to the hospital, but I don't want Alan to stop providing the relief his massage gives. We call Mom. She comes immediately.

We load ourselves into my car, which had been Dad's car up until the night he died. Mom is driving very carefully. Alan has his back up against the roof of the car as he stands over me offering me relief. As Mom slowly turns onto the highway, Alan protests that she needs to go faster or he will never make it. The hospital is fifty minutes away at a regular speed. She speeds up significantly, and we fly through the night down the winding road that leads to the hospital.

We invite Mom to stay with us for the first few hours. When the time comes closer she leaves to give us the privacy we said earlier we would want. About an hour later, when the birth is imminent, our room is full; this is a teaching hospital. Alan and I realize this birth will not be private or quiet. Mom might as well be in the gathered crowd.

Alan goes and finds Mom. She is thrilled to be invited into the room. When they tell us we have to leave the birthing room to go to the delivery room we tell Mom to come with us since the crowd is only growing larger.

Mom is with us when our baby is born.

Alan leans down and whispers into my ear, "It's a Sarah." My heart melts, dissolving any lingering uncertainty about the power of love, dissolving any resistance to acceptance. I turn toward Alan. Our eyes connect. A surge of energy passes between us, connecting us at a level beyond my imaginings, and propelling us into an experience of eternity, of no time, no place, of just being. Our eyes are drawn to the eyes of this new precious one who is placed in my arms. A sense of expansiveness flows through me as an eternal bond wraps around us. I feel my energy align with hers, a prelude of our ongoing sense of connection.

Mom falls in love with our little one, instantly creating a bond with Sarah that is profound.

———————

For the next several months, Mom is able to stick with the original plan of providing care for our baby while I go to school. I miss one week of school after the birth. Then the three of us head to Toronto every Thursday. The hallways of Emmanuel College are made of stone and so every sound echoes and reverberates off the walls of the central staircase that travels from the ground floor to the top floor. Mom decides to go to Queen's Park and push the stroller around there all day. She returns to the college when Sarah needs to nurse. I sit close to the door so she can slip into the room to give me the baby to feed.

In the second week of November, Mom phones me on the Thursday morning and tells me it is too cold for her to go and keep the cries of the baby out of the halls of the college. She will stay home and I can take the pump with me. I manage to pump three ounces of milk before I leave. I don't know how she will do it without more milk. But I leave trusting that both Mom and Sarah will be okay. I never ask what she feeds Sarah. I suspect it might be a water and sugar combo. I am just as glad not to know.

At the end of my first semester, Mom tells me she can't continue to provide care because she wants to take a job she has been offered. It is work at a private restaurant that is connected to the company Dad was president of when he died. She will be the hostess in a dining room for top executives. She loves the work and they love her.

By the spring of 1984, I am beginning to see our "real Mom" show up again. She had not fully returned after all the episodes that began more than a decade ago when she was so impacted by medication at the time of surgery. Now our "real Mom" is back more of the time. Her conversations are more interesting. She starts to talk about going to university. Her core strength, which dissipated through the early 1970s, is returning. I am delighted. I begin to actually enjoy most of our two-hour conversations each day. When her grief is woven into the mix it feels healthy and appropriate.

I now realize that one of the reasons Mom may have been so good during this time is that Betsy is back living at the farm. Months later her fiancé moves in as well. Mom actually met him before Betsy did. Mom adores him, which could also be adding to why she is doing so well.

It is fascinating to look back and realize the repeated evidence that Mom is usually in much better shape when Betsy is around. Betsy's birth brought Mom back to us and her presence seems to call to Mom's core personality, drawing her out in a way that is different from Mom's relationship with the rest of us.

On Labour Day weekend of 1984, Betsy and her fiancé are married at the farm.

At their wedding, Mom meets one of their bosses. He has a position that is similar to Dad's position in the business world. He invites Mom to dinner the next week.

On the way to the restaurant, he asks Mom to marry him. She says yes.

Six weeks later, on November 10, they are married. I am one of the officiants.

I have a horrible sick feeling in my stomach that no one should be officiating at this wedding because this marriage is not a good choice. It turns out to be an accurate assessment of what is to come. The sick feeling is the prelude to seventeen years of incredible dysfunction and despair, intermingled with moments of companionship between the two of them.

The Suicidal One is frequently back. The tiny voice of the Three-Year-Old periodically intersperses into the sad ramblings of the Suicidal One. The Flirty One, who constantly sounds drunk and immature, is a regular attender of life. The Partying One emerges once in a while when Mom chooses hard liquor rather than just wine or beer. Even the Wild One shows up, though it is rare; when she does, she erupts into conversations with terror-filled questions. The Aggressive One pops in and out of life regularly.

———————

In the fall of 1985, Mom and her second husband are living part-time in his condo and part-time at the farm. Mom's better when they are at the farm. Betsy and her husband are still living there. They see the struggles Mom is going through in this new relationship. Mom's husband decides that he cannot live at the farm. My heart breaks when I think of the farm being sold.

I head out to the farm one afternoon in late fall. No one is home. I pass the barn and walk down the lane that leads to the back meadow. The lane meanders between the creek and the field behind the barn. I head down the lane, and then pause close to the grove of trees just before the next field begins. I stop to listen to what is rising up inside of me. I know there is a well of tears deep within me, so deep that I cannot reach it. I am afraid that the time will come when those tears will come gushing out of me in a way that is uncontrollable. I would prefer if I could figure out how to release them at a time that is appropriate.

In a way that I don't understand, it feels like the farm is the place that holds the key to releasing the pain I carry within.

I have brought a journal with me. I find a place to sit to try to tap into what is causing me distress. I write my reflections:

In the stillness of this moment I hear echoes of laughter and the pounding of hooves of our horse racing down the field, a memory of incredible freedom from a summer sixteen years ago.

In the stillness I hear the calls of my family from nineteen years ago, "Mike!" … and I remember the sad eyes of our puppy as he struggles to the top of the ridge along the creek to be with us for one last moment before the poison he has been fed ends his too short life. He is one of the dogs in our area who is killed by thieves as they prepare to break into a number of homes. The family dogs at the targeted homes all die that week.

In the stillness I hear my own tears falling in the grove behind me—falling for my beloved cat that dies a senseless death by falling into a window-well beside my university apartment, strangled by the choke collar I put on him. Alan and I bury him here at home.

There have been so many people, so many dreams and memories ... but now the people are gone ... dried up like the tall weed before me standing stark without purpose.

The peach sky creates a silhouette that reflects the image of the tree of life. Like the tree, we are many different branches crossing paths, once in a while taking our strength from our common centre so we can reach out to the possibilities that lie beyond.

The sun goes down and sets upon an era that has been rich with joys and filled with sorrow still deep within the unbidden well of tears.

Soon I will dip into that well, to blend the sorrowful emotions held there, with the joy that surges through me, so that the richness of the bittersweet taste of life can be experienced.

Now the constant sweetness like artificial pink lemonade leaves a lingering taste of fear ... fear that the bitterness will come on its own and overwhelm me.

The decision is made. The farm will be sold. Sadness pours through me.

Mom and her husband buy a condo on the fifth floor of a high-rise in Toronto. Before they move in they sell that condo to buy a new house in a new subdivision. Mom invests all her amazing decorating talents to create a home. They sell that place before the house is finished because Mom's husband cannot tolerate the idea of living there. They buy another condo in the same building as before. This one is on the nineteenth floor. Somewhere in the midst of this upheaval of finding the right home that will satisfy Mom's husband, the farm is sold.

On January 9, 1986, the final sale papers will be signed. I feel the need to be at the farm on the last night that the farm will be ours. It feels important to me to be there for the ending and to be aware of a new era about to begin.

I want to be alone. I pack a sleeping bag and pillow and head to the farm. Like twenty years ago when we arrived, a huge snowstorm has filled in the laneway. The car gets stuck at the foot of the driveway, just like the moving van had years before. I walk up the lane unconcerned at the moment that my car is stuck, though I know it will be a pain in the morning. I still need to carry out all the treasures that have been set aside for me from our family home. If I can't get the car up the lane in the morning, it will be a lot of lugging.

It is dusk when I arrive. My brother and his family are safely ensconced in their trailer in the field where they will continue to live. Betsy is across the road on the far side of a field in a house they are renting from long-time neighbours.

I am alone in the home we have shared. I set out my sleeping bag in my bedroom and sit down to write:

I am sitting in my old room on this last night of this being our family farm. It is January 8, 1986. Memories rush back at me like streaks of light of a film in fast motion.

I hear echoes of our life. Memories of the footsteps of Mom, Dad, Janis and Betsy swirl through my mind, coming up the stairs behind the wall where my headboard used to lean. I can hear Mom's constant motion, in the kitchen, up the stairs, bustling to the laundry room. I hear hints of rhythms from the family room at the front of the house where Dad's drums were set up. I hear shouts of laughter from the fire pit and the pool outside my windows.

As I look out the windows, I soak up the landscape of my solitude, the places I often go to centre, now covered in a heavy snow, soon to be ours no more.

I sit in the stillness remembering the first day in this room, a day filled with dreams of all that will happen here. And now those dreams are filled with details that will be complete when I wake in the morning. Tears of sadness and gratitude accompany me through the night.

I awaken in this house that later today will no longer be ours. It is time to go. In the grey, early light of dawn I wander through the skeleton of our home and say my goodbyes, letting the memories whisper to my heart of the insights, learnings and connections made in this place that is home.

I am sad that Mom's husband cannot imagine living here. This is the first place I came after leaving the hospital when Sarah was born. This is where we gathered for a celebration of Dad's life after the larger community had gone home. This is where I came down every day for high school to have Mom "ooh" and "ahh" over my chosen outfit. This is where I came down the stairs in my wedding gown to be ignored by Mom because she was distressed that Grandma was here, rather than at the church. This is where I sat with Mom night after night as she found her way back to herself. This is a place filled with laughter and tears, confusion and insights. This is the place where so many memories are held. But now this place is being passed on to another family.

I leave my key on the kitchen counter. I carry the treasures that have been left for me out to my car at the end of the lane. I sit for a while at the end of the lane and wonder if there will ever be another place that feels so profoundly like home.

I FINALLY TAP INTO THE WELL OF UNSHED TEARS that I struggled to tap into during the final months on the farm. In the spring of 1986 during my ministry internship I have an experience that gives me access to what is going on deep within me.

It happens during the church event called the Week of Guided Prayer. I delve beyond the vacuum inside me that protects me from the pain I carry. Once I tap into those tears I am able to again connect to the source of light and love that is within all of us.

At the opening session of the Week of Guided Prayer, I follow the instructions of the leader to go deep within myself to connect to who I am. He suggests that we go down an elevator to the centre of our being.

When the doors of the elevator open to the centre deep within me, I am shocked to enter into a place that looks and feels like a war-torn landscape. The air is filled with dust. There is no clear pathway. Boulders ten times my size obliterate my capacity to see. I wander through the landscape seeking clarity of where I am to go. I stumble and my hand reaches out. I discover a smooth metal wall. I follow its contours until I begin to see sunlight peeking through the dust by a pile of rubble ahead of me. When I clamber up the rubble, I can see an end to the steel wall. Just beyond it, amidst the dust-filled air, I see a stronger light coming from the far side of the wall.

I begin to scramble up the pile of rubble. When I am part way there I hear the leader telling us to return our attention to the room.

During the week of prayer, with the guidance of my spiritual director, I return to the place of the war-torn landscape within me where I'm not thrilled to go. My director encourages me to go back to the edge of the steel wall. I climb further up the rock pile to the end of the steel wall. I discover that on the other side of the wall there is a meadow that is filled with glorious flowers. There is a river that sparkles in the sunlight and a rich lush forest that stands at the edge of the meadow. It is beautiful. The beauty that has always been here welcomes me.

When I enter the meadow it feels like a safe place. I move to the centre of the meadow. I remember this place that is filled with light. It is like the primordial garden filled with lush possibilities.

Here, I can face the realities of my life that have created the war-torn landscape deep within me. I sit down and lean against the trunk of an old, sturdy tree. I centre into the stillness and the energy of this place. I tap into the well of tears and allow them to rise.

The sound of a wail that echoes with lament emerges from deep within me. As it erupts it is carried away on the gentle breeze. It feels like it is releasing me from a cauldron of turmoil and angst that I have silently and unknowingly carried within me.

I release these feelings of struggle and torment that have created my inner war-torn landscape. I reaffirm a power within me that is clear and strong and filled with love.

My spiritual director helps me understand what I am experiencing. We meet daily in the tiny room at the edge of the chancel in the sanctuary. It feels safe here, far from the busyness of church life. Light streams through the coloured glass in the wall of windows. It is warm in the sunshine. This tiny space becomes a place of spiritual awakening for me.

It is here that my spiritual director shares an image, an idea that gives me a symbol to express my experience. It reflects the wisdom of the ages about the spiritual aspects of who we are.

On a scrap piece of paper she draws a diagram of three concentric circles, a small one in the centre surrounded by a medium-size circle, which is in turn surrounded by a larger circle. She labels each circle.

The smallest circle, or the inner circle, represents who we are as a beloved child of God. The medium-size circle represents our life experiences including the external expectations that we accumulate through our lifetime. The largest circle represents the stuff of life that swirls around us.

CONNECTING TO OUR AUTHENTIC SELF

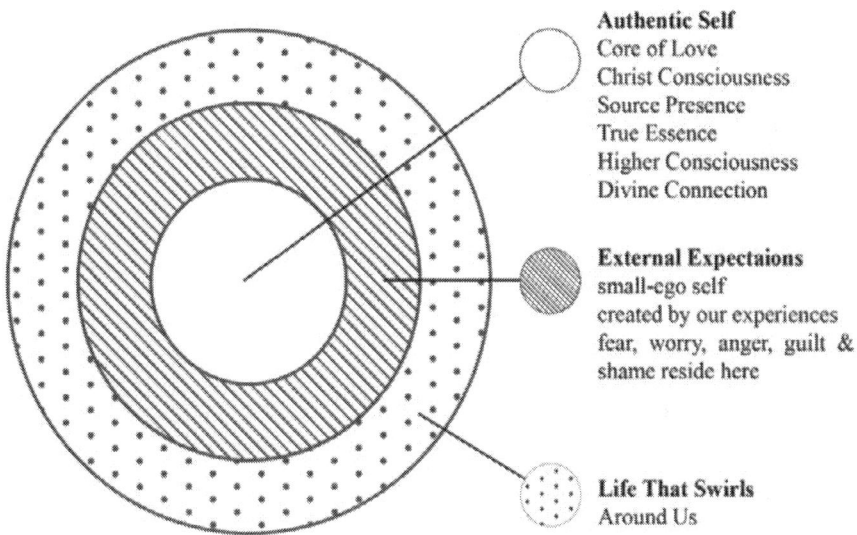

Authentic Self
Core of Love
Christ Consciousness
Source Presence
True Essence
Higher Consciousness
Divine Connection

External Expectaions
small-ego self
created by our experiences
fear, worry, anger, guilt &
shame reside here

Life That Swirls
Around Us

My spiritual director observes that most people live their lives in the circle of external expectations. She observes that this circle often covers over the inner circle where we connect to God and to who we truly are. As a result of living our lives in the circle of external expectations, we live our lives disconnected from the power of God's love and disconnected from our true essence, from our authentic self, from, in her words, who we are as a beloved child of God.

She goes on to explain that the goal of the spiritual journey is to move from the circle of external expectations into the inner circle where we remember who we are, where we remember our authentic self and our call in life, and are empowered to increase the creativity and love on this planet through our presence.

The diagram of the three concentric circles, and the understanding that the purpose of the spiritual journey is to reconnect to our authentic self, confirms experiences in my life and provides me with a clear way to explain my work and my perspective on life; it informs how I encourage people on their spiritual journey, and my choices as to how I show up moment by moment in my life.

A decade later, I expand the diagram to include how individuals can be in authentic community together one on one or in a Circle. The expanded diagrams shows a group of individuals seeking to connect to one another from their true essence in order to create a deeper sense of community.

CONNECTING AUTHENTIC SELF TO AUTHENTIC SELF

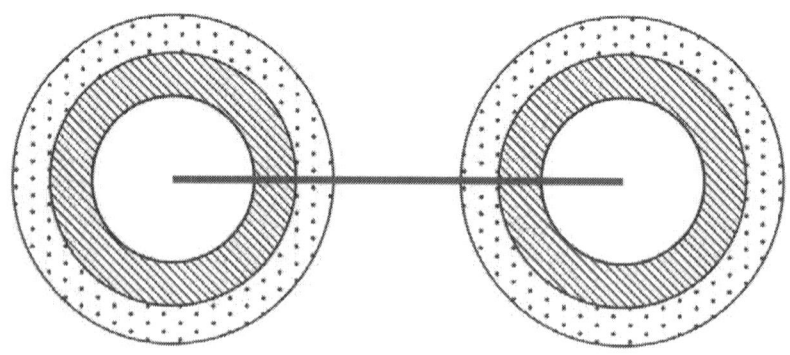

When I share this image of one on one connection, I note that if an individual is not able to connect to their authentic self, we can still choose to interact with them with the awareness that they are beloved and have a source of light and love within them, even though they may not be connected to it at the moment.

This new awareness confirms my memory of being a three-year-old and seeing the light of love in every person and every part of creation. For me such an understanding brings our life purpose into focus. We are to create the opportunity for love to expand and creativity and compassion to grow. We are to create space for the Kindom or the Realm of God to emerge in our midst, which happens when the power that reigns is love. This intention needs to be at the core of the narrative that informs our lives. We need a narrative that sees the goodness, connects to the energy of love, and calls us to live as ones who are committed to the common good, where resources are shared, gifts are celebrated, the Earth is respected and we listen deeply to the wisdom within us and amongst us. When we connect in community and really see one another, our inner capacities to cultivate the seeds of possibilities expand. When we gather in Circle we experience this profound sense of connection rooted in our shared agreements of how we will be in life-giving community together.

A CIRCLE OF CONNECTION

(HOLDING SPACE FOR MEANINGFUL CONVERSATION)

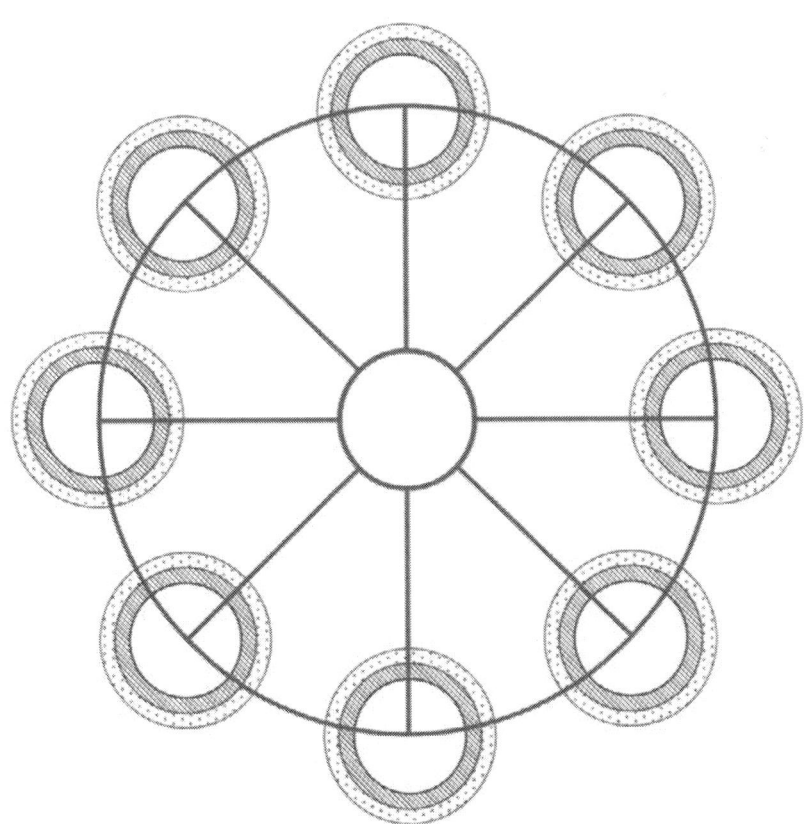

Years after I first share and teach this awareness of the power of creating community that is at the root of Authentic Connection Culture, some of the leaders of the Intentional Circles I train identify the difference between reacting to life from the middle circle of external expectations where our fears and wounds are held in contrast to how we respond to life when we connect from our authentic or true self. The difference described between reacting and responding is a helpful tool to use to be aware which perspective or circle we are plugged into, the one that is rooted in the insecurities of life or the one that roots us in a higher consciousness.

REACTING vs. RESPONDING	
Based on Middle Circle of External Expectations	*Based on Centre Circle of Authentic Self*
Life reflex, not conscious	Conscious, aware of choices
Automatic	Grounded, genuine
Objective "you" statements that come from the head and disconnect us from our own story by speaking from a detached perspective	Connected "I/we" statements that come from head and heart and connect to our own story by speaking from a personal perspective
I know I can fix you	I honour the wisdom in you
A sense of entitlement that blames and lacks ownership	Takes responsibility for self and focuses on the well-being of all
Difficult to disengage from demands and worries	Easy flow of energy toward possibilities and passions

When we are reacting rather than responding, we can choose to shift our stance so that we are connecting to our true essence which allows us to then actively participate in creating beloved community where we are all welcomed, honoured and celebrated.

My learnings about the spiritual journey during my internship prompt me to identify how our authentic self, our true essence, needs to be fully integrated into all aspects of our lives in order for us to have the capacity to enhance life to bring about the change we long for in a world where too often we have lost connection with what really matters, resulting in us barrelling down a pathway toward our own destruction. Connecting to the Divine within us, to the power that is love at the core of our being, sheds light on alternative pathways that lead to compassion and community.

One of the steps on this journey is recognizing our own gifts and listening for and trusting the wisdom we carry within us. For many of us this step is huge. I know I am not alone in feeling like life has taught me that what I say has little value and that I must keep my strengths hidden so that I do not appear boastful. Accepting who we are and that our voices are needed to find a way forward is counter-intuitive to the teachings of many of our childhoods, yet it is a critical step to once again reclaim the fullness of who we can be together.

MY YEAR-LONG INTERNSHIP is filled with learning opportunities that help me to better understand myself. There is one moment of discovery that particularly shocks me. It is prompted by a question from my supervisor. One day when we are preparing for a group we lead together, I suggest that it might be helpful to create a diagram of the main point of the chapter we are exploring. To me it seems like a simple way to express a clear understanding of a complex idea. I show him an example of the kind of diagram I am envisioning. But then I quickly withdraw the idea, suggesting that maybe it's a dumb idea.

My colleague looks at me and asks, "Who convinced you that you are stupid?"

I respond within a heartbeat without giving it any thought. "My sister Janis."

I am shocked by my answer. I think Janis would be shocked too.

When I give it some thought, I realize that when we were kids Janis often indicates that I'm not old enough to know something. I interpret that to mean that I am stupid or dumb. During our childhood Janis is not interested in listening to my stories. To her my stories are boring because she has already lived that part of her life. She wants me to listen to her stories.

In my mind I begin to think that my experiences and insights do not have value.

My experience is not particularly unusual; Janis and I are just eighteen months apart, with parents who do not teach us how to listen to one another as a healthy communication strategy. Learning how to communicate as kids does not seem to be a high priority in our culture.

I spend the year of my internship seeking to come to know and accept what my supervisor describes as my particular type of brilliance, my gifts that I am called to share that are at the core of my authentic self.

When my spiritual director gives me the diagram of the three concentric circles that identifies the central focus of our spiritual journey as reconnecting to who we are as a beloved child of God by disconnecting from external expectations that suck the life out of us, the pathway to do this work of accepting my insights and strengths becomes clearer.

———————————————

My internship is a time of profound shifts in my perspective about life and my understanding about myself. As a result, I am a changed person by the time I return to Emmanuel in the fall of 1986 to do my final year of my Master of Divinity degree.

Before I return I decide I am no longer going to approach essays or projects by trying to figure out how to satisfy my professors. I am going to do the work I need to do to get me ready to be a minister. I decide to stop fussing about my grades and focus more on what I need to learn and the areas that I long to develop in myself.

I get straight A's that year, which confirms for me that our best work happens when we allow the wisdom and creativity deep within to emerge rather than trying to fulfill what we think we "should" do to meet external expectations.

Even after spending a year with my supervisor encouraging me to acknowledge that my thoughts are of value, I remember an interesting moment as a returning student.

There is general agreement that one of the most difficult courses for Emmanuel students is the mandatory Philosophy of Religion course that is taught at the Jesuit College. Rumour has it that many students from Emmanuel just hope to get a passing grade. I have left the course to my final year. I remember coming out of the lecture hall one day with a group of other students who are considered to be academically astute. As we walk along the sidewalk I listen to them talk about how much of the lecture that day they don't understand.

I remember the thought that went through my head: "If they are confused, I must be really confused, because I think I understood everything he said."

At the end of the semester I sit with one of the doctoral students from the Philosophy of Religion class during a train ride home. For the entire ride I listen to all her insights and advanced knowledge. I know this role well from my years of listening to my sister Janis, of being the recipient of the knowledge of someone further along the journey of development.

The doctoral student tells me that she has received the second highest mark ever given for the Philosophy of Religion exam at the Jesuit college. She expounds on how amazing it is since it is such a difficult course. Then she wonders aloud who it might be who received a mark one percent higher than her mark because she can't think of anyone in the class who understands the work as well as she does. After exiting the train our paths begin to part as we walk across the parking lot. As we head our separate ways, I turn back and ask if she minds sharing her mark.

She doesn't hesitate. "Eighty-six percent."

I am stopped in my tracks for a fleeting moment. Then I smile my thanks and we both keep walking in opposite directions. After a few steps I hear her calling out to me asking what mark I received.

I respond over my shoulder, "Eighty-seven percent." I resist the urge to look back to see her response.

At graduation I receive the Philosophy of Religion award. I am told by a number of my friends they are delighted that I won the scholarship. The look in their eyes adds layers to their words. I see shock. I sense they are puzzled by this reality. This is an aspect of who I am that they have not known.

I am intrigued as I look at this pattern and perception that I have of myself of not being a particularly good thinker, because it keeps proving to be false. And yet this perception can still plague me to this day. If people don't understand what I am saying, at one time I regularly presumed it was because I did not know what I was talking about rather than considering that I may have a significant insight into a topic but need to find a different way to explain it or unpack it. It could be a new way to see things which is not readily grasped without enough input.

These days I am more likely to sense that my perception about life is different enough from how others see the world that people cannot hear me or take in what I am saying because what I am saying makes no sense in their worldview and so the concepts don't register. There are times when it feels like I am speaking a foreign language that is not understood. I work hard at trying to share my insights using language that will connect. At this stage in my life I trust that my contribution is worthwhile and that at some point in the conversations of life I may be more fully understood so long as I keep sharing my insights from a variety of perspectives in a variety of moments.

Experiences of not feeling heard or silencing my perspective because it seems so different from others inform the development of my life's work to ensure that we listen to all voices so that we are able to tap into the wisdom that is amongst us. Too often that wisdom is kept silent due to uncertainty and anticipation of being rejected. This reality is based in attitudes that infuse existing systems with lack of respect for alternative ways to see life. I know from experience that ideas like mine, which come from a perspective different than the predominant way of thinking in our culture, can be left on the sidelines of discussions when we strive to discern future possibilities.

My commitment to honour my different style of learning and alternative ways of engaging topics prompts me to make a request to do a reading course in the fall of 1986 when I return to Emmanuel after my internship. This will allow me to work one on one with a professor who will suggest a reading list for me to explore my topic of interest.

None of the professors understand what I am trying to focus on. The professor who ends up stuck with me is the newest person on staff, and so lowest on the totem pole. He has no choice but to take me on when all the other professors have tried and failed to get a handle on the topic I want to explore.

This new professor offers a number of reading options. None of them fit what I want to explore. He tells me that perhaps I need to write a paper on what I want to work on so that he will understand my focus.

The paper is extensive and it becomes my required work for the reading course. Instead of me reading, I write and the prof does the reading. After reading my paper no further readings come to his mind that would help me unpack this topic at a deeper level. Instead we spend our time together having great conversations.

The paper helps him to understand. He is surprised at my vehemence that I believe that, in order to be an effective minister, we need to not get caught in external expectations and definitions of the role of minister. I share with him that I believe that external expectations can cause us to create masks and façades that disconnect us from our authentic self, which results in a stronger probability that we will burn out and/or be ineffective. I am firm and clear that without connection to our authentic self (the inner circle of the concentric circles diagram) we will likely be tossed to and fro by the demands and the expectations of the whims of a multitude of people in a congregation rather than being led by the still, quiet voice within us or the passionate raging voice within us that calls us to engage life by living the way of love.

Ten years later, my professor from my reading course is the keynote speaker at a Conference Annual Meeting I attend. When we chat he tells me that my thesis has become a central concept of a course that is now mandatory at Emmanuel.

When I have led courses on this concept amongst colleagues who attended Emmanuel after me, I have heard the comment that not only was my core concept central to the course my professor led, it was the basis of the content of the course. Recently a colleague repeated a comment I have heard from others: the course by the professor I did my reading course with was the most significant and concrete course that helped them figure out how to be an effective and healthy minister.

———————————

In the final semester of my master's degree in the spring of 1987 I take a course on prayer from three professors. I am supposed to hand in three papers. I write one substantial paper only because as I engage different styles of prayer to write the three essays, it becomes apparent that something is trying to get my attention that is of far greater importance than successfully completing an essay for a due date. Fortunately my professors agree.

One of the methods of prayer that I explore is a method in which we invite an image to arise within us to give us insight into what is stirring inside us. It is this practice that finally makes clear to me what has been trying to get my attention.

When I try out this method of prayer of asking for an image to deepen my understanding of what the Spirit is trying to communicate to me, the image I receive is a big, hairy, masculine hand squeezing the life out of my heart. I spend time journalling to explore what the image means in my life. What emerges is that if I am ordained the big, hairy, masculine hand of patriarchal attitudes within the church will squeeze the life out of my heart. The interpretation of the image, combined with insights that emerged through other methods of prayer, nudge me to the awareness that I need to defer my ordination.

It is clear to me that I am not ready to immerse myself into the life of the church, which is deeply rooted in patriarchal attitudes. I need to become stronger within myself and clearer about my theology before I get the life squeezed out of me by prescribed expectations and systems of belief that are only just beginning to remember and celebrate the gifts of feminine energy, perspective and wisdom. I defer my ordination for an indefinite period of time, a decision that Alan chooses to support even though it baffles him.

WITHIN DAYS OF DEFERRING MY ORDINATION, Alan and I have a puzzling and profound experience. For thirty-six hours it feels like we are plunged into an alternate universe. During those thirty-six hours we decide that I will be ordained the next year. In looking back I wonder if I would have ever been ordained if the experience of that day and a half had not radically intruded in our lives. The message filling those hours is clear: ordination is not an option; I can pause but I can't stop moving toward my call.

The alternate universe experience starts one morning when Alan returns home shortly after leaving for work. He has been working incredibly long hours as one of the managers on a cash-crop farming operation. When other staff members get a day off when it rains, he does repair on the equipment. When the rain stops everyone gets back to work and Alan gets no breaks as he heads out in the fields as the operator of some of the larger and more complex equipment. He leaves early in the morning and comes home late into the night, hours after Sarah and I have gone to sleep.

But on this morning, he returns home almost immediately after leaving early for work. He tells me that his boss's wife just told him he has lost his job and we have to move out of their farmhouse we have been renovating. The job and the renovations were separate arrangements, but now they are being linked together. No job, no house, and no use of the barn. Alan will have to sell his sheep. We are stunned. This abrupt turn of events makes absolutely no sense. Up until now, Alan's work has been extremely appreciated.

We move into action to try to figure out what we will do next. We head to the nearby city to try to find a place to live that we can manage with no income between us. We look at the apartments where I lived when I went to university. It seems so bizarre to think of moving back here now that I am married with a child.

We find a house for rent we can likely afford. We would have the upstairs. It is totally open to the lower level, with no doors dividing the space and no separate entrance. After wandering through the upstairs level we check out the backyard. There is a patio area created from beer caps pushed into the ground.

We stand on the sidewalk in front of the house looking at our potential home. Huge sadness and anxiousness wash over me. Tears pour down my face as I stare at this place where Alan and Sarah and the recently discovered baby that I am carrying might end up living without me. I am waiting for the results from a medical test that is checking on suspicious signs that indicate I could have cancer. Most of my aunts died of cancer. I am not surprised the same might happen to me.

As I think about us moving here I scan the landscape of my mind, searching for positive implications. One good point is that moving here would bring us into the city where I did my internship. I ponder reconnecting with the congregation. I see a picture of the church and a picture of this house side by side in my mind's eye.

But then something strange happens. In this vision the pictures begin to move. The picture of the church moves off to the side so it can no longer be seen. The house fills my vision. I am shocked as a thought goes through my head. My perception, the interpretation overwhelming me in this dismal moment, is that if I live in this house, in this neighbourhood, there will be no place for me in the church.

I am astounded. I feel like someone has kicked me in the gut, thrusting all the air out of my lungs in one painful, emptying groan. I am startled by this thought. If *I* feel like I won't be welcome in the church because I live in these circumstances, my perception, which is that the church is a place of welcome where everyone will feel at home, explodes in a shattering moment of disruptive insight. Why is this thought entering my head that I won't feel welcome in the church? Why wouldn't I feel welcome? Where is this thought coming from? I have heard the charge against the church that it is not a place where the disenfranchised are comfortable. And now I am experiencing these feelings seeping into my perception. I feel sickened to think that I carry even an inkling of this perspective within me. It appears that it is so deeply rooted in the psyche of our culture that it erupts as judgment in my head even though it is the opposite of what I say I believe. This perception that some people are of less value than others has judged me and found me to be unworthy. This perception is screaming at my own betrayal. I am horrified to discover that such an interpretation is lurking deep within my psyche.

I had no idea how deeply the church is perceived to be rooted in the concept that does, shockingly, weave in and out of one strand of thinking in scripture that affirms those who are wealthy. I have focused on the much more predominant call in scripture to walk with all people and extend radical hospitality. But now a sick feeling of being judged as unworthy washes over me. A sick feeling washes over me that I have this sense of judgment within me. I wonder if what I am feeling would be an accurate experience for others from this neighbourhood or neighbourhoods like this across the country. My heart breaks at the thought.

If nothing else, this day is giving me a sobering insight into how the church is perceived. It shocks me and saddens me and demands that my call in ministry include a commitment to shift the culture of the church so that lingering echoes of judgmental thinking do not taint the ministry of creating life-giving community where everyone knows they are beloved.

At the end of hours filled with fear and painful realities, Alan and I ponder what to do. We realize that we need to stretch our thinking and imaginations to identify options we can live with by combining our wisdom to find the best solution in this difficult situation.

I make the commitment to be ordained the next year. Alan offers to go back to work to try to figure out what he needs to do to patch up his relationship with his boss so he can work there for one more year. We agree that we will move wherever the church wants to send us next year, rather than limiting where I can work so Alan can keep his job. Alan figures he can put up with a lot to ensure we have a place to live and income for the next year.

Alan goes to see his boss. His boss tells Alan he is confused. He says he has no idea what Alan is talking about. From his perspective Alan has not lost his job. The wife of the boss stands by and listens to the conversation. She makes no comment.

Alan and I are totally confused. There is no explanation for the anger that erupted from the wife of his boss that left Alan with the very clear picture that he no longer had a job, we no longer had a place to live, and our sheep would have to be sold. However, we are relieved to step back into the world we have lived in for the past three years, knowing that the decision has been made that we will only stay for one more year.

Later that week I have a miscarriage.

I also hear the results of the in-depth medical tests. I am clear. There is no sign of cancer.

That weekend I go to the Conference Annual Meeting where I was originally supposed to be ordained. I spend much of it in tears. The ups and downs, the struggles and the insights, have left me feeling unsettled and wishing I had followed the standard and expected course of action so that the future would now be known. However, that opportunity is not available to me. I bolster myself with the awareness that next year I will not put limits on where I will be settled so that Alan can keep his job. We will be moving to begin an adventure whose destination is unknown.

I settle in to savour this year of integration to prepare for ordination and for moving in a year's time to the congregation where I will be sent.

The year is filled with an abundance of time with Sarah who is now four years old. It is the first opportunity of extensive time to reflect on my style of parenting. I begin to notice why others look at me with surprise at how I engage with my child. I realize that I seem to be parenting differently than others around me. I focus on how amazing my child is, affirming her for who she is and what she does well. I shift her focus when she is spiralling into unhelpful choices. I seem to differ from other parents who are more focused than me on teaching correct skills and being compliant.

I create a story that I tell Sarah each night. It is the story of Charlie the Chipmunk. It always begins with, "Charlie the Chipmunk loves the little girl with big blue eyes and blond hair." It continues with Charlie naming all the wonderful things that she has done that day, noting the moments when she chose to be kind and creative rather than mean and grumpy. Sarah loves these stories. So does Marissa a few years later. And my grandkids gobble up any stories that begin with how much the little boy with brown hair and big blue eyes, or the little girl with blond hair and big blue eyes, is loved.

As babies, my daughters and my four grandkids also love to hear the song I wrote for them. It is the same song for each of them made personal by inserting their name. On the morning they are born each of my grandbabies is serenaded with the song that tells them how much I love them. As babies, all of them calm down and go to sleep in my arms when I sing it to them. Every once in a while my older grandkids still ask for their song.

There are many memories that well up within me from the year I take off before being ordained that reflect Sarah's character. Three in particular stand out.

One day when we are at kindergym, Sarah is totally engaged in walking on the beam, somersaulting on the mats, and trying to cartwheel across the floor. Suddenly she turns and runs to me.

She asks me, "If God lives inside of me, does that make me a house for God?"

I respond, "That is a great way to describe it, my love."

In the fall we go to the local fall fair. As we are leaving, I ask her if she would like to see the inside of an ambulance. She does. We go over. Just as we arrive there is a call on the radio for help in the arena where an elderly woman has fallen. We back out of the way. I take Sarah's hand to leave the park. She protests and moves to follow the ambulance attendant. When we get into the arena I tell her to stay out of the way. She leans in to see what is happening. Before I realize what she is doing she has moved in to put her hand on the shoulder of the woman. She is telling her she will be okay. The woman looks at her with gratitude.

During the year, I spend a significant amount of time in prayer each day. I am doing the ancient spiritual practice of the Ignatian Spiritual Exercises. I remember one day in particular. It is close to the end of the two hours of morning silence.   Sarah has been keeping herself engaged in play, which she does in a wonderful, independent way each day.

But then, oh so quietly, she begins to sing, "Jesus loves me this I know ..."

She looks over at me to see if I notice and is delighted to see that her song has brought my time of prayer to an end, meaning she can once again chatter about everything she sees, and plan great schemes for the two of us to share.

I choose to do the Ignatian Spiritual Exercises that year to help me in my discernment around ordination. The format for the exercises that I choose is designed to be integrated into everyday life for most of a year rather than over a forty-day silent retreat which is the traditional model. It means I spend three hours a day in prayer for ten months. I also choose to do two eight-day silent retreats. The primary focus of my year of prayer is around the centrality of relationships as we respond to our call to create the Kindom of God on Earth where the power that reigns is love. At the end of the intensive process, I am ready to be ordained. It has been a significant journey of developing understanding and refocusing my life so that I can clearly see what really matters.

LIFE WITH MOM BEGINS TO SPIRAL OUT OF CONTROL, creating a tapestry of good days and difficult days.

Mom and her husband have created a new home in the second high-rise condo. Mom has an amazing capacity to adapt to changes by leaving old expectations and dreams behind. On the surface Mom wears a mask of contentment. But life inside the condo is not good.

I can't count the number of times during Mom's second marriage that Alan and I plan to rearrange our home so Mom can come live with us. The tension with her husband continues to escalate, exacerbated I'm sure by (what I now understand as) the vicious cycle of Mom's alternate personalities that are playing a major role in her daily life. I suspect they are triggered by the abusive atmosphere.

More than once Mom has to get her husband's car out of the police compound where it has been towed because he is over the limit for alcohol consumption.

More than once when I ask her where she keeps a particular plate she tells me it has been broken. She eventually tells me that more than once her husband has thrown plates against the wall. She's surprised when I say that destroying things is a form of abuse. She denies it, saying he's just angry and needs to let off steam.

I ask her, "Has he ever thrown and broken anything of his?"

She looks puzzled. She thinks for a moment, then says, "No."

I tell her that ruining her property is considered a form of abuse. It's a threat that suggests that things will escalate.

For all that is happening behind closed doors, Mom is active in her community. She gets to know their neighbours from India, who introduce her to new culinary adventures. Mom also becomes the chair of the condo board of management, which is a complex role with more than twenty floors of condos and twenty condos on each floor. She has to take a university course before she can be chair, so that she understands all the detailed legal issues with which the board will deal. When we go to visit she is often called by the staff at the front desk to give clarity about a situation. At the end of our visits, she walks us down to the lobby. She always stops and chats with staff and checks on the plants that she has bought for the front seating area.

In the midst of the tumultuous life that Mom and her husband share, there are times when Mom is totally coherent and can engage in life.

In August of 1987, during my year of integration before my ordination, I have a second miscarriage, just three months after the last one. Both miscarriages happen within two days of taking the same prescription for pneumonia. After the second miscarriage I spend a number of days in the hospital with Alan at my side continuously supporting me as I face the reality of having only one child after four pregnancies. I lost a pregnancy before Sarah. This miscarriage has been a particularly difficult one requiring a blood transfusion.

I spend most of my time in the hospital with the curtain pulled around my bed, protecting myself from the world. Alan sits on a chair at the edge of the curtain, chatting alternately with me and others in the room. He sparks my curiosity. He encourages me to get up and walk around with my IV pole. He braids my hair to contain the chaotic knots that protrude from my head, which have been the least of our concerns up till now, then he pulls back the curtain and introduces me to the other three women in the room. Talking to them and walking around helps shift me out of the spiralling melancholy.

Once Alan brings me home and feels I am doing okay, he goes back to work, phoning to check in with me regularly. Mom does the same. Mid-way through that first week at home, Mom hears something in my voice that suggests to her that I am not well. She tells me she is coming up.

Mom lives twenty-five minutes away. She shocks me by arriving faster than I can imagine. I wonder if maybe I have been unconscious for a while because it feels like she arrives in less than ten minutes. Following Mom into the bedroom is our family doctor. He examines me, and then tells Mom to stay with me. He says I need time to rest and that it would be good to have someone to watch me. I didn't know that doctors still made house calls and certainly not during daily office hours. It's rare, but when Mom phoned the doctor's office before driving up it would have been clear to anyone who heard her that not coming was not an option. There are definitely times when Mom is extremely competent. That tendency quite often shows up as the Aggressive One.

Mom had to have times of great competency or I never would have agreed to her taking Sarah on a seven-hour train trip to the States to see Janis and her family at some point during 1987. In October of 2016, Janis reflected on a phone call I made to her after Mom and Sarah got on the train back in 1987. She said that I called her and asked her to please make sure to be intentional about providing Sarah with good eye contact because Mom won't give her the eye contact she needs. Janis told me on that night in October of 2016 that my request changed how she parented from that time forward. She realized she needed to be looking her kids in the eye. Once she made a point of looking her kids in the eye, it changed her relationship with them.

As I look back I realize that I learned about the importance of good eye contact from Scott. I used to watch him. I could see the difference it made to people to have someone totally focus on them. I learned firsthand from him what it feels like to have someone look you in the eye and see you. Really looking at people and seeing them has been an integral part of my life and it turns out that I learned it from the extra biological father in our family!

While there are memories of Mom being very capable and competent during this time, there are other memories of disruptive difficulties. One of the difficult times happens the night of my ordination in 1988.

I stand in the hallway to watch for Mom to arrive, hoping she might be good this night. I see her enter. I can tell by her walk that this is not a good night. She is self-absorbed and angry, totally opposite to our "real Mom."

After the service I watch Mom, knowing she is very unstable. I feel anxious because I don't normally have to deal with this extreme reality in public. And this is very public. As I look back to that moment, I would describe her as being a combination of battling characteristics from different personalities. The personality who likes to make extravagant plans combined with the one who is filled with rage both seem to want to take over. It is during the reception after the ordination service when people have the opportunity to greet the newly ordained ministers that the fullness of her instability is evident. A line of friends and family gathers in front of me. More than seventy of the people I invited are here. Then my mother blows in. She chats with everyone in the line as she makes her way past the line toward me. She is telling everyone to come with her because the party is happening somewhere else. People look both delighted and confused. But Mom has a reputation as a good hostess. People drop gifts and cards on the table beside me and say they will see me later.

Only they don't see me later because I do not know where Mom has taken them.

I never hear details of my party that I don't go to. Mom never questions me about why I didn't show up. Years later my daughter, who is there that night as a four-year-old, asks me if what my Mom did upset me.

I comment, "That's just Mom."

In retrospect, it is rather startling that I had grown accustomed to accepting something so inappropriate.

In spite of Mom's odd and over-the-top bizarre behaviour, the night of my ordination is a night of wonderful memories of intense sacred moments and profound gratitude for all who have journeyed with me to this time in my life.

After seeing Mom to her seat beside Alan and Sarah before the service, I return to the robing room. More than twenty of us are to be ordained or commissioned that night. Each of us has three people accompanying us, so the procession is huge. A banner is carried before us asking, "Whom Shall I Send?" There is a banner behind us that answers, "Send Me."

At the end of the service, during the recessional, a friend from seminary walks beside me. She was a doctoral student when I was at seminary. She has been the worship leader for the Conference Annual Meeting. The United Church hymn book published in the mid-1990s is filled with her songs. As she walks beside me at the end of the service, we are singing one of her hymns. As she belts it out full volume, she regularly turns around to make sure everyone is falling into place behind us. As she turns to look, she sings her song directly toward me. It feels like it is penetrating deeply into the very marrow of my bones. It is a special moment. I feel personally sent out, empowered by her blessing to go into the world and live the way of God's love, to make God's love known by living it. The hymn is "Go to the World" by Sylvia Dunstan.

———————

An added treasure to the memories of my ordination becomes evident a month later.

When I am leaving a huge three day United Church Women's Conference, I gather together all of Sarah's and my stuff and then pause to get changed into something more comfortable for the trip home. I put on the turquoise corduroy pants that I wore to the conference. They won't do up. A smile erupts onto my face. I realize that I am pregnant. That means I was pregnant on the night of my ordination. I realize that all four members of my family are in my life when I make my ordination vows, which feels like an affirmation of what is most important in my life. My family comes first.

My spiritual director is one of the people I invite to participate in my ordination service for the ritual of 'laying on of hands' in order to confirm my ordination. He and I both agree that being pregnant when I am ordained is a clear sign that my family is central to who I am. My supervisor from my internship, who is also part of the laying-on-of-hands ceremony, often comments that we have to be careful to ensure that we don't confuse serving the church with serving God.

So I am delighted when I realize I am pregnant. The mom in the next bedroom at the Women's Conference, who is also busily getting her kids organized to go home, is my classmate from seminary with whom I have shared maternity clothes. I tell her that I am pretty sure I will need to pick up the maternity clothes before we move in two weeks to the community where I am being sent as minister.

Once I speak this new reality out loud, I begin to wonder how the three churches are going to feel about a pregnant minister. They have never had a female minister before. They have never had a newly ordained minister before. I am the youngest minister they have ever had, and now, to top it off, I am pregnant.

On my third week in the congregation I announce that I am pregnant. I need to be in maternity clothes and so can't delay the announcement till a time when they know me better. With Sarah swinging off the pulpit, I share my good news. The response is applause, led by the woman who will become our daughters' adopted grandma.

We have moved to an amazing community in which to raise Sarah and Marissa. It feels like an extended family. It is this community that supports us during Marissa's birth. Plans are in place for the church secretary, who is already a very close friend, to pick up Sarah when we are ready to head to the hospital. The local road manager has told us to call when the time comes if the snow is heavy so he can drive ahead of us with the snow plow for the forty-five minutes to the hospital. It is a gift to have a caring community around us since we now live three and a half hours from family.

THE SEVEN AND A HALF YEARS IN THIS RURAL VILLAGE are filled with incredible opportunities for learning, expanding my skills and discovering who I am as minister.

The summer I arrive, the General Council of The United Church of Canada declares that sexual orientation will not preclude people from full membership, which includes ordination or commissioning in the church. To me it seems like an obvious declaration. To the community where I have just arrived, it is not an obvious stance. Earlier that year they sent petitions against the church adopting this policy. And while they were at it, they sent a petition requesting that the church overturn its policy to use inclusive language.

As this reality stares me in the face, I experience an overwhelming sense of turmoil and wonder why I have been sent here. The angst in the community over the next many months becomes the cause for numerous excruciating headaches. I ask someone at the Conference office why I was chosen for this place. I am told that I am specifically chosen to be settled here because they suspect that of all the places where ministers are being settled this one has the greatest potential for fall-out, depending on the direction of the General Council's decisions. They felt that I could connect with them through my commitment to prayer, since prayer is a central characteristic of their identity.

It turns out that their insight has some validity. When the news of the General Council hits the airwaves I immediately end my vacation and gather the elders of the churches together. The first thing I do is invite them to pray for guidance as to how to respond to the upset in the community in a way that will be helpful. People respond well to the letter we deliver to all the homes in the pastoral charge asking them not to react based on media reports. We agree to invite a guest who can explain the process and prayerful nature by which this decision has been made. Safe space is created for people to share their feelings, inviting the community to listen to one another with respect. Slowing down reactions and listening deeply makes a difference that allows us to stay together in community even though we don't all agree with this decision made at General Council. While the congregation beside us splits, with over half of their members forming a new non-denominational church, our pastoral charge has only two people withdraw their membership. Both of them stay active in the church community but do not feel comfortable being official members of The United Church of Canada.

Tensions are erupting within the boundaries of the pastoral charge around another topic when I arrive. Prior to my arrival, a Conference staff person bluntly tells them that no minister wants to deal with three congregations in one pastoral charge where a minister has to travel from one congregation to the next to lead worship and go to meetings, so they need to get their act together to amalgamate. When I arrive and discover their huge anxiety about having to give up their unique identities as two rural congregations and one village congregation, I promise them that I will not try to amalgamate them.

Their hackles calm down, leaving them open to the way I envision community. They begin sharing more and more activities: one Bible study for all three churches, one summer day camp with over a hundred people participating, one musical production that everyone participates in, and a roving dinner banquet that moves between all three church buildings when I become the chair Presbytery, the regional group of churches that work together.

Underneath all of the congenial sharing, one issue quietly churns, with a hope by many that it will never rise to the surface. But it does. Anger and discord erupt along with it. Sides are drawn and defences put in place. A request has been made to reconsider the percentage split that each congregation pays toward the pastoral charge expenses of the salaries for the minister and the secretary, and the costs of the house for the minister. I am astonished by the strong feelings. They feel like they are swamping us as we struggle to stay above the rising tides of turmoil.

In the midst of the rumbling I request they put the decision on hold since I am about to go on maternity leave. They agree.

The week before my maternity leave we are in the final days of preparation for the first musical production I direct while there. Months later the cast shares with me their horror that I had showed them how to do the can-can when I was in my ninth month of pregnancy with what turned out to be a nine-pound, fifteen-ounce baby.

Marissa is born the day before my thirty-fourth birthday. The church secretary arrives in the middle of the night to take Sarah home with her. Alan is battling the flu. I don't want him to massage me this time because all my labour is back pain. Two weeks ago the baby did a somersault, causing massive undulations in my belly that have placed her in an abnormal position for the birth. The roads are clear of snow, so we don't need to awaken the road manager who offered to drive ahead with a snow plow if needed.

When we arrive at the hospital they ask me if I need a wheelchair. They don't mention that the maternity ward is somewhere close to the other side of city. Part way there they need to find me a wheelchair.

When I get to the final stages of labour, things happen quickly. We are taken to the delivery room and told the doctor is on his way. They tell me to keep pushing because it will take a while. Something in me tells me not to. I wait for the doctor before I really push.

When the doctor arrives I push once. He tells me to stop because the cord is around the baby's neck. I stop. I am thankful I waited for his arrival. He tells me to push again. I do. Marissa is born.

She arrives with an ear-piercing scream filled with anger. I reach for her. I feel awful that she has had a difficult birth. So does she, and it appears she wants the world to know that what has just happened is unacceptable. As loudly as she protests she is also quickly responsive to a different option. She immediately nurses with a bold, strong latch. She nurses for a significant period of time, and then goes to sleep in my arms.

I am overwhelmed with a strong feeling of mother-bear-like protectiveness toward her. A passionate commitment rises within me to ensure that she has the space in her life to be the fullness of who she is, even when that means raging with a piercing cry to tell the world a change needs to happen—as she did with the startling scream that arose in the moment of her birth. As Alan and I stare into her face, a bond is formed that is powerful. When Sarah arrives the next day to meet her, the bond expands to encircle the four of us, each one independent and strong, each one tethered to the others by a longing for each of us to be supported to be our best self.

———————

Marissa teaches me a lot about life. She is clear about what she wants to do and what she does not want to do from the moment she is born. There are delightful memories from her years of growing up that capture her gifts and strengths expressed in her life as an adult.

From the time Marissa can crawl, if she doesn't like what is happening she won't stay and tolerate it. She crawls away as fast as she can and heads to her bedroom. She goes into her room and closes the door. Since she learns to walk at nine months old she's pretty young when this starts.

Marissa loves music. When she is two months old we decide to revive the musical I was directing while pregnant with her. Sarah, Marissa and I go to a rehearsal. I am sitting facing the cast as they run through the music. Marissa is on my lap. I realize that the singing is fading away. I look up from my choreography notes to see what is happening. They are staring at Marissa. It is clear to them that she knows this music and loves it. When they start to sing her face lights up and she begins to move.

Her love of music and movement flows through her life as a kid growing up. During our last months in this community where she was born, when the choirs do a special service where they sing songs from all the different musicals and cantatas we have shared during our years together, she sings along. She even sings the musical that we last performed when she was two months old, catching on quickly and with ease.

And then on Christmas Eve she asks to sing her first-ever solo in front of a packed church. She sings "Christmas is a Time for Love." There isn't a dry eye in the place as their "baby in the manse"—as a child is often called if born while their parents are living in the designated house for the minister—sings out with a crystal voice like a cherub angel.

When Marissa is in grade six her room is overflowing with stuff. Her Dad and I tell her she needs to clean her room. Each week that she doesn't clean her room she has to identify one thing she will give up as a consequence for not doing the task. Nine months later she has given up everything that is possible to give up. She has spent the school year with no phone calls to friends, no television, no dessert, no treats, no having friends over. The list goes on of all that she chooses to give up. The intriguing thing is this is the year she really finds herself. I watch her and marvel at her strong spirit and choice to do what is right for her. When the only thing that is left to give up is her music and dancing I put a stop to the process. Putting on music and filling the living room with movement has been what has grounded her and connected her to herself all year.

I declare, "Enough." She can't give up anything else.

She's content.

A month later her Dad cleans up her room. So long as she keeps it clean she gets everything back. She keeps it clean but continues to spend her time writing poetry, singing and dancing rather than reclaiming the activities she had given up.

Marissa is clear about boundaries and shows me how we can make sure our boundaries are not violated by others. She is much better at it than I am.

When I return from maternity leave after Marissa's birth the issue around the percentage split of financial commitments to be shared between the three churches has toned down. Everyone agrees it can wait until early in the new year for the annual congregational meetings. We commit to tackling this issue that festers beneath the surface of the relationships between the three congregations then.

As minister, I chair all the meetings. It's the only piece of advice my predecessor gave me: to keep chairing. This issue provides opportunity for me to learn about dealing with conflict in a way that builds bridges rather than creates war-torn landscapes in a community. One of my deepest hopes is to create life-giving community in which we can honestly and openly deal with issues without seeing one another as the enemy or on an opposing team. I long for us to recognize that we have the wisdom within us and amongst us to make a decision together. I am sure the direction will become evident as we listen deeply to all the perspectives and possibilities.

I learn from Mom to have patience to wait for the right moment and the right mood in order to arrive at a good decision. While the Aggressive One makes rapid decisions, if other alter personalities show up in the midst of Mom making a decision, the process is slowed down as all the differing perspectives have the opportunity to be expressed. The combination of the perspectives of all the alter personalities usually results in a much better decision than if Mom is led only by the quick decision-maker of the Aggressive One.

At each of the three congregations' meetings I ask people to prayerfully consider what percentage their congregation can offer toward the pastoral charge expenses. I invite them to look through their annual report, which includes their financial report, and pray. We sit together in silence for a fairly significant amount of time. I then ask each person to write down the percentage of the expenses they feel they can contribute as a congregation. I ask everyone to share their answer. I am repeatedly astounded by how close everyone comes in the percentage they identify. I do the same process with each of the congregations.

When it is time for our annual board meeting, which is a combination of the three congregations, seventy-five people show up. It is the largest possible number of people that can vote. It is a rare situation to have the full complement of people who can vote. The air is filled with a fighting spirit. Walls of defence are erected. As people enter it feels like they are prowling around each other prepared to pounce at the least provocation. I shake my head because in other situations where I see these same people they are all part of the same organizations and work together as a team. The territorial aggressiveness surprises me, waking me up to a reality that plays out too often in the arenas of our lives. The percentage split of expenses is the first item on the agenda since nothing will be accomplished well until we openly deal with the issue.

I am the only one who knows the percentage each congregation is willing to offer. I tell the crowd, who feel like they are gathered on a potential battlefield, that I will ask the Clerks of Session of each congregation to share their amount. I will write the amounts on the blackboard. I tell them no one is allowed to say anything until they can make a motion that honours each community.

The numbers are given. The amounts are posted on the board. I watch them. There is discomfort. Feet start to shuffle, but then there is stillness. No one seems to know what to do. The silence is finally broken by one of the clerks. We have waited for more than ninety seconds of silence.

In a slow voice he declares, "Well, I reckon if you add up those three figures it makes a hundred percent." He pauses. "It seems to me that we can make a motion to accept what each congregation has offered."

I ask him if he would like to make that motion. He does. The other two clerks second it together. The adrenalin in the room shifts from fighting mode to relief. The tension can almost be heard as it releases like the squeal of a helium balloon deflating.

I ask them if they have any ideas as to how they can help each other meet their new financial goals. Offers are made to help each other with annual fundraisers of turkey pot pies, fruit pies and dinners.

By the next agenda item it feels like we are a more cohesive community working together rather than guarding our territory.

A few years later someone wonders aloud if there are three separate congregations or just one congregation who happens to worship in three places. Years after that, when the time is right, they amalgamate with ease. Many years after that, I am invited back to be their anniversary speaker. After I speak they present me with the title of minister emeritus in honour of my years of service in their congregation and to the wider church.

IN MY SECOND YEAR IN THE RURAL VILLAGE I am invited to take on a number of roles in the wider church. One is to be incoming chair of the Presbytery. Presbytery is the group of churches in one county that have oversight of the pastoral charges in their area. The decision of the General Council in 1988 that sexual orientation is not a deciding factor in eligibility for ordination or commissioning has caused a huge rift in our Presbytery. As incoming chair I work with the current chair to identify ways to rebuild a sense of community. We decide that the first action is for me to lead two retreat days for ministers for the purpose of rebuilding bridges. The second action is to streamline business tasks and decision-making processes so that we have more time to build relationships. Within a few months the energy at our meetings shifts for the better. We find a way to be together in our differences, and relationships begin to build, stretching over a theological divide that was once considered too wide to reach across.

During my first year of ministry I have to take two one-week sessions of a mandatory course on rural ministry in southern Ontario. I dislike the format of the course of a group of experts teaching students insights that they feel they need to know. However, I love the opportunity to spend significant time with other newly ordained ministers as well as some seasoned ministers. The next year I am invited to be on the leadership team. I agree, but only if the leaders are willing to look at shifting the format. They are willing. We shift it in significant ways. The major change is to invite the participants to identify their own learning goals. The other team members who have been on the team since its inception resist, insisting that people won't know what they need to learn. I disagree and ask them to let me lead a process where we gather everyone's ideas, including the ideas of the leadership team. The team is delighted by the outcome; the participants become more engaged in the course now that they have input in developing it, rather than grumbling about the mandatory nature of the programme. Now it responds to learning needs we have identified together, which still include much of the original content, since the participants agree that those topics that the leaders suggest sound worthwhile. More than one person describes the programme as a source of some of the most formative learning about being a minister.

This idea of the importance of listening to all the voices and perspectives by creating space for all the wisdom amongst us to emerge becomes a recurring theme as I mature in my work as a minister. When people feel that they have input and that they are being listened to, there is far greater buy-in to whatever steps are being identified and decided upon.

I am delighted by the input of a guest during my third year on the rural ministry leadership team. He is working on his Doctorate of Ministry degree. His research focuses on a growing concern that ministers are experiencing a sense of deep and profound isolation. He travels to rural Scotland to test his theory that geographic isolation is a key factor in this disturbing phenomenon. What he discovers is that his hypothesis is wrong. The epidemic of feeling isolated in ministry has little to do with geography. Instead the source of the isolation is rooted in the degree to which the minister is living behind masks and façades based on their role and the expectations in their own minds and in their community.

His conclusion is consistent with the point in my reading course during my last year at Emmanuel: the more our work as a minister flows through our authentic self, the healthier we will be, resulting in our ministry being more effective; the more we wear masks, the more we will feel isolated and unhealthy.

The perspective of the importance of connecting to our authentic self continues to be central to my ministry. It is important to me that we not hide behind masks that project that all is well when there is conflict stirring that needs attention. However, due to the impact of having a mother with many personalities (which I don't understand in younger years), some of my patterns of engaging with issues of conflict are skewed based on distortions from my life experiences. As a result I don't always deal with conflict in a healthy, responsive way.

I develop a high tolerance for ignoring conflict because for me it has to first show itself to be a true conflict with long-lasting impact before I feel it is worthy of being addressed. Having been raised in a home with a person who could be disruptive and volatile, I learn to ignore signs of potential conflict if they feel fleeting. Issues periodically erupt but then disappear for a long time, which I now realize is because different issues resided with different alter personalities within Mom and so would sometimes go away for years on end.

As a child I develop a passion to deal with issues so they don't fester. However, I also develop a distorted sense of what constitutes a conflict worth dealing with and what is simply an issue that will likely go away, with the latter interpretation being my more likely response. Aware of this tendency in myself, I try to be intentional about taking note of grumbling issues in the church and engage them rather than anticipating that they will dissipate quickly like they did in my childhood by virtue of my mother shifting into a different personality. I learn to pay attention, rather than letting issues have a long-lasting rancorous impact due to lack of attention.

Central to my work of developing the tenets of Intentional Circles and Authentic Connection Culture is a sense of safety where we can speak our truth and deal with hard topics openly, trusting we have the wisdom within us and amongst us to deal with issues and as a result moving forward stronger. Life in the church provides lots of opportunity to practice and develop the skills to intentionally deal with conflict in a way that keeps us grounded in our true essence of love.

In the summer of 1990, I am on the periphery of a conflict beyond our community known in the media as the Oka Crisis, also known as the crisis at Kanehsatake. The Mohawk people create a barricade to stop the local community from bulldozing their sacred burial grounds in order to expand a golf course. I am the chair of the Division of Mission in Canada at the Presbytery level. I am asked to go to the local Native Friendship Centre to represent the Presbytery in this time of crisis. The experience challenges me to confront conflict by finding my voice and speaking from my core about the outrage within me toward behaviours that are a distortion of how we are called to be in relationship.

When I am at the Friendship Centre a woman begs me to use my power to ensure that required medicines are delivered to the people behind the barricades. Her mother-in-law needs her insulin. I am shocked to think of myself as having power, but her nudge helps to wake me up. She pleads with me to honour the two-row wampum. She shows me a wampum hanging on the wall. She teaches me that it represents the agreement of two nations to walk side by side and live in peace. The two nations represented in the two-row wampum are Canada and the First Nations of the Indigenous people who welcomed us and agreed to live in peace with us. I am shocked that this is the first time I have heard this concept.

Months later I host three people who were in the sacred burial land of the pines the morning that a police officer is shot in Kanehsatake. I spend two days with them, absorbing stories that I have known nothing about. I am shocked at all I do not know about our relationships with the Indigenous people on this land as a person educated here in Canada. What I do know is that as a church we apologized to First Nations people in 1986 for the way we treated them when we arrived on this land. I am glimpsing the unspoken wounds that are behind that apology.

When the people of the farming community where I serve protest the actions of the First Nations people in Kanehsatake I hear the passion in my voice when I tell them that I believe that they would be the first ones to arrive in our cemetery if someone were planning to bulldoze it. They are stunned. They stop talking about the situation, at least when I am in earshot.

I am learning to speak up and challenge preconceived notions as I realize that I have both the right and the responsibility to share what lies within my heart rather than continuously silence it.

In 1992, I am elected as a commissioner to General Council, the national court level of The United Church of Canada. I am excited to go. It is at this General Council meeting that the United Church elects Stan McKay, our first Moderator from one of Canada's First Nations.

I spend the first eight days of the General Council meeting watching and observing. The process feels like an incredible waste of valuable time as certain people keep going to the mic to make corrections to motions that sound to me like the dotting of "i's" and the crossing of "t's" rather than a good healthy engagement with the core issues that are being developed.

I go to the person who will be the chair of business at the next General Council meeting. I share with him that I am experiencing the process as a horribly effective way to silence the wisdom, insights and questions of people. I suggest that we need to develop a better way to engage topics of such importance. It is not acceptable from my perspective to rubber stamp reports and motions once they have been grammatically corrected.

Eighteen months later he tells me that when I spoke to him that day he thought that I was being a pain in the butt. But after the meeting my observations kept swirling through his mind, demanding attention. He has since developed a new way of dealing with the work of the General Council, with sessional committees first taking an in-depth look at motions and reports and then bringing their deeply considered recommendations to the full court. In this new process all the work of the Council is to be divided between four sessional committees to make sure everything is fully explored. No comments about grammar or tiny details will be allowed in the full court sessions. People are free to make notes and pass them to the sessional committee, but they are not allowed to use the microphone to modify tiny details. To this day we use aspects of this model, which creates space for in-depth conversation.

Early the next year I am asked to let my name stand for President of Conference. I am also asked by the senior staff person of The United Church of Canada to be one of four people to work on developing a new model for the structure and governance of the United Church. I say yes to working on the structure because of my passion to create space that supports significant conversations and good flow of communication so that everyone is kept in the loop.

I am elected as a commissioner again for the 1994 General Council, which means I will have the opportunity to be part of the new process that creates space for in-depth conversation around motions, a process that was developed in response to my frustration that we were not hearing all the voices and perspectives on important topics. I experience the new method that germinated from ideas offered as seed thoughts that are now showing signs of their first fruits. I am also there for the presentation of the recommendation for a new governance structure for the United Church that I helped to develop. While it is adopted by that General Council it will take another twenty-four years before its basic core concepts are fully supported for implementation.

The early years of ministry, just like the years of seminary, expand my insights, demand that I develop critical capacity to see unhealthy disruptions in our systems, sharpen my knowledge about the structure of the church, and encourage me to figure out how to best work within the existing structure to remove barriers to ensure creative and productive outcomes. All of this learning becomes fodder for the development of the principles and practices of Intentional Circles that provide the possibility of the emergence of Authentic Connection Culture.[6]

In the midst of all the learning, life at home continues to evolve.

---

[6] See Appendix.

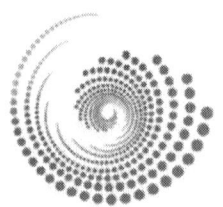

ON TWO OCCASSIONS MOM STAYS for an extended time when we live in the rural village. It is during the years she is married to her second husband. Once he drops her off after she has surgery. The other time is when he simply says he can't cope with her.

The one planned time that her husband drops Mom off at our home is after she has surgery for a bladder suspension. I have vivid memories of the last time Mom had surgery when her life was turned upside down back in 1971. I am not looking forward to the three weeks of anticipated recovery time. I understand why her husband can't cope with her. I just hope the impact of the medicine this time will be shorter-lived than the last time. At least she has told the medical team that she must never be given codeine again, which was the greatest culprit of the tumultuous difficulties at the time of her last surgery.

We don't experience a full year of hell like we did last time Mom had surgery, but it is definitely three weeks of hell. The medicine trips Mom into the demanding suicidal personality, with periodic shifts into the frantic terrorized personality. She demands my attention constantly.

One evening I tell her we have company and assure her she should be fine on her own for a while. When I go to check on her she has burned a hole in the sheet with the lamp and the mirror. She begs me to stay. This is the only time I see Alan reach his boiling point around care of Mom. He comes to find me since I have disappeared in the middle of hosting guests. I tell him Mom needs me. He is so furious at my unbalanced response to Mom he gets on his motorcycle and leaves. I go to our guests in the backyard and ask if they can please keep an eye on the dinner on the BBQ. I return to Mom. We get through the night, but Alan is clear: we can do lots for Mom, but there have to be boundaries when enough is enough.

The next day Mom gets up to sit on the front porch. She becomes frantic, declaring that she can see little green men. One of our guests from the night before who lives across the street is a nurse. She comes over and takes care of Mom until Mom calms down. I take Marissa, who is two years old, and Sarah, who is seven years old, into the house.

It is only now, after working on the development of my understanding of the many personalities within Mom that I realize that the one sitting on the front porch that day is the one I call the Wild One. At first I think that episode confirms that it is anesthetic that triggers the appearance of the Wild One. Maybe she isn't an actual personality. Maybe her response to the medication is a normal reaction. The nurse seemed to handle it well. I don't talk to my friend who is the nurse about it afterward so I don't really know what she thinks.

But then I remember that the Wild One actually shows up before Mom's surgery in 1971 and she shows up in the condo on the nineteenth floor when there is no surgery. A part of me would like to think that it is the anesthetic that prompts the emergence of the Wild One rather than her being a splinter personality created because of a crisis. But the timing doesn't line up. I still shudder to think what happened to her to create such a terror-filled personality.

After Mom goes home, Alan and I do extensive sorting out of our relationship.

We have been married for eleven years. Our life together takes a surprising turn when I feel called to ministry, which consumes six years of preparation, financial resources, and more time than we originally expect because we decide to have a baby in the middle of the process. Then I discern that I am not ready to be a minister, or maybe I won't be a minister at all. I take a year off. A year later I am ordained.

When we move to the rural village Alan is offered work immediately. It is good that he gets work right away since one of the stresses for a minister's family in a small rural community is that the spouse of the minister may not be able to find work.

Many things are working okay but there are still details for us to sort out. We are now living in a house that belongs to the church. The church office is in the basement. We are both deeply immersed in the life of the community. We have two children who are also busy in activities. We are experiencing both the joy and the demands of my work. And our marriage is feeling the pinches of all these changes and expectations.

I am aware that both Alan and I are wondering if our marriage might end up being a casualty in this new reality. We both suffer and struggle in silence, not knowing what to say. I finally decide that I am totally exhausted and drained from living behind a newly created façade that strives to appear happy and content as I struggle to fulfill the role of wife and mother based on what I think Alan expects, combined with trying to sort out the implications of my role as minister that is swamped by expectations that make no sense to me.

I feel lonely, conflicted and cut off from myself and from Alan. I come to a crisis point. I decide that I am tired of being who I think Alan wants me to be. I am going to simply be me and if that's not good enough for him, so be it. I can't keep losing myself. I'm prepared to lose the marriage if need be, but I'm not prepared to be a veneer-thin approximation of what I think others think I should be as a wife, mother or minister.

I drop the façade. I let go of the masks. I risk being me with all my boldness, creativity and big ideas. I start taking time for myself. I start saying no to as many things as I can. I start to anchor back into me rather than be adrift in a sea of presumptions.

In the midst of what I perceive to be my radical stance, Alan and I start talking again at a level deeper than day-to-day details. It's not long before I sense our feelings of love for each other reawakening and emerging from deep below the surface. I begin to recognize and acknowledge that it was the real me that Alan fell in love with, and so I wonder why I ever thought I couldn't be the real me.

Life teaches that when we need to learn a lesson, opportunities to learn it will keep showing up until we have fully integrated it into how we engage life. Clearly this is a lesson that I need to keep wrestling with in order to dig deeper into my capacity to not live behind masks, and to not be bound by external "shoulds" that conflict with my authentic inner wisdom.

Alan and I have a heart-to-heart conversation. We decide that divorce will not be an option for us. Instead of trying to figure out how we can exit the marriage with the least amount of trauma, we agree we will both be committed to making sure our relationship is healthy and strong and our communication is open and honest; we will focus our energy on figuring out how to have the kind of relationship we want rather than how we can either get out of it or endure it.

Our new united stance changes everything for me. I feel my core strength returning. My once foggy, reactive self is dissipating. My response to life is more fully rooted in love rather than fearful reactions.

My experience with Alan of discovering the value of sticking together to work through issues teaches me that when I am going to commit to a relationship at work, with friends or family, I need to know that the other person won't just walk away if issues arise. I need to know I can trust that there will be honesty and curiosity rather than judgment, and that there will be a willingness to work on our relationship. I am okay with relationships ending by circumstance or when there are abusive behaviours or bullying, but I am not okay with a significant relationship ending because we won't deal with our issues together. Open, honest conversations where we are willing to wrestle with how to be in relationship that honours each other as well as our self, provide key moments of growth and new awareness in my life.

Another huge learning for me over the years through my relationship with Alan is that it is critical that I not dump 'expectations' onto other people. 'Expectations' are part of the middle circle of the 'three concentric circles diagram,' which identifies how to be spiritually healthy by connecting to the inner circle, where we remember we are all beloved children of God, and by not living our lives from the middle circle of 'external expectations.' If I have expectations of others, they become their 'external expectations,' which I encourage people not to be guided by unless they align with their authentic self.

I learn that if I want to experience people in an authentic way, it is important to let go of preconceived notions about who I expect them to be. If I am critical of others based on the lens of my 'expectations,' I miss the richness of who they truly are. I learn that rather than having 'expectations' it is helpful to be committed to encouraging one another to strive to live our core values and to share our unique gifts, which enables us to grow toward the fullness of who we can be.

My relationship with my Mom keeps teaching me to work on relationships even if they shift and head off in surprising directions. Being curious and engaging at a deep level of compassion, even in the midst of what may feel like craziness, is worth it as we engage like archeologists sifting through the shifting sands to find the treasures hidden beneath.

————————————————

The next time I spend extensive time with Mom is in March 1993.

Alan, Sarah, Marissa and I spend a week with Mom at her place in Florida. Mom is not in a good space. One afternoon is particularly bad. Alan leaves the condo with the girls because Mom is extremely out of sorts. Anger is rolling off her. I stay since we both know that someone needs to be with her. It is only later that I understand why she is exhibiting such an array of weird, aggressive behaviours throughout the week. It is because of a piece of mail she receives just before our arrival.

The week before we fly down, my church secretary tackles a mass of accumulated mail in my office. Mom told me that any mail I receive for her could just be opened and then thrown out. I had a pile of unopened mail that should have all been unimportant. My secretary bundles it all up and sends it to Mom.

As it turns out I am glad the secretary sent the mail to Mom because in that pile of mail is the final letter on behalf of my half sister who has been trying to find her birth mother for the past eleven years. She has been told my address is their last lead. The letter has been in my home for several months, unopened. I'm glad I am not the one who opens that letter.

After opening the long-delayed letter, Mom makes contact with the agency to say she wants to open communication with her daughter who she put up for adoption. Plans are in place for the two of them to meet by phone the week we are in Florida. In retrospect, I understand why she is anxious and out of sorts all week.

On the Friday of our visit, we take the kids to see Janis and her kids.

While we are away for the day, Mom has her first conversation with Lynda, the daughter she put up for adoption forty-five years before. When we get back that evening Mom shares the full story of the events of the birth of her first child. She tells me she never wanted us to know in fear that we would think she could give us up too.

I sit and listen for hours. At the conclusion of the story my response is to say, "I know who the father is."

She glances at me with a dismissive and annoyed look and tells me, "You can't possibly know."

I tell her what I think. "It is the dad of a member in Mark's grade eight band, isn't it?"

She stares at me, then nods, and asks how I know. I tell her how I experienced the rising of her anxiety level every time he came to the house and how on the day she drove him home during the thunder storm I noticed her anxiety skyrocket.

Later, I ask her if the presence of the band member's dad in the neighbourhood had anything to do with the fact that she and Dad stopped bowling every Thursday night.

She looks at me, puzzled. "You noticed that? You were only six years old."

I tell her what I noticed: "You used to love to bowl but shortly after we moved you stopped your weekly ritual of pulling out your turquoise case that holds your bowling shoes. That bag has sat untouched in your closet for years."

She shakes her head, surprised. "You're right. His Dad is the father of my first baby. And you are also right that we stopped bowling because he and his wife joined the bowling league."

So Janis's thought that she shares when the three older siblings of our family are together in 2014 has validity: the encroachment of the father of Mom's first baby through his son's involvement in Mark's band probably plays a part in us moving to the farm, though we don't understand the implications at the time. It might even make some sense that his presence in our lives may have been one of the causes of Mom spiralling out of control emotionally in the early years at the farm as she once again faced a difficult part of her history.

One of the first things Mom does when she meets Lynda is to provide her with the medical history of her biological family on Mom's side. Mom is adamant that Lynda has the right to know her biological father's medical information. Since the father of Mom's first baby chooses not to meet his daughter, because he doesn't want to risk his family finding out about her, Mom and Lynda's father meet for an afternoon for Mom to gather all the information that she is passionate that their daughter has the right to know.

Mom is adamant about the importance of people knowing their own medical history based on their biological family. Mom's passion to ensure that Lynda knows her history is one of the reasons why I don't think our "real Mom" is aware that there is an extra biological father in our family. She always makes sure we all know the details of Dad's medical issues along with her own, so that we will know where we are at risk. I believe that if she had an inkling that there might be a different biological father amongst her children she would have found a way to ensure that his medical background and its potential impact were known.

In so many ways it is great to meet Lynda and include her in our lives. However, group dynamics change when an extra sibling shows up in a family. So while it is good, it is also hard because it means that those of us who grew up together, who have shared memories as well as DNA, rarely get together with just us.

Lynda's arrival, however, adds interest and deepens an ongoing conversation that Janis and I have been having for years, right back to when we were kids. We continuously wonder about the traits in the two of us that come from the different sides of our family. We identify traits we presume we get from Dad because they are traits that are not seen in our maternal cousins who exhibit characteristics that come from Mom. For much of our lives it has been curious to Janis and me that we are quite different from Mom's extended family. Lynda's traits reflect our maternal cousins and so confirm our observation that we have traits that must come from Dad.

It is even more puzzling to us as to why we are different from our brother and sister. We wonder if maybe we are more like Dad in personality and they are more like Dad in looks, especially in their very distinct bottom lip. We observe that the way we engage life feels different from the energy with which Mark and Betsy engage life.

Looking back, I am amazed at the ways we try to make sense of our genetic background. I did not know until recently that, based on other people's experiences, Janis and I are quite odd in our in-depth explorations and wonderings about our genetics that go back decades.

Lynda shows up in our lives right in the middle of the years of Mom's second marriage. It is a good time to welcome someone new into the family when the family is already in the midst of sorting out relationships with the addition of Mom's husband. Lynda and her kids create a bright spot in a time when we are trying to sort out how to be family.

The latter years of the twentieth century are not easy as a family but we work at our relationships to incorporate all the new shifts and changes and demands.

Three times during these years of Mom's second marriage, her husband takes her to the hospital where she is diagnosed as having an anxiety attack. She has no memories of the episodes leading to the emergency room visits. I do not know which personality would have been present, but her behaviour had to have been extreme for Mom's husband to feel he had no other choice than to get help for her.

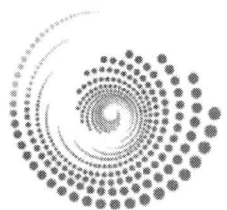

IN THE SPRING OF 1994, a colleague from Presbytery draws to my attention the fact that I am the lowest paid minister in the Presbytery. He observes that my pastoral charge is one of the few that is growing and that there are more people involved in programs in my church than any other churches in the area. He suggests I need to talk to the board about my level of remuneration. I am not comfortable initiating or even having this conversation. But he's right; it is a conversation that is needed.

I meet with the Ministry and Personnel Committee to tell them the statistics that have been brought to my attention. I also tell them that it has now become mandatory that new ministers coming to a church will have an increase in their financial support for continuing education funding. I ask them to consider increasing my funding for continuing education to the current required level they would have to pay if they called a new minister.

The committee agrees to increase my salary by $1,000, which means I am now only $500 lower than the person above me in the Presbytery. I accept. But then I am told that they are not going to increase my continuing education money. I remind them that there is a Conference motion stating that when I leave they will have to increase the continuing education financial support for their next minister. The answer is still no.

This is the moment when I realize I have changed and grown in the years I have been here, and though I always thought I would stay for an extended time, it feels like my dreams and visions for the church will be too much for them if they resist keeping up with a simple policy change like the level of remuneration for continuing education. I love them and I don't want to get to a place where I do not accept them or feel negative judgment toward them. But I need to be in a community that wants to keep growing and changing and deepening how to live its faith, including expanding generosity and celebrating abundance to be who we are called to be, rather than fearing scarcity of resources. I feel a strong nudge that it may be time to leave.

In August that year at General Council, a sampler of hymns for a new hymn book is introduced. When we sing the song "Here I am Lord" I begin to weep. It feels like a confirmation of my call to leave; I am called to go, as the song says, to where God leads me, and wherever that is, I will hold God's people in my heart, both those I've worked with in this congregation, and those I have yet to meet.

Alan and I begin to explore options of churches where we might move. I apply for a number of positions, including one for a Conference Executive Secretary. Although it is not their usual practice, they phone me to tell me why they are not going to interview me. I had been on the short list but when they thought about the job and who I am, they felt that the new increased focus on paperwork would slowly deaden my spark and my enthusiasm for engaging with people.

It is a huge process to discern where I feel called to go, including pondering which churches are large enough to handle my level of energy, which ones align with my vision of church, combined with where my family would like to live. When I enter into conversation with Downtown United Church in the community on two lakes, I experience nudges and strong feelings that this is the place.

Then on the way to my third interview when I am leaving the cottage where I stayed the night before, I sense a command deep within me to go to the water and stand by the lake before going to the interview. I do, even though my time is tight. Those thirty seconds change everything.

I go and stand on the shore of one of the lakes facing toward the place where the two lakes meet. I hear a voice rise up within me but also rush at me from across the lake, declaring, "I call you to these waters that this may be a place of healing."

I ask, "Who will it be a place of healing for?"

The answer is, "You and your family."

And, in what is almost an afterthought, but will be a key piece in how I respond to this call, these words are added: "And to walk as one with the people of Downtown United Church."

Looking back, what is clear is that this being a place of healing for me and my family meant more than my immediate family. Family in this call is the family of the human race where much healing is needed. It is about all who gather in this place to connect in meaningful community and be inspired by the ancient energy of this gathering place of peace. That is why I am called here: to be part of what is emerging in this place. In my understanding the church is called to be responsive to the hopes and deep longings of our community so that together we can awaken to the wholeness that enhances the well-being of all and focuses on the common good.

In January 1996, we move to this new community on the shores of two lakes.

The move is extremely demanding. Sarah and Marissa need lots of support as they transition into a new school in the middle of the school year. I am trying to sort out how to be in team ministry, which is far harder than I anticipated. We are missing our fifteen-year-old dog, who had to be put to sleep the day before we moved. Mom is constantly adding to the turmoil with escalating crises.

Alan is able to spend the first year setting up and running our home. He finishes the basement which creates the needed space for our family, helps me to set up my office at the church when he recognizes my exasperation after nine months of living out of boxes I never have time to empty, and builds a high wooden fence on one side of our house that provides me with longed-for privacy from the very friendly people who use the public pathway to the park beside our house. He establishes relationships with our neighbours. When I am at home in those early months I hide in the house, where I find some sense of balance in a world that feels like a fishbowl filled with crashing waves.

Soon after moving, Marissa and I agree to go with Mom to Florida. It surprises me that Marissa is willing because she and Mom do not have a good relationship. Mom is always blatantly overt about declaring that Sarah is her favourite grandchild.

Mom does the driving. I never drive long distances because I struggle to stay awake in a car.

It is during this trip that I first realize the full impact of Mom on my family and me. It is surprising it happens now because Mom is actually in pretty good shape. She isn't in my preferred state of "real Mom," but she is in one of her higher functioning states. I wonder now if we were mostly engaging the Aggressive One. She is the most interesting of the splinter personalities because she has more than one primary focus. The mean, directive streak is definitely present. I rationalize her demanding tendencies as a reasonable result of all the stress of the tumultuous relationship with her husband.

The tension in the car on the twenty-four-hour drive to Florida is palpable. Mom constantly gets annoyed with Marissa. I defend Marissa. Marissa retreats into herself and ignores us.

I find some tapes of John Denver music. The songs contain insights and themes about the new way the world can be when we connect to the power of love. I had not noticed this theme in his songs before. I need something to keep me grounded in a hopeful vision and distracted by the reality around me, so I keep playing the tapes over and over for the whole trip.

We stay in my cousin's extra trailer in Florida. All three of us are miserable. It is a relief each day when my cousin comes for happy hour when Mom at least appears to be pleasant. In the middle of the fourth day away, Mom receives a phone call from her husband's doctor. Her husband has been diagnosed with liver cancer. Mom tells me the doctor says she needs to come home right away. I tell her I will go pack. She says not to bother because she is going to fly home to be with him.

I'm incredulous. "What? You are planning on leaving, expecting that I will drive the twenty-four hours home when I'm not comfortable driving more than three hours because I get sleepy?"

She leaves me a map and heads off to the airport, hoping to get a flight home soon.

I am horrified on so many levels.

But it doesn't take long before a different feeling rises within me. Marissa and I start having a good time together. It feels like we are playing hooky. We get to go swimming when we want to swim, eat what we want to eat, and go to bed when we want to go to bed.

By the time we hit the road to drive the twenty-four hours home I am feeling such relief in my soul that I decide that the time of driving will be treated as one more new adventure. We have a great time. We stop all along the way. We don't drive the full distance Mom planned for the first day. We find out later that Mom is extremely upset when she calls the hotel she booked for the first day of our trip home and finds out we aren't there. We phoned and cancelled so she knows we aren't in trouble. But she has to sit with her feelings until we get home because we decide we aren't going to contact anyone on our trip.

The relief that I feel to not have to be with Mom is enormous. It shocks me because I have always just dealt with her without thinking about the implications or impact on my family and me. The trip teaches me a lot about choices I need to make as the demands to support Mom continue to increase.

Shortly after our trip to Florida, an episode happens outside of our family that gives me an objective rather than subjective glimpse into the impact of Mom on other people.

Mom agrees to stay with one of her good friends to care for her following surgery. Mom flies to somewhere on the east coast of the States and takes care of her friend for two weeks. Unlike Mom, with her love of beer and the odd glass of wine, her friend drinks liquor. When Mom comes home she tells me she doesn't know what happened but her friend never wants to see her again. One of the other women in their group of four friends also decides she never wants to see Mom again. But Mom has no idea what happened to cause the chasm in their friendship.

My guess would be that Mom joined her friend in a drink or two of liquor and as a result Mom probably behaved in ways that would have been shocking. The Partying One likely showed up. If Mom's friend happened to get mad at her, it might even be that the mean one who is part of the Aggressive One showed up to protect the Partying One. The mean one can slip further along the spectrum of the Aggressive One into the full-blown raging banshee if she is provoked. And Mom would have no memories of the episodes that caused the rift in this long-time relationship if they happened while she was in the Partying One personality.

There is never any opportunity to mend the relationship. Mom's former friend will not return any of her calls and never speaks to her again.

THE LATE NINETIES IS A TIME OF INCREDIBLE LEARNING for me. After the trip to Florida with Mom and Marissa, and my recognition that Mom impacts my life far more significantly than I realized, I become aware that I need to find ways to cope with the impact of Mom, the church and everyday life.

I become intentional about seeking strategies to be healthy and whole amidst the demands of my life. Something I heard years ago, which has turned out to be true in my experience, is that we are called to teach the things we need to learn. I definitely need to learn how to cope with the reality of life with Mom in the midst of the rest of my life. My exploration of tools, attitudes, perspectives and practices expands, benefitting my life and the lives of the people around me as we all deepen in our spiritual journeys and strengthen our capacity to be healthy in our relationships in community.

In the summer of 1994, before I feel called to the community on two lakes, I have an experience that gives a sense of direction to my explorations in the latter years of the nineties and beyond.

During a time of meditation in 1994, a focus emerges within me for a thesis for a doctoral degree. I am told during this time of prayer to focus on the "Re-awakening of Ancient and Alternative Wisdom." Instead of doing a doctoral degree, I am called to move. I live the focus of the thesis for the next decade and a half, seeking places where wisdom is emerging, both ancient and alternative.

Examples of the awakening of ancient and alternative wisdom begin to emerge in the 1996. I lead an eight-week session with my colleague to train people to be facilitators in a ministry of Intentional Circles where significant relationships have the opportunity to build and meaningful conversations happen. This type of ministry is often called Small Group Ministry, which is a description of a process rather than a description of the size of the group.

When the training is complete I encounter four women in three days who all use the exact same phrase in conversation with me. They all say to me "I am in a time of transition." Since this description of being in a time of transition reflects my experience, I offer an Intentional Circle called "Women in Transition." I learn much in this time of exploration with women who are in a time of transition. We are not sure where or what we are transitioning to, but we are certain that a journey toward somewhere new is happening. Within this Circle we connect to the ancient wisdom of Circle where we encounter alternative perspectives to what we have known.

Through the years of this Circle and the weekly Circle of Light meditation services I lead, my spiritual journey deepens. The experiences provide a strengthening of my core that is much needed to keep my life in balance, with demands coming at me from many different directions. I am introduced to a variety of spiritual practices that help to ground me, even in the moments when life with Mom feels broken or the demands of family and church life seem overwhelming.

Over these years I expand my repertoire of styles of meditation through the use of the labyrinth, drumming, visual journalling, chanting through song, dancing to listen to the wisdom of our bodies and a wide variety of expression through the arts. I also deepen my awareness of the transformative power of story and confirm the impact of working in the fields of our energy.

In the variety of places I have the opportunity to provide leadership I offer meditations that are visualizations. I invite people on a journey based on whatever I am experiencing, as Spirit leads me deep within to connect with my soul. Years later, I use similar practices in my consulting when I am facilitating what I call Significant Conversations and want to help people listen for the wisdom and creativity stirring deep within them.

I am including a sample of the types of images and phrases I use in meditation. Often the meditation is much less detailed than this one and includes open-ended invitations. This meditation is a full description of an experience of going deep within to the centre of my being. I will someday record and post meditations on my website to respond to the growing list of requests. If this is read slowly with pauses you may be able to engage the experience in a meaningful way.

I invite you to get comfortable.

Close your eyes,
or let your eyes be soft by looking at the floor.
Relax into this moment, noticing how wonderful it is
to feel the support of the furniture or the floor that upholds you.
In the same way, you are upheld by the power of love
that is constantly with you.

Notice your breath.
The word for breath in Hebrew is the same word as Spirit.

So breathe in deeply the gift of breath, the gift of Spirit
and let it fill your body with the warmth of relaxation.
Breathe out a sense of calm into our shared space.

Breathe in deeply the gift of breath, the gift of Spirit,
and let it fill your mind,
clearing away pathways from clutter so that you can think clearly.
Breathe out kindness into our shared space.

Breathe in deeply the gift of breath, the gift of Spirit,
and let it fill your heart,
creating greater capacity for compassion.
Breathe out compassion.

Breathe in deeply the gift of breath, the gift of Spirit,
and let it fill your abdomen,
awakening the creativity within you.
Breathe out wisdom into the circle.

And now take your point of consciousness
that usually sits behind your forehead
and intentionally pull back into the still point in your brain.
Feel the stillness, deep in this place within you.

Silence

And now let your point of consciousness move
to begin a journey to go deep down within yourself
to the very core of your being,
pausing first at the energy field of your heart.

Imagine you are walking with ease down a beautiful stone staircase
that travels down, down, down, down within you.

As you get to the area that is somewhere around
the level of your heart,
stop for a moment.

Intentionally choose to set down any baggage you are carrying,
all the things that we carry around in the midst of everyday life,
the demands and details, the schedules and responsibilities,
just set them down for now; you can come back later to pick them up.

Notice how much lighter you feel.
Look around to notice how you see differently
when the demands of life are not blocking your sight.

Look over the railing of the stone staircase.

Allow the beauty of what you see to fill you with nourishment.
There is a meadow that is filled with lush flowers.
At the far edge of the meadow there is a gentle moving river.
It sparkles with glittering sunlight.
Across from where you are standing you see a pathway
that leads into the forest that is rich in its hues and colours.
The space is filled with warm golden light.
It feels peaceful.

And now continue down the staircase,
moving deeper and deeper,
going down, down, down within you toward the centre of your being.

As you get close to the bottom of the staircase, there is a turn.
Pause just before you make that turn.

See if you can set down any of the other aspects of your life,
like your roles in life, the way you are described by your relationships
and the expectations that others have of you.
Set them down just for now.
They are an important part of your life,
but just for now let go of them so you feel as light and free as you can.

And continue down the staircase.

As you turn the corner you see a place of golden light before you.
Continue down the staircase to the bottom.

You feel yourself being welcomed into the place of light.

You move forward and enter into the light.
It feels like you are coming home,
coming home to You.
It feels familiar, it feels nourishing,

it feels good to return.

Here in this place you connect to a power,
a source of power that fills you.
You feel the light within you expanding
to connect to the light all around you.
And you know that the light is love.
You sense the light within you reaching out
and the light all around pouring in to fill you.
You feel replenished and clear, empowered to be you.

And then you hear words that resonate in your heart,
"You are beloved ... You are be-love-ed ...You are love ..."
words that come from the heavens in the story of Jesus's baptism,
words and understanding meant for us
throughout the moments of our lives.
You allow this certainty to seep into the very marrow of your bones,
the awareness that you are beloved, and you are love.

And with a sense of certainty
you move beyond the place of light.
You enter into the place you saw
while looking over the railing as you descended the stairs.
This is a place deep within you.
As you enter this place it is clear to you
this is a place that nourishes your soul.
Absorb how good it is to be in this place.
Look around. See details you couldn't see from above.

Notice the warmth of the light that is emanating everywhere.

Feel the gentle breeze.

Hear the sound of the flow of the river.

Hear the wind in the leaves of the forest.
Watch as the butterflies dance amongst the flowers in the meadow.

Find a place so you can sit down and be comfortable.

Allow yourself to be open to listen …
to see what is trying to emerge from deep within you.

What treasure within you wants to be noticed?

Silence

What wisdom or insight wants to be heard?

Silence

What is stirring deep within the intelligence of
your gut/womb, your heart, your mind?

Silence

Listen. Listen deeply. Listen gently.
Listen trusting whatever it is that is emerging.

Allow yourself to sit in stillness and quiet
to simply listen … for an extended time.

Silence

When this extended time of listening feels complete,
ask for a blessing for your journey.
Allow yourself to be open to receive
whatever rises into your awareness.

Silence

When you feel ready, stand up and go to the edge of the meadow.
As you stand there,
you see others come join you.
People emerge from all around the meadow,
people from all around the world.
A huge silent circle forms around the circumference of the meadow.
As you watch you begin to see streams of light
that connect each person to the people beside them.
You feel your heart opening and gentling.
Light flows out of your heart
and out of the hearts of everyone in the circle.
The streams of light connect in the centre,
filling the meadow with
the light emanating from everywhere.
You bask in the light.
It is the light of love that connects all of us.
You stand with others and savour this moment.

Silence

When it is time to leave, acknowledge your gratitude
for this time of connecting to the Divine energy
that is within you and all around you
… of connecting to the Christ Consciousness
that was in Jesus and waits to awaken in us
to teach us the way of love.

As others fade away into their everyday lives,
move back toward the place of light
you entered at the bottom of the stairs.

Pass through the light, feeling it fill you with power.

Begin to ascend the stairs.

As you get to the top of the stairs, pause for a moment
and allow any insights or blessings or gifts
that you have experienced or noticed
rise into your consciousness.

Take a moment of silence to give space for what wants to emerge.

Silence

And now allow yourself to become aware of the place where you are.

When you are ready, open your eyes.
Look around you with eyes that see with love.

Remember how it felt to be connected with your true essence,
with higher consciousness,
your authentic self,
with the divinity within you,
and be open to knowing that that place,
that feeling, is just a step away.

Allow yourself to imagine walking through
the moments of your life
connecting to that love,
being aware of the wholeness
and being open to the creative flow of energy.

THE CIRCLE OF LIGHT MEDITATION SERVICE happens weekly in response to people wanting help to centre and connect to the power of creativity, wholeness and love within them. The services draw a crowd—sometimes upwards of fifty or more people—confirming for me the deep longing we have to connect to this place of wholeness within.

In the first year in the community on two lakes, I also am intentional about doing my own personal work beyond what I do when I provide leadership. I venture into the realm of energy healing. I start by working with a woman who will become significant in my spiritual journey, my friend Lynn. She uses an in-depth process called One Brain. It is work that we do together right up until her death, constantly seeking ways to heal and strengthen our roots of creative wisdom, so that we can engage the world with the ability to respond with love rather than react from fear or negative judgment.

In those early years of working with Lynn, my colleague in ministry becomes a source for me to be aware of the healing that I need to do in my life. He manages to push my buttons or trigger me more often than anyone I have ever met. A trigger is a place within us that needs healing. He seems to be able to readily help me identify my inner wounds that keep tripping me up. It is truly a great gift, albeit painful to have wounds exposed. But if we don't enter back into the wounds and tend to them, they will continue to divert our energy from what we are intended to accomplish with our lives.

After three years of work with Lynn, my colleague is no longer able to regularly push my buttons because the wounds are significantly healed; learnings have been identified and healing has happened. The process is similar to the way we heal from a wound physically; the pus and infection in a wound is cleared out and tended to by creating an environment for healing, until the once-wounded flesh is renewed. Although a scar may remain to remind us of lessons learned, the pain and tenderness are gone. Now I can more fully engage with my dynamically creative and demanding partner from a place of wholeness and wisdom rather than being tripped up by the periodic emergence of pain and reaction.

Another step of my journey of developing skills and spiritual awareness happens when I spend time with alternative healers in the community. I learn about their work by exploring and experiencing how they help people to be spiritually well.

Two years into my time here, I think back to my call to come to the community on two lakes so "that this may be a place of healing." If I am called to be part of the reawakening of this place as one of healing and creativity, what will my role be? Since more than one healer and artist has told me they wonder why they are here, maybe getting people together will help build bridges for something new to emerge.

We plan two events. At the end of the second event it is clear this is not yet the time to develop the idea of a collaborative of creative people and alternative healers. The development of a hub for creativity and healing will emerge later.

But there is an incident during the second gathering of healers and artists that keeps demanding I remember it as I write this book.

I arrive late at the second gathering for healers and creative people due to a very odd beginning to the evening. Spirit is intruding on my choice of clothing for the evening, an experience I have never had before. I am being nudged to wear my red sweater. It is only October and I never wear my red sweater until Christmas, so I am resisting the nudge. I try on a multitude of outfits. None of them feel right. As much as I am particular about what I wear to ensure that it will be comfortable, this is ridiculous. I finally give in and put on my red sweater. I figure I might as well pair it with my moss green wool pants and my holly berry earrings since that's what I usually wear it with. With a sigh of acceptance, I hop in the car and head to the gathering.

When I arrive I let myself in. The host's dog greets me at the door, which is odd because her basset hound normally sleeps through everything and has never before greeted me at the door. The dog follows me as I deposit my coat. I trip over the dog as I try to make my way to the huge central kitchen where everyone has gathered. I arrive just as they have formed a circle to officially begin the evening. A space is made for me in the circle. I apologize with my eyes. As I adjust into my place, the dog causes me to stumble as he winds around my legs to settle by my ankles.

I struggle to centre and ground. The dog's head is on my foot and is adding to the heat that my red sweater and green wool pants are generating. Perspiration is beading on my forehead and in other more uncomfortable places.

As I stand in the circle overwhelmed by the heat my body is generating, an old memory surfaces.

It is a winter's day. I am very young. Mom dresses me in a brown snowsuit, a wool hat, big fluffy mittens attached by a string, and white winter boots that do up with moveable buckles which frustrate me because there is a difference between the tightness on each foot. She puts up the hood of the snowsuit and ties it under my chin. I'm guessing it's the winter I turn one because she picks me up and carries me outside. She sets me on the ground. I stand in one place. Even if I do know how to walk I can't move in this overstuffed contraption Mom has stuffed me into. I feel like I am in a pressure cooker. It isn't long before sweat is breaking out on the top of my head. The sweat begins to pop out on other parts of my body. When the sweat drips on my forehead my overheated body begins to chill from the wintery air. The sweat attracts the bitter cold. The cold is now finding its way inside my monstrous snowsuit. Sweating with heat and shivering with chills is not pleasant. I finally plunk down on the snow bank behind me and wait impatiently for whatever length of time I will have to endure this agony. It looks like it will be a while. Dad, Mark and Janis are having a great time on our backyard ice rink. Mom is standing on the sidelines cheering their game of hockey. I'm off by the shed where the roses grow on a trellis in the summer, feeling like I am becoming a simmering puddle.

My mind wanders back to the present moment. The opening circle at the gathering of alternative healers is finally complete. I feel a sense of relief as I nudge the dog off my foot and I can once again move. When I look up, our guest speaker for the evening is coming toward me from across the circle. She clearly has a sense of purpose.

She introduces herself, asks me who I am, and then tells me an intriguing story.

She says, "I was startled earlier today when I was in my studio preparing for this evening. A journal that has sat on my bookshelves for years suddenly fell off the shelf that is packed full of my lifetime of journals. When the book landed it was open. I picked it up and checked to see what journal it was. It was a dream journal from twenty-five years ago.

"I read the dream recorded on the open page.

"It was a dream of a woman I will someday meet. The woman will be wearing a red sweater. She will have a basset hound at her feet. In the dream I am told that this woman with the red sweater who has a basset hound at her feet will make a significant difference in the world in the years to come through a book she will write. My task is to make this woman aware of the task she will be called upon to do, so that when the time is right she will respond. So I am here to tell you that you need to listen and respond when you feel that there is a book you are supposed to write."

The two of us look deeply into each other's eyes. She nods her head, pats my shoulder, puts her other hand on her heart, and then turns and walks away.

I am stunned as I stand in the middle of the hubbub. I shake my head, trying to dislodge the barrage of rational thoughts that are quickly judging this mystical moment. I settle into a stillness that is calm, now aware of why Spirit may have interfered in my choice of outfit for the evening.

The memories of that night nudge me in this time of writing, encouraging me any time I wonder if this book will be worthwhile for others. I remind myself that it might not be this project that will make a difference. Perhaps this will just be a first step toward a further call in my life. Or perhaps another woman with a red sweater and basset hound will show up in the dreamer's life and the message is for her. Whatever the future holds, I trust that the path will be illuminated and identifiable if there is work I am to do.

Through these early years in the community on two lakes where creative energy nudges me to see deeply into life, I continue to meet people who offer an alternative and often ancient way of listening for guidance and wisdom.

A major new understanding and insight comes from the teaching of an Elder from the First Nations community close by. He shares his wisdom about the perspective and practices of the Medicine Wheel to enhance decision-making and discernment within community. The teaching confirms what I have been discovering. The wisdom that he shares impacts my work and my relationship with Mom. It is a teaching rooted in the understanding of the importance of hearing the different perspectives that are carried within the circle of community. I write about this teaching in an article:

> It is an Elder of the First Nations community near my home who teaches many of us about the wisdom he's been given about the Medicine Wheel. A key concept in the teaching is the importance of hearing the wisdom of all perspectives within a community when we need to resolve an issue or find a way forward that will be life-giving to the community. When a decision is required, the process is to listen to the insights of each of the seven clans. There is recognition that each clan

has one-seventh of the perspective required to make wise choices. When the wisdom of all seven clans has been shared, time is given for all the clans to digest the different perspectives. Then the community gathers again to hear more input, and then maybe again. Only when it feels like all the perspectives have been heard does the way forward become clear, a way some call the eighth way, which is the way of the Creator. To arrive at this place of awareness, conversation is filled with pauses in order to allow wisdom to emerge. The use of a talking piece, such as a stone or feather, invites people to listen deeply as others share their thoughts. People are encouraged to only consider what they are called to share when the talking piece is handed to them rather than developing their answer while others are speaking. This practice contrasts with the tendency in our culture where ideas and responses are mulled over while others share their perspective. We think about what we are going to say rather than listening to what others are saying. In many ways for me, the use of the talking piece, or "peace," models the experience it promotes, of talking for the purpose of finding a peaceful and wise way forward.

The wisdom of the Medicine Wheel strategy for communal decision-making confirms my experience with Mom of the importance of listening to the multitude of perspectives within her so that she can discover a way forward that is rooted in wisdom. Of course, at this point in the journey I am not aware that Mom is dealing with a series of personalities, but I am aware that there are times when she needs time to allow the richness of insights to emerge.

In the midst of this time of intensive learning I go to a week-long training workshop with four women from the congregation as part of my continuing education that all ministers must do. The focus of the training is to explore the concepts and practices of attitudinal healing. I love the story in our textbook of a medical team who experiences the mother of one of their patients as very difficult.[7] Every time she enters their office the people on staff become tense. When they take time to talk about what is happening they realize they are all lobbing energy at this woman that they wouldn't want thrown at them. They collectively decide to change how they interact with her. Instead of aggressively throwing cannonball-like energy, they imagine sending roses to cover her path or cotton balls to greet her with a gentle touch.

After deciding to shift their own energy, the staff discovers that instead of the frustrated energy that used to fill their working space when the mom was present, now their working space is filled with positive energy even when she is there. People in the office are not sure if the woman changes at all, but they know they are changed, and as a result the angst in their shared space lessens. When this woman leaves their clinic for the last time she tells the head staff person that she is sad to be leaving because she has so enjoyed the staff.

I learn to be aware of the kind of energy I am sending at people. It impacts us. I tell a story in a sermon of a time I am stuck behind someone who is turning left at a set of lights at a busy corner in our town. Though I see many opportunities for the car in front of me to make a left turn, the driver waits until the light is yellow. There is no way that I will make it through this light. I witness myself lobbing cannonball-like aggressive energy at the driver. When I notice, I stop sending the cannonballs. I connect at a heart level with the other driver and ask for forgiveness. I then intentionally choose positive energy to send toward the driver. I realize that my negative judgment does not enhance their life or mine in any way.

The insights from this course on attitudinal healing confirm what I already know: that our energy matters. I appreciate that this insight is now a conscious thought rather than just a wondering. I

---

[7] Trout, Susan S. *To See Differently: Personal Growth and Being of Service Through Attitudinal Healing* (Alexandria, VA: Three Roses Press, 1990).

become even more intentional about how I engage with Mom in our relationship and how I engage in community.

In another course my imagination is captured by an image shared by author Carolyn Myss, who talks about how we have choices about how we use our energy. She invites us to think of our energy as being like one hundred plugs on an old telephone switchboard. We are the switchboard operator, so we get to choose where we will plug in our energy. Will it be in the past, the present or the future?

My friend Lynn once asked me to intuitively feel into my energy to see if I can sense how much of it is plugged into my past. The number that arises surprises me. It is thirty-seven. I have thirty-seven percent of my energy plugged into past experiences, so thirty-seven plugs on my switchboard of energy are busy flowing back to a reality that no longer exists except in my memory. Therefore thirty-seven percent of my energy is not available to connect to the present moment.

In the lecture, Myss talks about how we can choose where we plug in our energy. She teaches us to notice if there are places we can unplug our energy, like from a moment in the past, so that we can be more fully present.

I practice this strategy each day as I leave work. My drive home is only four minutes. I check in with myself in the church parking lot to notice where I need to disconnect my energy from my work before I arrive home to be with my family. I check to see if there is energy flowing out of me to some lingering moment of the day. Once I identify where my energy is being sent, I check to see if there is anything I can immediately learn from that moment or any decision I can immediately make about how I will deal with it. If not, I imagine myself unplugging all the plugs that are still connected to those moments of my workday, acknowledging I will come back later to see what I need to learn or decide.

I start my drive home. About ten seconds into my drive, I have to disconnect those plugs again, and then again in fifty seconds, and then at the two-minute mark, and again at three and a half minutes.

Finally, as I climb out of my car, I definitively acknowledge that I will come back to tend to the issue that is making my stomach churn, but for now I surround it with light and love and bring my energy into the present moment before I open the door.

I unplug from the past so that I can plug as much of my energy as possible into the present moment to connect first with Marissa and Sarah as they come home from school, then with Mom as I make dinner, and later with Alan when we sit before dinner to catch up on our day. I will likely need to leave immediately after dinner to return to the church, so during these precious few hours I want my energy to be present and available to connect to these people I love.

I incorporate teachings around being conscious of our energy into the enquiry groups I lead for kids in grade nine, which involve a hundred kids over twelve years. When we spend the night in the church for the Easter vigil we gather in the sanctuary before the vigil begins and form a circle. I share insights about how to create lives filled with life-giving energy rooted in love rather than allowing our energy to be consumed by fear or hatred, which is a recurring theme in the life of Jesus.

I ask everyone to put their left arm into the circle. I invite them to think positive thoughts about themselves and our group. I then direct them to place their right hand on the extended arm of the person beside them and push down to see how strong their resistance is. Usually arms bounce down a bit but basically stay in a raised position.

Then I ask them, just for a moment, to think negative thoughts about themselves and about our group. I tell them to test the strength in their arms now. Every arm pushes down easily. There is no strength or resistance.

The kids are always amazed. As soon as they have a chance to debrief the experience and what they have learned about the power of their thoughts and how their thoughts connect to their energy and their strength, I invite them to think positive thoughts once again. As they intentionally think positive thoughts, the strength in their arms is even stronger.

The awareness that the power of my thoughts radically impacts the level of strength I am able to bring to situations in life, combined with my resolve to actively ensure that I am keeping myself strong through a variety of spiritual practices, is key to my experience of enjoying my life with a sense of wholeness. I experience a sense of wholeness even in the midst of a multitude of demands, like the piles of the stuff we are encouraged to think we need, the constant expectations of church, the demanding requirements of parenting and partnering, and the need to respond to my Mom, who is amazing some of the time and unravelling other times. The need to strengthen our connection to the power of love within us is confirmed again and again by the things I learn and experience.

DURING THIS DECADE OF LEARNING I engage with other opportunities to expand my understanding of life. Though there are many pathways of learning, one is particularly significant.

On the computer late one night, I follow a series of intriguing links. This unexpected trail leads me to a symposium called "The Eagle and the Condor Symposium: Awakening the Dreamer, Changing the Dream." I read about how the eagle and condor are part of an ancient prophecy. For five hundred years the eagle, representing intelligence, will fly alone in the sky through the period of time when we develop science and technology. After the five hundred years, the eagle and the condor will once again fly together. The condor represents the heart and the importance of relationship, which are at the core of the wisdom of Indigenous people. When the two fly together our world will again experience the wisdom of the heart and the mind combined, which will initiate a renewed way of being on Earth. We are now in the time of the eagle and the condor flying together.

My imagination sparkles with enthusiasm at finding a way to respond to my longing to connect to the awakening of a new vision, a new story. I love the goal of the symposium. It weaves together three key strands of life that at this point in history are often treated separately and presented as being in competition with each other. The goal of the symposium is "to create a human presence on Earth that is environmentally sustainable, socially just and spiritually fulfilling."[8]

For me this goal is a reflection of beloved images from Isaiah's vision in the Old Testament in the Bible of a time when the deserts will blossom (environmentally sustainable), swords will be turned into

---

[8] See Pachamama Alliance: Awakening the Dreamer Symposium, www.pachamama.org/engage/awakening-the-dream.

ploughshares so all will be fed (socially just), and the natural enemies of the wolf and the lamb will lie down together in safe relationships (spiritually fulfilling).

I send an email to the organization asking if there are people in Canada who can lead these symposiums. The next morning I get a reply. Two people from Canada were trained that weekend. I am asked if I am close to where they live. We live three hours apart. I contact these newly trained facilitators to arrange for a symposium at the church. Their response is delayed by a day as they make their way home from the training. Two years later I am trained as a facilitator.

At a special Eagle and Condor Symposium I meet elders from all over Turtle Island—which is North America. While many provide incredible teachings, one particularly catches my attention. He talks about the importance of all people reconnecting to their hearts as we move through this time of transformation. Years later I hear him speak again. He now teaches about the importance of women connecting to the wisdom of the womb as a central key to the healing and shifts needed on the planet. I have been referring to such an experience as listening to the wisdom of our guts, which is central to my understanding of creating a culture of authentic connection rooted in connecting to the wisdom deep within our cores.

Over this decade of learning, scholars and speakers whose work I integrate into my thinking and my descriptions of life confirm the way I approach life.

There are thirteen theological understandings that for me are integral to the foundation of Authentic Connection Culture. These theological concepts are significant to the way I engage life as I explore and expand my understanding of how to be spiritually healthy and balanced in a world that longs to be a reflection of love and wholeness.

HOW TO BE SPIRITUALLY HEALTHY
IN ORDER TO REFLECT LOVE AND WHOLENESS

1) Celebrate the awareness that we are born in blessing, and ensure that the foundational stories we lift up carry the message of love.

2) Recognize the gift of the blessed unrest that is happening in the world through grassroots movements as a sign of the new way that is emerging.

3) Be aware that we are capable of conscious evolution, and so we are key players in deciding the direction in this time of great turning and change.

4) Incorporate the gift of integral spirituality that gathers together the wisdom of the ages by combining the insights of the sciences with best practices for the spiritual journey.

5) Connect to the perspective that God or the Divine is both within and beyond all of life, which encourages us to see goodness and choose the way of love.

6) Know that compassion is at the root of all world religions, confirming that it is an innate human capacity.

7) Be open to the emergence of creativity, wisdom and new ways of seeing life that are part of the significant evolution we are currently experiencing.

8) Accept that we are deeply and profoundly connected.

9) Integrate the awareness that it is our task to move more fully toward living from the Divine love within us.

10) Awaken to the Christ Consciousness within, to the universal consciousness of love.

11) Recognize that love is a choice and that when we are in fear we are disconnected from love.

12) Connect to opportunities for collaboration to create a world focused on everyone's well-being.

13) Create safe space to practice healthy community where we can risk being vulnerable, brave and creative so that we allow the world to be filled with possibilities and wisdom.

The shifts in my thinking, combined with the impact of deepening spiritual practices, help me to articulate my perspective about finding and living wholeness even in brokenness. It also helps me be clearer about how to be in relationship with Mom in a way that is caring of her, my family and my own state of being.

What is abundantly clear in my journey is that the support of an engaging, mature community is a critical piece in creating a healthy, life-giving spiritual journey. The power of creating healthy community becomes central to my work. While I am aware of this central focus in my work long before coming to the community on two lakes, my experience here deepens my understanding of how to create community where we expand our capacity to engage in authentic connection with our self and who we are capable of being personally, and with each other and who we are capable of being as a global community.

The centrality of the power of community weaves into an experience I had on the night of my first conversation with the contact person at Downtown United Church in the community on two lakes around their search for a new minister. When I make the call I am sitting in a hotel room paid for by Big City United Church after just completing my second interview with them.

Although I know I do not fit Big City United Church, the second interview is a time of significant learning for me. The workshop I lead in the second interview confirms for me the transforming power of an intentional healthy community. The impact of the workshop becomes a guiding beacon to remind me to trust in sharing our stories and being intentional to create safe and open community. It inspires my work in the development of Intentional Circles that are rooted in Authentic Connection Culture whose process is refined during my years at Downtown United Church.

Plans for the second interview with Big City United Church begin when I receive a call requesting that I prepare a workshop for the search committee. I shake my head, knowing I am not a good match for this congregation. I ask for guidance in prayer as to what to do. The answer comes back, "Go and be the fullness of who you are, Karen."

I tell the person who calls me from Big City United Church that I will come for the second interview but I don't think I am the right fit. She actually agrees with me. But she says it will be good for them to engage further with someone who brings an alternative perspective to traditional church, and who knows what might happen. She would love it if I am chosen to be their minister.

I develop a workshop rooted in what I will later describe as Authentic Connection Culture. I anticipate that the process of the workshop will be demanding as people are invited to enter unknown territory together. On the night I present the workshop I invite the committee to shift their location from around their thick board table to a circle of chairs. I lead the group through a series of exercises that intentionally push their level of comfort by exploring their faith through sharing their own stories and listening deeply to hold the space for others to do the same. I invite them to express themselves using crayons and construction paper and to anoint each other with water, confirming each one as beloved.

As they gather around the homemade cookies that I brought to complete our time together, the woman who has been my contact comes over to me. She tells me that something amazing is happening. She points to a group of people who are standing together in the corner. She shares that the young man has just told other members of the committee that during the past many months when the committee has been meeting on a weekly basis, he and his wife have been going through a difficult pregnancy, and that it has been hard to continue coming each week. During the birth of their child his wife was in danger. Until tonight he has not felt comfortable to share their difficulties in the group, or even to share the joy of the birth.

As the woman and I stand together and watch, I sense barriers cracking open as people shift and connect at a deeper level. Her comment to me as I leave is that the experience of this night has the potential to impact this community for a long time, even though I won't be there to help it grow.

Intentional Circles provide opportunity to create a renewed Culture of Authentic Connection. Once we experience it, we know when we are not in it by its absence. As humans, we have a deep longing to connect at a significant level with each other and with who we truly are, but in order for this to happen, we need to intentionally create a safe environment where people can be brave so that their stories are told, their wisdom shared and their gifts added to the work of creating a world rooted in love.

OVER A PERIOD OF FIFTEEN YEARS, I learn much about creating healthy life-giving Circles. We identify the ways that Authentic Connection Culture emerges in Intentional Circles by experiencing and noticing what works and what does not work. My relationship with Mom, including how her mental health challenges can make it difficult to connect at an authentic level, informs the development of the principles and practices of Circles. The concept of connecting authentically with ourselves and with others continues to be my understanding of the primary source of the power of Circles. However, it is also through my relationship with my Mom that I learn the importance of listening to diverse voices, perspectives and stories. When we do take the time to listen to more voices we begin to recognize that we do not always accurately arrive at a helpful final conclusion without extra time for more thoughts to be heard.

My awareness is that authentic connection and listening deeply have the power to impact our lives and the world around us in a positive, transformative way. I develop a definition that reflects this way of connection in a fractured world.

AUTHENTIC CONNECTION CULTURE emerges from an intentional way
of being which includes the following practices:
✓ listen deeply;
✓ connect to Wisdom within us and amongst us;
✓ honour our own and each other's gifts;
✓ share laughter and tears, joys and struggles comfortably;
✓ create a safe space where we can be brave and speak
from our heart, mind, experience and soul;
✓ commit to action for ongoing transformation

as we respond to our life purpose and call;
✓ encourage, support and be accountable to one another
as we seek to live a vision of wholeness;
✓ honour creativity and discover clarity emerging in our midst;
✓ deal honestly and kindly with issues before they fester;
✓ follow the flow of energy to align ourselves with pathways
that honour who we are and how the Spirit calls us to be.

This shift in culture away from
being consumers and individualistic emerges
as we connect to our core wisdom and creativity
at the centre of our authentic self
which compels us to develop healthy life-giving community.

When we are able to find stability within our core where we connect to our true self, we are much more likely to bring about the change in the world that we long for and seek. Our voice and insights are stronger and become channels for our vision of wholeness and goodness for our self, our family, our community, our world.

One of the wonderful aspects about delving into and practicing how to engage in relationships authentically in Intentional Circles is that this way of engaging becomes a way of life. This renewed culture begins to permeate other situations as a result of the influence of one or two people who carry this wisdom. There is a ripple effect as more and more people redevelop their skills and attitudes that contribute to creating a culture where everyone belongs, everyone's needs are considered, and together we commit to the common good.

To reflect on the task of engaging at an authentic level, I identify the points of pain that Authentic Connection Culture can alleviate. When these pain points are in a team, group, family or organization, developing new strategies for communication and engagement has the potential to revitalize purpose, intrinsic motivation, relationships and creativity.

STEPS TO CREATE A CULTURE OF CONNECTION

ACKNOWLEDGING PAIN POINTS
AUTHENTIC CONNECTION CULTURE CAN ALLEVIATE

X   People are disconnected from others = sense of isolation
X   Constant sense of pushing rather than a synergistic flow
X   Not intrinsically motivated, always needing external
    affirmation
X   Emergence of new ideas at a standstill
X   Rumbles below the surface
X   No significant conversations
X   Lack of a sense of community or being a team
X   Disconnected from inspiration and creativity
X   No shared laughter but lots of feelings of entitlement
X   Judgment and blame running rampant
X   Hiding behind masks, façades and walls
X   No sense of shared responsibility
X   Overwhelmed by external demands

13-POINT SYSTEM
TO CREATE A CULTURE OF CONNECTION

THE PILLARS to create a renewed culture are:
*   Connection to authentic self = connection to wisdom
    and future possibilities
*   Trust we have the answers amongst us = developing
    deep listening
*   Create safe space where people can be brave = tapping
    emerging ideas and concepts
*   Celebrating a diversity of perspectives = creative steps
    forward

THE PRACTICES to develop a renewed culture are:
*   Develop a community agreement to create a safe
    environment where people can be brave and bold.

- Listen deeply and with curiosity to self and others.
- Allow wisdom to emerge from deep within.
- Use responsible "I" to share your story and perspective.
- Speak truth simply and responsibly to deal with issues.
- Choose an idea to develop (prototype ideas), then assess, clarify and either correct it or move to prototyping another idea to create an environment where it is safe to fail.

THE PRODUCTIVITY resulting from following the practices and developing the pillars are:
- Significant conversations where future possibilities emerge
- Community of connection and creativity
- Synergistic flow = meaningful and purposeful lives

I realize that helping a group function well by following the "Steps to Create a Culture of Connection" isn't enough. I develop a 13-Step Connection Strategy for self and community called "From Disconnected to Connected" to identify the inner shifts needed to be authentically engaged. This inner work is critical to creating a culture of connection to help make the shifts that are needed in our world today. The response to the "pain points" needs to be at both an individual level and a community level so that transformative creativity can emerge to develop healthy, collaborative and cooperative groups.

FROM DISCONNECTED TO CONNECTED
A 13-STEP CONNECTION STRATEGY
FOR SELF AND COMMUNITY

13 Steps to Connect to the Power of
Transformation, Meaning, Purpose and the Authenticity
Within Each of Us to Enhance Our Life Together in Community:

1) Connect authentically with self and others.

> Disconnect from expectations that are external or in opposition to your true self; disconnect from building walls within that separate you from *You* and from the people around you; disconnect from wearing masks to hide behind.

2) Develop intrinsic motivation.

> Disconnect from insecurity, judgment and the need for external affirmation, which can destabilize our connection to our core.

3) Release, lament and claim the insights.

> Disconnect from being a victim to old wounds.

4) See differently.

> Disconnect from dumping energetic garbage on others or ourselves.

5) Expand compassion, curiosity and laughter.

> Disconnect from our small-ego self, which focuses on defending territory, a sense of entitlement and personal desires as the highest goal.

6) Speak truth simply.

> Disconnect from blame and judgment.

7) Listen for inner guidance.

> Disconnect from dishonouring and ignoring inner wisdom.

8) Reclaim power and purpose.

> Disconnect from wandering through life feeling powerless.

9) Energize the vision and longings that emerge from deep within.

Disconnect from focusing on and energizing what we don't want to grow.

10) Create authentic relationships of connection.
Disconnect from being fearful and phony.

11) Engage in significant conversations that include laughter, tears and lots of wonderings.
Disconnect from shallow, veneer-thin dialogue filled with catty comments and opinions that are declared as "the" answer.

12) Tap into the wisdom and creativity of future possibilities.
Disconnect from dependence on logic and past experience as the only valued guides.

13) Live your call: trust your intuition and gut response.
Disconnect from living the life you think you "should" live and start living the life your passion calls you to live.

The 13 steps invite us on a deepening journey, which shifts our focus to plug into the core of power within us and releases us from being limited by the voices of judgment, fear and cynicism in our heads.

Another process where I define steps to shift from toxic relationships to authentic connection culture is:

9 STEPS TO THE SHIFT FROM TOXIC RELATIONSHIPS
TO AUTHENTIC CONNECTION CULTURE:

1) Connect to the core authentic essence in you and others.

2) Recognize, celebrate and encourage the gifts in you and others.

3) Honour what wants to emerge by getting small-ego self out of the way.

4) Trust inner wisdom and listen to intuitive gut responses.

5)   Let kindness and honesty lead you.

6)   Follow the flow of energy.

7)   Awaken to the perspective of possibilities, wholeness and the well-being of all.

8)   Allow space for divine inspiration.

9)   Live your purpose and collaborate with others to co-create the world as an amazing community.

The next step in the development of my thinking is to summarize the keys to unlocking this culture:

THREE KEYS TO AUTHENTIC CONNECTION WITH SELF

CONNECT to the energy of love and authenticity at your core.
DISCONNECT from the drama, small-ego self
and expectations that drain you.
RECONNECT to the wisdom, light and gifts
in you and in those you encounter.

Unlock greater capacity for peace and possibilities
in you and in the world!

THREE KEYS TO AUTHENTIC CONNECTION WITHIN COMMUNITY

CONNECT to authentic power and intrinsic motivation.
DISCONNECT from the distractions of drama, small-ego self
and the voices of judgment, fear and cynicism.
RECONNECT to the gifts and inner wisdom
in you and in those you encounter.

Unlock a renewed culture of fulfilled people
and a healthier, creative environment!

DURING THE FIFTEEN YEARS OF LEARNING about staying balanced and connected to the place of wholeness within, I continue to take care of Mom.

The next time Mom comes to stay with us is just before her husband is admitted to a hospice home in the final weeks of his life in October 2000. When the doctor called Mom while we were in Florida to say her husband had liver cancer, it was anticipated that he would die very quickly. As she has for all the family members who are diagnosed with cancer, Mom becomes the ever-attentive nurse. But her husband lives for another three years; all of them are difficult years. Mom needs a lot of moral support. She keeps slipping in and out of her different personalities, although at the time I don't understand what is happening other than she is once again falling apart on a regular basis. By the end Mom is exhausted and expresses her extreme agitation in a way we have not encountered before.

Mom and her husband have a social worker to support them during the months of palliative care. I meet her more than once. She calls me one night at 7:00 p.m., just weeks before Mom's husband dies.

Mom has locked herself in the bathroom. She is screaming and throwing things against the mirror. The support person doesn't need to tell me much. I can hear the screaming and the shattering of objects. This is the first time that I am conscious of meeting the part of the Aggressive One that I describe as the raging banshee. She is absolutely wild, cursing and screaming that she hates her husband. Her words are combined with animal-like sounds.

The support person asks if we can come. I turn to Alan, tell him what is happening and ask him if he will go. I turn back to the phone and say that my husband will come right away but it will be a two-hour drive. She asks me to stay on the phone with her. Mom calms down when she hears I am on the phone, but then gets worked up again and screams for the rest of Alan's two-hour trip. While Mom screams, the support person and I make arrangements for Mom's husband to be transferred to the hospice. Using her mobile phone so she can stay on Mom's phone with me, the social worker makes arrangements for him to be picked up right away. He is gone by the time Alan arrives.

I hear Alan enter the condo. I listen as he speaks to Mom with the calming voice I have heard him use with a frightened animal. Mom eventually opens the bathroom door after being assured that her husband is gone. Alan helps her gather some of her things and then stands back when she becomes a whirlwind of frantic activity that grabs things and throws them into a suitcase. He guides her to the truck to bring her to our home.

Two days later, when Mom starts to emerge from the state she has been in, she is puzzled. She demands to be taken to wherever her husband has been taken. I drive Mom the two and a half hours to the hospice home.

On that first day Mom asks me to stay with her husband so she can go out to buy a few things that they will need. One of the items she wants to buy is a cellphone for me so she can reach me anytime. I'm not totally sure I want to be reached that easily, but I agree. Mom manages to get me a great cellphone number, with the same final four digits as my home phone. Her choice shows a level of organizational detail and clarity that surprises me considering the past two days of upset. She also picks up special lotions and oils for her husband, plus chocolates and a fruit basket for the staff.

Mom is shockingly alert for all she went through two days earlier, of which she doesn't seem to have any memories. When I leave that night she is enjoying making sure her husband is comfortable and cared for. She becomes a beloved volunteer caregiver at the home over the next five weeks as he is dying.

Mom's husband's funeral happens on November 7, 2000, the day that George W. Bush is elected President of the United States. By then Janis has lived in the States for a long time, so we spend the evening watching the news, an interesting pastime for a family with differing political perspectives, but it gives us a focus.

My strongest feeling at the death of Mom's husband is relief. I am, however, sad for our kids. He has been their grandfather. In so many ways he was kind and gentle and oh-so-caring of them. They have wonderful memories of trips on the train to the Canadian National Exhibition that include purchases of large stuffed animals when the games did not successfully provide them with one. There are memories of big Christmas parties at the condo, along with a special birthday party when Mom turned sixty, ensuring that they got to hang out with their cousins.

The week after his funeral, Mom and I fly to Montreal with his casket to bury him by his first wife. Before the service we meet with his family, including his son. The conversations are filled with topics that echo the discussions with Mom's husband over the past seventeen years. There are strong beliefs in this family that are deeply rooted in a theology that focuses on how unworthy we are, how much we have sinned and that we are likely going to end up in hell. Mom's husband did not like this theology, but even though his two priests, a nun and I offered him an alternative perspective rooted in the understanding that we are profoundly loved by God, he held fast to his childhood beliefs. His family does too. I spend my time with them observing. I am genuinely interested in getting to know them before I do the service. It becomes clear in listening to them that like Mom's second husband they are not interested in a different way of seeing life. Their childhood beliefs are deeply ingrained. I preside over the service, which is woven full of statements about how profoundly God loves us and how when we die we are embraced by that love. They listen politely. When the service is over there is a part of me that is relieved when they head back to their everyday lives. Their absence allows me to disengage from my sadness that this understanding of life, that we are all sinners who will end up in hell, is still prevalent.

That night Mom and I enjoy the cobblestone streets of old Montreal. We go out to dinner at an amazing restaurant and then see a play. It feels like our "real Mom" is present. We have a delightful time together. We kid about Mom someday being like the lead in the play we see called *Driving Miss Daisy*, where the main character hates having to depend on her driver to help her. Mom declares that she will never be like that because she will accept the changes of life with grace. For all her expectations of how she will be in later years, the play foreshadows Mom's frustration when she can no longer be independent.

On December 9 and 10, Mom and I go to an inn for one of our two-day spa retreats, a practice her husband started years ago. He paid for Mom and me to go to a spa at least once a year. He told me that the two-day retreats accomplish a few things: they give him a break; they help Mom to relax; and they provide him with a way to thank me for all that I do for Mom and therefore for him.

On the first night of our December spa retreat, as Mom and I eat the delightful, creative desserts set before us, Mom tells me she met a man a few months earlier and they've become friends. They met when she was trying to sell her sister's condo. He called for details as a possible purchaser. Her sister, who she lived with at nineteen when she was pregnant, died earlier in the year, after receiving the usual incredible support from Mom. Mom was helping her sister's daughter by being the contact person for the sale of the condo which is in the building where Mom lives.

Mom and this man hit it off on the phone, enjoying rich conversations around music and politics and life. Their connection was probably a real gift to her in the midst of all she was doing to care for her husband.

Since her husband has now died, this new friend wants Mom to come to Florida to stay with him. My first reaction is shock. As I listen to Mom's description of him, it sounds to me like he is bossy and demanding.

I ask her what she is going to do. She shares that she thinks she will go to Florida to meet him in person. She asks me what I think. I pause for a moment, trying to figure out what to say. Although I am clear that it is not my place to fix her life, she has asked my thoughts. I tell her that I don't know about her, but I still need time to get over the impact of her last relationship.

A month later, in January 2001, Mom heads to Florida to stay with this new man in her life. I suggest she might want to stay at a place of her own. He insists that she stay with him. Mom responds in a way that is typical of other times in her life when she makes a rapid life choice with a sense of enthusiastic gusto that leaves the rest of us shaking our heads with astonishment. She decides to move into his condo. He is recovering from major heart surgery, so it is better if he can stay close to home. I groan for so many reasons.

Mom and I still speak regularly on the phone. Every call she asks me if I want to meet this new man in her life.

I am clear. "No, I am still recovering from your relationship with your last husband."

It is only later that I find out that he can hear all our conversations because Mom has me on speakerphone.

A few months into their relationship, they move back to Canada, sell Mom's condo and buy a home on a lake two hours east of our home in a town where he used to live.

I begin to realize just how good Mom sounds. She seems stable. She sounds more like our "real Mom" than she has in years. It is delightful to have a conversation with her. I had grown accustomed to long conversations in which we predominately seek solutions for her daily issues. But now she usually sounds happy.

In July, after the two of them have settled in Canada in their new home by the lake, I decide I am ready to meet her new husband. It takes him a while to warm up to me after the multitude of times I refused to meet him. We end up quite liking each other. As time goes on, Mom becomes even more chatty and engaging.

Only once do I get a frantic call from Mom during her years with her third husband. She calls and begs me to tell him that the way she is behaving is normal. To me it actually is normal, more normal than the way she has been for the last few years.

He tells me bluntly and firmly, "There is nothing normal about the way your Mom has been acting for the past five days." The phone call ends.

It is something of a relief to have someone who refuses to accept this behaviour that has been so normal for us.

I'm not sure which personality is present over the five days, but since Mom sounds whiny and fearful I suspect that he is seeing glimpses of the suicidal personality.

Over the years Mom is with him, she is more like our "real Mom" than she has been in a long time. I am grateful for his ability to ground her.

It is only after many months of sorting through the personalities that I realize it is probably the personality of the Angelic Presence who is present throughout this marriage. Mom's focus during these years is consistent with the Angelic Presence who is serene, content, focuses on the people immediately around her and does not engage in the wider community. The people she engages with during this time are her hairdresser, her cleaning lady, her handyman and the two little girls she reads to in order to help them learn how to read. They all adore her, as we hear regularly from them and see evidence of in their continued contact with her over the years.

The Angelic Presence is the one who comes to provide respite for the host personality from the turmoil of the other alter personalities. When Mom meets her third husband she has just gone through seventeen years of hell with her second husband. It makes sense that the five years with her third husband were all a time of respite for the host personality. In the time of respite the Angelic Presence comes to tend to life.

IT IS GOOD MOM IS WELL THROUGH THESE YEARS because we are going through a tough time in the church. My colleague is being reviewed. Divisive camps are forming, even though both my colleague and I encourage people not to create pockets of perspectives that divide them.

I learn much over these next years, developing a deepening awareness of energy, a broader understanding of the power of stories to heal, and greater clarity about boundaries.

As I walk with the congregation during the months of the review, and then the review of the review, I feel a heaviness of energy that contrasts with the energy of the early years when the ministry of the church expanded as my colleague and I develop their vision with them. I sense angst swirling amongst us, racing uncontrolled through our gatherings, creating wounds and sadness that are palpable.

Over the years I have become sensitive to the energy within and amongst us. I feel it deeply.

One of the ways the awareness of energy has increased has been through being with people at the time of death. After crossing over with Dad at the time of his death, I have similar experiences with other people. I also have a number of experiences of connecting to people heart to heart in the last hours of their lives. These episodes have cracked open my awareness of how we can connect at a level far deeper than a surface level, through far more than words alone. They teach me how to connect with people at the core place within us where we connect to Love.

One experience happens in the middle of the night when I am on call at the hospital. The phone rings in the stillness of the midnight hour. The voice on the other end of the line is a nurse in ICU asking me to come.

When I arrive I am led into a room with three people in their eighties—a man in a coma and two women at his bedside. The two women are introduced to me as his wife and sister. They ask me to say a prayer for the man. I do. They return to chatting. I stay at the far side of the bed and look down at the man. I try communicating with him heart to heart, a form of communication in which no words are spoken aloud but a connection is made. I ask him what he needs before he can go. It is clear to me, almost as clear as if he had spoken aloud, that he'd like his sister to leave the room so he can be with his wife alone. Do I have the right to ask her to leave? Well, let's see. I suggest to the two women that it might be good for the wife to be alone with her husband without his sister there for a moment. The sister leaves. I stay because he tells me to.

I ask again through heart communication, "What do you need?"

He says he wants his wife to kiss him and tell him she loves him. I make that suggestion to his wife. She does it. Then she stands there and stares at him like she is obligated to because of my encouragement to focus on him. I ask him what he needs now. The response from his heart to mine is that he wants his sister to come back in. I go and get her. The two women begin to chat again. I ask him if there is anything else he would like.

He says, "No." Not in words, but the message is strong.

I ask him if he likes Psalm 23. He indicates that it would be nice to hear as he goes.

I stand by him and wait for that time. It comes in a few minutes. I interrupt and tell the chatting women that he is crossing over. I invite them to join hands with me and join me in saying the words of the psalm.

As we get to the line "he leadeth me beside still waters," the man slips away into life beyond death. I continue to the end of the psalm, knowing the two women do not realize that he has left.

I have significant experiences with a couple of other people when I am with them in their dying moments.

I see one man head toward a meadow with a hill where there is a large luscious tree on top. A whole group of people are standing by the tree waiting for him. His wife agrees that makes sense for who he is.

Another man goes to a plateau that looks like a place in the Grand Canyon. I do not see anyone there to greet him, but I sense that he isn't alone. His wife agrees it is a perfect place for him.

I also have experiences where I feel the presence or the energy of a person in the room after they have crossed over to life beyond death. Their presence feels like a warm hug they are wrapping around the ones they love. It is a comforting feeling.

My awareness of energy is something that I have become sensitive to. The energy swirling through the congregation during the time of the review feels uncomfortable at a very profound level.

I realize that we need to figure out a way for healing to begin. I work with a retired minister in the congregation for whom I have incredible respect. We develop a process to engage people in conversation in an environment that is supportive and healthy. We meet with groups of people in homes, asking them to reflect on seven steps. Each step is based on an open-ended question. Two hundred and fifty people meet in twenty-five circles which are called Listening Circles. The process is so successful in shifting both the culture and the feeling in the congregation that it becomes the basis of my consulting work a decade later.

By the time the Listening Circles are complete and the report has been presented and adopted as a map for our way forward together, I am exhausted. In April 2004 I realize I am going to crack if I don't get some relief from the constant barrage of demands that keep creating mountains of work.

I check online for a course. I find one on adaptive leadership that will take place next week. I call. I am told they are full and there are already five people on a waiting list, so it is highly unlikely that I will get to go. Two days later, just before the event begins, I hear there is space for me. I go.

The Moderator of the United Church, Peter Short, is one of the leaders at the event. He invites us to find one verse of a hymn that captures our sense of who we are called to be as the church. Seven of us will have the chance to share our verse and have the group sing it back to us. I am one of the seven chosen. The group sings the verse to me. Tears pour down my face.

The song and the community begin to revive me, giving me a hand to grab on to instead of slipping toward the abyss. I am familiar with this experience from the times I have been present to others, trying to help them from becoming lost in the tunnels of darkness. The words that help to revive me come from a hymn sung to the tune we know as "Danny Boy." The hymn is called "We Shall Go Out With Hope of Resurrection." It speaks of engaging the world with a sense of hope and wholeness even in the midst of the brokenness. It expresses poetic images of creating a tapestry of wholeness that weaves us together in circles of love.

At the end of the course we are assigned a companion for the year to share stories and learnings about adaptive leadership. I am paired with an amazing partner who supports me, challenges me and helps me ask myself significant questions.

When I return from the week away, I am anxiously aware that my colleague of over eight years is leaving soon. We do not have plans in place to find extra staff to alleviate the burden of work. There are ongoing day-to-day realities of a large church that need to be attended to and there are still remnants of turmoil that require further steps for us to be able to move forward. I also want to be intentional about the church celebrating all the good my colleague and I did together as we say good-bye.

It is a demanding spring. I vividly remember the angst of one board meeting in July of 2004. I am supposed to be leaving for vacation the next day, a schedule that has already been extended to accommodate the meeting. That night the board decides that a letter has to be written right away to send to the congregation to explain where we are in our journey. The board wants me to do it before I leave.

I am at the end of my rope.

However, I agree to stay the extra days to write the letter on two conditions: that when I leave for holidays I tack on two extra weeks to the dates of my vacation in recognition of my delayed exit and the workload of the past eighteen months, and that each board member commit to ensure that I am not called while I am away. It means they have to take responsibility for the church on their own, with no minister. My colleague has left and the new half-time person we have found will not start their short-term contract until September when I get back. They agree. By the time the difficult-to-write but important letter is complete, I feel like I am going to explode from the pressure that has been slowly building inside of me. It is now at boiling point.

After I take the final letter to the church, I call Alan at work to ask him if he is willing to take our trailer out to the provincial park for me that night. I desperately need to get away.

For the next nine days I am completely alone. I do not listen to music. I do not read books. I barely think. I talk to no one. I allow myself to merge with the forest beside my campsite. It isn't until the fifth day that I even walk down the trail to be nourished by the lake. I simply sit in the campsite, barely moving, staring into the trees, allowing time for my depleted stores of energy to connect to the source of love's power in order to be refilled.

As the days unfold, the power at my core has the opportunity to be charged. In this time of healing solitude I become aware that during the past many months, in the midst of the crashing and rumbling that felt as disruptive as an earthquake, there has been a sense of wholeness that never completely left me. Now with my power reserves topped up, the wholeness within me is again filling the landscape of my soul rather than being diminished to a tiny still point in the middle of chaos.

By the time I return to the church that fall, I am ready to develop a relationship with the new part-time person who will take care of some of the ministerial tasks. He is a gift as he supports the work, and me, as I continue to heal from the impact of the last two years.

IN THE SUMMER OF 2005, five years after Mom and her new husband's relationship begins, her husband ends up in the hospital for an extended stay. He's already had several heart surgeries. It is determined that he will need to be in a nursing home when he leaves the hospital. He and Mom decide it will be best to find a place for each of them in the community where we live, so Mom can be close to me.

However, Mom's husband dies unexpectedly in August while he is still in hospital.

Mom is coping well. She is good the day of the annual family reunion that she hosts each year. We meet at her home on the lake. Part way through the afternoon we gather around the pond on the lawn for a celebration of life service that I conduct for her husband. All day long Mom is welcoming and hospitable.

Mom is good when she decides she will still move. She is good as we pick out her new condo that is right around the corner from us. She is good while she sells the house on the lake, including all the furniture, because the buyers love what she had chosen. She thinks it will be fun to buy new furniture for her new home. She is good as we go from place to place to place to choose custom furniture. She is right; it *is* fun. We have a delightful time together. She is good when we pick out four shades of moss green for her condo to match the quilt her husband asked me to choose for her birthday earlier that year. She is good while we choose her new kitchen and all the new ceiling lights for the house and all the new flooring. She is good in the week leading up to moving out of her home. She is good on Friday, October 28 when I speak with her before heading out to lead a retreat for the weekend. She is good until the morning of Sunday, October 30, when she is leaving the house she has lived in with her third husband to move to the community where I live.

She calls me at 6:00 a.m. that morning. I am in her area leading the weekend leadership retreat. Plans are in place for me to meet her so we can travel to my home in a convoy. At some point during our 6 a.m. to 8:30 a.m. phone call Mom begins to splinter. She crumbles as I listen.

I don't know how to describe it. It feels like she is disintegrating. She speaks of audio hallucinations. She tells me about jewellery that has been lost showing up that morning. She weeps and sobs and declares she does not feel she will be capable of driving later that day. I tell her I will make alternative arrangements.

I don't realize at the time but later I understand that a completely new and different personality is emerging in the face of this change in her life. It takes a while to be able to fully see the new personality, although at the time I think of it as a manifestation of a mood or a state.

Her physical deterioration is the most obvious aspect of the splintering. By December 4, thirty-five days after she moves, when Mom goes to the church to see me conduct my first of five interviews with Canadian icon Gordon Lightfoot, she can no longer walk on her own.[9] She needs a wheelchair in order to get around in public places.

By early November Alan is almost carrying Mom up and down the stairs in our home as he provides support for her. I sit with her to feed her tiny morsels of food to tempt her nonexistent appetite. We focus on getting her condo ready that is just around the corner from our home. It is a big job. The whole condo needs updating. Walls are coming down in several places and a new kitchen is being installed. There is new flooring to put in everywhere. Her new furniture is being custom made, with twists and changes in the schedule of its arrival. Mom lives with us for seven weeks while the work is being done, which is four weeks longer than anticipated.

---

[9] For an article by me about one of my interviews with Gordon search https://broadview.org Gordon Lightfoot

During this time, it is confirmed for me that the behaviour of slurring words and incoherent thoughts, which some of the family have presumed to be a sign of her drinking heavily over the years, happens even when alcohol is not consumed. This continues to be my experience during the final years of Mom's life—such behaviours are not necessarily indicative of her drinking.

By the new year, a new personality, who is extremely focused on and obsessive about the minute details of an already overly organized life, becomes the primary way that Mom engages the world. I now refer to this personality as the Mundane Organizer. Intermingled with this demanding, and what I experience as boring, way of interacting is the suicidal personality who regularly shows up declaring her life is not worth living.

The emergence of this new personality of the Mundane Organizer provides Mom with a strengthened resolve. By the time her condo is ready she is getting around with greater ease and is back to eating. When she moves into her new home she immediately launches into an intensive time of setting up. Her home must be set up in a very particular way, so she does not want us to help other than to lug boxes around. Mom has had glaucoma for years. She is concerned that the time will come when she will be blind, so everything in her house has to be organized in preparation for that possibility. All drawers are lined with an amazing product that ensures nothing will slide out of place. She needs to know exactly where to find something even if she has her eyes closed. Then she'll know she will be able to cope if she goes blind.

The first time I realize how much the glaucoma impacts Mom is when we are in Israel in 1999. We are going through the Children's Memorial at the Holocaust Remembrance Center. It is painfully stark. To walk through this museum in Israel that honours all the children who died in the death camps is a gut-wrenching experience.

Mom is walking behind me and grabs at my arm, clutching at me repeatedly. I'm annoyed. I want to focus on this experience. When we get out she tells me she couldn't see anything, saying it was like there was a thick fog that was so dense she couldn't even see me in front of her. I feel horrible that I felt annoyed. I had no idea that dim light was so difficult for her.

The last time that Mom and I go to our favourite spa we cannot stay in the parlour of the original house like we usually do because the hallways at that end of the complex are dark with periodic splashes of natural light. The combination of darkness and light means Mom loses all sense of depth perception and ability to navigate. We choose a room in the new building where the light is constant. It means Mom can manage to get from our room down the elevator to the waiting room for her spa treatments. If she wants to go anywhere else I need to help her.

The fear of becoming blind adds to Mom's lifelong commitment to keep an organized home. Even though she is living with constant pain from the back injury in earlier years and the fibromyalgia she is diagnosed with recently, Mom manages to get an incredible amount of work accomplished in a day while still leaving time for the mystery novels she devours and the crossword puzzles she does daily to keep her mind alert.

Periodically a thin veneer of the "real Mom" emerges to spend time with me, but it is once again rare. Glimpses of the "real Mom" do show up in her interactions with my daughter Sarah, with my sister Betsy, with members of the Liberal Party for whom she is an incredible phone volunteer. She also shows up when she is fulfilling her task of being a pastoral care provider for the church, in her ministry of hospitality at the welcoming table in the atrium each Sunday, and when she is on duty with the social service team at the church to respond to some of the most vulnerable people in our community.

As minister of the church I actually have to remove Mom from the social service team because I find out she is going way overboard to provide help for people. One time she invites a couple to her home to give them supplies for their new place from her own cupboards.

This is an example of Mom's generosity, her horror at injustice, and her commitment to care for people. But when she loans someone several hundred dollars who will never be able to pay her back because he uses the money on his addiction rather than rent, I redirect her attention to people who need emotional rather than physical support. She becomes pastoral care caller extraordinaire.

She is delighted on the day she becomes an official member of the church. It has been many years since she has had an active membership in a United Church congregation. The times she is active in a church since Dad's death are in the Catholic Church with her second husband. When her picture is taken before the service she insists I be in it with her, which will be odd in the photo directory since it is supposed to be a picture of the new member. It's the best picture of the two of us during those years. I use my half of it as my professional picture for years.

During the service I officially introduce Mom to the congregation as a member, just as I have introduced four other people. Normally at that moment the congregation applauds to welcome the new member and then the new member goes to sit down. Not so with Mom. Mom requests that I give her my mic. It's attached to my ears, so it's difficult to share. When I realize that this is not going to deter her from speaking to the congregation I lean in and turn the mic toward her.

Mom is delightful in her spontaneous speech. She affirms both the congregation and their amazing minister. I feel slightly embarrassed by her public affirmation of me. I thank her and invite her to sit. The congregation applauds again as she returns to her seat. I shake my head with the surprise of her unexpected comments and smile at the way she sometimes engages life with a startling boldness.

The spring after moving, Mom becomes the chair of the management board of the building where she lives. She accomplishes many of the same tasks that she did at the high-rise in Toronto when she was in a similar position there; all the hallway carpets are replaced and walls painted, security is increased, beautiful plants fill the entryway, though here they are gorgeous silk ones since she doesn't have the capacity to care for live plants. She also plans a multitude of social events to create a sense of community. I am aware of every event because I make the posters.

However, before long she decides she doesn't want to cope with what she experiences as the narrow-minded attitudes of the people who live in the building. She completes her term, resigns from the board and rarely attends the events she initiated.

She does, however, become caregiver to the woman down the hall who is struggling with the early stages of dementia. The woman is extremely lonely and lacks the ability to feed herself properly. Mom somewhat likes the company of her neighbour, but she is annoyed that she is the one who has to take care of her. I suggest that she not take care of her and leave it to the woman's family. Mom is horrified because the woman's family comes so rarely. To Mom it is not acceptable to leave someone without good ongoing support.

ON A PERSONAL DAY-TO-DAY LEVEL, many of Mom's and my interactions over the next six years are filled with organizational details and demands to attend to Mom's needs. She regularly extends invitations for us to gather as family at her home. At the gatherings she is often not able to carry on a conversation, let alone follow through with the preparations she has planned. Alan, Sarah and I pitch in and engage with her while we take care of tasks, hoping we can elicit the part of her that has a good sense of humour and loves to be playful. It doesn't always work, but it makes us feel better to try to get her fun side to emerge, rather than resign ourselves to being consumed by what feels like a shattered atmosphere.

Along with caring for Mom and my family, I engage in activities associated with my work for somewhere around sixty hours a week. Some of the hours are done after my family goes to bed at night or before they get up in the morning so that I can spend as much time with them as possible. I love that some of my work has flexible hours that allow me to be available at odd times of the day to attend the sports events or theatrical productions our daughters are involved in. I spend most of my Fridays, my day off, responding to the details of Mom's life. I try to arrange for our regular daily calls to happen at a time when my family does not need my attention.

I often find myself telling Mom things like, "No, I am not going to make sure your one hundred and eighty-three emails in your inbox are all properly saved and put in folders when I have over twenty thousand emails in my inbox that I have no time to clear out." We laugh together a lot. We also argue, particularly when she demands that I do unreasonable things like read all the mail that is delivered to her home, even when it is advertising. I tell her I receive the same things and just throw them out. She does not agree and requests that I read the material before throwing it away. I read her highlights before I toss every single one of the letters into the recycle bin. However, that is better than having to deal with her being anxious about something she thinks she needs to do, which is what happens when she reads the advertising on her own.

We spend an enormous amount of time preparing lists of what she wants to happen to all her things when she dies. We go over all her contact information to make sure I will know what I am doing when the time comes to be one of her executors. I've never seen someone so organized. I feel my sister and I are quite capable of opening the designated box that contains every last detail we could possibly need. But she insists we keep having the conversation. I regularly distract her with questions that prompt her to tell me more stories of her life or the things she has learned as a voracious reader. It keeps our times together from spiralling into complete boredom.

Mom arranges for Alan to replace her much-loved handyman from her last community. Most of what Alan does he does as a member of the family rather than as her employee. He lets her pay him for larger tasks to satisfy her desire to pay her way, but he refuses to take anything, except maybe a beer, for the day-to-day support she needs.

Mom phones Alan at work, often several times a day. He suggests she make a list so he can come up regularly and take care of everything. But she can't manage to make a list and wait for his arrival. All her needs are immediate. Alan, Sarah and I each go up to the condo a couple times a week to bring things she has asked for, to open jars, or to help her accomplish something. But once we arrive, she often slips into a personality who just wants company and so will distract us from getting the task done. But then, when the Mundane Organizer personality shows up the next morning, the need once again becomes immediate.

I have heard stories from Alan that more than once, after he has gone up to Mom's condo to do something like take up salt for her water softener, she calls him at work the next day and says things like,

"I had some bags of salt brought up yesterday for my water softener, so now I need you to come to fill it."

Alan calmly reminds her, "Mom, I am the one who brought up the salt, and I have filled your water softener, so you are set to go." At the time we do not know we are dealing with different personalities.

The cycle is tiring. In the midst of the demanding cycle, Sarah and I take up prepared meals, knowing that no matter Mom's mood she needs to eat.

We try to keep a good balance between Mom's need for organization and the desire to hang out together. At one point Alan and I arrange to spend a specific evening with her every week just to visit. We quickly discover that doesn't work because it depends on which personality is present as to whether she wants company at all, since not all personalities are as sociable as others.

And so we go back to the pattern of Alan going several times a week, with Sarah and me running in with groceries, dinner, beer or books throughout the week. Each of us stays to visit if that is what she wants and we have the time.

In our multiple calls throughout the day, Mom often whines in frustration that she has no sense of purpose. Sometimes we can strategize about what she wants to do, but the pain in her body significantly limits what she is able to do. Together we try to find ways that she can still make a difference without putting too many demands on her body.

Other times, depending on the personality, I find myself getting stern when she says she has nothing to live for. I remind her that she can choose to focus on what she can do, rather than on what she can't. When I don't wallow with her she seems to shift out of that mode sooner.

There are days when her greatest passion is to ensure that her family knows all the medical information that we might need. The details include both hers and Dad's, which is one of the things that confirms for me that she was not aware of the extra biological father in the family. In these moments it is the new personality of the Mundane Organizer who is present.

Over the years, in the midst of our daily conversations, I learn skills about how to encourage dialogue that includes greater dimensions. My skills develop when I decide that it would be good to have conversations in which Mom and I have back-and-forth dialogue rather than a one-sided exchange, so that we can be mutually supportive of each other.

To develop the pattern I start to insert things into our conversation about what is happening in my day. At first I feel like I am pushing them into our conversations like a wedge as I try to create space, but in time we develop a healthy rhythm that begins with her sharing, usually followed by some time for me to share. We both develop our skills of listening by holding space for each other and honouring the concept of "no fixing" unless we have been asked for help. These skills become core principles and practices to create Intentional Circles.

―――――――――――――――

In March of 2006, Mom invites Betsy's family and my family to spend the weekend as her guest at an inn. There is a spa and a huge indoor games area for all ages. The state Mom is in when we arrive does not bode well for the weekend. Alan describes it as Mom being a basket case. In mechanical terms, if a piece of equipment comes to the shop as a basket case it means all the pieces are broken apart so need to be carried in a basket. It feels like Mom is broken apart. I decide that with so many other family members around, perhaps it is a good time for me to book a number of spa treatments. And so I do.

Dinner on Saturday night is planned as a surprise birthday celebration for my fiftieth birthday. It is such a wonderful gesture. But in the midst of it, Mom is really struggling. She tries to ground herself by getting one person to have an in-depth conversation with her. This is often Mom's strategy in a group when she is not receiving the attention she needs. She withdraws from the group and focuses intensely on one person, whether they want to be part of the group conversation or not.

I remember former Moderator of The United Church of Canada, Walter Farquharson, sharing an insight into the way different people like to engage with others. Over dinner one night he told me about a workshop that he did with his wife.

They tell the group that there are three styles of engaging in a group. Some people like to be part of a conversation with the whole group. Some people like to be in a conversation one on one with another person. Some people like to be alone in a crowd.

They ask everyone at the workshop who prefers to be alone in a crowd to go into the sanctuary. Some individuals get up and wander to the sanctuary. When you look in the sanctuary, each person is in a different area checking out the things around them or sitting quietly alone.

Then they invite everyone who likes to talk in pairs to go to the library. A group of people get up and walk in pairs toward the library. When you look in the room, you see people in pairs turned toward each other, chatting with lots of energy.

Then they ask if everyone left in the circle likes to be in a group conversation. Everyone nods. The conversation begins. One woman almost immediately starts to try to talk to the person beside her. The group protests, saying she belongs in the pair room. She denies it. The conversation continues. Before long she turns to the person on her other side to make a comment. The group declares that she really is a pair person. She gets up and heads to the library. My awareness is that when she arrives everyone else is already in pairs so her preference will not be responded to in that room either.

The awareness of different preferences for engaging in a group helps me understand people better. When I lead groups I make sure I provide some time to work alone through journalling or meditation, and some time to talk in pairs so that those who have a preference for those styles have their longing satisfied enough that they can participate in a group conversation when the time comes.

We can all move in and out of the different preferences. At times we will have different preferences in different situations or moments of our lives.

What I realize about Mom is that she continuously provides me with learning about the different styles since her personalities each have their own preferred way of engaging. For example, there are two personalities who don't function well when they don't get enough one on one conversation, the Flirty One and the Suicidal One. When she is in those personalities, she tries to withdraw someone from the group conversation in order to have a one on one interaction. Since my most natural preferred style is to be part of a group conversation, I always feel like I am being rude when I am the one Mom tries to talk to without the others.

During dinner at the inn on the night she has planned the surprise celebration for my birthday, Mom begins to fall apart. She shifts into a dramatic personality filled with sighs and the need for assurance that she is of value. Betsy and I leave with her so others can stay and enjoy their dessert.

When we get her back to her room, Mom curls up on her bed and starts to wail that she just wants to die because she has no purpose in life. I speak with her firmly, pointing out all the things she does have to live for, including the family all around her for whom she has created this weekend.

Fifteen minutes in, Betsy gets up and declares, "This is ridiculous." She leaves the room.

I wonder if Betsy leaves because of Mom's behaviour or because she thinks what I am doing to try to shift Mom is ridiculous. Whichever it is, within two years I start to think it is ridiculous to sit and try to converse with Mom in this state. That night I stay, not knowing what else to do.

I have experiences with a person who often speaks of suicide in my professional work. My colleagues help me to gain a sense of detachment that gives me clarity as to how to respond in ways that do not enmesh me in the person's feelings of being a victim, so that I can help the person realize they have choices.

From the time I am fifteen until I am fifty, I can't find that kind of detachment capacity within me in relation to Mom.

I am, however, clear about what to say to Mom when she talks about feeling like she does not get enough affirmation from the world around her, which is another common complaint that feels like a demand. It frustrates me when she and other women of her generation expect external validation rather than trusting their inner value. Being taught that it is appropriate to have an expectation of, or desire for, external validation is a significant way people learn to ignore their inner awareness of their own value.

In working with the "three concentric circles" concept, which includes both the authentic self and external expectations, I develop an awareness of the need to shift away from seeking external approval in order to move toward knowing within ourselves that we are of value. When we seek external approval and when we focus on needing to be empowered by something outside of us, it diminishes our capacity to know and affirm our own goodness.

I appreciate how the practice of the Daily Examen from Ignatian Spirituality helps me to listen to my inner awareness. It shows me my strengths and value rather than demanding that others identify my worth from an external perspective.

I recall using the Daily Examen practice on a day years ago when I am judging myself harshly. I have been a bear to everyone I engage that day. By the end of the day, I am ravaged with guilt, certain that negativity has consumed the day. When I ask for the grace to see my day through the eyes of love, which is the first step of the Daily Examen practice, I am taken to a moment that lasts less than two minutes. I see myself with Marissa. I am changing her diaper. I pause in the midst of the crazy demands of the day and focus totally on her, tickling her belly, looking deep into her eyes and telling her I love her. By the end of the day, I have forgotten that precious moment. I am too consumed by guilt about all that I did not handle well to remember that moment of grace. It feels like a blessing when that moment is brought to my attention through the Daily Examen prayer. It reminds me of actions I can expand and repeat to ensure that the way of love is woven into my days.

I often find myself reminding Mom, like I did that night at the inn, that her power does not come from external affirmations but rather from a deep inner knowing rooted in her authenticity. It has the capacity to bring her peace through acceptance of herself, rather than ensnaring her in a destructive pattern of judgment based on what she thinks she "should" do.

I sit with Mom for another forty-five minutes after my sister leaves that night at the inn. Mom finally exhausts herself with her wailing and falls asleep.

By the time I return to my birthday party the dining room is empty.

Life continues to unfold with good days and bad days with Mom, with moments of shared laughter that delight me and with times of feeling overwhelmed by her demands and needs.

IN FEBRUARY OF 2007, in her sixth week of a vacation in Florida, Mom is not doing well. She has an abscessed tooth and has been given pain medication. One of Janis's daughters has been staying with her, but she and Janis think Mom needs more support. Me.

As I prepare to go to be with Mom, my friend, who is also the church administrator, asks me if I will take this time to write my book.

I am surprised. "My book? I didn't know I have a book to write."

Three others hear the suggestion and agree it is time.

When I arrive in Florida Janis drives me the three hours from the airport to where Mom is staying. On the way I tell her about this encouragement to write my book. She agrees.

I'm puzzled about the focus of this book which people are clear I am to write. Janis encourages me to write about what I have learned through my life and my work that holds the potential of being of interest to other ministers. I decide I will buy a notebook, put pen to paper and see what emerges.

I'm glad I have this idea of writing a book to give focus to my days. Mom functions better when there is a schedule and a purpose to each day. My desire to go to the beach to write provides her with the opportunity to take care of me by making a picnic lunch and to encourage me in the project. Helping me makes her feel more settled. While I am gone for six hours of writing each day Mom has time to rest so that the two of us can share dinner. The extra rest makes a difference in her recovery from the medications.

Each day I go and sit by the ocean. I have two chairs, one to sit on and one for my feet, plus an umbrella, a small cooler that acts as a table, a large selection of food and two empty notebooks with pens.

The first story I write is about the experience in the meadow when I am three years old when I see light coming from within everything and everyone.

The stories and poetry I write on the beach and for months after, reflect a peak time when my insights about creating healthy community, encouraging people's gifts, and guiding people to see the seeds of wisdom they carry within them burst open like blossoms, filling the garden of my life with beauty, colour and diversity.

I realize that what I am writing is a handbook of stories and poetry that provides practical insights, attitudes and approaches to creating life-giving community and how to be open to the transformative energies that are so desperately needed in our world. This is my favourite poem:

> The Poetry of the Cosmos
>> sings deep in our soul
>
> listen … listen …
> it is waiting to be heard …
>> awakened in stillness
>> carried on the breeze in the trees
>> heard in the songs of the birds
>>> and in the sound of laughter shared
>
> The Poetry of the Cosmos
>> twirls in our midst
>>> calling us to life and laughter and play
> inviting us into a dance of joy
>> beyond the ego borders
>>> that limit and sever connection
>>>> by the power of fear
>
> The Poetry of the Cosmos
>> beckons us to trust and delight

in this world of awe-filling experiences
that continuously present themselves
if we are open to see

The Poetry of the Cosmos
connects to the song of our hearts
and weaves together the passions of our souls
to create a tapestry filled with boldness
of colours and textures, shapes and intricacies
that are beyond the limitations
we place on our imaginings

The Poetry of the Cosmos
is all around us and deep within us

listen … listen …
and let it lead us in a joyful dance
into life filled with the abundance of
resources shared
creation honoured
each one known to be loved
and wholeness lived

The Poetry of the Cosmos
is amongst us
standing on the tiptoe of anticipation
for the moment of our awakening.

The poetry I write during this time in my life feels like a balm to my sometimes ravaged soul. A second poem from that winter's warm retreat:

Cracks of brilliance
splinter through the trees
radiating the world with light

wind gently moves through the leaves
waves lap upon the shore
a day filled with translucence
a day filled with awe-inspiring beauty
a day that holds the potential
of shared laughter
new insight
profound connection
joy and sorrow
infused with possibilities

Will we notice?
Will we allow ourselves to be engaged
or will this day dwindle away
unnoticed in its beauty
endured and tolerated
as a different day
is awaited with impatience
that day when there's enough money
to buy the toys presumed
to be needed for happiness
when the people we detest
are gone from our everyday lives
when we have the control
we seek and strive for

Shallow days
of waiting with impatience and anger
while days of accumulated
richness and beauty
go by unnoticed.

Later in 2007, just before our extended family gathers for Christmas dinner, Mom completely falls apart. She has reached a crisis point and for a short period of time exhibits some of the deepest despair I have ever heard her express.

I speak with her on the phone to make plans for her to come over for Christmas dinner. She begs me to come be with her even though she knows the extended family is arriving at our home any moment. I talk to her for as long as I can. She speaks yet again about having no life purpose. I suggest that maybe she start thinking about a trip to Africa.

When she hears my suggestion to refocus on something she has been interested in for a long time, she shifts out of the despair and immediately goes to a high. She is totally excited about going to Africa. She kidded about going to Africa all through our growing-up years. When the phone rang during her active volunteer years in the late 1970s, she asked us to take a message and tell whoever is calling that she has gone to Africa. She laughs with delight at this possibility she never imagined would happen.

We get off the phone. Marissa, who still lives at home, goes to pick up Mom. Marissa's presence shifts Mom to an even higher state of excitement.

Betsy and Mark, who don't have the opportunity to spend much face-to-face time with Mom, notice that she doesn't seem like herself; they describe her as spacey and down. It is interesting to hear their perspective because to me she is functioning better than she has since moving here in 2005. The excitement of the trip to Africa is causing her to be more engaged than she has been in months.

To keep Mom focused on something positive over the next few months we have a great time making all the arrangements for the two of us to go to South Africa in January 2009 for twenty-five days.

In January 2008, Mom goes to Janis's home in Florida. When I talk to Mom on the phone I think she is sounding better than she has in a long time. I wonder if the sunshine is helping. However, Janis tells me that Mom can never come to her home again without me because she can't cope with Mom on her own.

It is interesting to hear the assessment of my siblings as to how Mom is doing. I realize I am probably too close to the situation to be able to properly assess her. I went through such a difficult time with her for those seven weeks when she first moved away from her home on the lake to come live here in our community. I wonder if I have lost perspective on how much she has deteriorated in the past few years. Compared to those early months, she is doing well. Compared to when others saw her last, she has diminished capacities.

IN AUGUST OF 2008, LIFE SHIFTS AGAIN.

In late August I spend a day with Mom at her condo to collect information for the surgery she is to undergo to remove the cancer spots from her face. I asked the doctor about using an alternative method to putting her to sleep since she doesn't do well with anesthetic.

As we sit at her dining table looking at the glorious tree out her fourth-storey window, we have the most amazing conversation. Mom is totally clear that day. Her presence is more grounded and even less attached to small-ego self than the one we call the "real Mom." It is a euphoric experience for me. It is like I am talking to the eternal part of Mom where only love resides. She is kind and attentive and speaks in a tone that holds no edges. At the time I interpret her presence to be that of our "real Mom."

In looking back I realize that this is a good example of the personality I call the Angelic Presence. It is in this conversation that all my support of Mom over the years takes on a whole new understanding. As I collect medical information from her about her reactions to medications, she tells me she has never been suicidal in her life. I am absolutely stunned. She is insistent. She has no memories of the kinds of experiences that I am describing to her of being so distraught that she speaks about wanting to die.

She smiles at me lovingly. She tells me that, if she ever has such an episode in her life again, I have her permission to record it so that I can show her what she doesn't remember. But she can't imagine ever feeling that way.

Up to this point in our life, no one in the family realizes that Mom does not have memories of the bizarre realities that we experience.

In that moment I decide that I will never again allow myself to be fully engaged when Mom is suicidal. I will connect her with help in the community at an organization where I have helped train the volunteers, but I won't personally engage her in the times of suicidal distress. If Mom doesn't remember all that I have done all these years then I am simply not going to do it anymore. It intrigues me that after I stop engaging with the extreme part of the suicidal personality, she rarely appears. A groan of anguish arises in me when I acknowledge a lesson I have known for years: depriving a situation of energy can stop it from growing. This awareness is a critical aspect of what Mom teaches me about wholeness: focus on whatever it is that you want to grow; don't focus on what you don't want to grow.

I learn from Mom how to shift focus to give attention to the ways she is functioning well rather than the difficult moments. This is how I engage with my kids and grandkids: I focus on what is good and shift people away from inappropriate behaviours, without making a big fuss about what I do not want to encourage. I also use this approach in my ministry by asking people to identify the things that inspire and excite them so they can choose to pour their energy into what they want to grow.

If it is true that Mom's suicidal tendencies show up less when they do not get attention, I wonder … how do we deal with the issues of the world without adding our energy to the situations we do not want to grow? That thought is often on my mind when I see us give politicians, wealthy people and people of influence attention for inappropriate behaviour. Are we exacerbating a situation we actually hope will stop?

Becoming aware of the fact that Mom does not have memories of some of the most difficult times of her life nudges me to wonder what might be going on in Mom's life. Leaving her to make significant choices in her life when she does not know all the details of her life becomes a concern that sits at the back of my mind. Of course, in 2010 I learn that not having full memories has been the reality for her entire life. I also learn that the host personality has been there to pass on required information, although in looking back I realize she seems to provide less information for the Angelic Presence since the host personality is on respite time when she is present. At the time, in 2008, all I know is there are gaps in Mom's memory of significant moments of her life.

In late August 2008, a member of our extended family asks us to gather information about anyone in our family who has exhibited signs of mental illness or is known for strange behaviour. The information is required to help with a possible diagnosis of bipolar. While we gather information, my siblings and I begin to wonder if perhaps Mom exhibits the symptoms of rapid cycling bipolar disorder.

Janis, Mark, Betsy and I write to Mom's doctor to share our observations, questions and experiences of Mom, along with our hope that there may be something to help Mom. I gather everyone's thoughts to write a combined report.

In rereading the report now, I am shocked that in 2008 we do not consider that dissociative identity disorder might fit what we have experienced with Mom throughout our lives.

As I am preparing the letter for her doctor, Mom contacts me to say she is in severe pain. I call an ambulance. I travel with her in the ambulance to the hospital. Mom continues to be in the state of clarity that I refer to as the Angelic Presence. The hospital staff responds to her with great concern and care. I watch her engage with each person who enters her cubicle in a manner that focuses on them with kindness. We have more than one doctor taking care of her as they intently seek to figure out the source of her pain. Mom stays calm and is extremely helpful as she engages with the staff.

Mom is diagnosed with an obstructed bowel, and admitted to the hospital.

After telling the emergency room doctor, in front of Mom, about our concern that she might be dealing with some undiagnosed mental illness, I deliver the letter my siblings and I have written to her doctor. We hope the medical community might be able to respond to our concern that she may be experiencing the impact of rapid cycling bipolar while Mom is in hospital. It is a long letter detailing all the circumstances that lead us to express the concern that Mom may have a mental illness for which we hope there could be medical help.

Below are excerpts from the letter we give to the doctor. I have included the emails from my siblings because they are primary sources about the story of our Mom, written from perspectives that are different from mine. My stories in that letter are already documented in this story.

In the cover letter, I tell the doctor that first we want to note that our mother is a much-loved woman in the wider community. We tell him that people speak of her with great enthusiasm because of all her energy and positive outlook. As kids we have gone through our lives thinking that the behaviour we will describe is just Mom, justified by the stress or grief or illness she is dealing with at different points in her life. We never consider that there could be something wrong that could be managed with the right medical care. Though many professionals and other adults have seen glimpses of the behaviours we will describe, the full picture has never been put together until now. We share this information with love and with the hope that whatever years she has remaining can be years filled with Mom being our real Mom, who, as the years go on, we experience less and less.

By Mark

September 6, 2008

Karen,

At the age of 56, these are some of my memories of Mom's behaviours:

- In 1955, when we moved out of an apartment to our first house, I was three years old. Mom was very concerned about her image and what people thought of her at that time. I remember Mom and Dad fighting fairly often and sometimes severe arguments. I remember Mom drinking beer every day at that time. I remember Dad working late and going away golfing on the weekends. I remember Mom saying she was sick quite often. I remember having the feeling that Mom was anxious and nervous a lot. I remember her being involved in the PTA and that her status was always important to her. All of this was prior to our aunt's death when we are kids. I also remember Mom always being overly concerned with death, dying and sickness. I remember Dad taking us to church every Sunday and Mom not going very often.

- In the early sixties we have moved to a new suburban home. Mom's status is even more important to her than ever. She still seems to have a preoccupation with death to the point where it begins to scare me.

- When we move to the farm, I am a teenager. I begin spending more time away from home with friends. Mom still seems to be preoccupied with sickness and death, which began after she almost died in August 1956. I was getting to the point where I didn't want to hear it anymore. I began to pull further and further away until I moved out west. Also, drinking was commonplace; she called it having her beer before supper. Dad spent more and more time at work and on the golf course.

As I got older and could understand more, here are some things I noticed from late teen years till now:

- Mom's mood swings increased dramatically over the years. She could be very happy or extremely mean. She could be her "good old self" or she could just be a weeping mass of self-pitying misery. There were four

Moms and I never knew which one to expect when I phoned or visited.

- Her illnesses seemed to increase and I got the feeling she was looking for pity and attention. I began to grow callous towards her.

- Sometimes Mom's behaviour was bizarre: heavy drinking, smoking, swearing, meanness, crazy talking. The next day there would be no indication that she realized she had done any of these things.

- Mom is extremely adept at covering up these types of behaviours.

- One time Mom came to visit with plans to spend time with her grandkids. After she had been with us for less than half the time, we arranged for her husband to come and get her because she couldn't function.

- My wish for Mom has always been that she be content and happy. When she married her second husband, she seemed more interested in his business title and social position than him. After her second husband died, I hoped she would find peace, but she ran off with her third husband. After he died, I hoped again she would find peace, but she hasn't.

- In October 2007, I went to visit her for three days. During that time I saw incredible mood swings. One minute she was going to buy a new car, the next minute she was crying and saying how much she hated God for causing all these problems in her life. She fell on the floor and would not let me help her up. She told me she didn't drink anymore but was drinking most of the time I was there. She told me she loved me and was proud of me, then a little later told me I was lazy, that I didn't try very hard and then asked me if I was happy while I was cleaning up her broken glass of beer off the floor. I became so upset I had to leave and go for a walk. I could not understand why she was the way she was.

- Mom has upset and hurt me so many times over the years that I don't want to take her phone calls anymore and will only talk to her in the early mornings when she seems more like her normal self. I am convinced she has severe emotional problems and has had them as long as I can remember. I love her very much and hope this helps.

By Janis

September 6, 2008

In 1968, our energetic and loving mother became ill, suffering unexplained pain. She stopped cooking, getting dressed and generally spent most of her days crying. I understood that eventually her doctors did exploratory surgery that removed her gallbladder. Her erratic behaviour the year before the surgery was explained as allergies to the pain medication she had been given for the gallbladder pain. It was before the surgery that I remember a particularly bad night where she asked me to stay up until my father came home so that I could insist that he divorce her. She wanted me to tell him that her life was not worth living and she blamed him. My father acted like this was normal behaviour that should be ignored.

After I left home I avoided spending time with Mom as

my presence seemed to bring out her insecurities. She did not develop relationships with my children as they avoided spending time with her. In the early nineties I spent time in the Florida Keys, visiting my mother on the way there and on the way home. She was physically ill during the first visit and could barely maintain a conversation. So on the way back I phoned ahead a few minutes before I was due to arrive to make sure she was well and expecting a visit from us. She sounded fine on the phone, so we went to her home expecting lunch and a visit.

We arrived and there was no answer at the door, but it was open and so we let ourselves in. My mother was on the floor sobbing and crying that her husband had left her. She was unintelligible and seemed unaware of her surroundings and was talking about suicide. I waited until her husband came home and then called after I got home. When I couldn't reach her for twenty-four hours I called the police and asked them to check on her. She was fine, just hadn't wanted to talk to me.

These behaviours are routine for family members and in sharp contrast to the public face of our Mom. She can be energetic and kind and caring to others. People usually love her and enjoy her company. So I was surprised when my in-law children came to me after spending time with her last New Year's and told me they thought she was emotionally disturbed and needed help. It was at this point that my sisters and I stopped making excuses for her actions and began looking for answers.

I appreciate any help that can be given to my mother as

she is suffering and I would like to see her enjoy a sense of peace that she has not ever had in her life.

Betsy sends me an email as well. In it she shares that she has experienced Mom as depressed and disoriented at times and that when she is in these states she is not able to communicate clearly. She observes that Mom can be impulsive about life-changing decisions. She notes that she supports what I am doing to try to help Mom and thanks me for being there for her.

The doctor responds to our concern by putting Mom on a medication to see if it will make a difference. It does! It is amazing. We have our "real Mom!" She is delightful, engaging, caring and filled with fun. Janis has a memory of a particular conversation with Mom during this time when Mom tells her she has no memories of the different incidences we describe in the letter to the doctor. All four of Mom's children make sure we contact her as often as possible because we enjoy having her present. It is great! Even though Mom is having awful bouts of vomiting and diarrhea, which often are the outcome of her taking medicine, she is coping well and enjoying the time with her children.

It is during this time that Mom tells me she is sad to hear the stories of what we have gone through all our lives with this disruptive reality she cannot remember. She expresses particular anguish when she learns that her last husband and I once spoke about her odd behaviour. Her agitation comes from the fact that she always thought the two of them had no secrets and so she can't imagine him not telling her. When I tell her she was part of the conversation when we discussed her odd behaviour, she becomes very quiet.

After five weeks, the ethereal experience of connecting to Mom begins to dissipate. Her anger erupts—an anger directed at me for saying whatever it was I said that prompted the doctor to put her on the medicine that is creating such a negative reaction in her. With much sadness I agree that the choice to take or not take the medicine is hers.

She doesn't know what we are losing. She wants to feel physically better, which I understand. The reaction has been quite horrific. She stops taking the medicine. Life returns to what has been our normal.

In looking back at that experience in the fall of 2008, a new perspective emerges as I write this book. I now realize that when Mom first went on the medication she was in the personality of the Angelic Presence. This is a personality who is totally clear and connected to the core of love within her. When she makes an appearance in our lives she tends to stay around for a fairly solid period of time. I now wonder if our sense of having our "real Mom" present wasn't the result of the medication at all, but rather the result of the delightful personality of the Angelic Presence staying with us for the month.

This explanation of the month being filled with encounters with the Angelic Presence seems more likely in my mind than the medicine having a positive impact. Mom had immediate negative physical responses to the medication. She coped with them in the beginning, which is an odd thing for our "real Mom" to do. Mom usually won't continue a medication that makes her ill. Plus, I can't imagine that the medicine had much of a chance to make a difference since her body immediately rejected it.

I now suspect that after a month of vomiting and diarrhea the raging banshee part of the Aggressive One intruded, declaring with ferocious anger "ENOUGH," no matter how much the Angelic Presence is willing to tolerate the physical discomfort.

By OCTOBER 30, 2008, on her third anniversary of moving to the community where I live, Mom is again living predominately out of the new personality that formed during the first weeks of living here. The adventure to South Africa planned for early 2009 is cancelled for medical reasons. Life settles back into the tedious and demanding rhythm of helping Mom care for herself while savouring the odd conversation that is funny or supportive or filled with glimpses of possibilities.

In the midst of the reality of life with Mom I make sure that our conversations include memories and descriptions of the gift of who Mom is: teacher, volunteer, caregiver, engager of young children, supporter of others. I don't want those memories to fade into oblivion for her or for me.

There are times when Mom gets mad at me when she thinks I'm saying I know what is best for her. It's strange because I am careful not to offer solutions to her; I play the part of sounding board so she can solve her own problems. However, with deeper awareness of the complexities within Mom, I now think it was hard on her for me to remind her of things she previously said about a topic. Earlier comments may have come from a different personality than the one currently engaging in the conversation. I now wonder if my reminders of what she said earlier seemed to her like an opinion coming from me rather than an earlier opinion that was her own.

Perhaps this sounds convoluted, but it actually brings clarity to me about what might have been going on when Mom would get mad at me for not listening to her perspective. One of the greatest skills Mom hones in me is to listen and to remember what has been said so that we can link all the ideas together. In my mind, I am trying to link all of Mom's perspectives together—another skill that I learn from Mom that

I use extensively in my work as a facilitator of significant conversations. I now realize that it seemed to her like I was not hearing what she was saying in that moment from the perspective of that personality. Of course, at this stage I am not yet aware that she has different personalities and neither is she. What I remember is feeling confused by her aggressive attitude when she'd get mad at me for thinking I know what's best for her life.

It is amazing the way perception provides such different understandings of what is happening in the midst of the moments of life. It's why I believe we have to learn to not project our interpretations or expectations onto someone else. Our interpretations and expectations can leave us in a constant state of judgment toward one another rather than being curious and savouring the gift of the richness of a multitude of perspectives. We need to be aware of our own worldview, so that we can be open to the worldview of others.

Mom judges me as bossy, while my perception is that I am trying to be helpful. The different perspectives she has identified on a topic are often divergent; I feel a sense of responsibility to remind her of those other thoughts so she doesn't make a decision that she will regret later. Mom has a history of quick decisions that have lingering negative impacts. Even so, I am intentional about being careful to leave the final decision to her.

However, once our minds begin to chatter with judgment and negative stories about someone, like Mom's did about me, it takes intentional effort to not use that lens to judge one another.

In 2007, when I am writing my yet-to-be published first book, I tell the story of a time when I have negative feelings toward three different people. I remember looking at all three people to see if they were reflecting something about me that I don't like. I don't find anything. But then I am awakened in the middle of the night and prompted to take note of a particular book that is beside my bed. I open it and glance through the chapter headings. The title of the seventh chapter jumps out at me. It is about how life mirrors back to us the lessons we need to learn. I turn to the chapter. The second type of lesson we often need to learn emerges from the things we judge negatively in the world. So I reflect on the three people that I have negative feelings toward and ask in a time of meditation to be clear why I judge them harshly. The answer emerges quickly: I negatively judge people when I feel like they are not being team players.

I immediately realize that though being a team player may be a good thing, it is not my place to judge others for not fulfilling my expectation. Once I let go of that judgment I am amazed how all three relationships shift for the better. I am again able to see and experience the gift of each person now that my negative judgmental chatter has been silenced. And in seeing their gifts I am able to affirm the positive seeds that are within them and focus on those as they blossom, rather than smothering that potential with a blanket of negativity. As I observe the process, I am keenly aware that the person who is changed is me, though I suspect that all of us benefit from the shift.

In our daily conversations, Mom and I do have our struggles but they weave in and out of moments of fun and encouragement. Our conversations are filled with her being my strongest cheerleader. I often smile to myself because she regularly expresses anger about the expectations that other people place on me without acknowledging that she has a ton of expectations of things she wants me to do for her.

I share with her stories of the things I am doing. She repeatedly says she thinks I am an amazing person. While it is nice to hear her compliments I am aware from Don Miguel Ruiz's teachings in *The Four Agreements* that we are encouraged not to take things personally, whether they are good or bad.[10] It is important that we not use external affirmations to validate ourselves. I do acknowledge, however, that I struggle to not take these compliments personally; there is a little girl within me who still loves to be told by my Mom that I am doing well.

---

[10] Miguel Ruiz, Don. *The Four Agreements: A Practical Guide to Personal Freedom* (San Rafael, CA: Amber-Allen Publishing, 1997).

Talking about my life during my daily calls to Mom ensures that our conversations are not consumed with her daily needs. Janis and Mark tell me that their conversations with Mom are filled with medical details of her life, with her expressing little or no interest in their life. I refuse to accept that as an appropriate pattern since our conversations happen two or five or seven times a day. We learn a lot about how we can hold space for each other so that we can both share.

In May 2009, Mom will be turning eighty years old. I contact my siblings and we agree to plan a surprise party together for her at my home.

Janis suggests that we have the event catered rather than us doing all the work. She will make that her contribution. I make arrangements to hire staff and rent serving supplies. I am able to get all the contact information for Mom's friends and family from Mom's phonebook. Betsy sends out the invitations. Mark's wife bakes buns. Lynda plans to arrange for a bouquet of balloons to identify the house outside. Sarah and her husband bake and decorate the slab cake large enough to feed eighty. We ask everyone to wear yellow to echo the yellow roses and yellow rose bushes her kids have given her over the years as a sign of love. We arrange for a picture to be taken of each person with Mom. A bouquet of yellow roses is positioned at Mom's shoulder in each picture.

Everyone shows up: new friends from here, friends from the lake, friends from the farm and family from far and wide. Every one of Mom's kids is there and almost every one of her nieces and nephews.

I have invited dignitaries since that sort of thing is important to Mom. The mayor comes and presents her with a certificate celebrating her birthday. Our provincial and federal representatives bring certificates signed by the Premier and the Prime Minister.

And Mom is absolutely amazing! She looks stunning. She is totally present. For the whole party it is our "real Mom" who shows up. She is engaging, funny, interested in other people and delighted by all we have done. She teases people, including the dignitaries who are not Liberals. She tells them she definitely did not vote for them. They laugh with her.

It is truly a great day, a day of celebrating a woman who is worthy of being celebrated.

IN THE SPRING OF 2010, just after the snow has melted, Mom and I go out to run errands on a beautiful sunny day. Each time we arrive at a location, Mom asks for her bundle buggy to carry her items. I realize that she is using the buggy to support her walking. When we get back in the car after our fifth stop, I ask her if she would consider getting a walker. She says the buggy is fine. I acknowledge that is probably true most of the time, but it will look odd for her to walk down the aisle pushing her bundle buggy at the opera house where we are going in a few weeks for a show, even with its lovely peach canvas liner she had made for it. She laughs at the image and agrees that perhaps it is time to get a walker, so long as it is set up so that she can stand up straight. She hates how so many people walk hunched over their walker.

I immediately turn the car around and head to the medical supply store in town. She's delighted and sees it as an unexpected adventure. I have learned from Mom over the years to notice when energy is flowing because that is the time to follow where it is leading. That day it leads us to purchase a walker while Mom is open to the idea.

In July of 2010, I am away for a week at a course led by an organization called Encountering World Religions. I get a call from the hospital to say Mom has been brought in for observation because she fell after being bumped by a car in a parking lot. I shake my head, knowing that she needs to not go out on her own but persists. They tell me she's not too bad, but they want to keep her in for at least a few hours. I call Marissa to see if she can check on Mom. Marissa is not willing to deal with her Grandma, but she is willing to leave work and take over Sarah's daycare centre so Sarah can go to the hospital.

I wander around in the hall outside of the lecture room, waiting impatiently to hear Sarah's assessment of the situation. Just when I've decided I will head home, Sarah and Mom phone. They tell me to stay and finish the course. Sarah will stay with Grandma, and Marissa will stay with the kids. I am comfortable leaving Mom in Sarah's care. She's done so much with Mom, like driving her to specialist appointments in Toronto even when it meant stopping on the side of the highway to feed Sarah's newborn. Sarah knows Mom's quirky ways well. She calls and talks to Mom at least once a day and sees her several times a week. They will be fine.

Although the injury Mom sustains is not severe, from that time on it is clear to all of us that she is not doing well. We encourage Mom to stop driving and take us up on our multitude of offers to chauffeur her where she needs to go or use a taxi or the service in town that provides rides for seniors. Though we drive her to most places, she holds on to the keys of her car for six more months.

Then she suddenly declares that she will only give up her car if I am willing to buy it. We do not need an extra car, but having learned to respond quickly when Mom comes up with a good idea, we agree. We settle on a price. We feel it is high but worth it to get the keys out of Mom's reach. We draw up a plan together to pay for the car over a number of months.

During the fall of 2010 Mom spends a lot of time in her condo. Her mobility and her eyesight are both depleting. She is beginning to talk about feeling a presence with her in the condo. The raging banshee trickster part of the Aggressive One seems to be playing tricks on her quite regularly now. Mom puts things on the hall table in preparation to do errands, but when she returns the items are no longer there. She wanders around until she finds them. It leaves her feeling that she is not alone in her home.

It is during this time that Mom talks about feeling a sense of contact with Dad and her other two husbands. She also describes a moment of seeing a presence in the condo. Though she is alone, she sees someone standing in the doorway to her bedroom in the middle of the night. She gets up. She is disoriented. She falls and lands between the bed and the night table. She presses her alarm button and I am called and told she needs help. I wake Alan. He gets dressed and goes over. He's gone for a long time. He stays to clean up because she didn't make it to the bathroom in time earlier that night. Her stomach and intestines had both been in a state of disruption. This is not the only time Alan cleans up vomit and diarrhea for Mom.

It is in October of 2010 that the incident happens that clarifies for me what we have been dealing with over the years. It is late on an evening in October when Mom morphs through four of her most common personalities, allowing me to realize that I recognize every one. These different personalities have been wandering through my life as long as I can remember. She morphs from the wounded Three-Year-Old who asks why everyone wants to hurt her, to the raging twelve-year-old who hates her Daddy, to the Flirty One who loves her Daddy, to the Suicidal One who just wants to die. The moment ends with a bland voice, leaving me in a state of astonishment. Much later I realize that the bland voice is one of the facets of the host personality. She is the only one who could make the choice to share this experience with me. She is the only one who knows about the many personalities.

For the next many months, I watch and observe as I respond to Mom's conflicting needs. I am amazed at what we have not seen. Now it is so clear.

I wish I could talk to her about the many personalities, but at this stage in 2010, I have no idea what part of her knows about the different personalities. I am not yet aware of the concept of a host personality who feeds the other personalities the information they require to be able to function on a day-to-day basis. This is what I do know: the personality that I now call the Angelic Presence tells me in 2008 that she has no memories of the tough stuff of her life; there is a partying personality that does not have memories of her behaviour the night before, which is an observation made by both Mark and me for many years; and for the most part, memories do not pass between the personalities. I can't have a conversation with Mom about realities and events for which she has no memories or awareness.

I do not know for sure why the host personality makes the decision to intentionally and boldly show me the "many personalities." As I look back to that moment in 2010, I wonder if the host personality decides to show me because she realizes her body is deteriorating rapidly. She could have chosen to not share the information with me, but that is not consistent with Mom's constant desire to provide people with understanding and knowledge based on her life experiences.

It strikes me that the host personality's desire to share insights into the many personalities had to be very strong for her to sustain that intention from 6:49 p.m. when I received the first call from the raging banshee part of the host personality until I arrive at her door at 9:18 p.m. I don't think it was a sudden decision. I think she must have thought about it long and hard. Even when I arrive at the condo she stared at me in silence and seemed to be assessing me before she showed me the distinctiveness of the personalities. I think it was a very intentional decision to provide insight and understanding into this reality that significantly impacts her life, my life, and the lives of others.

IN EARLY 2011, the demands on my time at the church escalate. I am directing the musical *Jesus Christ Superstar.*

At my first interview with Downtown United Church in the spring of 1995, the music director took me on a tour of the church. I shared with him that very first time I met him that someday I want to direct *Jesus Christ Superstar.* He told me it is a demanding show because of the number of powerful soloists that are required but said that we can probably work up to it. In 2010, he declares that he thinks we are ready to tackle this musical I have wanted to do for so long.

I anticipate that it will be a good production. We have phenomenal talent and the music director is incredible. But just as we are about to go into rehearsals I think about this production that I have loved from the time I was a teenager, and I realize that the basic story it tells of the last week of Jesus's life, is no longer enough for me. If a story does not show how transformation is possible in our lives, what difference does it make? It's not enough to tell a story from long ago. There has to be a clear connection to our lives today.

The royalties are paid for, the parts are cast, and the music books have arrived. I feel sick in the pit of my stomach. What am I going to do to shift the focus without changing one word of the story? An idea captures my imagination. Ways of visually showing the journey of transformation that leads to a greater sense of wholeness emerge, erupting so fast I barely have time to write them down.

The show opens with people moving about, ignoring one another as they focus on their distracted lives and their cellphones. The scene is a busy city street. In the centre of the stage, on a stand that looks like an old fountain, there is a man talking to friends. It is Jesus. He is wearing a sparkling rainbow-striped vest that I refer to as the

Christ vest. For me it is a reflection of the Christ Consciousness, the divine connection he boldly lives, showing by his life and by his choices how the challenging and demanding power of love changes us and changes the world around us.

The people who walk by are carrying baggage. The baggage is labelled with words like "fear," "greed," "guilt," "shame," and "judgment." As Jesus continues to teach in this oasis in the midst of the grinding world around him, more people slow down to listen to what he is saying. Bit by bit, more and more gather. As they listen they hand him their bags marked with fear, hatred, isolation, jealousy, greed and more.

There is a brick gateway a third of the way back on the stage. It is covered with graffiti reflecting the values of a consumer society. The tenement houses at the back of the stage are dilapidated. A homeless person sleeps on the street. A pile of garbage has created a raised pathway for people to walk upon. Looking down on this derelict scene are the palace and the temple, each one a building that reflects power and wealth, places of separation from the life that goes on below them.

There is a PowerPoint display shifting from image to image throughout the production, reflecting the pain, the brokenheartedness, and the distortions of our humanity in our consumer world.

In the scene where Jesus is overwhelmed by people demanding to be healed, the screen changes with the beat of the music; images shift and change to twelve different statues from around the world that reflect the anguish and horror of the Holocaust, filled with people reaching out and pleading.

During the scene of the thirty-nine lashes when Jesus is whipped, there are thirty-nine images of the pain in our world today: from ducks covered in oil, to children alone in despair, to families behind barbed wire in refugee camps, to the dropping of the atomic bomb.

The cross for the crucifixion is created from the pillars at the edge of the gates that carry the messages of the destructive impact of greed for power, for control and for money. It is nailed together with a block of wood that says "FEAR."

The script ends with the death of Jesus. The music continues as the cast act out the impact of the story.

After the death everyone but Peter and Mary leave. The body has been carried out and they are left alone at the foot of the cross. Moments pass. Mary notices that Jesus's vest is on the ground, stripped from him when he was whipped. She picks it up and hugs it. Peter reaches for it and helps her to put it on.

Then Mary notices that Peter has something beneath his shirt. She pulls on it. It is a scarf made of the same material as the Christ vest. Others come back onto the stage in mourning. Mary and Peter show them that they each have a Christ scarf inside their layers of clothing. People are amazed and hug each other, realizing that the Christ Consciousness or Spirit that was in Jesus is in them too.

The leaders of the temple and Pilate of the Roman government come out on stage and look down on the crowd from their high places. The child in the crowd stands on the fountain base where Jesus taught. She shows the local leaders that they each have a Christ scarf as well. Then she beckons to Pilate, who comes to her. She takes the sash that has been worn throughout the story and turns it over to show the Christ scarf there as well.

Then the little child amongst them gives directions with her hands, prompting people to move into action just like the scripture in the book of Isaiah where it says that a little child will lead us.

Everyone works together. The cross is dismantled by the political and temple leaders, and the wood labelled "FEAR" is put on the garbage heap. The tenement houses are cleaned up and flowers planted. The palace and the temple become places for local art. The pile of garbage becomes the place for a community garden. The graffiti is removed from the walls of the gateway. The base of the fountain becomes a park laden with a picnic feast for all to share.

As the transformation is completed, the audience is shown that in their booklets they each have a bookmark that is made with a piece of the Christ scarf, indicating that the consciousness of love is in them too.

In the end Jesus comes back onto the stage. Judas also comes out and Jesus shows Judas that he has the presence of the Christ energy of love in him as well.

There is no elaborate opportunity for the cast to bow. No one person receives the spotlight over anyone else. Everyone is equal. They bow together and then head down the three aisles, shaking hands with the people as a way of passing the peace.

The show is demanding but so worthwhile.

———————————

Directing *Jesus Christ Superstar* has meant my attention has been significantly consumed by the show. I don't see Mom as often, though we still speak regularly on the phone. Mom plans to come every night of the show. She manages to make it to two out of four shows and brings friends with her each time.

But once the show is over it is clear that Mom has been feeling the loss of my attention.

In April of 2011, Mom's doctor requests that I accompany Mom for an appointment with him. It is an odd request since I have been going to her appointments for years. He wants to give us the report from the different specialists we have been seeing for the past many months. Mom is quite cantankerous. Apparently she told the doctor she would come by herself to hear the report. He refuses to book the appointment until I say I can come.

We go to his office at 5:00 p.m. on Thursday, April 28, the night after the twenty-eighth anniversary of Dad's death. It is the night before the royal wedding. Mom and I are planning to spend the night together so we can get up early to watch the wedding of William and Kate, like we did for Charles and Diana's wedding years before.

We go into the doctor's office. I have strict orders from Mom that I am not to say anything. She will respond to the doctor. The doctor enters. He looks at the two of us, and then shares results of all the appointments and the multitude of tests.

He turns to Mom and says, "You have an aneurysm. It is at the top of your heart. It is six centimetres wide and ten centimetres long. There is nothing we can do about it. It is too large to operate on at this stage of your life. When it bursts, which it will, you will die within fifteen seconds."

I bite my tongue. He looks at me. I am silent, as per Mom's request, as he shares the results.

Mom thanks him and leaves. She pauses just down the hall to chat with someone.

I turn back to the doctor. "I didn't speak because Mom wanted to be the one to engage the information from the tests. I want to update you about Mom possibly having a mental illness. I am now pretty sure Mom has dissociative identity disorder. Mom chose to morph through four different personalities in less than five minutes, as though she wanted me to see what we have been dealing with all these years. I was shocked to realize that I recognized each one of the personalities and that I have engaged them all my life. I know a doctor has to make a diagnosis, but I know it is difficult to diagnose. I am convinced that intervention through medication is not the best choice for Mom, so I am not suggesting you need to do anything."

Mom barks my name. I turn and move to catch up with her. I glance back at the doctor, who is watching us leave.

In the car I ask Mom if she wants to go out for dinner. We go to the nicest restaurant in town and share a feast. Mom is quiet but polite. We share some memories that make us smile, like all the times we have gone to a spa together, and some of the fun things we have done. A smile is all we can manage. We finish eating and make our way to the car in silence.

Back at her condo, we climb into her large bed together. It is early, but we want to get some sleep before we wake up for the wedding celebrations. Instead, it is hours before we sleep.

We lie facing each other.

I ask bluntly, "How are you feeling about this reality the doctor shared with you?" There is no response. "… that sometime in the future your aneurysm will suddenly burst … and when it does you will die right away?"

After a long silence, I ask, "Is there anything you want to do to prepare for your death?"

She looks deep into my eyes. She says she feels that she did some good things with her life. She says she doesn't want to die, but since she will, this is a good way to go.

I look at her, remembering the multitude of hours I have sat with her, listening to her longing to die. There is a part of me that is relieved to hear her response. I wrap my arms around her. She finally falls asleep at 2:00 a.m.

The alarm goes off at 4:00 a.m. to alert us to the beginning of the wedding celebrations. I am alone in the bed. Mom has gotten up and wandered out to the living room. I join her on the couch. She is clearly distressed. In her angst she falls back to sleep. With my arm wrapped around her, I watch the wedding alone.

OVER THE NEXT MONTHS, MOM FALLS SEVERAL TIMES. One day the two of us attempt to get her up from the floor. Our attempts are filled with laughter as it becomes abundantly clear that we cannot get her up on our own.

I try to figure out how to get non-emergency help. I finally find out how to call the fire department without dialing 911, which a city worker assures me is the correct place to seek such help. We await their arrival with a sense of playfulness rooted in Mom's delight in the firefighters' provocative fundraising calendar that had been created in our community. We lie on the floor waiting together, identifying good memories of the life we have shared.

Eventually two firefighters arrive. Both the man and the woman are wonderful with Mom. They are gentle as they lift her with ease back onto her bed, and ensure that she has not been hurt.

Even with the concern about the falls I am glad I am able to convince Mom to go on our annual camping trip that summer. It is the first and last time in the summer of 2011 that she spends much time outside. Alan sets up our trailer at a local provincial park. He comes out to check on us regularly, knowing it is hard for me to do anything but care for Mom in this setting that is not her everyday environment. We stay for as long as Mom can tolerate, soaking up the sun and nibbling on some of her favourite foods.

On Sunday, October 23, 2011, the office administrator from the church comes to find me in the middle of the Jazz Sunday celebration. She tells me my Mom called to say she has fallen and can't get up. Since I know I can't get her up and Alan is out on his motorcycle and Sarah is away for the day, I call Marissa and ask if she and her fiancé can go and help Grandma. She agrees that they will go up and get her off the floor. They even stay for a little while to visit and have a beer with Mom, which is good because it is the first time they have seen her since their engagement in early September.

The next day, my brother Mark has a major stroke. It paralyzes his left side. His wife calls me. Our conversations are ongoing all week, with regular updates throughout each day, sometimes hour by hour.

Mark asks me to tell Mom that we cannot talk to him. I feel uncomfortable telling her no one can talk to him since I have spoken to him, but I understand the need to limit the number of people who make contact.

Mom, however, does not understand. She is livid. From her perspective, as his mother she has every right, no matter the limitations, to speak to him.

Mom manages to figure out which hospital he is in, which would have taken some effort since he is not in the hospital local to where he lives. She calls him on Tuesday night. Mark tells me the conversation turns out to be a wonderful gift for him. It's filled with lots of understanding and forgiveness.

In a second conversation, however, Mom is in an alternate personality and within minutes of the start of the conversation Mark's blood pressure soars. The staff is alerted to a potential crisis by alarms going off indicating his blood pressure is rising at an alarming rate.

Mark's wife calls and tells me I have to stop Mom from phoning Mark. I groan but I call Mom. She is not happy. I talk about it not being about her but Mark. While she can understand that others might not be able to call, she cannot imagine why his mother can't call. I hold firm to the request and tell her she can't call. Over the years I have felt that I had to develop an ability to set boundaries with Mom if the needs of others were being significantly disrupted by her erratic behaviour. She is mad, but she doesn't call again.

———————————————

On Friday morning, Mom calls me earlier than usual. It is still dark out. She awakens me from a sound sleep. She has decided she needs to go to the hospital. The sense of not feeling well that has plagued her all fall is now too much to handle. She tells me she is going to press the button on her emergency alert system. She wants me to know I will be receiving a call. Her desire to be independent and organized is still guiding her actions.

I scramble out of bed to get dressed. The call comes. I tell them yes, please send an ambulance.

When I arrive, the ambulance attendants already have Mom on a stretcher in the hallway outside her home. I am sad that I wasn't there when they took her out of her home. I have a feeling deep inside that she will not return. I had the same feeling the last time I saw Dad, though with him it made no sense. He was a healthy, vibrant fifty-six year old. As he was leaving our home late on an evening in April 1983, the thought crossed my mind that I would never see him again. I scolded myself for thinking such a thing. I turned, refusing to watch his taillights disappear into the night. I never saw him alive again.

And now here I am, standing in the hallway of my mother's condo, thinking, "This is it, she's never coming home again." I have learned not to ignore such feelings.

We spend all day Friday in the emergency ward. Mom is in a cantankerous mood that periodically explodes into raging anger. She is in excruciating pain for a multitude of reasons. From my perspective, the staff does not seem sympathetic. She knows that some of the pain could be alleviated by a catheter because she has had difficulty urinating since her bladder suspension. She requests a catheter. The staff says no. They tell me to take her to the toilet, which means getting her into a wheelchair because the pain is too unbearable for her to walk. I repeatedly take her to the toilet, but she has no success at alleviating the pent-up pressure for over seven hours.

The ward is not busy that day. This experience is radically different from the time I brought Mom in with what turned out to be a bowel obstruction. But that time Mom was in her Angelic Presence personality who is engaging and kind. This time she is the Aggressive

One, almost at the end of the spectrum of the raging banshee. She is demanding and gruff.

As I compare these contrasting experiences of the ways the staff interact with Mom, I wonder how much they reflect the boomerang theory: what goes around comes around, so the energy you put out into the world is the energy you receive back. It seems like the contrast between the two experiences of the staff's response to Mom may have been impacted by the two radically different personalities.

As hard as this reality is, it becomes a gift of insight that vividly reminds me to be aware of how I engage with people. I need to ensure that I don't continually send out negative energy and that I don't get caught in the rebound effect of others' negative energy. We get to choose our attitude. We can choose to not exacerbate negative energy by not adding in our own negative energy. In the hospital that day the staff seems to choose to reflect Mom's negative, grumpy attitude back to her.

Just before the staff on the ward is about to change I am told the order has been written to put a catheter in since we can't seem to solve Mom's problem. A new nurse comes and brings a ray of sunshine with her. When she inserts the catheter she is amazed at how significantly the bag fills with fluid. Her attitude toward Mom is one of extreme sympathy and concern about the amount of pain Mom must have been in all day.

Mom is admitted for observation.

Shortly after 4:00 a.m. on Saturday morning Mom calls me. She is spitting mad. We try to figure out what can be done so that her situation will be more bearable. By 5:30 a.m. she has called three times. A nurse comes into the room during the third call and tells Mom it isn't appropriate to call someone at this hour.

I ask Mom if she wants me to come.

She says, "No, I can handle it."

I feel badly for her, but I also feel badly for the nurses. I know how overwhelming her anger can be.

After leading a day-long workshop on Saturday I go to the hospital. Sarah, Marissa and Alan have been in to see her during the day. Mom and I visit for three hours. She's happy by the time I leave.

When I arrive the next day after the church service, she is definitely not happy. She grumbles at me. There are times she tells me she totally understands that I can't be with her all the time and that she's proud of me for the work that I do. At other times she is mad at me for not being with her all the time. It depends on the personality that is present.

This time she is mad at me for not being there all the time. She is so mad, she tells me to go home. I refuse. She says she's not going to talk to me. I tell her that is fine; the two of us can sit and read our novels together in silence.

Part way through the afternoon I open a package of dark semi-sweet chocolate. I know Mom hasn't eaten anything in two days. I slide a piece of the dark chocolate onto her tray while I keep reading. She picks it up and nibbles on the treat.

Eventually there is only one piece left. She says she doesn't want anymore, and then asks me about my book. We start to chat but are interrupted when a nurse comes in. After the quiet the two of us have shared all afternoon I am shocked by Mom's anger at the nurse. The nurse asks me to leave for a moment so that she can take Mom's vitals.

When the nurse comes out I tell her that Mom's behaviour is unusual, which it is considering the fact that she doesn't usually act like this around other people. I go back into the room.

Mom tells me I need to go home to have dinner with my family. I give her a hug and kiss and tell her I love her. She takes my hand and looks at it while she says, "I don't think I am going to be able to do any more travelling. I want you to take the trips that we have planned, especially the one to Hawaii that Dad and I didn't get around to before he died."

I look at her and say, "I will carry you with me whenever I travel. If I do get to Hawaii I'll carry both of you with me."

I move toward the door. I turn back and say, "I love you, Mom."

She smiles at me and says, "I love you too."

I leave and head home to be with my family for dinner.

After dinner we follow through on our plan for the whole family to meet at Sarah's to carve pumpkins with grandkids.

It's October 30. I realize on the way to Sarah's that it is the sixth anniversary of Mom moving here.

At 7:56 I suggest that we call Mom at the hospital before the phone lines block incoming calls to the rooms for the night. I put her on speakerphone. The eight of us, representing three generations, shout and scream and tell her all we are doing. She laughs on the other end of the line.

Then we all shout over top of each other, "We love you, Grandma! We love you, Mom! Good night! We love you!" The call ends with her response, "I love you too!"

Alan, Marissa and I arrive home just after 9:00 p.m. At 9:17 the phone rings. It is a nurse from the hospital. She confirms who I am.

Then she says, "I'm so sorry to have to tell you: your mother just died."

I thank her and hang up. I turn to Alan and Marissa and tell them. We look at each other and decide we will drive out to Sarah's to let her know.

Just weeks before, on Thanksgiving Sunday, Alan and I made our way to the homes of our daughters to tell them their other Grandma died. And now, twenty-one days later, we are on the road to tell of the death of the last grandparent.

Marissa isn't sure if she wants to go to the hospital, but she does want to be there when Sarah is told.

In the first hour I am functioning in a need-to-do mode. We drive to Sarah's and tell her. She has always been so close to this Grandma. Marissa had been close to their other Grandma. She is very supportive of Sarah now. It is decided that we will all go to the hospital. The girls will drive together in one car and Alan and me in another car.

When we arrive in the hospital room it is clear Mom is gone. Not one sign of one personality remains. She is like an empty shell that had contained so many diverse and hard and wonderful aspects. Now her body lies empty. I don't feel her presence in the room at all like I have at the time of other deaths. What I feel is absence.

The nurse tells us details. The last time they checked on her she was sitting up in bed reading, which is such a familiar pose for Mom. Memories of the multitude of times I walked into a room and watched her take off her reading glasses to engage in conversation flash through my mind. Memories of the number of times I took her glasses off and set aside her book because she had fallen asleep reading flood through my mind.

The nurse tells us we can stay as long as we want. She says that when we are done they will take her down to the morgue. I tell her, "No, she is not being taken to the morgue." She protests that they can't get staff from the funeral home there until the morning. I tell her I know we can arrange for someone to come during the night.

Then she tells me they can't have Mom pronounced dead until the morning when her family doctor can come. I look at her with a raised eyebrow. "You have no doctors in the building?"

I tell them that if they can't have a doctor come, we will wait in the room until morning. They leave.

I am clear that this body that has carried all the personalities of my Mom, this body that has carried the amazingly resilient spirit of my Mom, is not going to be covered up and left here in a cold area alone.

I call the funeral home to tell them Mom has died and that we will be calling them in the next eight hours for her to be picked up.

A half hour later the doctor arrives. It is Mom's doctor. We talk for a little while. I tell him she went quickly, just as he said she would. We don't talk about what I shared with him when we left his office that day back in April about my thoughts about Mom's mental health challenges. I wonder if he is curious since he doesn't get a chance to hear more details. Now we will never get the chance to talk about it again. This is his last action as Mom's doctor.

When he leaves, the four of us stand around the bed and talk in low voices. Tears rise up and spill to my cheeks, creating a constantly flowing stream.

I hold Mom's hand, a hand that has looked old all my life. The rest of her looked young right up until Dad died, but her hands always looked old.

I look at the blankness of her face and remember the different portrayals of different personalities. I marvel at all she carried within her.

I am grateful for her presence in my life. I am grateful for all she has taught me. I am grateful for the way she has been my champion and the champion of so many people down through the years.

There is a part of me that is grateful that she won't need any more constant care. I'm intrigued to notice that I don't feel any guilt about that thought.

It is after 11:30 before I am ready to make any calls. I start by calling Janis. She says she will let Mark know in the morning. He's still in hospital. I will call Betsy right away and Janis will call Lynda. Everyone else can wait until morning, including the nieces and nephews she has been so significant to throughout their lives.

By 1:30 a.m. I call the funeral home to let them know they can come and get her.

The two funeral directors enter the room with a stretcher. I know them well. It is two women. I work with them often. I do more funerals in town than any other minister, particularly the funerals that are the result of a tragedy for families that have no church connection. These difficult funerals create a strong bond between those of us who work together on them, since they are so emotionally difficult.

There is a quilt on top of the stretcher. The rest of my family leaves the room. I stay to watch Mom be transferred. They handle her with a loving gentleness that I appreciate.

After wrapping the quilt around her, they wheel her out to the hall. I tell them I want us to travel down with them to see her put in the car. When we get to the basement we pass the door of the morgue. I am glad this is one final thing I can do for Mom, to make sure she leaves with dignity, surrounded by people who love her.

The four of us watch them put her in the car. We stay and watch as they drive away. I have stood with many families and watched their loved ones driven away in a funeral coach. The moment is a significant one for me. I know it is important to observe all the steps of saying goodbye.

I sleep deeply that night knowing I will not be abruptly awakened by the regular morning call from Mom, calls that could come before dawn if she was distressed. The morning after Mom's death, I awaken naturally. It is morning. Sunlight is pouring in the window. I am rested.

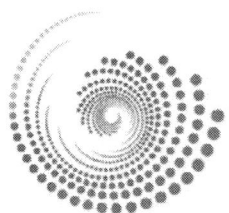

ON THE MORNING AFTER MOM'S DEATH the first thing I do is go to the funeral home. The staff is wonderful. They tell me about the day Mom came to plan her funeral. She was full of fun. They tell me that she made one decision that they were to note I could change if I want to. I ask what it is. They say they have to show me. I am led into the casket room. They point to a unique casket. I immediately say, "There is no way I am choosing something different. It is perfect for her."

It is shiny metal. I see it as the turquoise of the Mustang car we shared when I went to university. Some see it as moss green, like the colour that fills her home. I take the pillow with me to her condo to find something for her to wear that will complement the unique champagne colour.

When my sisters arrive we develop more of the arrangements together. I discover quite quickly that no one wants to talk about the difficult times with Mom. I never wanted to talk much about them when Mom was alive, but now I want to talk and share the depth of my experience with Mom. No one will listen. They want to focus on what was good. I am frustrated because I spent a lifetime focusing on what was good in Mom and now I want to talk about what was hard for me to deal with. But there is another part of me that is simply glad to hear other people talk about what I always saw as the good in Mom.

The days of planning are not without their trials and frustrations. They are also filled with memories of the fun of choosing pictures and planning a service to reflect the gifts of Mom's life.

On the day of the service to celebrate Mom's life, the church is full of nieces and nephews, friends of long ago and new friends. The choir is part of the service to honour Mom's love of music. Mom wanted me to do the entire funeral service, but I did not think that I could give it the attention it needs. My colleague in ministry leads the service and my family and I add embellishments that celebrate the gift of Mom.

Janis delivers a lovely eulogy. She is caring and kind toward all the significant people in Mom's life. She describes all the amazing things Mom has done. It warms my heart to sit and listen to her name all the positives of Mom's life after listening to her struggles with Mom for years.

When I speak, I reflect on how I saw Mom live her faith as an expression of the vision of Isaiah—a vision and dream of the time when all the Earth will live in peace and every person will be cared for and honoured.

Betsy dances the most incredible dance wearing expansive, swirling angel wings that for me feel like the flow of the life Mom sought to live but lost in the final years. The wings feel like an expression of Mom's energy of love, which defines her state now. After all, the only thing that is eternal is love. I like to think of her energy flowing around us to embrace us all.

The feast after the service is a reflection of Mom's gift of radical hospitality. It is filled with all the treats Mom served in her home: from pineapple-upside-down-cake, to an array of olives, to shrimp and avocados, Strubb pickles and fresh veggies, along with strawberries with sour cream and brown sugar for dipping. The party is a delight, filled with pictures of Mom through the decades and the music she loved.

I invite all my siblings to gather for dinner at our home that night. Betsy invites our cousin, who is Mom's godson. We feast, laugh and toast with Mom's wine to honour how she has been an incredible gift in our lives even in the midst of the struggles.

The next morning, we follow behind the funeral coach as Mom's body is driven to the cemetery in the town by the farm where Dad is buried and her third husband's ashes had been placed.

Although we anticipate that the service at the cemetery will be an intimate circle of family, a large circle of old neighbours from twenty-five years ago gathers. I lead this part of the ritual to celebrate Mom's life.

At the end of the service, everyone is given a yellow rose, as per Mom's request. The significance of the yellow rose in our family began in the fall of 1971 when Mom was in the hospital. I arrange for four yellow roses to be delivered to her room with a card that says they are from her four children with love, signed with our first and middle names.

And now, we stand in a circle of many people, each one holding a yellow rose around Mom's casket. I watch as the casket is lowered into the earth. I throw the first yellow rose into the hole as a sign of my love. I smile with gratitude for all that we have shared as I watch the multitude of yellow roses dance their way to the top of her casket. They gather in an extravagant bouquet, with flowers pointing every which way. It feels like an expression of the love and light and chaotic energy that Mom shared through her life.

I wait while the backhoe fills in the hole, watching until the task is complete to ensure that her body is held safely deep within the heart of the earth.

I then turn away from this significant place where my parents have been laid to rest. I go to where my sisters are standing to see if they want to go to the farm where we grew up. I had contacted the family who reside there to ask if we could come to wander around what was once our family farm. They agreed.

We head down the highway and travel together down the side road of our childhood.

When the family arrives at the farm, we are welcomed with a generous hospitality that reflects the tone when we lived there. We are invited to roam about freely.

We enter the kitchen area of the house and marvel at how things have not changed. I turn and head up the stairs, turning right to enter "my" room. The built-in furniture is still there! I ask if I can look under the vanity. Though puzzled, the new owner says yes. And there in my teenage writing is the list of all the boys I liked, starting in grade two and going up through the years. I invite my daughters to see my memory log. I already have a record of the list from the last night we owned the farm, which I spent there alone.

I stand at my one-time bedroom window and remember the times I spent in the orchard below, seeking refuge on the swing or high in the apple tree to re-centre myself in all that is good. I remember how it felt to swing high and sing at the top of my lungs when life seemed to be falling apart. I remember the experience of sitting on the ancient limb of the apple tree to look out over the field and feel the calm that emanated from the tall, rustling grasses. I remember the sound of the whip-poor-will penetrating my night times with a steadfast assurance that life keeps evolving even in the midst of chaos.

After stepping briefly into each room I leave the house and wander toward the barn. It feels familiar, rich with scents and the feel of wonderful relationships with animals that lumbered through our lives.

I head out beyond the barn into the woods, following a well-remembered path by the stream, allowing memories, filled with poignancy and love of this place, to emerge. This is a place that holds meaning and insights. There is a richness here that fills my soul with peace and a sense of being grounded that infiltrates my dreams and my meditations.

I feel at peace in this place in a way that nourishes a longing in my soul. Memories awaken with the assurance of connection and creativity. I feel complete in a way that I have not for a long time. This is home. This is a place of peace for me. I love this land. It nourishes my soul.

A year after Mom's death I sit and remember her. I eat the final piece of semi-sweet dark chocolate that I have carried in my purse for a year. I nibble on it like Mom did on that last afternoon. I am aware of its taste bursting in my mouth as a toast to the life Mom and I shared … it is both bitter and sweet.

Piecing Together The Fragments

Four significant pathways emerge as my life shifts and changes after Mom's death. The pathways beckon me on a journey that feels like I am weaving together fragmented pieces to allow greater wholeness to emerge in my work and in my personal life. They are like spirals leading me deeper and deeper into the centre of my authentic self.

THE FIRST PATHWAY is filled with stories of moments that reconnect me to the energy of the mystical, magical experience in the meadow when I am three.

On Tuesday, November 1, 2011, two days after Mom's death, on the day that is All Saints' Day, when we remember and honour ancestors whose love and encouragement still surround us, I receive an email that sends a spark through me. It says it is the final notice for a pilgrimage to Hawaii. It is startling to receive this email two days after Mom asks me to travel to Hawaii on behalf of her and Dad. A friend is one of the leaders. I immediately send her a note telling her of Mom's death—she knew Mom because she stayed with her once—and to say that I am interested in finding out about the pilgrimage to Hawaii.

Cracks leading to unexpected detours keep shattering open to provide glimpses of possibilities that surprise me in their potential to disrupt life as I have known it.

One surprise happens on November 17, 2011 during a meeting with the friend I will travel with during my sabbatical in the summer of 2012. She is the chair of the new visioning process that we have just developed for the congregation where I have served since 1996.

I hear myself begin a sentence; I have no idea where it is going. "I want you to know (*hmmm, I wonder what I want her know*) that when you are leading this visioning process, it is very important that the congregation really think about what they want (*well, of course it is, since that's what visioning is about, so I wonder what my point is*), because (*here it comes*) by the time we implement the visioning plan ... I will no longer be on staff. (*Oh ... My ... Well ...!*)"

Two months before, during a time of prayerful reflection, a message arose in me to stop asking if it is time for me to leave the congregation. The message is clear that when the time comes for me to leave I will know.

Well, I guess the time has come. It's odd that I find out that it is time to leave by declaring it to someone. Usually I have time on my own to consider a sense of call, though typically the time I allow for pondering it is truncated into a matter of hours rather than the days or weeks I plan for myself. I feel a sense of call so definitively I have never been able to sit with it longer than five hours without sharing it with Alan. Experience has taught me that when a call comes, it is strong, clear and not to be ignored.

I have never not done what I feel called to do, even when it means major changes in my life. Although Alan isn't always thrilled with the potential implications of what I am called to do, he is always supportive. This time the call has left no time to ponder. It has come as a declaration not to be denied.

I am intrigued that less than three weeks after Mom's death my life is taking a radical turn in a direction that is not clear. I know what is ending. I do not know what is beginning.

What I do sense is that I will stay with the congregation until April 2013.

Later I discover that our mortgage will be paid off in February 2013 and my car loan will be paid off in March 2013. It turns out that Mom's estate is finalized in January 2013. By the designated date of departure of April 2013 from Downtown United Church, a date chosen purely based on intuition, my largest financial commitments are complete and renewed personal finances are available.

Along with the plans being developed for my sabbatical starting in June, plans are put in place for the trip to Hawaii in the winter of 2012. I take the cash value of $683 out of the life insurance that Dad bought when I was two months old. It is a symbolic acknowledgement of Mom and Dad's connection to the Hawaii trip. I told Mom I will carry them in my heart, but this way they also contribute to the costs from a source of funding they developed many years ago.

When I share the itinerary of the spiritual pilgrimage in Hawaii, two of my friends, Lynn and Kathie, declare they are coming with me. I had anticipated travelling alone because Alan has little interest in travelling, though he anticipates that someday he will go on one major trip—just not this one.

Being in Hawaii is a powerful journey. I am glad I have companions with me with whom I can reflect. The itinerary is not one that Mom and Dad would have chosen, but it is the right trip for me. It provides a multitude of opportunities to explore with others the types of spiritual experiences I have had throughout my life.

When we arrive in March of 2012 on the island of Kauai where Mom and Dad so wanted to travel, the young Kahuna, the traditional leader of the tribal community, shares with our extensive group that there is an ancient prophecy of a time when a large group of people of a specific number, which is exactly our number, will come to the island of Kauai from all over the world. Their arrival will herald the reawakening of the golden age of Lemuria.

The story of Lemuria is more ancient than the story of Atlantis. It is of a land in the Pacific Ocean where the people lived in peace. The land was swallowed up by the sea. Yet its rituals are still found on the islands around the Pacific Rim, which suggests they all originally came from the same culture. It is prophesized that the time will come when the peace known in the time of Lemuria will return.

The mystical story about Lemuria connects to my childhood ponderings about living in peace. I know deep within me it is possible. Being here with these healers and visionaries from all over the world deepens my connection to the reawakening of the ancient dream of wholeness, which activates the song of my soul.

Something happens in me on this mountainous island in the sea. I awaken to something I do not fully understand. As we journey to places of ancient healing and insight, I experience myself being cracked open. It is a cracking open that I have prepared for in moments of my life: on the gnarled branch of the old apple tree at the farm, on the rock out in Georgian Bay where I sit and listen for hours as a child, in the image from the meadow of golden light that wraps around my life.

Here on this island I connect to a profound silence within me. The silence carries energy like the ancient and alternative wisdom that Spirit invited me to explore when I considered completing a Doctor of Ministry. Instead I was called to the community on two lakes.

Now, on this island of ancient people, when I speak in this community of spiritual companions, I hear myself speaking from a place of profound silence within me that is filled with insights that words struggle to express. It is a voice filled with a resonance that is different from my everyday voice. And yet it is my voice, a voice that has waited and prepared for the time when it will be heard in the midst of everyday life. It is a voice that emerges as I tap into levels of myself that I have not known. It echoes with the invitation to be aware that there is a higher consciousness that connects us and calls us to a time of transformation and awakening on a personal and communal level.

My experiences with Mom, both on a personal level of seeking to create healthy connection between us even in the midst of brokenness, and on a political level by watching her demand that as a community we work together for the good of all, awaken a passion within me that is expressed through this new depth of voice.

The years following Mom's death provide me with opportunities to explore a deeper awareness of what is trying to emerge from the place of profound silence within me. This silence continually beckons me to listen for the ancient and alternative wisdom that we so desperately need in our world.

While we are on the island of Kauai, a torrential rainfall disrupts life. We hear reports that it is a rainfall that is causing floods all over the Earth. It feels like a time when the world is being washed clean from the grime of past choices that have led us away from the wholeness that is possible.

───────────────

In June of 2012 I go to Scotland, having chosen with my travel companion to not go to India or Peru as we considered but rather to return to our Celtic roots.

A calling surged through me
to return to an unknown but often-dreamed-of land.
A land that carries the wisdom
of my Celtic spiritual roots:
of a perspective that we are born in blessing rather than sin,
where all of life is considered sacred,
and moments are filled with prayers of gratitude.

It feels like coming home
to a place where I've never been;
a connection that grabs at my heart
tugging at my roots to expand
into the rich loam
where heather grows
and hills roll,
where craggy mountains create bubbling creeks
and roadside waterfalls.

This feels like the land of my soul.
And yet I do not know for sure
that this is the place of my ancestors:
England—yes
Ireland—yes
Scotland—uncertain but maybe.
My heart says yes.
My soul has found its place.

I feel my life spiralling deeper
connecting to a power
that nourishes and transforms.

There is an energy here
awakening me
as the ocean winds blow across the land.
Energy surges through me
on the tiny island where mammoth crystals
have risen to create space
for a magical, musical symphony of life.
Pathways charge my footsteps
and lead to unsuspected vistas
that open my wonderings to new possibilities.

There is connection here on the isle of Iona.
I respond to a nudge to wander
the ancient cemetery
to notice the ones laid to rest.
It is a surge of demanding energy
I rarely experience in a cemetery.

Scotland
a land of coming home
a land that speaks to my core
a land that calls to the bold vision that stirs within
and empowers me to be the fullness of who I am.

Scotland. This is the place where I want to bring Alan. Like me, he
will be drawn by the power of the land.

IN AUGUST 2012 I GO TO ENGLAND with a large group of colleagues for my second year at the Greenbelt Festival of Faith, the Arts and Social Justice. While our ten days together are amazingly rich in conversation and experiences, it is the ten days after the festival that provide significant renewal after the years of extensively incorporating care for Mom into my day-to-day life. The ten days after my colleagues leave is a time of transformation and awakening. I am glad I follow the nudge to spend extra time in England. This time allows for a significant realignment to emerge in my life, created by deepened connection to the mystical realm where we are continuously empowered by the energy of love in the moments of life.

I had a conversation with my Dad about "nudges" during my late teens, which continues to impact my life on a regular basis. He told me that it is important to always listen to the nudges that I get in life. He said that if you stop listening, the nudges will stop coming. He shared stories of business deals that would have fallen through if he had not followed a nudge to make a phone call. I learn the power of that lesson again and again in my life.

The most powerful affirmation of the importance of following a nudge happens shortly after I am ordained. I am walking through the kitchen in late afternoon when I am nudged to call a young mom whose baby died of crib death months before. I wonder if I have time. I look at the clock and know the time is tight before my kids will come barrelling through the door. I decide to call to at least set up an appointment to get together. The phone rings three times before she answers. We make plans to get together in a few days. Four months later she tells me that when I called that day she had a bottle of whisky in one hand and the first handful of pills in her other hand. A pile of pills sat on the table in front of her waiting to provide a lethal dose. When the phone rang she considered not answering. She stared at the phone, not moving. Then she felt a strong nudge to answer. Today, almost thirty years later, she is a Grandma who hangs out with her grandkids rather than being a suicide statistic.

Extending my trip to England by ten days after the Greenbelt Festival is one of the times when I follow a nudge even though it feels odd. It is a nudge that sends me barrelling down a pathway that confirms for me, within the context of community, that I am not alone in the profound spiritual experiences that are continuously part of my life.

All my life I have sensed a mystical, loving energy that playfully calls us to see through eyes of love, inviting us to see life differently from the limitations of the teachings of our society. While I have journeyed far into this awareness in conversations with others, these final ten days in England create the opportunity to have experiences that confirm even more deeply my sense of the world.

It is this awareness of a power greater than we see with our eyes that sustains me through the years when Mom is going through difficult times. And now, because of Mom's encouragement to travel, I have a multitude of mountaintop spiritual experiences filled with the transformative power to change people as we awaken to what is possible.

The ten-day trip begins with time alone, a need I learn to respond to in kindergarten. After saying goodbye to my colleagues at the end of the Greenbelt Festival I hop on a train and head to the town of Bath. I have a room booked at a bed and breakfast. After a bus tour of the area, I book myself into the spa with hot springs that are available to enjoy in a multitude of ways.

It is difficult to put into words the shifts that happen to me that day.

One moment stands out in my memories. I am in the outside pool on the top of the building that is filled with healing waters. Periodically the jets come on and the pool swirls with renewed energy, stirring the water around the forty to fifty people who are sharing the experience.

Everyone else is with someone. I am comfortable being alone. Though alone, I have a strong sense that we are all connected. At one point I turn away from the crowd to look toward an ancient mound that I can see from the pool. I first saw these amazing systems of mounds earlier in the day when I was on the train. There is something about them. They feel like they are filled with an energy that is mystical. As I watch, surrounded by the warm healing waters, the moon rises over the hill. It is not quite a full moon, but it is brilliant. The moment feels magical, like there are powers on this Earth of which we are not aware.

When I was in England a year ago, I felt this magical, mystical energy. It was particularly strong during the time I spent at Stonehenge and the day I spent at Glastonbury with a friend. In Glastonbury we wandered around the grounds of the Chalice Well, the place that legend says is at the edge of Avalon, the land beyond the veil that separates the realms of earth and heaven from Arthurian legends.

We entered into a pool of clear healing waters that come from the well. There we shared a ritual of reaffirming and remembering our baptism. We are both ordained ministers. The moment is significant, just as it had been significant more than a decade before when two other minister friends and I reaffirmed and remembered our baptism with full immersion in the Jordan River in Israel.

Later that day in Glastonbury we made the journey up the Tor, a hill that can be seen for miles in the Somerset landscape. It too is identified by legends in Celtic mythology as a place of spiritual impact.

I bring my attention back to the present moment as I soak in the healing waters in the town of Bath. The hillside that now fills my view feels like a source of the life-giving, restorative energy that I am absorbing.

After the nourishing experience of being submerged in the warm healing waters I leave the spa at closing time. I wander out onto the streets, not knowing where I will go. I follow others to see where they go.

I arrive at a square in the centre of the village. The warm light from a restaurant window beckons to me with a sense of welcome as darkness descends on the village. I sit alone looking out at the square and enjoy the most incredible meal.

I get a taxi back to my room.

After arriving at my room I go outside to sit under the ancient tree in the yard. It is 11:00 p.m. I know Alan will be sitting out on our back deck for cocktail time that we share each evening. It is our wedding anniversary. I sit in the moonlight that is creating silhouettes of the branches of the ancient tree and I feel connected to Alan. I am very aware of the two of us being together as we sit under a shared moon thousands of miles away and several time zones apart.

The next day I head by train to a town that I can't find on a map of England. Part way there it dawns on me that I am about to be welcomed by a woman whom I will not recognize, having never met her in person before. We have communicated by email over the past year. A year ago she arranged for my friend and me to take her place in a group who gather in Stonehenge at sunrise for a circle of prayer for peace on Earth. Now she will meet me in this tiny place that does not show up on a map. I am to stay with her for eight days.

I ask another passenger how large the station is at the next stop. He says it is a small station. When the train stops, I get off. The platform is empty. The train pulls away. I look across the tracks and see a lone woman dressed in white. I know it is the person I am to meet. We greet each other across the tracks. She says she will drive around.

We feel an instant sense of connection. I clamber into her van. Our first stop is at a crop circle close to where she lives. The crops have been slow coming off this year, so there are still all seven crop circles that showed up in this area this year. The plan is to visit all of them.

The next eight days are astonishing. My guide on the journey lives on the estate of a highly accomplished painter. I wander through the rooms amazed at his work. The painting that captures my attention is the one of Princess Diana. I am told the story of the day she comes to the estate. She is so delighted by the serene setting she takes off her shoes and runs up the mound of the hillside at the back of the house by the pond. I have a picture of my footprints in the morning dew on that same hillside.

I won't be staying on the estate but rather in a cottage next door at the home of the deceased painter's daughter. I am rarely in the cottage because my days are filled with an incredible journey.

Let me give you some glimpses of what turns out to be a profound spiritual experience, knowing that words alone will struggle to capture the depth of what happens. The experience is similar in its power to the mystical experience I had when I was three in the meadow.

Over the eight days I spend significant time in eight crop circles. There are seven circles when I first arrive but an eighth one appears on the morning after my arrival. We are the second pair of people to enter that circle after its presence has been shared through the crop circle network.

My guide describes crop circles as a kiss from heaven. The intricacy of their design fills me with astonishment. I stare at the detail and patterns, amazed. I hear a story about friends of my companion who spent the night on one of the systems of mounds that create a hillside at the edge of a field. They were awakened in the middle of the night by activity and lights on the field below them. They catch the activity on film. The next morning at sunrise they see the outline of a new and very complex crop circle.

I don't know how crop circles are created. A kiss from heaven feels like a wonderful poetic expression. What I do know is that when I am in a crop circle something happens inside that strengthens my core, expands my capacity for compassion, and increases my delight in life in a way that is similar to, but more than, the impact of art and music and walking deep in the forest.

One day in particular is incredible. It includes being in two ancient standing stone circles, one circle made of petrified wood, two crop circles and three sound journeys.

The day begins with a gathering at sunrise amidst the ancient standing stones of Stonehenge. Special arrangements have to be made a year in advance for a group of people to enter the circle of stones at Stonehenge outside the time the general public is there. The general public is only allowed on a path around the outskirts of the stones. During public hours no one enters the circle of stones.

We gather as a group of twelve. At the same time other people are gathering in seven ancient stone circles around the world. The groups connect energetically for a time of prayer for peace on Earth.

Two huge gongs are brought into the circle with us. The centre altar is filled with candles and crystals and symbols of peace. The time of prayer takes me to a different realm of awareness. I am not aware of time. It feels like I am floating in energy that is the source of all that is. Though there is movement, there is a deep calm filled with the feeling of stillness. There is a sense of detachment from life, yet connection at a profound level.

When the guards of Stonehenge arrive and stand quietly on the pathway where the public generally has to stay, their presence alerts us that our time is up and we need to leave before the public is allowed in. We head out in silence.

We stop at a local restaurant. We have a boisterous breakfast together filled with the power of our early morning excursion.

Next we drive to Woodhenge, which I have never heard of before. It is an ancient circle created by petrified stumps of trees. We spread out blankets in the middle of the circular pathways for a picnic lunch. Three of us, my guide, her friend and I, rise after lunch and move in a dance amongst the pathways. The two of them carry crystal bowls that fill the air with a song that feels like deep connection to the message of love.

After our picnic we head to Avebury, a village that sits in the middle of a circle of standing stones. A small community hall has been rented for the afternoon for an event that is open to anyone. It is a two-hour sound journey that weaves together the music of the gongs, the crystal bowls, wooden flutes and other instruments that I do not recognize.

Again I am transported to a different realm of life that is filled with golden light, like my first experience in the meadow at three years of age.

Later we wander amongst the ancient standing stones. We go beyond the circle of stones to the field just outside the village where there is another crop circle. Again we make a contribution to a farmer whose crop has been diminished by the presence of the crop circle to thank them for their willingness to allow us to enter the field. Entering requires a pathway through the crop, further limiting the yield. Crop circles change location each year. We contribute to the loss of crop with a sense of gratitude for what is gained by being in the field. As we wander through the complex design of several circles we can hear the combines droning in the background, making their way through the field leaving this area until the end of the harvest.

My guide, her friend and I get separated from the rest of the group. We know that at some point everyone is heading to another crop circle somewhere nearby. When we return to the community hall they have all left—even though there is much cleanup to be done. Irritated that we are left alone to tend to the tasks, the three of us fill the van with all the musical instruments and remnants of the shared food, then tidy the hall. It feels odd to shift into the frustration of everyday, mundane details. Even amongst this community that spends an incredible amount of time in prayer and doing healing work for themselves and the world, there are ordinary problems.

The hour of frustrated cleanup feels like a disruption in the midst of an amazing day. But I learn something significant about myself that urges me to be aware of the need to ensure that people around me feel honoured and respected and not put upon. It is actually a lesson my family has been trying to teach me for years by protesting any time I move into organizing mode to make plans for everyone to prepare an event. I am often told they are not my minions to tell what to do. It is okay at church, they tell me, I am expected to be an organizer there. But it is not okay at home. I need to stop dumping expectations on them. The day in the village at the centre of a circle of standing stones provides me with insights into how it feels to be expected to take care of tasks without consultation.

We are finally able to head away from Avebury. A sense of exasperation travels with us for a few miles but I treasure the insights about the importance of not dumping expectations on others that become their external expectations.

Everyday lessons in the midst of a day of spiritual nourishment remind me that all of life is about spirituality, because all of life is about creating healthy relationships. My definition for spirituality is that it is about healthy, life-giving relationships with self, other, Earth and God in whatever way people experience God. Being intentional about our spirituality includes being intentional about the everyday details.

It is getting dark. We wonder if we will be able to locate the crop circle that is supposed to be the most phenomenal circle of the year. Driving slowing down a country lane we spot what looks like a pathway into a field. We drive further up the road on a hill so we can look back to see if we have found the circle.

It is there and it is startling. It is in the shape of a Rubik's Cube. We head back down the road and climb out of the van.

Of all the experiences I have during these eight days, this is the most awe-inspiring.

We make our way through the tall crop. The path is narrow. It is difficult to get a full sense of the circle because it is so complex, with far more tall areas within it than other patterns where there are often wide-open spaces. We wander around trying to get a sense of the breadth and design.

We come to a standstill in the depth of the silence of the night, somewhere close to the centre of the circle.

Energy is surging through me and dancing amongst us. We hold the moment in stillness.

Then my guide lifts her crystal bowl and begins to play. Her friend joins her. We stand looking toward the hillside mound that rises at the edge of the field.

As the notes penetrate my heart, the two women begin to sing. It is a song that feels ancient. Its words fill me with hope. It is repetitive. I join in. It reflects the power of the rising wisdom of women.

In a moment of crescendo, the moon begins to peak over the hillside mound. It is the night of the full moon. As it rises to the fullness of its glory, its beauty and presence capture our voices.

We stand in silence, amazed.

When the moon is fully exposed the song continues.

I feel a sense of oneness with all creation that is primordial and profound. I feel the feminine energy that is giving birth to a new way that is held in the hearts of people around the world. Tears of gratitude and joy pour down my face for all who have carried and lived this message, for all who have demanded that everyone is welcome in all aspects of the circle of life, for all who have modelled a way of cooperation and collaboration, for all who have focused on goodness even when life feels broken. I think of Mom and so many women with gratitude, for their standing up for a different way than the status quo of our society.

I am grateful for this ancient and alternative wisdom that is emerging around the globe. It is happening in all aspects of life. As we awaken to the longing for wholeness and birthing a new way, this ancient and alternative wisdom is also weaving into the masculine energies and thought patterns that reside within us all, illuminating new possibilities of how to live collaboratively and compassionately on our planet home.

We leave the circle, though we long to stay.

My guide and I go for dinner in Merlin, which is named after the wizard of Arthurian legend. Since the day has been filled with magical experiences it feels appropriate.

Although it is late when we arrive home, my guide tells me she wants to bring the day to a close by leading me on my own sound journey. It will help all the insights and wisdom of the day rise to consciousness.

She sits cross-legged amidst an array of crystal bowls. She encourages me to lie on the couch where I can gaze out the window to see the hillside mound and the full moon.

I have no idea how long the journey lasts. It feels timeless.

At the end she anoints my head with fragrant oil. I slowly come out of a state that feels like deep connection with the Divine. I sit up, and then slowly stand. I give her a hug. We stand in a splash of moonlight heart to heart.

I whisper, "Thank you."

I leave the house to wander through the moonlight to my cottage down the road. I feel like I am in a cocoon of safety as space is created within me for what feels like imaginal cells doing their work. It is the imaginal cells within the cocoon that create the transformational energy for a caterpillar to become a butterfly. It feels like I am going through such a transformation of awakening to new possibilities and ways of being. Like the caterpillar in the cocoon, I don't fully understand what is happening, but it feels like the right next step in my journey.

I FOLLOW ANOTHER NUDGE after my return from England. The event Spirit is adamant I participate in is called *Awakened World 2012: Engaged Spirituality*. Mom would have loved the focus. Her passion for a just and caring world informs my deep longing for us to wake up to the vision of compassion that encompasses all of life and to not be consumed by a system that responds to the needs of some rather than the needs of all.

I write an article that provides a glimpse into my experience at this event. It is published in *The United Church Observer* in the "Spirit Story" section in April 2013.

The woman in the next seat to me reminds me of the fear and despair many people live with today. We chat when we first get on the plane in New York City. When she hears about the Awakened World Conference I am travelling to, she seems intrigued by the ideas of global citizenship and engaged spirituality that the conference will address. But when she realizes that genuinely caring for others and the Earth might threaten her comfortable lifestyle and status, she becomes angry. She rages at me about taxes for people who don't deserve support. "I feel like the world that I deserve is disintegrating," she declares. She puts on her headset and the conversation ends.

I am on my way to Rome to connect with two hundred people from around the world who, like me, see hope emerging as we awaken in our capacity to create the kind of world for which we long. We will gather for ten days of deep conversation and profound silence, adding our combined wisdom to a global movement toward wholeness and well-being for all.

Our group includes many well-known people, including the granddaughter of Gandhi, the economic adviser to the G20 finance ministers, the founding editor of *Kosmos Journal*, and a number of well-known authors. But it also includes ordinary people like me who are committed to personal and collective transformation through engaged spirituality.

The week unfolds with signs of new life as well as birthing pains. Those who are accustomed to presenting solutions rather than listening to others slowly discover the gift of hearing the voices of everyone. The shift, in my experience, requires long conversations in the hallways and over the dinner table to help some of the powerful men become aware that we need more than the voice of one expert. I am not sure they are convinced that this style of deep listening will work in a world where change is in imminent demand. But for the week they contain themselves and try to listen, although I can feel their impatience bristling through the room.

In the midst of the process of deep listening and conversation, there are sacred moments. A man from China and a man from Tibet, two countries in conflict, stand and hug each other. A young Japanese woman, whose grandfather inspired over 200,000 peace poles around the world, speaks of the day the 2011 tsunami races toward the coastline of her country and the Fukushima nuclear plant. While others run in fear, she offers a prayer of gratitude to the Earth, bending down to a tiny yellow flower and asking for its forgiveness—this one who has no legs to run. A Buddhist monk from Korea invites us to sing the song that has inspired her journey. The room fills with the song "Amazing Grace" in a multitude of languages. A pastor from the Southern States publically apologizes to his wife and daughter and the women in the room after listening to author Joan Chittister speak passionately and clearly about the insidious nature of sexism and white privilege that is present in our gathering. It's the first time he really gets it and so he chooses to acknowledge what he has not known before.

We all agree that greater well-being begins by reconnecting to our authentic selves, our true selves, which we find by being in communion with God, the Sacred, the Source. Only then is healing of the Earth possible. Spiritual practice is what makes this transformation happen; it is the key to opening us to the eternal power of love.

Moving from the fear and despair of my encounter with the woman on the airplane, to engaging with people who believe we can create a world of peace, is like moving through Holy Week. Obstacles are rolled away. New life emerges. Profound commitment grows for a vision of how the world can be when we live the fullness of our humanity and the fullness of our divinity.

The experience confirms what I have learned through my church community over the past seventeen years: it is critically important in these times to create an intentional culture where people listen deeply, speak from the heart, do not try to fix each other, and make space to engage inner wisdom.

It is amazing to discover that the longing of my heart resonates with the longings of so many others from so many different places.

Hope deepens.

During the ten days we are together we present our insights in two public forums to local politicians, at city hall in Rome and later in Florence. On the last full day of our work we are asked to do one final report to identify the actions that we need to put in place to bring about the transformation we have talked about throughout the ten days. I am asked to report on the actions we need to commit to in the field of spirituality.

I am the least known presenter and the only woman on this final panel. I am asked to share first. I stayed awake for much of the night to synthesize what I heard in our group about the actions we need to engage when we leave. When I finish presenting, the other presenters laugh and say "ditto." Their reports focus on specific projects and less on the ideological shifts that I identify.

I present my report in seven categories:

RECONCILING WITH THE OTHER
- Build tolerance and respect through understanding. If we are treated with respect and dignity, we respond that way.
- Recognize that education is critical in making sure we carry forward the goal of understanding each other.
- Educate ourselves so that we start the transformation within ourselves.
- Reconcile with one another by shifting from tolerance to acceptance to appreciation to celebration.

STAYING FOCUSED ON THE CULTURAL SHIFT
- Be clear that the overall goal we seek to achieve is "a world that works for everyone" because that helps us let go of petty issues instead of grimly holding on to what has been.
- Trust that Spirit is at work creating harmony and peace.
- Keep our hearts in the process through regular use of spiritual practices such as meditation.

WORKING TOGETHER
- Strengthen the web of interconnections. We are all seeking the same thing but the pieces are disassociated.
- Recognize that we are all responsible to "repattern," to shift from a pattern of violence and dualism toward synergy and co-creation where we are constantly asking the question: what can we co-create together?
- Change the system, as the minds of children are being formed by the system. Without changing the system we won't be able to create conditions where people can reconcile or move toward a vision of wholeness for all.

PROCESSES OF RECONCILIATION
- Support mediation within community rather than in courts.
- Grow a garden together (God created a garden, we created religions).
- Respond to basic needs.
- Forgive because forgiveness provides freedom rather than being imprisoned in the past.
- Be engaged because when we each play our part, we all help the solution to grow. We need our solutions to spread readily like a virus that we keep sharing.

A KEY TO THIS WORK IS KNOWING OURSELVES
- Start with knowing who we are. Imagine the impact if we each do our individual work and embody it so that everywhere we show up, we are not just seeing love, we are the source of love.

- Do our real work in ourselves to be the best we can be. Every day we need to look for what we can improve. (Someone suggested we need to compete with ourselves.)

EMPOWERED SELVES

- Remain in hope and personal power, believing in our own potential to hold space for change. One way to do that is to celebrate what others are doing rather than being overwhelmed by the fact that you are not doing the same thing they are successfully doing. We need to be a community that encourages one another rather than competes with one another or judges ourselves through comparison, which limits our capacity to see the good we are doing.
- Reconcile with our self, in our divinity and our humanity. When we do this, it leaks out and affects others.
- Treat ourselves with the respect we extend to others.
- Recognize that when we reconcile with another, we reconcile with self.

QUESTIONS TO PONDER

- How do we practise what we preach, even when faced with a powerful force that destroys people's dignity? How do we apply the notion of reconciliation without eliminating opponents?
- If we totally shift to a non-dualistic worldview, how do we continue to communicate with people who have a dualistic perspective? A non-dualistic worldview refers to an essential sense of wholeness, completeness, or unity of life. It is an awareness of all of life being interconnected.

Being amongst such an incredible group of change-makers from around the globe further ignites my passion for transformation and for the awakening of imaginal cells that will help the people of the world to metamorphose, just like the imaginal cells help the caterpillar become a butterfly.

———————

Six months after returning from Italy I leave Downtown United Church. My last day is April 7, 2013, after over seventeen years of providing leadership for the ministry of this dynamic and creative congregation.

THE SECOND PATHWAY BEGINS TO EMERGE and spiral toward the centre. It focuses less on my personal journey and more on enhancing skills and language to develop people's understanding, awareness and experiences of the depth and power of Intentional Circles and Authentic Connection Culture.

On April 8, 2013, I am aware that it is the first day of the rest of my life and I don't yet have clarity as to my path. I follow nudges that often surprise me, including travelling to meet teachers and engage in communities of learners. As a result, my work deepens, rooted in a sense of connection to wholeness even in the midst of the brokenness of the world. I feel supported and guided.

In the fall of 2014, I have a profound experience when I clearly articulate the passion that motivates me. I am invited by the new mayor of our community to provide the invocation for the inauguration of the city council. The writing of this invocation is a turning point for me. I hear myself articulating how my passion can impact the world.

The words for the invocation pour out of me with a power that captures with clarity the understanding that stirs deep within me. It is deeply connected to all the learning that I have experienced through Mom as well as the alternative perspectives and wisdom I have connected to since the late 1990s. I do little editing to my first version because it feels like it resonates with what I am called to say. It reflects the need for us to awaken to the ancient and alternative wisdom that longs to emerge in each of our personal lives, in our relationships throughout the city and beyond to the world.

It is December 1, 2014 when I share this invocation in the council chambers. I feel centred and grounded when I rise to offer these words:

In this time of invocation we begin with gratitude,
by thanking each of you
for responding to the call
to offer yourself in service to this community;
to offer yourself as ones who seek to be open to the future possibilities
of the new story that is longing to emerge.

We pause on this night to take note of this incredible moment ...
I invite us to notice our breath as we breathe deeply ...
breathing the gift of breath, the gift of Spirit ...
feeling our being expand ...
feeling our hearts gentle ...
feeling our minds open ...
being very aware of where we are ...
the sacredness of the place where we are and the time that is now.

This place where we gather, on the shores of two lakes,
gives birth to new life
through the narrow place where the two lakes meet.
It is a sacred place filled with creativity.
It is a place known from ancient times
as a powerful place of gathering in peace.
There is an energy here that nourishes and revitalizes
and will guide us, if we listen.

And so I encourage you as the council
to create space for the gift of the energy of this place,
pausing often in your work to listen to the wisdom
that is longing to emerge
from the land, the wind, the waters and the people.

You stand in a powerful place but also in a powerful time,
for this is a time of new beginnings, not just as a council,
but a time when we, in our global community,

are letting go of the old story of domination and control
and moving into a new story rooted in collaboration;
rooted in images of wholeness
of life being like a community garden
rather than like a machine that is driven.
One of our many creative people in our community,
pianist and author Michael Jones, notes that
we are in a new time of
"crafting a world where life can thrive."[11]

We are in the midst of a time of transition and transformation:
it is a time of letting go of belief in our limitations
to shift toward belief in possibilities;
a time of shifting from resource extraction to eco-sustainability;
a time of moving from fear to rejoicing in our diversity;
a time of identifying well-being not by accumulation of wealth,
but by the health of our community and natural environment.
It is a time of moving from hoarding to sharing;
from passive to active citizenship;
a time of cooperation and partnership.
This is a time for us to listen deeply to the story of this place,
to listen to the deep longing of humanity
so that together we journey toward
creating life-giving community.

Creative Energy,
Wisdom of Ancestors and Spirit,
Holy Presence that calls us to journey together toward wholeness:
Come and be known whenever this council gathers;

---

[11] Jones, Michael. *The Soul of Place: Re-Imagining Leadership Through Nature, Art and Community* (Victoria, BC: Friesen Press, 2014). Jones, Michael. *Artful Leadership; Awakening the Commons of the Imagination* (Victoria, BC: Trafford Publishing, 2006).

Come and fill the space
with gentleness that inspires
a spirit of life-giving collaborative community.

May blessings be poured upon and awakened within
these ones who have been chosen to serve;
blessings of creativity, of wisdom,
of being people who listen deeply and share honestly.

As you work together as members of this council,
may you see and celebrate the gifts and the light in each other;
may you listen for the deep wisdom that longs to emerge amongst you;
may you trust and anticipate that together
you will find a way forward that is filled with possibilities
that will honour the energy of the land and the lakes,
the wind and the sun.
May you be guided to honour this place of gathering
by deepening a sense of celebration of life.

And we, as the people of this city,
will hold you in our prayers,
surround you with grace,
and encourage you with our thoughts.

And now mayor and council members,
may you go forth into this calling with a daring and bold vision.
Go in peace.
And all that you do,
may you do it by the power of light and love
that is deep in the core of your being,
may you do it by the power of the Spirit and the energy of this land
that awaken wisdom and creativity
and call us to wholeness.

May it be so. Amen!

As I speak the invocation I hear and feel my voice emerging from the place of silence deep within me that I connected to in Hawaii.

———————————

In December 2014, I am prompted to begin to write a second book with a similar focus to the book I wrote on the beach in Florida in 2007. The 2014 book is entitled *The Mystical, Magical Power Within: Keys to Authentic Connection*. In early 2015 I tentatively rename the book *Creating Circle Culture: The Reawakening of Ancient and Alternative Wisdom*. Seventeen of twenty-five chapters are written. Preliminary editing is done.

In early February of 2015, while I am working on the book, I feel another nudge in my life. The nudge is rooted in the awareness that my life's work, which I am writing about in my book, may be particularly helpful in the time of transition we are experiencing in The United Church of Canada.

In the life of the United Church we are actively discerning our role in the world as carriers of the Gospel vision of wholeness and well-being for all. We are seeking to identify how our call can best serve the world around us in the midst of the fact that our people and our financial resources are diminishing.

As the church restructures to respond to a changing world around us, I feel nudged to re-open a conversation colleagues and church members have had with me over the years about someday letting my name stand for Moderator, which is the spiritual leader of the Canadian-wide United Church.

Through a series of conversations and times of prayerful meditation it is discerned within community that now is the time to follow these nudges and let my name stand for Moderator at the upcoming meeting of General Council in August 2015. Regardless of whether this is the time to serve as Moderator, colleagues and others are encouraging me by observing that the perspective I bring would enrich the conversation of the church at the national level.

On a cold winter's day in late February, as I am driving home from a weekend retreat where I have shared that I will allow my name to stand for Moderator, the traffic suddenly slows. The reason is surprising.

A family of three white wolves—one large, one medium and one small—is walking in the centre of the highway. I am filled with astonishment, joy and wonder. The white animals showing up around the globe are said by Indigenous Elders to indicate the dawning of the new story, when the old story of consumerism and extraction will give way to collaboration and honouring of the Earth and the wisdom of the heart. A central component of the new story is a new way of engaging with one another that involves deep listening and holding space for our creativity to inspire us. In this moment of awe as the wolves walk toward me within a foot of my car, it feels like the presence of the three white wolves is a sacred experience.

I later learn that Elders teach that Wolf represents the power to achieve balance in life between the physical and the spiritual, a deep connection with intuition, and awareness of the importance of social connection. Wolf emits intelligence and leadership.

The number three represented by the three wolves resonates with the energy of optimism, joy, inspiration, creativity, communication, expansion, broad-minded thinking and love through imagination. The spiritual significance of the number three is the power of the Trinity and indicates that there is divine protection, help and guidance.

The Trinity in my understanding is a mystical expression of God, Christ and Spirit. God as Creator is the source of the energy of life, which is love—an energy that infuses all of life. Christ refers to the Christ Consciousness that Jesus lived, and that we are all called to awaken to and develop in our lives. This consciousness sees through the eyes of love and calls us into action when love is obscured, resulting in us being authentic to our true self. Spirit is the energy that dances and twirls within us and amongst us, awakening us to our gifts and our callings, inspiring us to live the fullness of our capacity while rooting our lives in the demanding and creative power of love.

Seeing the three wolves on my path feels like a confirmation of the call to let my name stand as Moderator where leadership skills are critical and strong connection to the power of God's guidance is essential.

Two months later I become a nominee for Moderator. The twelve nominees are asked to introduce themselves in both formal and informal ways. One informal question is about a favourite movie. I respond:

> There is a movie that has resonated with me since I was a child. It is a story of a girl who sees the world differently than the people around her. When others see limitations she sees possibilities. Where others feel disgruntled she discovers the positive aspects and focuses on those. She encourages people to choose what is life-giving rather than only doing what they think is expected of them. She refuses to accept preconceived labels for people and instead sees the goodness in them. She protests perspectives based on fear and lifts up joy as an alternative option. As the movie unfolds, the community slowly shifts. Walls begin to crumble. Relationships build. Possibilities emerge. At the end of the movie, she is faced with her own despair. The now-transformed community rallies around her to remind her of the joy and potential for goodness in life. *Pollyanna* is a story of choosing to see the potential for goodness, a key step toward being the change we want to see in the world.

My formal introduction takes days to write. Below are key points:

> My vision for the church is rooted in my vision for the world. It is a dynamic vision of relationships grounded in trust and respect that animate the longing for wholeness and well-being that is stirring amongst us.

As we stand at the edge of the tenth decade of The United Church of Canada we find ourselves living in times of overwhelming disruption and amazing potential. In many ways, life as we've known it is ending. But are we dying, or might the pain and turmoil be connected to giving birth? In Isaiah's vision we are nudged by a question from God: "I am doing a new thing! Can you not see it?" We need to see the new thing God is doing. In these times when the familiar patterns and structures of our common life are radically shifting within the church and beyond, it is critical that we not be consumed by fear but rather see this as an opportunity for new possibilities to emerge.

In the midst of global turmoil there is also a global spiritual awakening. We see it in the 'blessed unrest' that is gathering people together for meaningful conversations, in people seeking authentic connections and right relations, and in a longing for respectful sharing of resources that do not devastate the Earth. We also see it in churches engaging new practices and perspectives.

As the church, we can more fully be part of this spiritual awakening, if we are willing. It will require us to be intentional about our inner work, clearing out attitudes that hold us in fear, despair and limitation so that love, joy and inspiration can guide us to a new vision. Through anticipation of new life we shift from focus on survival and fear of death of the church to focus on the new way God is calling us. We are charged to be God's love in action and to see possibilities infused with hope, knowing that whatever we give energy to will grow.

Our diminishing financial and people resources provide a catalyst to reimagine how we will be church. The world is crying out for meaning and connection. We have the capacity to create safe places for important conversations that need to happen in our neighbourhoods and in our lives. There are evolutionary efforts being made in the world and in our churches. We need to partner with people and groups to support positive initiatives that align with our goals for community of deep gratitude, compassion and wonder.

A central aspect of the work we will be doing in the coming years will be to develop relationships to shift how we interact. Can we risk engaging in decision-making in new ways, so that more voices will be heard through consensus building? Can we enter into relationships without the constraints of grasping for the way we have always done things? Can we see the light of love in everyone?

Can we move forward empowered by vision rather than fear, stay open to creative possibilities and be willing to be led by Spirit? Our hope is rooted in the trust that we are being called "to participate more energetically and faithfully in God's new creation." (*United in God's Work Report to GC42*)

Each candidate addresses the council, which is a crowd of over 500 people on location and livestreamed throughout the country. At five minutes and thirty seconds, the mic is turned off. We have to connect with people's hearts and minds within our span of allotted time. I begin with a story from my childhood:

The summer I am seven, my older sister and I make up a game where each of us choose members for an imaginary family, going back and forth to take turns.

Janis chooses famous people.
I choose people I know, until she picks John Lennon.
Then I claim Paul McCartney.
Her response: "But I want all the Beatles."

I think for a moment, and then say, "Okay, you pick anyone you want for your family, and my family will be everyone else."

"You don't want people in prison."
"Yes I do."

"You don't want people who live on the street."
"Yes I do."

The list continues, punctuated with my adamant "Yes I do."

That childhood game still impacts my life.

I look at strangers and think, "You don't know it, but I chose you to be in my family! … and you … and you … and you. I chose all of you to be in my family!"

The church gets it! Our crest declares, "That all may be one" and "All my relations."

Relationship, rooted in authentic connection, is a key to transformation. In the work ahead of us as the church, it is critical that we evolve by focusing on being relational … and *not* try to fix things from the mechanical perspective of the modern twentieth century.

A primary focus of my ministry has been to develop Intentional Circles so that meaningful conversations can happen to build relationships that open us to the wisdom within us and amongst us. Over the years I fine-tuned how to create safe life-giving Circles. In the midst of this work I have witnessed a new culture emerging. I describe it as Authentic Connection Culture.

In the culture created in Intentional Circles: 1) we create a non-anxious environment where it is safe to be authentic and courageous; 2) we listen deeply for the wisdom and creativity within us and amongst us so future possibilities emerge; 3) we allow love to guide us rather than fear; 4) we make space for joy, gratitude, respect and encouragement to thrive; 5) and we focus on what we *can* do.

Authentic Connection Culture creates space for the Christ Spirit to crack us open and align us with the energy of love. Although the culture of Intentional Circles is developed through spiritual and community practices … it is more than a system. It is a way of life. It can become the way we engage with the world.

I have seen the practices and principles of Intentional Circles *transform* lives, circumstances and congregations.

For the past decade I have worked in Circles with people from around the globe connected to The Art of Hosting Meaningful Conversations who are passionate, like me, about the potential for transformation in our world, our communities, our organizations.

So, when I read the reports for this General Council meeting I am encouraged by the commitment to renewal and transformation they contain. I am also deeply aware of the incredible time of transition we are entering as the church when we will need to inspire each other to be led by vision and Spirit, encourage each other to be open to new possibilities, and show up with a willingness to listen deeply and share stories of hope.

There is a spiritual awakening happening around the world and *we* get to be part of it! We have the opportunity to work with people everywhere who are committed to creating human lives that are environmentally sustainable, socially just, spiritually fulfilling and committed to creating cultures and practices of trust.

Evidence abounds, including in our workbook, that Spirit is at work in the world, guiding us toward the Kindom of God where relationships matter and the power that reigns is love.

As we journey forward together, may we listen deeply for Spirit ... an energy and presence that will challenge us, demand much of us, open us to joy and renewed life, and send us out to engage the world with the transformative power of love!

The reflections I share as a nominee for Moderator point to the impact of Mom and Dad on my life. They taught me about the importance of having a bold vision for my life as well as for the life of the community. They taught me about the importance of not allowing that vision to be obscured by fear that is often evoked by change. Mom taught me about the concept, articulated in the closing words of my speech, to "engage the world with the transformative power of love." She taught me to trust the power of love even when life is crashing down around us.

Many people's lives are richer because their path crossed Mom's life path, and mine is one of them. She taught me much about the power of change, compassion, creativity and community.

When the list of the names that will be on the third ballot for Moderator are read I am not on it, which means I will not be Moderator. I immediately hear a clear message. I am told that I am called in a different direction. I am told that there is something else I need to focus on. In that moment I am curious as to what that will be, but experience has taught me that when the new direction emerges I will know. Now, in 2017, I am aware that if I had been Moderator I would have struggled to find time to focus on the impact of all the shifts and changes of this unwinding story. I am glad I have the time to unpack the significance of this story.

THE THIRD PATHWAY OF MY EVOLVING JOURNEY arrives like a bulldozer creating a swath of upheaval on the landscape of our lives. It is the news of the shocking implications from the DNA test result that disrupts our lives in the early morning of April 18, 2016.

Janis and I connect periodically after the early morning call when our stories confirm the DNA science which determines that Scott is Janis's biological father. Both of our lives are so busy there isn't time for an in-depth conversation about how we are dealing with this new reality.

After the shocking DNA news, questions keep demanding my attention, even in the midst of a gruelling schedule. The disconcerting feeling of being off-kilter, because Janis and I might not be full sisters, never leaves me. My datebook shows that, along with other work, I facilitate thirty-two Circles between April and June, including a day of storytelling to identify ways the church can engage the neighbourhood. Typically I facilitate an average of ten to fifteen Circles in a two-month period, not thirty-two.

From April to June, I also co-facilitate a two-day retreat for clergy and I am the worship coordinator for a two-day Conference Annual Meeting, a gathering of over four hundred people. In May I help to organize the grand opening celebration of the newly named Centre for Community at a church where I have been consulting for the past two and a half years.

In early May our fourth grandbaby is born to Marissa. At the birth of each of our four grandchildren we have been invited to meet them right away. When the call comes to announce this birth we are asked to make chicken and fried rice before coming, which follows a tradition begun at the birth of our first grandbaby of bringing in favourite homemade meals to the hospital. Alan heads out to the BBQ at 1:00 in the morning while I go to the kitchen to chop vegetables and cook rice. When we arrive with our gift of food we are delighted to discover that Alan is our new grandson's middle name; this newest and last grandchild will carry his grandfather's name while the youngest child in our daughter Sarah's family shares my middle name of Celeste.

During these incredibly demanding two months, my energy keeps diverting to ponder the new reality of an extra biological father in our family. My mind keeps chewing on the pieces of the story that I know, trying to illicit other insights that will help me understand what might have happened decades before.

In the midst of the churning and the wondering and the heavy schedule, I am dealing with another heartbreaking reality. The day after the call from Janis that disrupted our lives, my beloved friend Lynn calls to tell me she has two large abdominal masses. It has been seven years since her last bout with cancer. On the phone that day she asks me if I will preside at her funeral. The cancer is quickly leading to her death. From April to June I spend as much time as I can with Lynn and her family. When I am with them I set aside this mystery that feels like it is consuming me. I want to focus on the tender moments of my friend's dying days.

In the middle of June, Janis texts to say she is coming to Canada to meet her newly discovered family. She hopes she can stay with me on the night of her arrival.

After all the turmoil of the past two months, it is good for Janis and me to be able to physically reach out and hug each other. We talk long into the night, sharing memories and wonderings, including exploring my strong sense that Mom and Dad did not know that Dad is not Janis's biological father.

During our late night conversation, Janis shares memories from her new cousin about Scott. As I listen to descriptions of him, the thought swirls through my mind that he is the kind of father that makes sense for who I am.

In the morning Janis prepares to head out to meet her cousin. From the beginning I feel discombobulated anytime she speaks of having a cousin that isn't mine. It doesn't feel right.

Before she leaves, we go for a quick visit to each of the homes of my daughters. While I read a story to my grandkids, Sarah asks her Aunt Jan how she is feeling about all that is happening. I listen as best as I can above the sound of my own reading. I don't catch all that is said, but one moment jumps out at me. I hear Janis exclaim that it is odd to think of not having any full siblings.

My gut wrenches. A strong feeling surges through me, rising in silent protest. "It isn't true. I am sure you have a full sibling."

With a sense of overwhelming grief I also acknowledge that it might be true that she doesn't have any full siblings. Whatever the outcome, it will demand that I reimagine and reinterpret who I am, whether I am not Janis's sister or I am not Dad's daughter.

Simmering grief has become a companion in the past months and not only as a result of this radical new reality in our lives.

On the morning of Christmas Eve 2015, our brother Mark died at sixty-three years of age. He had his first stroke the week before Mom died in October 2011, followed by another stroke and bypass surgery two and a half years later. Even though he had been dealing with medical difficulties for a while, his death is a shock. And now, not having him around to check in with about all the new details that are emerging makes the loss of him even more acute.

The reality of Lynn's impending death causes grief to walk with me through the moments of day-to-day life.

Throughout the five days in Canada, Janis keeps me up to date on where she is and who she is meeting. She sends pictures of her new aunt, Scott's half sister, along with memories from her aunt and three new cousins. The cousins include the aunt's daughter as well as another set of cousins who are sister and brother. The brother remembers babysitting us as kids at Scott's cottage. Janis also sends details of the family genealogy from Greg, the cousin she first meets who has traced the Macdonald family back to the 900s. It is his extensive knowledge of the family DNA that helps him figure out that Janis has to have a Macdonald parent.

Another of Janis's stops is to see our younger sister. While Janis is there, Betsy receives the results of her DNA test. Her report identifies Janis and Betsy as half sisters. The news indicates that they share only one parent, which would be Mom.

In the early hours of Tuesday, June 21, while Janis is still in Canada on her short five-day trip, my phone startles me awake. The call is to inform me that my friend Lynn has just died.

When I hear the news I am camping. In the midst of all that has been happening I decided to go on my annual camping retreat with my friend Tanis, knowing I needed to take care of myself, to refresh myself and reconnect to myself. I had offered to go with Janis on her travels but she wanted to go alone. I am glad for the three days of rest before having to face Lynn's death.

I drive toward Lynn's home in the early hours of the summer solstice. As I travel down an empty four-lane highway, a black wolf saunters out in front of me and slips away into the marsh at the side of the highway. It feels like I am seeing Lynn slip away, leaving an echo of the memories of her wisdom. The wolf is a symbol of freedom. Lynn is free, which has been her deepest longing in the past many weeks.

Her death is a relief, yet sobs crash through me to echo in the cool morning air. They are tears of joy that she has freedom, tears of gratitude for all we have shared, and tears of grief for the loss of our daily contact. In recent years we had chatted on the phone most days and gone swimming two or three times a week, a time filled with healing and laughter and spiritual companionship.

For a long time we have both worked out our thoughts and feelings about life in our conversations together. I have been missing her, as the landscape of my life shifts through the reality of an extra biological father in our family.

Over the next three days, I immerse myself in writing the service to celebrate Lynn's life, trying to capture the depth of her gift to the world, to ensure that it reflects the understandings, learnings and insights that have been important to her. Grief overwhelms me, and I wonder if I will be able to get through the service without significantly breaking down. It doesn't bother me to have tears when I am leading a service, but uncontrolled sobs will not be helpful.

Then I remember that when Lynn and I were together back in May, while we were lying on the bed in the camping trailer looking out the window at the sky and the trees, she told me she would be standing right beside me surrounding me with her love when the time comes for the service.

Lynn's celebration of life service is on Saturday, June 25, Mom and Dad's wedding anniversary. After leading the service and connecting with all the people who love Lynn, I feel totally drained. I head home, seeking a place of peace and quiet to process how I am doing and what I need.

I feel like I have been bombarded from every direction through these past six months. Shifts and changes keep coming, demanding my energy and commitment to delve deeply into the dynamics of life. Once things started to unravel, an unrelenting momentum propelled them along, opening new possibilities and uncovering the richness of new insights and perspectives, creating new pathways to deepen my understanding of life.

Normally, this is a journey I embrace in life. But for just a while I would like to pause, to have time to ponder or to simply sit without any thoughts at all.

FOUR DAYS LATER, ON WEDNESDAY JUNE 29 at 12:10 p.m., I check emails in preparation for an afternoon meeting. A message from Family Tree DNA pops up. My DNA test results have arrived.

A charge goes through me. I click on the report and go to the section that identifies relatives. I hold my breath in anticipation of information that will significantly impact my life.

I stare at the information.

Janis is listed as my full sister. Betsy is identified as my half sister.

I exhale loudly into the room.

The family friend we called 'uncle' Scott is my father too …

I feel something shift inside of me; it's like my core is strengthening and expanding, becoming a magnet to attract fragmented pieces back to the centre. It feels like pieces of my life that have never quite lined up now make sense. They begin to click into place.

At 12:11 I call Janis. She picks up right away. I tell her I have received my DNA results and she responds with a tone that indicates her impatience to know.

"And …?"

"I'm your full sister. 'Uncle' Scott is my father too."

She's thrilled, proclaiming loudly to the person beside her, "I have a full sister!"

When we hang up after talking about who needs to be told right away, I pause for a moment to take note of what is happening.

Then I reach for the phone and call Alan to tell him. It feels like a sacred moment. We allow this awareness to move between us after all the turmoil and demands we have shared around caring for Mom.

Somewhere in the conversation, Alan tells me, "Well, I love you no matter what," and laughs.

His comment is a gift. His laughter reminds me that it is me he loves no matter what my background. His words and tone ground me, realigning the pieces that shifted off the pillar within me when Janis first told me she had a different father than the one who raised us.

I continue to feel a shift happening in me, as I claim this new reality and allow me to be me.

Next, I call our daughters. We talk about what this means regarding their actual relatedness to different aunts and cousins. We are intrigued to note that the cousin they feel closest to is the one they spent the most time with, who it turns out is a half cousin. Relationship and shared memories have impacted their sense of closeness more than DNA.

In many ways this is true for Janis and me as well. It's not just that we have the same DNA.

As kids, Janis and I spend a lot of time together. We share a bedroom where we share our dreams long into the night. One dream is to create a village of homes from the shale rock down by the creek near our home. Those conversations peter away after we go and actually try to build our dream village. Years later, it is a delight to wander through Janis's home and see how she has incorporated many of our childhood decorating ideas into her décor.

As university students, Janis and I live together for more than a year. For our weddings, we are each other's lead bridesmaid. As adult women with adult kids, we spend blocks of time together visiting in each other's homes for special occasions or just to hang out.

So the closeness between Janis and me is rooted in more than just shared DNA. Our closeness is also about memories and opportunities through which our relationship develops.

As all these thoughts bombard me, I reach for the phone and call Betsy. Janis reminded me that Betsy will receive the email from Family Tree DNA with updates on people she is related to, but I want to be the one to tell her.

Betsy doesn't answer. I leave a message asking her to call me.

It isn't long before I receive an email from my new "first cousin once removed" who identified Janis as a Macdonald. Greg welcomes me to the family, which is a delight, though also somewhat disconcerting.

Janis and I continue to have quick conversations back and forth, updating each other as the story is shared.

Then, just before 3 p.m., caller ID alerts me to a call coming in from Betsy. I excuse myself from my meeting to take her call.

Betsy begins by saying she is sorry she missed my call. She is leaving again in a few minutes but my message sounded important, so she has taken the time to phone back.

I tell her, "I have received my DNA test results, and you will have an email sharing the results."

She responds casually, saying, "Okay, what does yours say?"

I hesitate for a moment and then reply, "Janis and I are full sisters. You and I are half sisters."

"What?"

It sounds like I have just punched her in the gut.

Her response echoes through me, reverberating deep in my soul.

I apologize. "I'm sorry we haven't talked since Janis shared her news. I've thought all along that this is a real possibility."

"Why? What made you think that?"

"Well, Janis and I have always been so much alike, and you and Mark are so much alike, and not just in personality. It is more of a deep feeling, an awareness of a different type of energy. I couldn't imagine that Janis and I are not full sisters. It didn't make sense of my life."

"You mean you felt it intuitively?"

"Yes."

With distress, she exclaims, "Well how do I know whether or not I am Dad's daughter?"

I laugh, and then quickly realize that is probably not the best response when my beloved sister is wailing.

I tell her, "Oh Betsy, there is no doubt you are Dad's daughter. All you have to do is look at your bottom lip. It is identical to Dad's and Mark's. It is very distinct."

She isn't convinced. "Well, I don't see it. It's hard when you are looking at just yourself in the mirror."

I feel my heart break, wishing this all could have happened when Mark was still alive.

I hear myself say something that I've never thought before. It rises up in me and exits my mouth before my brain can grab it and process it.

"Betsy, you are the one who brought Mom back to us. She was fading away after the death of her youngest sister, but when she got pregnant with you, she came back. Mom always told us that Dad was the one who really wanted another baby. When Mom almost died because of complications from a pregnancy when I was six months old, the doctors told Mom and Dad they shouldn't have any more children. I think Dad knew that if he didn't do something he would lose her to the depression that was consuming her. He might lose her through the pregnancy like he almost did five years earlier, but I now wonder if he thought it was a risk worth taking because if he didn't do something, he would lose her for sure. Betsy, you are a reflection of Dad's love for Mom."

Frustrated by limited time, Betsy says she has to go because she has a class to teach. When she speaks, her tone has changed from the anguish of the earlier part of the conversation. She sounds more settled but still filled with questions. We say we will talk again soon.

Later in the evening of the day when we find out that Janis and I are full sisters, Janis tells me that she and one of her daughters have figured out when she was likely conceived based on her birth date. It would have been around November 20.

I ask her to wait for a second while I check something.

When I come back on the line, I say, "Actually I suspect you were conceived on November 28—the day of the Grey Cup party in 1953."

Mom and Dad and their friends always had a big party for Grey Cup Sunday where alcohol was consumed in larger than normal quantities. Mom was okay drinking wine or beer. Hard liquor, however, was the trigger for Mom to flip into her uninhibited personality of the Partying One, the one I believe is intimate with Scott.

So the Grey Cup party of 1953 fits the date of Janis's birth of August 1954.

Since Mom has two children by Scott, people have jumped to the conclusion that the two of them had an ongoing affair. I do not think that is the case. Janis would have been conceived at a party where alcohol was flowing. When Mom is the Partying One, she is lively and flirtatious, but also disoriented and vocally unhappy with her life. From my experience, she acted in a way that demanded attention, perhaps leading others to suspect that she lacks it in the rest of her life. In Scott she finds someone who listens and understands her.

I also begin to suspect that Scott had celiac disease, which leads me to reflect on another impact of alcohol on their intimate moments. Let me explain.

From stories I have heard from Scott's sister about difficulties he had with his stomach all his life, I suspect that he had celiac disease. My suspicion may seem based on vague details. However, when you consider that celiac disease is a genetically transmitted disease and we have not been able to identify anyone who is an obvious candidate to have passed the disease to members of Janis's family and mine, it makes sense that we inherited that tendency from our biological father.

And here's the key point as to why I wonder if alcohol played more of an impact on the relationship between Mom and Scott: as a person with celiac disease, I know from experience that people who are celiac are extremely susceptible to intoxication from alcohol with grains that originally had gluten in them, which is most alcohol.

Research says that the gluten is gone, but there is acknowledgement that the impact of such alcohol is strong for people who are celiac.

Scott's sister told me that he rarely drank, except at parties. So the combination of Mom shifting to her flirtatious partying personality as a result of consuming alcohol, and the possibility of Scott being more impacted by the consumption of alcohol than an average person because of celiac disease, creates a scenario not common in everyday life.

I suspect that their intimate encounters are only at parties where alcohol is consumed. I can imagine that they wander off to chat as buddies. As more hard liquor is consumed, unplanned choices are made.

Eighteen months after the 1953 Grey Cup party the gang would have been together at Scott's cottage for the Victoria Day long weekend in 1955. Mom could once again partake in the social drinking because she is neither pregnant nor nursing as she has been at all the parties since the Grey Cup party of 1953.

The date of the May 24th Victoria Day weekend celebration is nine months before my birthday of February 1956.

TWO DAYS AFTER I LEARN that Scott is my biological father, Alan and I head out for a Canada Day celebration weekend with another couple. It is an extended weekend filled with camping (or glamping, which better describes the plush way that we camp), going out on our ATVs, and creating amazing food. On the first night, as we sit around the campfire under a star-filled sky, I tell our friends about my DNA test results. It is good to be able to share, in one sitting, the fullness of this story, going right back to Janis finding out about being a Macdonald. They listen attentively and ask lots of questions.

The next morning, when I step out of the trailer, the husband in the couple asks me, "So who are you this morning?" I smile at him, appreciating the acknowledgment of his interest in the long story I told the night before.

The weekend provides lots of processing time. When I am on the ATV I can sit in my own little world without distractions, supported as I lean into the strong back of my husband. As we fly down wooded paths filled with luscious foliage nestled beside glistening lakes, memories pop in and out of my head.

One memory is that if people called me by the wrong name when I was younger, they consistently called me Heather—a good Scottish name. I also remember that there were kids in my high school class who had the last name of Macdonald. I wonder if any of them are related to me.

When I wake up in the morning I check my emails. I am intrigued that I have a notification that I have been tagged on a Facebook picture from August 2015, eleven months earlier when I was a nominee for Moderator.

The comment says, "I know Karen. I went to high school with her."

I don't recognize the person's name. I check the profile pictures on her page. On the fifth picture, I look into a face I recognize as a Macdonald from high school.

I shake my head, startled. She is someone I have had no contact with since high school.

This whole experience has deepened my awareness of how intricately all of life is interconnected. One of the ways that I experience this profound connection is in how the thoughts and wonderings of my mind keep physically showing up in my life. It happens several times that weekend, with the Facebook moment being a significant one. I think about the Macdonald kids in high school, and one shows up on Facebook the next day.

There is another simple moment when my thoughts show up in a physical way when we are out on the ATV. Shortly after one of our rides begins, we stop to meet someone and see the property they have just purchased. I am frustrated by the stop. I want to keep riding so I have time to ponder.

However, we are stopped, so I figure I might as well shift away from grumbling.

A thought flits into my head: "Well, maybe I can at least find a store nearby so I can buy the lighter we need."

I glance around, but all the stores are permanently closed.

To let go of my sense of frustration, I intentionally gaze over the landscape to absorb the setting. We are standing on a lush, large lawn with cute, quaint cabins facing a sparkling lake. I breathe deeply and relax, enjoying the warm sunshine and cool breeze. I glance around, noticing light emanating all around me.

Something catches my eye in the grass in front of me. I bend down. It is a lighter.

It is early evening on the third day after arriving home from our ATV weekend. Alan is away fishing with his four brothers. I am savouring my time at home alone. I groan when I notice we have a phone message. I wonder if I have to check it right away. Then I realize it could be six days old. I listen to it. It is from my cousin. His mother was Mom's youngest sister who was killed in the car crash. His message says he's spoken to Janis and wants to know more information. He asks me to call him.

Since the message came in three days ago, I call him immediately.

He asks me if I have spoken to Janis recently. I say, "Yes."

"So you know what's going on—that you two have a different father than your Dad?"

"Yes, I've been part of figuring that out."

His response is, "Well I don't get it. How can that be?" He sounds agitated.

I understand his feelings. Though we all spent a lot of time together when we were growing up, my siblings and I didn't talk about what went on in our home when no one else was there. The story he is about to hear will be new to him.

I tell him about my experiences with the many personalities of Mom, about the mental health challenges that I believe she lived with for most of her life. Again I hear myself declare that I don't think she knew we are Scott's daughters and that Dad didn't know either.

I tell him what I have told others: "I don't think the personality that partnered with Scott actually carried her own memories at all, somewhat like, but more than, a person who is drunk doesn't remember all that they do."

My doorbell rings. My dinner has arrived. My cousin says we can talk later.

I sit out on the back deck enjoying the quiet of the evening wondering what it must be like for my cousin to hear my perception of Mom's mental health challenges for the first time. Since Alan is away, I am alone with my thoughts. The night grows dark. I sit and savour the stillness.

At 9:35 the phone rings. The beeps indicate it is a long-distance call. I can't get from the deck to the phone before the machine answers. I finish my dinner, and then check my phone. The last call was from an area code I don't recognize. I figure out it is from the area where the sister of the cousin I spoke to earlier lives. I call the number.

It is my cousin, and she is extremely upset. She is adamant that what she heard from her brother can't be true and that I must be wrong. It can't be true because my Mom, her aunt, is the one who saved her life. She is clear she does not want to take her beloved aunt off the pedestal she has had her on for years.

We engage in conversation for an hour and a half. By the end of the call, she acknowledges that she has experienced the different states in Mom over the years, particularly when they have been drinking. More than once in her memory it seemed like Mom wanted to talk about things my cousin didn't want to hear, so she suggested that they go to bed.

I tell her about the depth of Mom's struggle and remind her that even in the midst of all that Mom personally dealt with, she was still an incredible pillar of strength for others. I share my thoughts with her: "You and your brother are not the only ones she helped so much. She helped lots of people. So instead of seeing this as some indication that she's not worthy of high regard because she had two children with someone other than her husband, I think the way she helped so many people, combined with her personal struggles, is a testimony to the incredible person she was."

My cousin ends the call by confirming that she was most concerned about Janis and me and that it is good we are okay.

Over the next three weeks, I have the opportunity to meet, or in some instances re-meet, a few of the Macdonald clan that I now know are part of my family. It feels comfortable and dynamic to be with them, like our energies align in a way that feels familiar.

On July 10, I meet Greg, my new "first cousin once removed" who contacted Janis to explain the Macdonald connection.

It is good to connect and to hear Greg's story about the details of his life. We sit and piece together the stories of our childhoods and beyond, delving into who Scott was for each of us. Greg has memories of playing with Janis and me at Scott's cottage. He recognizes a picture of Janis as a kid that I have in our home.

The next week I drive to his home. We spend the day immersed in the work he has done to create our massive family tree. He has identified lineage that goes back to the 900s. He shares that according to ancestry research eighty percent of the people with the Macdonald name in the world are not actually from the lineage of the kings and chieftains. Only twenty percent are from the original line. Many of the rest have taken on the name of their leader or land owner generations before. We are part of the twenty percent who carry the DNA of the chieftains. Our family tree includes lots of royalty, leaders and chiefs. The geographical area of our clan includes both Iona and the Isle of Mull which were the key places I travelled when I went to Scotland. No wonder I felt the strong sense of coming home to a place I'd never been before. No wonder I was drawn to wander in the cemetery on Iona that is filled with my ancestors.

Later in the afternoon, his wife and I head out to their glorious deck that overlooks a lake. We have a wonderful chat about our years of discovering who we are as women.

One of the things that I share with my new cousin's wife is my wonderings about the impact of my DNA from Scott, combined with the influence of my Dad as a role model. Both were astute business people with different styles. I'm glad that I have the influence of both of them in my life.

I tell her a story. It is the story when Alan and I decide, while on our honeymoon, to start our own business. On the Sunday we return home, we spend the day with Dad, sharing our vision and dream of our own business with him. Dad is totally absorbed. He had once tried to start his own business and so he has lots of ideas. He advises us on the steps we need to take to start a business. His suggestions are woven through with great caution to ensure that the business will be viable. Steps include researching the market and starting small as we both continue to work.

Alan and I listen intently to Dad's wisdom. Then we listen to our own wisdom late into the night. We decide Alan will go to work the next day and tell them he is leaving. I will continue to work at the dealership.

When we call Dad Monday night he is shocked but impressed with our bold step. Two weeks after we marry we go down to one salary and Alan begins developing our woodworking business.

Scott is different. Like Dad, he was a visionary, but from the stories I know he was bolder in action as one who lived with a vivid sense of enthusiasm. While the Dad who raised me taught me to consider all cautionary steps while building a vision, I wonder if the DNA from my biological father compels me to be willing to take risks that often lead to wonderful new evolutions in my life.

The day of sharing stories ends with Greg piping me out to "Amazing Grace." In many ways, this journey is filled with amazing grace that is deepening my understanding of me.

A week later, I visit Scott's only surviving sibling, a sister. Greg and his wife go as well.

When I arrive at the door, I am welcomed by a feisty, delightful woman. "Karen, I presume?" I nod. "I guess I'm your aunt."

It is clear that she is ticked at her brother Scott. Her daughter confirms, during another afternoon of conversation between cousins, that finding out about Janis was a novelty for her mother. By the time the news is known about my connection to the family, Scott's sister is primarily focused on being furious at her brother.

The afternoon I meet Scott's sister she tells me how perturbed she is with her brother.

Later, my new aunt's daughter arrives. She is my first cousin, though not a full cousin. Scott and his sister have different mothers.

Scott's mother, my grandmother, died when Scott was very young. Even so, I see physical similarities between this new cousin and me.

For my whole life, I always looked so much like Mom I didn't wonder where I got my looks from because I was sure I knew; I just looked like Mom. It is uncanny to now see physical similarities with people beyond the family I have known. It provides greater awareness of who I am—a visual clarity that I didn't know I was missing. But it does finally explain my peculiar nose, which was the one tiny part about my looks that I have wondered about all my life. It is clear that I got my nose from Scott.

Seeing myself in the face of a stranger is a powerful experience. It feels like fragmented pieces coming together.

Though my experience is not anywhere near as stark, I understand something of how my half sister Lynda might have felt the day we met in 1993. I am the first member of the family Lynda meets when she finds Mom after eleven years of searching. On that morning when Lynda and her Mom get out of the car, she stares at me, and exclaims, "Look Mom, someone with the same hair as me. And the same colour eyes as me!"

Then she gives me a bouquet of two dozen red roses. The only thing I have to give her is a partial reflection of what she has seen of herself in a lifetime of mirrors.

A later conversation with my new aunt contributes to feeling like the magnet within my core is drawing fragmented pieces home. I ask her how she would describe the characteristics of the Macdonald clan that she saw in her brother. She names his kindness, the way he supported people, his success, and his ever-present charm. She goes on to say that when she thinks back on Scott's life, what is clear is that people really liked him; the whole family knew they could depend on him to help. He was loyal; he still had friends from his childhood when he died in his early fifties.

Her description of Scott fits my memories. As a kid, I spend my time watching people. I notice that whenever anyone is talking to Scott, he gives them his full attention. He had a way of making people feel special. I always love when our families got together at the cottage and when he and his wife came for the evening parties at our home. I miss him when all that stopped. I miss his two kids as well, particularly his daughter, with whom I feel a strong sense of affinity. But it is Scott I miss the most.

In the early days of living with this new reality of my biological father not being my Dad, I have the opportunity to be with a group of young people I adore.

I am at the wedding of one of the kids I confirmed during my years at Downtown United Church. The wedding party is filled with other kids from their enquiry group. It is good to be with them.

During the rehearsal dinner, one of them asks what's happening in my life. I say, "I will tell you sometime, but it is too lengthy a story to go into tonight." I am asked for a quick overview statement. I offer a glimpse: "I have just found out that my sister and I have a different father than the Dad who raised us. We discovered it through a DNA test."

An hour later, a couple of them lead me to a chair amongst some couches they have pulled together into a circle. There's a large group of them gathered. They plunk me down and lean in to listen to my story.

As they listen and ask probing questions, tears well up in my eyes. This is how we spent our time during their group when they were teenagers—listening deeply to one another and holding space so that the storyteller could speak their insights in a safe community. I feel grounded and grateful for their interest, their compassion, and their ability to create healthy, life-giving community.

THE FOURTH PATHWAY OF MY EMERGING JOURNEY takes hold of my life in the last week of July 2016 while Alan and I are camping for our two-week holiday. I tell Alan I have to start to write. A book is emerging. I find myself rehearsing the opening line. It is time to write it.

That night we have an intriguing experience. While we sit quietly by the fire, both absorbed in our thoughts, a beautiful, healthy fox emerges from the bushes around our campsite. We have a circle of solar lights around the fire pit. The fox walks into the campsite between the circle of lights and the fire. The fox is within reaching distance of us. We are stunned and astonished. We have encountered many animals while camping. But we are shocked by how close this one comes and how nonchalantly it meanders through the campsite.

The next day I check the Internet for the spiritual meaning of Fox. According to Indigenous wisdom, the energy of Fox provides guidance to find our way around obstacles. It is an indication of being in a time when discernment is required to see through deception, and for clarity in tricky situations. It is a call to pay attention. Fox indicates that we may be challenged, but we have the strength to learn the lessons that are ours to learn.

The arrival of the fox seems particularly timely as I begin to explore how to share a story that has significantly impacted my life, but it is not just my story.

Later in the week I contact my sister Betsy to see if we might get together while we are camping in her neck of the woods. Their lives are busy, but we find an afternoon that works. It is good to be together and to confirm what Betsy has been clear about as the DNA test results came in: to us, the DNA results don't change anything. We are still fully connected sisters.

Betsy and I, along with our husbands, go out for lunch, meander around a fruit and vegetable market together, and spend time at a specialty coffee shop. The afternoon is filled with rich conversation.

———————

As the days unravel, I spend time working on my book. I find myself living in the memories of my teen years when I first consciously and significantly experience Mom's difficulties. At page seventy-five of the handwritten version of this book, Alan and I go to a gathering with his family. During the party I have several conversations about this new reality in my life.

One conversation is with a sister-in-law. She is puzzled as to why anyone would want to do a DNA test. I explain the reason for Janis doing a DNA test. Then I share with her that I will be working on writing this story while I am alone at their cottage next week.

She looks at me and asks, "You really feel you need to write about this?"

Good question. A feeling of certainty that this is important, not just for me, but also for others, flows through me.

I also have a significant conversation with Alan's older sister. I share the story from a different perspective with her. I talk about all the amazing ways her brother Alan stepped up to help take care of Mom and provide support for me over the years.

It feels good to share this perspective of the story with her. No one in Alan's family knows all that he has done over the past many years. They couldn't know. We have never talked about it until now.

The party is amazing. The next day is filled with shifting emotions. It is a day of tears and joy, shock and sadness.

We stay overnight in our trailer. In the morning our youngest niece tells us her mother wants us to come up and have coffee with them.

Over coffee Alan's youngest sister reaches down beside the chair where I am sitting and pulls up a small black case. She hands me the case. I immediately recognize it. It is the clarinet Dad and Mom gave me for my eighteenth birthday. I sold it to Alan's sister years before. Alan and I needed to raise money to fix my car to drive to the nearby city to do my internship. It had been Dad's last car. I sold anything I could so that I could repair and keep that car. There was a sense of Dad's presence in the car that I found supportive, comforting and encouraging as I prepared to be a minister.

As I hold the case I have not seen in years, tears pour down my face to speak on my behalf.

On the drive home I think of the three pieces of jewellery, also gifts from my parents, which are sitting on my dresser waiting to be repaired. The first is the gold necklace watch that Scott gave me when I was eight. The second is a gold bangle that Dad gave me when I was eleven. The third is a gold spiral necklace that Mom picked out for me. The spiral necklace has become a signature piece of jewellery for me in my adult years as a reflection of the spiritual journey that spirals out from our centre to carry light and love into the world.

Three pieces of gold jewellery: one from my biological father, one from my Dad, one from my Mom. And now this fourth gift of the clarinet, a gift from my parents who raised me, who knew the intricacies of my everyday life and the things that I love. It seems right that there are four precious gifts from these three significant people in my life.

On the way home the day after the party, I check my emails one last time in preparation for a weeklong writing retreat. The second email is from my sister Betsy. The subject line is "sad news." With apprehension I open it.

She has just heard that in July our family farmhouse burned down. Shock surges through me. Tears swamp me. Grief overwhelms me.

For the past week, I have been writing stories that all happened at the farmhouse. The power of that place and its profound impact on my life has filled the hours of writing. The farm provided me with a sense of being grounded when my world, impacted by an emotionally and mentally unstable mother, crashed around me. During the past week of writing stories of the difficulties with Mom during the early seventies, I entered back into a multitude of memories, feeling myself there in our home.

I feel raw and overwhelmed. I share my despair and shock with Alan until words are choked by tears.

A few hours later, after the trailer has been set up in the driveway, Alan and I sit down together on the front deck of the cottage. This is where I will spend the week alone to write.

After an hour of numbness, sobs rise up in me. At first, I try to contain them, but they erupt with a power that defies my attempt to squash them.

Alan kneels in front of me and holds me as I cry. He reminds me I still have the memories of my family home. He's right.

I am grateful we were able to go to the farm on the day we buried Mom in 2011. That day of walking through the house and out on the land confirms that my memories of our home are accurate. I can return to our family home and be there anytime I choose. The tears begin to subside.

Alan and I sit in the silence of the night as the stars fill the sky. In the stillness, a new awareness nudges its way into my thoughts.

I realize that it is four years ago this week that I spent five days at this cottage with two friends: Lynn, my friend who died in June, and our friend Kathie, who travelled with the two of us to Hawaii. We came to celebrate Lynn's seventieth birthday. It was a week filled with new insights and great healing as the three of us shared our unique healing processes. We entered deeply into our lives to clear away any lingering wounds. It was a time of preparation to move more fully into our roles as elders, with Lynn leading the way.

Memories of that powerful week and our deep friendship send tears rolling down my cheeks—tears of joy and grief but also a profound awareness of how quickly life can change.

Although tears come to me quickly in my life, they rarely last more than a moment. I find this deluge of tears to be extremely disconcerting. I groan, thinking how I repeatedly encourage people to not hold back their tears. I try to acknowledge the wisdom I share with others about the power and importance of tears. What is clear is that I have no choice about these tears. They just keep coming.

Alan suggests we go to the trailer where we can get comfortable to cuddle. I put on a CD of the hits of Simon and Garfunkel. The song "Bridge Over Troubled Water" fills the air, soothing me in this melancholic moment.

As I lean into Alan's arms, I am aware I am not alone as I grieve. I am gently held in love.

———————————

After Alan leaves the cottage on Monday night to go home to work for the week, I enter a silent retreat and this story.

The whole week is an experience of prayer. I listen for guidance and try to be open to what is emerging. Prayer for me is about listening deeply beyond the clatter of everyday life so that insights, questions and wisdom can emerge. I enter into this week of silent prayer knowing I am changed by prayer. Sometimes the change prayer brings is demanding and challenging, sometimes it is soothing and nourishing. Whenever I spend significant time in prayer, the gifts of the Spirit—joy, patience, courage and gentleness—awaken more fully within me. They nourish the landscape of my inner being, filling it with beauty, creativity and glorious colour.

Each morning I sit in quiet solitude on the deck. One day the sunlight is particularly strong, so I put up the huge umbrella to block some of the intensity. As I sit drinking my tea, a small bird swoops down toward me. I watch its antics. After a few moments, I realize it is not a bird. It is a bat. It keeps coming closer each time it swoops down, coming under the umbrella several times, then back around to come toward me again. I sit and watch for a time until I can no longer handle how close it is flying to me. I scurry back to the trailer with my hand over my long hair. When I look back the bat is nowhere to be seen.

I again turn to the Internet to research the spiritual meaning of an animal. Bat is a symbol of intuition, rebirth and inner depth. It is a highly social creature with strong family ties. Bat coming into my life indicates a time of challenge that will demand one hundred percent commitment to spiritual growth. It will be a time of initiation as I journey toward my highest potential.

Since this spiritual meaning of Bat resonates so strongly, I decide to check out Loon and Hummingbird as well. All summer, hummingbirds keep showing up in places where I don't normally see them. While the loon is a common presence at the cottage, this year the loons keep coming right up into the swimming area in front of the cottage rather than staying out farther on the lake.

Hummingbird is described as a call to enjoy life and the journey. That feels like a good perspective to hold: enjoy this journey.

Loon symbolizes tranquility and the reawakening of old hopes. According to Black Feather, also known as David J. Nagy, the presence of Loon heralds a time of diving within, accessing other dimensions of our universal self, and gleaning wisdom from events that we otherwise wouldn't experience in our ordinary waking life.

Diving deep within and gleaning wisdom from events that come from a perspective beyond everyday life feels like a good description of this unfolding experience of telling my story.

As I finish writing the description of the symbolism of Loon, I hear a noise outside that sounds like it is out of place. I go out to check.

It takes a moment to find where the sound is coming from, but then I see it. It's a loon flying overhead, heading away from the water. It is filling the sky with its unique sound. I have only ever heard its call from the water. Now it is flying directly over me with its trilling sound filling the air, heading toward the east, the direction of the dawning of a new day. It feels significant.

Four animals, each one bringing a call to awakening: to go deep, to trust my discernment, and to journey with joy. They seem like the perfect companions for this journey of new perspectives and insights into who I am in this time of pausing to look back to see influences in my life of which, until late June of this year, I was not aware.

Fox, in particular, seems like a good companion. Writing the book provides me with the opportunity to sort through details and delve deeper into the untold story of Mom's life and mine to draw together the fragmented and fractured pieces in a way that feels authentic and clarifying.

It is a time for me to reflect deeply on how Mom's ever-changing mental state helps me learn the importance of finding ways to create healthy relationships that enable people to work together so that future possibilities can emerge, even in the midst of changing dynamics and demanding interconnections.

Fox feels like an incredible gift because of the energy it brings. According to Indigenous teachings, when Fox showed up in my life, on the day I realized I had to write this book, it came to make me aware that I need to be open to guidance around obstacles, to pay attention, to trust my discernment to see clearly in tricky situations, and to realize I have the strength to learn the lessons that are mine to learn. That feels right as I explore how the multitude of threads weave together to create a tapestry of life filled not only with fractured realities but also insights and wisdom that illuminate pathways to wholeness.

PERCEIVING THE BEAUTY

OF A MENDED MIRROR

WHILE I AM WRITING this book on seeing wholeness despite brokenness in the world, the iconic Canadian storyteller Stuart McLean dies. His words resonate:

> It is not said enough so I will say it again: the world is a good place, full of good people, and when we act out of that, when we act out of hope and optimism, and faith in our fellow human, we act out of our best selves, and we are capable of doing great things and of contributing to the greater good.
>
> Hope and optimism are not synonymous with naivety. We should be looking to the future with flinty and steely eyes, for sure, but they should be wide open with hope, not squinting in fear.

So true Stuart, so very true.

A new awareness emerging through this story is a sense of gratitude that my core strength of optimism finally makes sense, and has validity for who I am. For much of my life I have kept my optimistic strength somewhat contained, which I suspect some people will be shocked to hear since I am known as an optimistic person. But that optimism and ability to see possibilities have always been held back to a certain degree.

I have been squashing my optimism and an inner strength in me because I assessed them as unacceptable to others.

A colleague who often challenged my level of optimism and my inclination to focus primarily on what is good once told me he was stunned to discover how strong I am. He thought my optimism resided in a lack of awareness of reality but he realizes that my strength resides in my deep awareness of the goodness of the world in spite of its brokenness. He described me as being like an iron fist in a velvet glove, who is strong and firm about the gentleness that is possible amongst us. I now understand my strong core is because of my Macdonald DNA.

I am aware that, when this inner strength comes out, it feels less mature than other parts of me. Of course it does. It is a part of me that I have judged harshly. I have kept it in the depths of my being rather than allowing it to develop in a healthy and appropriate manner. I have kept it hidden rather than let it infuse the landscape of my life with a gentle acceptance of the gift of strength. Now I do not have to contain the part of me that, in the family in which I grew up, felt too strong, too kind, too expressive, too much.

When I meet another new cousin, a full cousin, I see a reflection of my core strength and big presence in her. She feels familiar to me as soon as we meet. Our energies align.

The day I meet her I go to her home for lunch. When I sit down at the table I am quite struck by the fact that she has set the table exactly how Mom taught me to properly set a table. A year later when she is visiting Janis, Janis mentions that Mom's name is Ellie. It turns out our cousin has a very clear memory of Mom. Ellie invites her to help set the table at the cottage, but it has to be done just so. Our cousin remembers running around to find matching jars to hold fresh-picked wildflowers and how Mom taught her to intentionally place all the utensils and glasses in relation to the dinner plate and side plate just as she taught us.

The more time I spend with our cousins, the more I settle into this part of me that I have kept at the edges of my life. As time goes on I find myself connecting to this core strength in each of my new family members.

Early in 2017, I am astonished how much I am continuing to uncover insights into the impact of Mom's mental health challenges and the new awareness of my DNA on both my life and my life's work. I keep wrestling with new insights as layers of understanding emerge that were not possible to see until the most recent layer had been exposed. The work of unpacking this story demands that I not be satisfied with simply putting together the pieces of the puzzle. A completed puzzle will only provide a flat and thin picture of details. This work is demanding that I delve much more deeply into who I am and how I am called to be in life.

In February of 2017 I become concerned about a pain in my chest. I wonder if this journey has been more stressful than I realize. I have lived with the concern of heart disease because my Dad died young of a heart attack. I now know that my biological father dealt with extensive heart disease at an even earlier age. The pain concerns me from a physical perspective, but I wonder if there is an emotional component to it as well. I am aware that I am plunging into unchartered territories.

During one of the late-night conversations with my friend Tanis, I tell her that I am experiencing chest pain. While I talk to her I realize that there is something deeper going on.

I am surprised when I say, "I feel as though I am dying." Very quickly that changes to "at least a part of me is dying."

As the conversation continues, I acknowledge it is true: there is part of me that needs to die to some lifelong perceptions of me. They now need to adjust. There are layers of new understanding cracking me open to see life differently and engage life more fully. There are parts of me that have to be released and be allowed to die.

I also acknowledge that these thoughts of dying may be triggered by an experience in mid-December 2016.

It happens when I am driving early one morning when the visibility is extremely poor due to fog. At the side of the four-lane highway there is a billboard sign with neon lettering announcing that six kilometres down the highway the right lane is blocked. By the time I arrive at the place where part of the highway is blocked, visibility is much better. I pull in behind the lineup of cars in the left lane that is at a standstill.

I glance back in my rearview mirror, assuring myself that I can see a long way back and so from a long way back people will be able to see me. After a moment of watching, a transport truck comes into view. I watch, expecting it to slow down. It doesn't. It continues to barrel right at me. I inch forward and try to get closer to the guardrails, but I know it will make only a minor difference. But that difference may have been enough. When the truck gets to me it swings into the right lane. At one point I can see the tractor beside me and the trailer on an angle behind me. I am sure that my car and the row of cars in front of me are about to be creamed. In that moment I am aware that I have already had sixty years of living but others in front of me may be much younger. I feel sick for the driver of the truck. The trailer begins to shift. Its back end jackknifes toward the shoulder of the road rather than in the direction of the lineup of cars. As I stare at this potential nightmare unfolding, a car pulls up beside me, just missing me. The truck does not lose complete control but continues to progress forward. Somehow the car finds a space to squeeze in.

A part of me is amazed at how calm I remain.

A second tractor-trailer speeds into view. It is not slowing down. It swings into the right lane, barely getting around me. But as soon as it does, a car pulls up to fill the narrow gap between the truck and me. I'm not sure where the tractor-trailer and the car go, but a space is created for a second car to squeeze into the scenario, fishtailing as it goes.

When the short line of cars in front of me begins to move, I am puzzled. Where have the two transport trucks and three cars gone? Somehow they must have stopped in the short space before they reached the tow trucks in the right lane at high speed.

For the next many days I am conscious that it is astonishing that I am still alive. I find myself being aware of what my family and friends would have been doing to plan my funeral if things had turned out the way they appeared to be heading.

During the days that follow, I am aware of how calm I felt knowing that my life could end. I had a sense of completion and richness about my life. In that moment of possible ending, there is a clear thought in my mind: I hope that the accumulation of my life experiences will have a lingering, positive impact through this book as well as through my relationships. I hope the people with whom I have shared my perspective on the importance of authentic connection can tap into the power of transformation that is so needed in our world.

As I feel the pains in my chest, I am aware that my death is on my mind. And no matter how accepting I would have been if my life had ended that day on the highway, the pain in my chest demands to be noticed.

When I go to Tanis's home to help her after eye surgery, she offers to help me go into the pain to see if there are emotional realities mixed in, but only after I phone my doctor and set up an appointment.

She leads me in the process of pulling back from my third eye that loves to provide probable answers. I take my point of consciousness down into the region of my heart. Once I am deeply inside my body she invites me to sense where the pain is radiating from. We both sense a tiny dark spot on the lower left corner of my heart, almost hidden because it is so tucked away.

She encourages me to go into the spot to explore the feelings that are there. With her guidance I energetically spiral into this small place. There, I discover I am carrying thoughts and questions that have never entered my head before.

The question that weaves through this place is, "What if?" What if I didn't have a mother with many personalities and mental health challenges who consumed so much of my life? What if I had known who my father is? What if I had been able to fully claim the core strength within me? What if I had been free to explore the world to discover my own pathway rather than feel bound to my mother?

Tears pour down my face as I acknowledge these "what if" questions. I feel a sense of sadness well up in me for the things that were not part of my life. I acknowledge the anguish that has been exposed. Acknowledging this sense of loss, of what might have been, eases the pain. The sadness dissipates quickly.

A few minutes after the experience, I feel a band of tension across my chest again. Tanis lightheartedly suggests it is probably my fifteen-year-old self who wants to know that I am free to choose how to live from this time forward. I acknowledge I am free to choose my own pathway. The pain lessens.

The questions of regret do not consume me. They simply help me to know and recognize another layer of my story.

The stress test at the hospital later that week indicates I do not show symptoms of heart disease.

Late on an evening in March 2017, when the second draft of the book is close to completion, Alan and I are sitting in our swivel chairs looking out the living room window. The planet Venus is shining brightly. It has been with us each evening for the past several months. We sit in silence in the glow of candlelight as we sip sherry.

Something stirs on the quiet street of our subdivision. I lean forward. My breath catches in my throat. A fox is walking down the centre of our street. We've never seen a wild animal in our neighbourhood beyond the usual squirrels, bunnies, chipmunks and skunks.

A fox. One came at the beginning of the journey of the writing of this book and now one comes as if to herald the ending.

This time I see the fox three times as it weaves in and out of yards on the street, emerging from shadows that hide it for a moment to again be illuminated by the gentle glow of the street lamps. The number three, the power of the Trinity, feels like it is supporting the awakening seeds of positive transformation that reside deep within all of life.

A sigh emerges from my being. Yes, there have been many lessons on this journey, along with tricky realities that required discernment as Fox's presence indicates. In the midst of it, I have uncovered strength within me to learn the lessons that are mine to learn.

As I ponder the book, do I feel as though my interpretations of all the details identified in this story are correct? That was not my goal. The reason I began to write this book was to delve into my store of memories to see if I could piece together fragments—to see if I could make some sense of the new information of an extra biological father in our family.

I have been writing in order to explore my story by bringing shadowy, little-remembered aspects into the light in order to discover the authenticity of wholeness even in the midst of brokenness. For me it has been a gift to explore the strands of memories and the themes that weave together to create a reflection of life that continues to inspire me.

The intricacies of insights that I have stumbled upon in the process of writing this book make me think of the work of sculptors, who carefully remove pieces of the mass that is before them to allow what is longing to be known to emerge and become visible, or of an archeologist who sifts through the sands of time to discover the story that has come before.

That's how this process feels in my life as I keep searching for deepening awareness of how this story impacts my life. I want the fullness and wholeness of who I am, and the fullness and wholeness of who I experienced Mom to be, to become visible, to not be lost under the rubble of quick assessment or judgment. In so many ways Mom taught me about being open to love breaking into our midst, to fill the broken moments of our lives with light to lead us away from paralyzing fear and infuse us with mobilizing hope.

In spite of all the turmoil and upheaval that engaging with Mom demanded throughout my life, there are days when I still miss her. She was my fiercest champion and constant companion in life. I am still learning from her. I love my Mom. A deep sigh rises within me as I acknowledge that I am grateful to her for all the lessons learned, even the ones that came with discord and demands. She taught me much about the depth of the fragmented human psyche, which we all struggle with to different degrees as we seek wholeness within us and amongst us.

As difficult as the personalities have been to deal with, as difficult as the weird behaviour and crazy-making-realities that we lived with were, it seems to me that it is because of these personalities that we were able to experience our "real Mom" both in our family and in the wider community.

In an odd way, I am grateful to them.

Without them would our "real Mom" have been able to do all she did in the world? They held so much of her pain, leaving her free to function at a level that made a profound difference in the world.

I am grateful to them because, in my interpretation, without the many personalities Janis and I, in our current genetic form, would not exist. There might have been other children in the marriage of Ellie and Max, but I wouldn't be the "me" I am today. I am glad to be me and to have sisters of different sorts with whom to journey into deeper understanding.

Another subtle theme that has reconfirmed gratitude in me while writing this book is the power of place to soothe, console and heal. The places of this book are the cause of many powerful moments: sitting on the rock in Georgian Bay that allows me to find myself; the swing in the old apple orchard that allows chaos to flow through me; the rolling hills of England that speak of ancient energy seeking to imbue life; the Mediterranean Sea crashing in the distance in Israel as the dove flies down on Mom and me like a blessing that declares we are beloved; the tiny room with a wall of windows that is a sanctuary from the busyness of the church; the woods that revive me during solitary camping; the hillsides of Scotland with their sense of homecoming; the rock in Hawaii that emanates ancient wisdom; my bedroom at the farm with its feeling of retreat; the crop circles that realign the flow of balance and harmony; the pathway through the forest by the meandering creek of my home; and the meadow filled with golden light. Each one is a powerful place of transformation and insight.

In the summer of 2016, when I receive the email from Betsy saying our family farmhouse has burned down, an eruption of deep despair fills me with a profound sense of emptiness. I am shocked by the strength of my feelings. When Janis arrives in Canada for her mother-in-law's funeral in October of that year, the first place she goes to is the farm. She needs to see the ashes of our family home. When she arrives she is overjoyed to discover that the house did not burn to the ground. There is damage to two walls in the combination dining and living room and to the bedrooms above, which were our two bedrooms. All the windows on that side of the house are blown out. The house has been gutted, but it has not burned to the ground.

When we meet for dinner that night she shows me the pictures of our family home. I weep for joy that the structure that has framed our lives still stands.

The tattered structure in the picture feels like a reflection of the journey of my soul: sometimes bearing the burden of wounds that overwhelm yet constantly providing stability and core strength.

Inner strength even in the midst of brokenness, like a mended mirror sparkling with strands of golden repair, reflects the complexity and richness of the wholeness that is possible.

IN THE EARLY HOURS OF THE MORNING OF JUNE 30, 2016, less than eighteen hours after I find out that Scott is my biological father, I have a vivid, dream-like vision. It is a powerful experience that brings me peace.

I sense the presence of Dad and Scott. I see them walk toward me. They stop in front of me. They look at me with eyes filled with love. They are standing side by side, shoulder to shoulder.

Dad speaks to me, "Daughter of mine." It feels like a blessing. It is naming what is true.

Then Scott says to me, "Daughter of mine," but with a slightly different tone on the 'mine.'

They glance at each other. Dad puts his arm around Scott. Scott puts his arm around Dad's back. They turn to look at me and communicate a sense of deep love for me. There is a strong feeling that they are proud of me and pleased for me.

I stare back at them. I absorb the gift of their presence and the gift of their love infused with acceptance of me and each other.

Mom walks into the moment. She looks like our real Mom.

She nods at me and smiles. The moment feels significant. It feels like she is affirming my understanding and interpretation of the events that surrounded this surprising new information of an extra biological father in our family. It feels like her nod confirms that Scott was her partner with some personalities and that Dad was her partner with her core personality.

The scene fades.

Then I glimpse the three of them standing together. Mom stands closest to me at Dad's right side. Scott stands on Dad's left side. It is clear that there was and is a strong sense of connection and support for Mom from both of them. They are a team together. My wholeness comes from all three of them.

Their presence together nudges me to be aware of a core of strength awakening within me. A warm feeling flows through me. It is filled with acceptance of my story and our story as a family.

I am whole and strong and have something of the best of each of them in me.

The vision feels like a reflection of the spiritual journey of life. We keep being cracked open to deepening awareness and circling deeper into love. We are awakened to our brokenness, and in our awakening we are cracked open to greater capacity for compassion to expand, for creativity to emerge, for relationships to deepen, and for respectful sharing to be our way of living. As we spiral into the transforming power of love, we discover the wholeness that is amongst us, too often covered over by the rubble of our lives.

As we reconnect to the power of love, we are compelled to be part of mending the world—to become a place where no one is considered to be of greater value than another, where we work together to develop solutions that honour the Earth and each other, where we seek to listen to the intelligence of many voices, and where love both empowers us and challenges us to walk a pathway together that leads to loving wholeness, with wisdom and profound hope as our guides.

Choosing to ensure that in our lives and in our world there is space for the resilience of beauty, curiosity, healing and wonder to emerge energizes us to evolve our capacity for joy, creativity, collaboration and authentic connection. These capacities enable us to move toward our purpose of mending our Earth community.

A key step on this journey will be reconciliation, of listening deeply to honour the stories of brokenness so that we can intentionally learn and move forward together to build right relations.

As the writing of this book draws to a close two years after the writing began, I have another dream-like vision that is filled with a sense of reconciliation which is both powerful and shocking.

It is a cool September evening in 2018.

I am alone on our back deck. My gaze is drawn to the star-filled sky. I snuggle beneath layers of blankets, warm though the night air is cold. A wind is rustling the leaves of the huge maple that umbrellas our yard, a tree that began as a tiny seedling in our garden twenty-two years ago.

I feel myself drawn into a deep place where the layers of life and the veil between this life and the next lift.

I feel the presence of Mom and Dad and Scott. They are standing on my left. Then Lynn and a dear friend and colleague, who died the month before Mom, come and stand on my right. The six of us form a partial circle. It is odd to me that the circle is not complete. Then my brother Mark walks in. Seven of us stand together in this circle that fills with love, encouragement, gratitude and requests for forgiveness. We hold the space together allowing time for the depth of the healing and restoration that is happening.

And then, we are swarmed by other relatives.

The first one to step forward is my Grandpa, Mom's Dad.

He speaks to me. "Thank you. In writing your book you have helped me to understand my role in the wounds of this story. Please forgive me for my lack of support to your Mom and how that has impacted the lives of others."

I look to my Mom. Grandpa does too. Mom responds to me, "Don't worry, we have already reconciled."

And then I am shocked as my uncle steps into the circle and approaches me. He is Mom's eldest brother. I only knew him as a scarecrow figure who sat unengaged by the world and ignored by Mom—the one whose actions I suspect were the cause of Mom's first splinter personality. He looks at me with love in his eyes. He looks different. He has a greater sense of peace. He smells different, with no lingering scent of whisky.

He reaches out to me and holds the upper part of my arms as he speaks. "Thank you for helping me see … I'm sorry … Please forgive me … I love you."

He hugs me as I weep. Though he has never hugged me before, it feels right.

A multitude of family members come into the circle: my grandmothers, my aunt who snubbed my Mom for being an unwed mother though providing her with a place to stay, my aunt killed by the police chase who I have missed since I was four. Mom's siblings all pour into the circle. A murmur swells, echoing an ancient prayer: "Thank you; I'm sorry; please forgive me; I love you." I add my voice to the refrain.

These are the four phrases of the ancient Hawaiian practice called Ho'oponopono that reminds us we are all connected and we can heal ourselves and each other when we understand that the wounds within us affect all of us. The words of the prayer invite us to take responsibility for the brokenness amongst us.

A huge circle is formed that is layers deep. I am at the inner edge surrounded by this whole crowd of ancestors. Healing is happening; the angst and the anger, the brokenness and the impact of choices, are lifting. Energy is pulsing through the circle: the energy of possibility, of gratitude, of deeply knowing the importance of the telling of the story so awareness can awaken, cracking open hearts to make space for forgiveness and reconciliation.

As the scene begins to fade, I hear a whisper that lingers in my head. "Thank you. Thank you for being the sharer and the carrier of this story's wisdom."

I feel my awareness returning to the cool September evening. My nose is cold and the tracks of tears down my face are chilly. I once again hear the sound of the wind in the trees. I look up and see that the stars are brighter now as the darkness deepens. I sit there stunned by what just happened.

I have never experienced a vision or sense of presence quite like this before. It was powerful, shocking and life-giving. Connecting to grandparents, aunts and my uncle feels like loose ends being woven into the beauty of the tapestry of life. Their energy felt free from the struggles and the ego issues of this lifetime. They were their eternal selves and exuded the love that has always been at the core of their being.

I am grateful. Long-forgotten memories emerge of when I experienced moments of connecting to their love in this lifetime. It is like a shower of blessings awakening me to more clearly see the presence of love in everyday moments.

I feel blessed. It feels like healing has gone deep into the roots of my family.

Fourteen days after I have this vision, I share the experience with my friend from seminary. We are sitting on the back deck on a beautiful autumn afternoon. When I complete the story we hold the space in silence with a sense of awe. My eye is caught by a dog walking alone beside the bushes that separate the schoolyard from the park behind our house. It walks directly toward me, and then shifts to the right so I can see its profile. It's a fox! It stops and surveys the area, turning to look at where I am sitting. With a sense of calm certainty, it strolls toward the pathway beside our house to head out of the park.

I am astonished. A fox came when it was time to start writing the book, walking right into our campsite in the summer of 2016. A fox came on a cold blistery night when I felt I had completed the full draft of the book in the winter of 2017. A fox now comes and stands in my life in the midst of a brilliant sunny afternoon immediately after I tell the story of the vision of reconciliation, the experience that feels like the story of this book is now complete in the autumn of 2018.

It feels like Fox is here for all of us as our new story continues to emerge and unwind. Its presence is an indication of being in a time when discernment is required to enable us to see through deception and see clearly in tricky situations. Fox indicates that we may be challenged, but we have the strength to learn the lessons that are ours to learn: good energy as we walk through these turbulent and wonderful times in which we live.

After months of being a midwife to the development and emergence of this story, I end with words Mom loved. It is a commissioning I use often to send us out into a broken world to be ones who are reflections of the way of love, because that, my Beloved Ones, is the point of life.

"And now let us go forth into the world
with a daring and tender love.
The world is waiting.
Let us go in peace.
And in all that we do,
may we do it nourished by the power of love
that is deep within every one of us.

And as we journey
may we see the face of Love in everyone we meet
and may everyone we meet see the face of Love in us."

May this be so as we connect to our authentic power and awaken the gifts amongst us of creativity, resilience, wholeness and wisdom!

CONVERSATIONS FOR BOOK CIRCLES
A CIRCLE OF CONNECTION
(HOLDING SPACE FOR MEANINGFUL CONVERSATION)

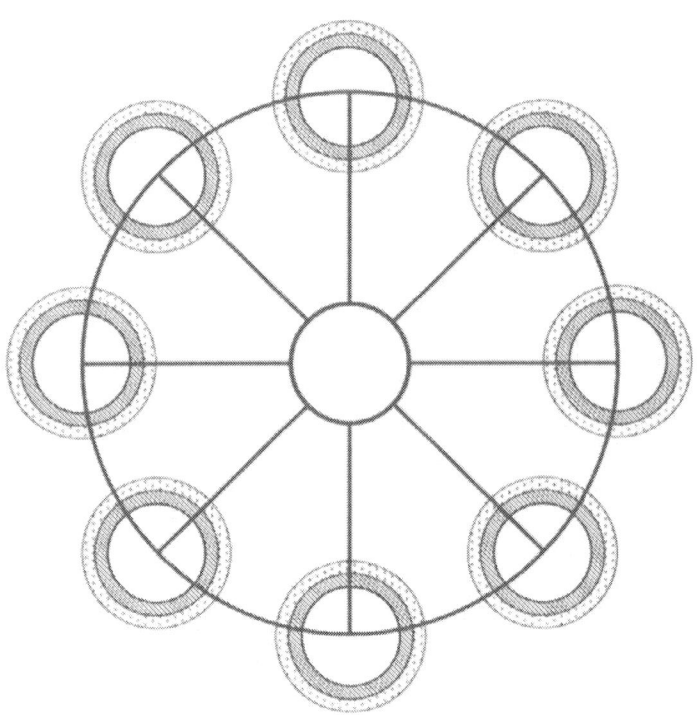

SIGNIFICANT CONVERSATIONS FOR BOOK CIRCLES
BASED ON HOW *THE MENDED MIRROR*
INTERSECTS WITH YOUR LIFE

In Intentional Circles we create space for the wisdom within us and amongst us to emerge. When we gather in Circle it is an intentional time to ponder the intricacies of life based on our experiences, questions and wonderings. In Circle we do not engage in debate as though we expect there to be one right answer. Instead we listen deeply to the layers of insight and weave them together to continuously create a tapestry that is an expression of the beauty of life filled with complexities, joys, sorrows, possibilities.

The conversation starters below are an invitation to consider concepts, ideas, thoughts or experiences expressed in the book from the perspective of how they intersect with your life. Choose ones that nudge at you. Each person in the Circle can choose a different question or topic to share how it intersects with their life, or you can delve deeply into one topic.

As you enter into Circle, seek to hold space for each other so that you can each name your own insights, your own wonderings. Do not try to fix each other or correct each other. Simply hold the space and receive the gift of one another's sharing. Listen deeply with the purpose to understand rather than respond. Allow there to be silence in your midst rather than chatter to fill the spaces.

When it feels like you are ready to enter into Significant Conversation together you might invite one another to enter into Intentional Circle with the invitation:

We are invited to offer our names into the Circle
to indicate our willingness
to be together in life-giving community
where we can trust that we can be authentic and honest,
where our stories will not be shared beyond this Circle,

where we will not criticize or correct
each other but rather be curious together,
where we will hold space to listen deeply
to the wisdom within us and amongst us.
If you are willing to be together in this way,
offer your name into the Circle
(offer your name into the Circle by going left around the circle).

At the conclusion of Book Circle, there is the reading of the commissioning Mom loved, offered as an invitation to say together to close your time in Circle. They are the words with which the book ends.

HOW DOES THIS STORY
INTERSECT WITH YOUR LIFE AND EXPERIENCE?

Pick a topic or topics that speak to you individually or as a group to reflect on how the concepts, memories or experiences in the book intersect with your life. Share a story or an experience from your life that connects with one of the themes in the book. For example:

1) Different stories in the book resonate with different people because they are familiar, like an echo of their experiences in life. If that is so for you, how do the stories, experiences or feelings described in the book align with your story? For example:

   a) Have you ever felt like you were living behind a mask or a façade? If yes, what mask or façade have you lived behind and why?

   b) Is there a core of strength within you that you keep a lid on in order to fit in? If yes, what is the strength you hide within you and what happened in your life that taught you it was wise to not share the fullness of your power?

   c) Were there experiences in your childhood that have caused you to be passionate about something as an adult, and if so what is it you are passionate about and why? (An example is seen in the book of the passion to create healthy, life-giving community that first awakened through difficult experiences in kindergarten and grade two.)

2) Identify insights, concepts or thoughts in the book that particularly make sense to you or express perspectives that align with your awareness of life.

3) Share an experience from your life when you felt like your style of intelligence was not appropriate or undervalued.

4) Have you had a person in your life who has struggled with mental health challenges? Have you had the experience of becoming aware of a mental health issue after simply coping with it for many years because it was not understood? If so, what was your experience like?

5) Have you had experiences that helped you to understand or identify the impact of DNA/genetic influences? If yes, in what ways have you experienced the impact of DNA awareness?

6) Do any of the memories in the story evoke memories for you? If yes, which ones? (For example, did you watch Ed Sullivan on Sunday night or wear go-go boots or find time alone as a kid to recharge yourself?)

7) What understandings or interpretations in the book are contrary to your wisdom about life? What is your perspective?

8) Does the concept of connecting to your "authentic self" or "true essence" resonate with your life? If so, share a story or an experience from your life.

9) Are there topics in the book that you want to know more about? If so, what?

10) Are there topics in the book that you know something about and want to share?

NOTICE WHAT YOU NOTICE

Notice what you notice is a process used in the Ignatian Spiritual Exercises that encourages us to read until something catches our attention. We are then invited to sit with what has caught our attention to see what it is we are being nudged to notice.

Below are a series of quotes from the book. See if one section particularly draws you. Then slowly read what has caught your attention to notice what you notice. Trust that what jumps out at you is worth pondering. Allow insights, thoughts and perspectives to emerge.

As you read through the quotes and concepts, allow yourself to wonder:

- o   Do any quotes or words resonate with me?
- o   When I notice something, how does the word or thought or concept interact with my life?
- o   Do any of the statements align with my experience?
- o   Is this a thought or concept that cracks open my understanding, and if so how?
- o   Are there concepts I want to further explore?
- o   How is this word or thought speaking to me?

I remember choosing a story from the Bible that I had drawn on many times before to provide people with an experience of this way of being open to what Wisdom longs for us to know.

Normally when I use this particular story, what catches my attention is the moment when Jesus stands up to the storm and declares "Be still!" Those are words that often speak to my life, providing me with the reminder to be still in the midst of the whirling demands of life in order to centre myself.

But this time, when life is crashing apart in the church, the phrase in the story that catches my attention is "cushion." Cushion? I sit with it, puzzled. Then I realize that in the story, in the middle of a raging storm, Jesus lays his head on a cushion. What I am being nudged to notice is that I am not sleeping well. I work until long past midnight night after night and then rise with the sun. I need to notice that I am definitely heading toward difficulty. I need to put my head on a cushion and sleep, even in the midst of a raging storm.

Listening for what speaks to you, even if it does not align with the fullness of the text, is an invitation to create space for your own wisdom about your life to emerge. Enjoy as you notice what you notice!

A) LIFE LESSONS

a) In my life's work and during the writing of this book, I identify lessons I have learned from my Mom about finding wholeness in the midst of brokenness.

13 Life Lessons that have emerged
through my relationship with my Mom:

o Deal with issues when they arise.
o Follow the flow of energy. If you meet resistance, be like a river and keep searching for a place that allows you to move with ease so that you are flowing with the energy of life rather than fighting the underlying currents.
o Choose to see differently by shifting your focus.
o Listen for, and to, inner wisdom and intuition.
o Pause so that as many people as possible know where we are trying to go.
o Trust that there is goodness trying to emerge.
o Reconnect to your core essence and the Divine.
o See the light within yourself and others, even if you have to look beneath the rubble.
o Allow curiosity to lead you rather than judgment or expectations.
o Listen for the wisdom of all the perspectives.

o Stop "shoulding" on yourself.
o Let gratitude and beauty fill you.
o Focus on what you want to grow.

b) Throughout the book, life lessons about self-care and spiritual well-being are identified. The quote below describes the impact of camping alone for nine days when I am completely done in and need to be recharged.

As the days unfold, the power at my core has the opportunity to be charged. In this time of healing solitude I become aware that during the past many months, in the midst of the crashing and rumbling that felt as disruptive as an earthquake, there has been a sense of wholeness that never completely left me. Now, with my power reserves topped up, the wholeness within me is again filling the landscape of my soul rather than being diminished to a tiny still point in the middle of chaos.

B) THE POWER AND IMPORTANCE OF SHARING OUR STORIES

a) When we risk being open, vulnerable and honest about our struggles and our joys, the fullness of who we are emerges and connects us to one another at a profound, authentic level. Sharing our stories allows us to take the risk of coming out from behind masks that separate us from one another and from ourselves. Experience has taught me that the pattern of hiding behind masks and disconnecting from authentically engaging in life is at the root of some of our greatest struggles in the times in which we live. We are experiencing an epidemic of loneliness rooted in the destructive powers of judgment, shame, blame and guilt. We are experiencing a culture that is numb to some of the deepest travesties of human history as we soothe ourselves with over-consumption of things, addictive substances and repeated mindless patterns. Too often, we are cut off from the roots of meaning at the core of our being as we strive to survive by fulfilling shallow expectations, rather than allowing ourselves to be nourished by the richness of wisdom and the vision of collaboration that is deep within us. Sharing our stories connects us at the deep level of our profound longing for community, creativity, compassion and acceptance.

b) I continue to be amazed at the power of untold stories. They create energetic havoc when we walk through this world carrying the burden of our silence.

c) The power of sharing our stories is a power that can change the world. Sharing our stories releases creative energy, which allows future possibilities to emerge rather than allowing untold and unexamined stories to quietly suck the life out of us by nursing unacknowledged wounds of the past.

d) Throughout my life, I have learned again and again that though life can be demanding and appear to be fractured or even crushed, somewhere in the midst of the rubble, there is goodness and a longing to be whole that yearns to emerge amongst us. This is a story about finding wholeness even in the midst of brokenness. It explores how to connect to the power of wholeness, the power of love, in the midst of the brokenness in our world today.

e) I am aware from experience that the weight of secrets is a burden that has the potential to become lighter when we can find a safe place to share. It's intriguing to me to notice how many people tell me one of their parents also lives with mental health challenges when I share my story. Sharing our stories connects us at the level of authenticity, which has the potential to dispel the feeling of being isolated and alone.

C) AUTHENTIC CONNECTION COMMUNITY

a) My central learnings that impact my life are the awareness that:

1) When we connect to our true essence, to our authentic self, we connect to a reservoir of power deep within us that is filled with love and creativity.

2) When we risk connecting to one another in a deeply authentic way, we see life differently; no longer are we bound by small-ego thinking that is rooted in limitations, entitlement and the compulsion to protect our territory, rather we see creative possibilities, abundance and incredible goodness.

3) When we connect at an authentic level as a community by creating a commons where everyone is respected and belongs, the wisdom within us and amongst us has the opportunity to emerge to enable us to recognize future possibilities that can enhance life if we work together.

b) One of my hopes for one Earth community is that we awaken more fully to the transformational power of love, a power that longs to engage our passions, teaches us to celebrate diversity, and compels us to risk imagining a way of being together that leads to wholeness. Awakening to this power within equips us to co-create a world committed to the well-being of all. For me this story of connecting to wholeness even in the midst of brokenness, of experiencing resilience even when life shows up with difficulties, deepens our hope as we work together to mend the world.

c) We are to create the opportunity for love to expand and creativity and compassion to grow. We are to create space for the Kindom or the Realm of God to emerge in our midst, which happens when the power that reigns is love. This intention needs to be at the core of the narrative that informs our lives. We need a narrative that sees the goodness, connects to the energy of love, and calls us to live as ones who are committed to the common good, where resources are shared, gifts are celebrated, the Earth is respected and we listen deeply to the wisdom within us and amongst us. When we connect in community and really see one another, our inner capacities to cultivate the seeds of possibilities expand.

D) OUR SHARED JOURNEY

While this is the story of my ongoing journey home to who I am, rerouted by unexpected detours, it is also a glimpse into our shared story as humans as we seek to: be in healthy relationship with ourselves, with each other and with the Earth; create space for love to emerge, for acceptance to expand, for possibilities of an alternative vision to be considered, and for creativity to be our response when pathways to wholeness and the common good become obscured.

E) REACTING VERSUS RESPONDING

REACTING vs. RESPONDING	
Based on Middle Circle of External Expectations	*Based on Centre Circle of Authentic Self*
Life reflex, not conscious	Conscious, aware of choices
Automatic	Grounded, genuine
Objective "you" statements that come from the head and disconnect us from our	Connected "I/we" statements that come from head and heart and connect to our own story by

own story by speaking from a detached perspective	speaking from a personal perspective
I know I can fix you	I honour the wisdom in you
A sense of entitlement that lacks ownership and blames	Takes responsibility for self and focuses on the well-being of all
Difficult to disengage from demands and worries	Easy flow of energy toward possibilities and passions

F) BOOK DEDICATION: TO ALL ON THE JOURNEY TO WHOLENESS

WHOLENESS:
Coming home to ourselves;
connecting to the Wisdom within us and amongst us
to create Community that reflects our True Essence,
imbuing the world with hope through the power
of the Universal Consciousness of Love
found deep within the centre of who we are.

Through Authentic Connection to Self, Community and the Earth,
through recognizing the Earth, one another and ourselves as Beloved,
through acknowledging and honouring our oneness with all of life,
through deep listening and deepening conversation,
through alignment with the flow of life-giving energy,
—we expand our capacity to create Community and the Commons
where together we imagine and engage possibilities
to journey toward a transformed way of being
rooted in and empowered by love
creating space for the emergence of
a lived vision of the well-being of all.

As a result of connecting in a deeply authentic way
we see life differently;

no longer are we bound by small-ego thinking that is rooted in
limitations, entitlement, blame
and the compulsion to protect our territory;
rather we see creative possibilities, interconnection,
abundance and incredible goodness.
We shift from an ego to an ecological perspective
in order to become resilient and sustainable
in all aspects of life—
economics, ethics, academics, decision-making and politics—
which all reflect the way we engage in relationships
at personal, local and global levels.

The journey to wholeness awakens us
to the light that emanates from the centre of all of life,
which longs to illuminate a pathway forward
that is empowered by love.
While this light is often covered over by
the demands, destruction, brokenness and noise of life,
it is not extinguished; it remains constant in its essence and presence.
The experience of wholeness,
arising from developing
an intentional Culture of Authentic Connection,
is a way of being when we choose to see
our self, one another, the Earth, and all of life
with eyes of love and with hearts open to possibilities.

G) CREATING AUTHENTIC CULTURE THROUGH INTENTIONAL CIRCLES

a) Authentic Connection Culture emerges from an intentional
way of being in which we:
    ✓ listen deeply;
  ✓ connect to Wisdom within us and amongst us;
   ✓ honour our own and each other's gifts;
 ✓ share laughter and tears, joys and struggles comfortably;
  ✓ create a safe space where we can be brave and speak

from our heart, mind, experience and soul;
✓ commit to action for ongoing transformation
as we respond to our life purpose and call;
✓ encourage, support and be accountable to one another
as we seek to live a vision of wholeness;
✓ honour creativity and discover clarity emerging in our midst;
✓ deal honestly and kindly with issues before they fester;
✓ follow the flow of energy to align ourselves with pathways
that honour who we are and how the Spirit calls us to be.

This shift in culture away from
being consumers and individualistic emerges
as we connect to our core wisdom and creativity
at the centre of our authentic self
which compels us to develop healthy life-giving community.

b) From Disconnected To Connected:
A 13-Step Connection Strategy For Self And Community

13 Steps to Connect to the Power of Transformation,
Meaning, Purpose and the Authenticity Within Each of Us to
Enhance Our Life Together in Community:

1) Connect authentically with self and others.
Disconnect from expectations that are external or in
opposition to your true self, disconnect from building walls
within that separate you from *You* and from the people
around you, disconnect from wearing masks to hide behind.

2) Develop intrinsic motivation.
Disconnect from insecurity, judgment and the need for
external affirmation, which can destabilize our connection to
our core.

3) Release, lament and claim the insights.
Disconnect from being a victim to old wounds.

4) See differently.

Disconnect from dumping energetic garbage on others or ourselves.

5) Expand compassion, curiosity and laughter.
Disconnect from our small-ego self, which focuses on defending territory, a sense of entitlement and personal desires as the highest goal.

6) Speak truth simply.
Disconnect from blame and judgment.

7) Listen for inner guidance.
Disconnect from dishonouring and ignoring inner wisdom.

8) Reclaim power and purpose.
Disconnect from wandering through life feeling powerless.

9) Energize the vision and longings that emerge from deep within.
Disconnect from focusing on and energizing what we don't want to grow.

10) Create authentic relationships of connection.
Disconnect from being fearful and phony.

11) Engage in significant conversations that include laughter and tears and lots of wonderings.
Disconnect from shallow, veneer-thin dialogue filled with catty comments and opinions that are declared as "the" answer.

12) Tap into the wisdom and creativity of future possibilities.
Disconnect from dependence on logic and past experience as the only valued guides.

13) Live your call: trust your intuition and gut response.
Disconnect from living the life you think you "should" live and start living the life your passion calls you to live.

CLOSING OF THE BOOK CIRCLE CONVERSATION

As Book Circle draws to a close, consider saying together the commissioning Mom loved:

And now let us go forth into the world
with a daring and tender love.
The world is waiting.
Let us go in peace.
And in all that we do,
may we do it nourished by the power of love
that is deep within every one of us.

As we journey
may we see the face of Love in everyone we meet
and may everyone we meet see the face of Love in us.

May this be so
as we connect to our authentic power
and awaken the gifts amongst us
of creativity, resilience, wholeness and wisdom!

APPENDIX & RESOURCES

DOWNLOADING RESOURCES:

While *The Mended Mirror* is copyrighted, Karen Celeste Hilfman encourages you to use the content and resources in it extensively. Go to www.AuthenticConnectionCulture.com to download the outlines and descriptions of the components of Authentic Connection Culture and Intentional Circles. You can also download the outline for Book Circles. Please share them freely. If you would like a small section of the book to share with others for teaching purposes, contact Karen through her website so she can send it to you. Karen thanks you in advance for always crediting her with these resources by including her name and website.

PRACTICES AND PRINCIPLES OF INTENTIONAL CIRCLES TO CREATE AUTHENTIC CONNECTION CULTURE

1) Engage from the place of authenticity and connection to the sacred, the place of wisdom deep within from which we respond to life rather than react to life.

2) Develop clarity within the group about action and purpose to support our call to co-create a world of wholeness and well-being for all.

3) Honour insights that arise from our intuitive capacity by listening deeply to our gut responses, and by speaking from our heart.

4) Celebrate and claim each person's unique gifts and tenderly hold each other in our limitations.

5) Develop an intentional agreement on how to be in community and agree to its intentions each time we meet.

6) Make the group a priority so that we are present and engaged as we are able.

7) Recognize that the wisdom of everyone is needed—individuals' contributions as well as the group wisdom that will flow through people; since every voice counts, space is created for every voice to be heard.

8) Include time for check-in at the beginning of each gathering so that we reconnect at a heart level through sharing brief stories or insights (with no cross-conversation). This provides opportunity to find our voices as we speak into the circle about a personal perspective or experience. This sets the tone of the gathering in which we want to hear the many perspectives and for people to share their wisdom even when it is counter to others. We are less likely to get "group speak" or one voice dominating when all voices have opened the Circle.

9) Commit to using the responsible "I/we" rather than using "you" statements; speaking about our own story from a personal perspective rather than a detached second-person perspective moves us out of judgment or presumptions about others and empowers us to change our reality through self-responsibility and acceptance, engaging our hearts and wisdom more fully.

10) Intentionally include opportunity for evaluation to enable the group to honestly assess how we are doing, so that relationships can deepen and the group is continuously revitalized.

11) Create a space that is life-giving and safe for the full spectrum of who we are to show up.

12) Challenge and shift negative energy and limiting beliefs.

13) Take note when people are absent, and arrange for someone to contact them. This ensures that the person who is absent and the people in the group all know that when they aren't there they are missed; people know that they belong when they will be missed.

My Work as a Consultant
and Facilitator of Significant Conversations

PURPOSE:

To provide opportunities for a community/organization to engage in Significant Conversations for the purpose of discerning future possibilities in order to be responsive to the deep longing we all have to live lives that are creative, meaningful and have a positive impact in the world. *(Note: the purpose and the goals are developed to fit each community based on their focus.)*

GOALS:

My 4-Step Visioning Process (Listening Circles, Conversation Circle, Discernment Circle, and Consensus Circle) develops a renewed sense of purpose and generates excitement about future possibilities for the community/organization.

The processes create a culture that is safe and respectful for people to share their wisdom and creativity, to enhance the vision that longs to emerge.

The insights and ideas gathered through the input of many people provide direction to identify next steps.

The processes result in people being committed to and enthusiastic about the identified vision and the emerging steps forward because they are rooted in their combined creativity and wisdom.

GRATITUDE & STORIES
OF COMPANIONS ON THE JOURNEY

FAMILY AND FRIENDS

Alan, my love, always, and cherished life companion: I am so grateful for the incredible supportive impact you have on my life. I have been able to develop my life's work with a dedication that would not have been possible without your major role in raising our kids together, caring for our home, and responding to Mom's needs. You keep me grounded, challenge me when I get off-centered, and step into my life with support when you know that without help I cannot do what I long to do. I treasure our cocktail-hour conversations, elaborate cooking schemes, camping expeditions, and our common love of being alone, including living independent lives while connecting in the centre that is our home. You fill me up, for which I will always be grateful.

Our beloved daughters Sarah and Marissa and their families, including our incredibly amazing and delectable four grandchildren: you inspire me every day by living the moments of your lives rooted in love for others and for self, within family and beyond. Your lives reflect strength and insight by honouring and encouraging one another and allowing love to flow in bold, bright splashes of colour filled with hugs and debates, creativity and commitment. You are all part of the circle of my greatest teachers in life. You fill me with a profound sense of delight and contentment. I love you all!

Mom, one of my greatest teachers in life, playing a role well beyond that of mother: from you I have learned much about acceptance and the amazing capacity we have within us for resilience. You continue to inspire me and fill my life with memories of shared moments that are rich in lively insights, laughter, compassion and a commitment to create a world focused on the well-being of all. Thank you, with love and gratitude to you my teacher, companion and mother.

Dad, forever my Dad: by your example you taught me to laugh in the midst of life, to be curious enough to get to know people, to trust my intuition, to seek a broad spectrum of perspectives, to enjoy time alone, to engage in questions about the meaning of life, to wonder about possibilities, to trust in the power of positive thinking, to be creative when seeking solutions, to savour the complexity of music, to delight in the things I love to do, to understand the importance of being good at hospitality by upholding Mom as an incredible example, and to be comfortable in my own skin. I love you, Dad.

Janis, my longest life companion: sharer of dreams and questions, insights and connection, thank you. I love that our relationship is filled with support and encouragement. Both were indispensable in the writing of this book. When you called and exclaimed with enthusiasm, "You wrote this story for me! I now understand my life so much more … You helped me make sense of it!" you filled me with assurance that the work of writing this book is worth it if only for you and me. I cherish our memories of wondering for so many years about where we get our characteristics. I so enjoy our discussions about being moms and grandmas. I delight in our significant friendship and the awareness of the gift we treasure of being sisters as adult women together. You inspire me and fill my life with joy.

Betsy, my adored sister: deep gratitude for how your life work aligns with mine, providing rich discussions and support between us. In your creativity, curiosity and teaching that invite people to engage life fully, you are a gift to your community and to us as family. I delight in your groundedness and commitment to building community. Watching Mom care for you when you were a baby gave me a window into the soul of a mother's love. I am so glad you came along and filled our lives with a joyful and beautiful dance.

Mark: as my brother you have taught me much about life. Although in many ways we journeyed alone through the difficult years, there was a sense of connection that was not expressed in words until our adult years. I treasure the times we shared of long and wondering conversations in person and by phone. Your encouragement means a lot to me and our love for each other warms my heart.

The three sisters: Janis, Betsy and me, whose lives reflect the gifts and strengths of our parents; with Dad's passion for the spiritual journey weaving in and out of each of our lives, and Mom's commitment to support people on the journey being an integral part of each of us in different ways; each one of us a reflection of Mom and Dad.

Scott: although you lived on the periphery of my life, your capacity to be present to people taught me at a young age how I want to show up in the world. Knowing you are my biological father makes sense of the pieces of my life that I could never quite sort out. I am grateful for my memories of you as a kind, charismatic and attentive man who laughed, listened and cared.

Lynda: you arrived in our family later in life, yet you were always there in Mom's heart. You provided new opportunities for us to discover what it means to be family and provided Janis and me with lots of insights into our ongoing discussions and wonderings about genetic impact on who we are. It is a gift to be aware of your connection to our family. There is richness in knowing the fullness of our story. And it is a delight to know you and all your family.

The members of my new family who have had the opportunity to extend welcome ... my new auntie, cousins, and their families: it has been such a gift to find you; you help me connect to a part of me I did not fully accept or understand. My life is richer for having you in it. I love my renewed social life of concerts and dinners, horse races and travel. Thank you, Deb and Auntie. Particular thanks to our cousin Greg, for figuring out the details of our connection to the Macdonald clan and opening a doorway to understanding and relationships that I am glad I did not miss.

Lynn, my beloved spiritual companion, teacher, healer and friend: for the hours of deep conversation and healing, for the fun of engaging life together, for your faith in me, thank you. I missed you as this story unfolded, but I felt your love strong and sure. You are held close in my heart.

Tanis, spiritual buddy, companion on the emerging journey explored in the book: thank you for holding space with me as I sorted through the multitude of tangled strands of the story of the shocking DNA test result to create room for memories to emerge and pieces of the story to begin to link together. The moments of discovery and excitement were delightful, as insights and connections would pop out of wonderings, ponderings, conversations and healing to provide new understanding.

Janet, fellow journeyer whom I first met as a facilitator of The Eagle and Condor Symposium—Awakening the Dreamer Changing the Dream: for the multitude of times you have encouraged me in my life's work, thank you. You have been a blessing on the journey.

To all my family and friends who are now part of the cloud of witnesses and the wisdom circle of my ancestors: thank you for showing up throughout the writing of the book, including in the huge gathering of reconciliation at the end; my grandmothers and grandfather, aunts and uncles, brother Mark, beloved friends and colleagues Lynn and Fred, and my parents Mom, Dad and Scott.

To the many companions on the journey toward wholeness who have walked with me in learning, discovering, discernment and development of awareness, those acknowledged by name or by circumstance in the stories in the book, as well as the multitude of others who have been catalysts for learning by providing experiences of the awakening power and gift of intentional relationships, thank you. Thank you for the multitude of times we gather together in Circles created through the commitment to listen deeply and hold space for each other to honour insights, gifts and our combined wisdom.

THE BOOK TEAM

Peggy Goddard, a phenomenal friend and an amazing writing companion on the journey of the emergence of this story: you have been dedicated beyond imagining in your support of this project through your prodding, questioning, and seeing deeply into what I was not saying, editing with me again and again and again and again, finding places where even a tiny point was not clear or the depth of the story was not being told. Thank you, my friend. My gratitude for the role you played in helping this book be written creates a feeling in my heart of profound, overflowing appreciation.

Carolyn Pogue, a friend who knows me well and a wonderful editor: with your encouragement, I have reflected deeply on how it is that I am a strong woman and strong leader considering the demanding realities of a mother with many personalities. At your insistence I have also reflected on how I have been able to gracefully accept the awareness that my Dad is not my father. Doubling the number of words by the second draft is due to you urging me to tell the fullness of my story. It has been a healing journey and a time of reclaiming strength because of your encouragement to delve deeper. Thank you.

Julie McGonegal, amazing editor, guide and new friend: you have been a gift in these final stages of the development of the book, from sharing the power of the impact of the book on your daily life, to challenging my colloquialisms, to engaging with me to find a clearer way to share an idea, your input has been rich and encouraged me to see that my story can touch others in beneficial ways. Thank you for sitting beside me at a church meeting and showing interest in my work.

Anitta Hamming, artist and friend: thank you for the painting of the mended mirror. It captures my imaginings with a wonderful energy. I love how the images all connect with my very real day-to-day life to acknowledge that it is a reflection of my life—with the mirror frame, candleholder and tabletop all made by Alan, the necklace, in the shape of a spiral to reflect the experience of the spiritual journey, is from Mom, the scarf is like the ones my mother-in-law made in the colours of a scarf that Betsy gave me that I love. I am wearing the scarf she gave me and the necklace Mom gave me in my author's picture. The colour of the wall is the exact colour in our family room. The candle is burning so that we can see the light deep within that will illuminate our daily lives if we don't cover it over with all the demands and expectations of life. The fractures in the mirror emerged in my mind with clarity, along with the golden enhancement to celebrate the wisdom and insights from the journey of life. You captured it all perfectly! Thank you for creating the sketches to reflect the stages of the development of the mended mirror for the five sections of the book, using images from the workshop where the mirror was made— downstairs in our basement. You are amazing.

Pegi Eyers, entering the process at the very end, bringing far more than just the formatting set up of the interior and cover of the book that I was seeking: thank you for your amazing technical ability but also for your creativity, questions and knowledge shared with an inspiring passion.

Mia, keeper of the up-to-date version of the book, feedback provider on the first draft, editor of the earlier yet-to-be published books: thank you.

Brian, confirmer of my understandings of Mom's many personalities based on your life work in the area of mental health: thank you. Your passion to support and encourage is a gift in my life as one of many who has been listened to by your gift of compassion.

Readers Mia, Joan, Tanis, Bev, Betty, Sarah, Janis, Deb, Wayne and Marike who took the time to slug through some of the earliest versions of the book: thank you! Listeners, who have sat and held space as I have shared glimpses of the story, each time discovering a new insight as I spoke: thank you.

AUTHORS AND THINKERS WHO HAVE INSPIRED AND ENCOURAGED ME

Phyllis Tickle: I deeply appreciate Phyllis's clarity that we are living in a time of emergence, a time of letting go of the parts of our past that have immobilized the deepening of our spiritual journey in order to make space for something new to emerge. As she reflects in her book *The Great Emergence: How Christianity is Changing and Why,* this will be a new era for the Christian faith that will lead us in unexpected ways toward the necessary shifts in the chaos of these times in which we live.[12] It was a joy to speak one on one with Phyllis for two and half hours on an occasion that was both an interview but also a chance for us to speak as two women who are passionate about the changes that are coming in our world—changes that will be for the good.[13]

Barbara Marx Hubbard: The teachings that Barbara shares of this being a time of conscious evolution have been helpful in my thinking. I like her invitation to consider what it would be like to be in labour but not know you are pregnant. The experience would probably feel like you are dying. In these times of great pain and upheaval, we are in the midst of giving birth to something new. In Barbara's work she identifies the new spiral of evolution of this time when we are able to consciously choose the kind of world we want to co-create. In different conversations, Barbara has encouraged me in my work of developing a

---

[12] Tickle, Phyllis. *The Great Emergence: How Christianity is Changing and Why* (Grand Rapids, MI: Baker Books Publishing Group, 2008).

[13] For my interview with Phyllis Tickle, see www.ucobserver.org/interviews/2012/12/interview_phyllis_tickle/.

culture for meaningful conversations, since such opportunities for connection will be a key to the world shifting toward the wholeness that is possible. This shift will happen as our connectivity with each other and with Divine love expand.[14]

Alanna Mitchell: Alanna is one of many authors who has inspired me around the need to awaken to our impact on climate change and the need to shift the stories we tell ourselves so that we don't get mired in perspectives that immobilize us. When Alanna was writing the epilogue to her book *Sea Sick*, she came straight from the airport to Wisdom Circle in the community on two lakes after a long plane ride from one of the places of her research. That night she reflected on finding a way forward. She identified the wisdom of physician Monica Sharma who works with the United Nations, delving deeply into how to shift the stories and the thinking behind some of the greatest atrocities in the world today. A key aspect that Alanna lifts up is to first identify what we value and then reflect on our ongoing behaviour to determine if it reflects what we say is important. She asks us two questions: "What do you stand for? What story do you tell yourself about why you are here?" She notes, "This is a call for wisdom, not for logic; for hope rather than despair. It is about taking a stand and then acting on it—being fully human at a time when we need it most."[15]

Matthew Fox: When I first read Matthew's list in his book *Original Blessing* that identifies the shifts from theology rooted in original sin to theology rooted in the understanding that we are born as blessing, I was delighted to find a clear expression of key aspects of my

---

[14] For my interview with Barbara Hubbard, see www.ucobserver.org/interviews/2013/12/barbara_hubbard/.

[15] Mitchell, Alannah. *Sea Sick: The Global Ocean in Crisis* (Toronto, ON: McClelland & Stewart Ltd, 2009), 202.

theology.[16] When Matt came to the community on two lakes in 2006 he brought his yet-to-be published manuscript on *The A.W.E. Project, Reinventing Education, Reinventing the Human*.[17] In it he identifies "10 C's" to balance the "3 R's" of education. The 10 C's are Cosmology, Contemplation, Co-creation, Chaos, Compassion, Courage, Critical Consciousness, Community, Ceremony and Celebration, Character and Chakra Development. I again experienced a sense of resonating with what he wrote of the importance of awakening creativity so that together we can imagine a different way of being in relationship in this world. When I saw Matt at the Parliament of the World's Religions in 2018 I shared my current work of this book with him. He again affirmed the importance of sharing my thinking.

David Korten: I find it extremely helpful when people identify the shifts of what we are moving from and what we are moving toward. David does this well. While I have engaged in invigorating conversation with him a few times, most recently at the Parliament of the World's Religions, it is his charts that trace the shifts we need to be going through that continuously speak to me and encourage me in my work. In his book *The Great Turning: From Empire to Earth Community* he identifies shifts in cultural, economic and political perspectives to move away from empire toward Earth community.[18] Examples of those shifts include moving from relationships of domination to relationships of partnership; from hoarding to sharing; from competition for individual advantage to cooperation for mutual advantage; from a belief in our limitations to a belief in our possibilities.

---

[16] Fox, Matthew. *Original Blessing: A Primer in Creation Spirituality* (New York, NY: Jeremy P. Tarcher/Putnam, 1983 and 2000 edition).
[17] Fox, Matthew. *The A.W.E. Project, Reinventing Education, Reinventing the Human* (unpublished, 2006).
[18] Korten, David C. *The Great Turning: From Empire to Earth Community* (Bloomfield, CT: Kumarian Press Inc., 2006).

Jack and Christine Spong: While I have heard John Spong speak a number of times, it was when he was five feet from where I sat, standing on the chancel in the Downtown United Church in the community on two lakes, that he most caught my imagination. He was speaking about his book *Jesus for the Non-Religious*.[19] He talked about how we live on a spectrum that consists of humanity at one end and divinity at the other end. Jesus lived far along the spectrum to live the divinity within him. But it is a journey we are all on. We are all invited to allow the power of divine love to inform our lives and mould who we are in the world. In this way we allow the light of love that is within us to be shared with the world. The more we live connected to divine love, the more we are actively engaged in co-creating a world rooted in God's vision of well-being for all. It has been Christine who has repeatedly encouraged me to write my books and connected me with other young (at the time) thinkers and leaders of churches so that we could support and inspire each other.

Christina Baldwin: When I was at the advanced training in *The Circle Way*, I had a one on one conversation with Christina, one of the founders of this style of engaging in meaningful conversations.[20] I asked her if I could simply teach her work and stop trying to develop my work. She told me that I could not. She pointed out that I was the one who brought the phrase "Circle Culture" to the weeklong retreat, and now everyone was using it because they know what that culture feels like and the transforming power it contains. So no, I cannot just teach her work. I need to develop my own. Her wisdom came at a critical time when the development of the keys of Authentic Connection Culture could have been abandoned.

[19] Spong, John Shelby. *Jesus for the Non-Religious* (New York, NY: HarperCollins, 2007).
[20] Baldwin, Christina and Linnea, Ann. *The Circle Way: A Leader in Every Chair* (San Francisco, CA: Berrett-Koehler Publishers, Inc., 2010).

Harrison Owen: I followed a nudge to go to a multi-day workshop led by Peter Block, Walter Brueggemann, Angeles Arrien, Michael Jones and Harrison Owen. Harrison led us in an Open Space session. My question that I offered to the group was how Open Space strategies can be incorporated into day-to-day life. When I read my topic into the circle Harrison told me we needed to talk because few people understand that it can be a way of life rather than just a process. We talked during my topic time because no one else was sparked by the topic. He asked me how it was that I saw the potential to integrate these concepts into day-to-day life. I shared with him about my work being more than a process for gathering in Circles but also a philosophical perspective and attitude that has transformative power. Harrison told me about a book that he had written that focused on this awareness. At the next training that I went to for The Art of Hosting, copies of that book, *The Practice of Peace,* were given to everyone.[21] He encouraged me to attend the annual global gathering of Open Space, which is where I was first introduced to the global community of The Art of Hosting Meaningful Conversations, an incredible gathering of people who willingly share resources and support as we all work around the globe to create space for the significant conversations that are needed in the world today.[22]

Mariposa Roundtable members Michael Jones, Daphne Mainprize, Mark Douglas, Kim Fedderson, and Ted Reeve: thank you for the significant ongoing five-year conversation around creating a commons where a sense of belonging and respect fosters a culture of meaningful conversations and relationships that then create opportunities for transformative possibilities to emerge to reflect our common longing for engagement and healthy life-giving community for all.   Our conversations have been a real joy in my life. Thank you.

---

[21] Owen, Harrison. *The Practice of Peace* (Circle Pines, MN: Human Systems Dynamics Institute, 2004).
[22] See www.artofhosting.org.

PRAISE FOR *THE MENDED MIRROR* FULL TEXT

After I read this book, I told myself never to forget it. Its powerful vision of the authentic life—where the fullness of who we are meant to be emerges out of brokenness—is more critical than ever in this age of artifice. This is a story that beckons us to return to our roots—both familial roots and ancient spiritual roots—so that we can move into a present defined by deep, loving connection. It's more than a memoir about a mother with mental illness, it's a testament to the transformation that awaits humanity on the other side of egoism. There's hardly a person alive who doesn't need this book.

Julie McGonegal, PhD, author of
Imagining Justice: The Politics of Postcolonial Forgiveness and Reconciliation

Karen Celeste Hilfman is a master story-teller. Sensitively alive to the subtlest inner feelings and nuances of inner guidance, she leads us to experience with her a powerful transformation and understanding of authentic connection from multiple perspectives. Her inner strength and "call to be in life" stand as an example to all of us that no matter how dire our experience of brokenness, it breaks us wide open, as well, to healing and growth. Her story is interspersed with teachings on group healing dynamics and authentic connection. We learn from her experience as well as feel with her to the heart of what really matters.

Dr. Nancy Roof, Founding Editor
Kosmos Journal for Global Transformation

This is a stunning piece of work by Karen Celeste Hilfman. As a writer and teacher of memoir, I know something of what this entails: first the living of it and then the art of it. Karen's voice shows us the journey of compassion as she comes to understand the multiple facets and personalities of her mother, and her own determination to use this experience of the fractured self to integrate her own being. Bravo—as in brave.

Christina Baldwin, author of
Storycatcher: Making Sense of our Lives through the Power and Practice of Story

The Mended Mirror is searing autobiography, keen analysis, and a very uncomfortable metaphor for the world today. It is a serious read, not for the faint-hearted—but with rich rewards for those who persevere.

Harrison Owen,
Originator of Open Space Technology

The Mended Mirror weaves together memoir, spirituality and the courage, love and frustration of a unique family life. It brings together Wise Woman teachings, lessons from a mother's fragmented life, and a glimpse of other ways of being in the world. Karen Celeste Hilfman's deft fingers create both tapestry and mosaic that will resonate with readers seeking ways to re-craft their own lives. I highly recommend this book for study groups, writers and seekers of wholeness.

Carolyn Pogue, author of
Hilwie's Bread

The complexity and insights of the story of *The Mended Mirror* continue to both amaze me and inform me about living life authentically. My mind wanders through the story again and again, allowing the details and the lessons to speak to me. Karen shows us how to persevere even when life feels broken. I appreciate the encouragement to peel back the layers of life to connect to our core, a peaceful core that cannot be taken from us. This book has impacted the way I see life and relationships and how together we need to and can create caring, engaged community.

Peggy Goddard,
Hospital Leadership Development and Health Care Management

The Mended Mirror is inspirational. Part searing memoir, part spiritual wisdom, and wholly entrancing, this book invites us to glean deep insight from the pains and challenges of our lives. Whether you are spiritual or not, Christian or not, interested in psychology or not, interested in memoirs or not, this captivating story will intrigue you and uplift your soul. Karen explores her harrowing personal journey with clarity, confidence and humility, demonstrating how to find wholeness in brokenness, no matter what. Her book exposes how she learned the powerful lessons she offers us to live by: to hear all voices, include all people, really listen, to let the wisdom within and amongst lead the outcome, and always to look through the eyes of love. This is a book for everyone.

Tanis Day, PhD, author of
The Whole You:
Healing and Transformation through Energy Awareness

Karen is a masterful storyteller. She shares how growing up with a mother with many personalities impacted her life and her spiritual journey. In reading, I found myself riveted by both aspects of this story—what would we discover next about her mother's life and what would we discover about Karen's experience. Karen writes with love, honesty, vulnerability and authenticity. I found myself drawn into her insight and brilliance. This book goes beyond an interesting read to be inspiring to people dealing with challenges in their lives, to people who have learned to follow their intuitive nudges and to anyone wondering how to bring love and curiosity to those members of our families or close circles that we might describe as difficult or challenging. By touching the spaces deep inside her, Karen's story will touch places deep inside of the reader.

Kathy Jourdain, author of
A Worldview Intelligence Approach to
Building Trust and Relationship at the Speed of Change

The Mended Mirror is a beautifully written and gripping family story and compelling account of what awaits us in the deeply human journey from brokenness to wholeness. What it brings home is how in a universe where there could be nothing, there is something—a light that fills us with goodness, beauty and love.

Michael Jones, author of
The Soul of Place: Reimagining Leadership
through Nature, Art and Community

ABOUT THE AUTHOR

Karen Celeste Hilfman was born in Toronto, Canada. She has lived in eight places all within three hours of the city.

Karen has a Bachelor of Arts in English and Drama and a Masters of Divinity. She has directed dramas and a multitude of musicals with intergenerational casts, drawing on her degrees and years of being in a dance troupe. She is an ordained minister with The United Church of Canada and was a lead minister in congregations for 25 years. She now works at the regional level of the church to support and encourage the evolution of communities of faith that are adapting to the changing times in which we live. Karen is also a consultant who facilitates Significant Conversations and a coach of Authentic Connection Culture. You can read more about her work at www.AuthenticConnectionCulture.com.

Karen lives with her husband Alan in Orillia, Ontario, where their daughters Sarah and Marissa and families live close by. They connect often for barbecued and smoked dinners, bonfires, camping trips, hikes and random moments when they happily show up in the same place.

Karen's passion for wholeness continues to inform her deep longing for us to fully awaken to the incredible possibilities that emerge— as we shift how we are in relationship in our personal, local and global communities—when we choose to be grounded in, and led by, the powers of creativity, love and wisdom.

Manufactured by Amazon.ca
Bolton, ON